REMEMBER THE POOR

REMEMBER THE POOR

Paul, Poverty, and the Greco-Roman World

Bruce W. Longenecker

WILLIAM B. EERDMANS PUBLISHING COMPANY

GRAND RAPIDS, MICHIGAN / CAMBRIDGE, U.K.

Published 2010 by ·

Wm. B. Eerdmans Publishing Co.

2140 Oak Industrial Drive N.E., Grand Rapids, Michigan 49505 /

P.O. Box 163, Cambridge CB3 9PU U.K.

Printed in the United States of America

16 15 14 13 12 11 10   7 6 5 4 3 2 1

Library of Congress Cataloging-in-Publication Data

Longenecker, Bruce W.

   Remember the poor: Paul, poverty, and the Greco-Roman world /

   Bruce W. Longenecker.

       p.   cm.

   Includes bibliographical references.

   ISBN 978-0-8028-6373-7 (pbk.: alk. paper)

     1. Church work with the poor. 2. Poverty — Religious aspects — Christianity.

     3. Poverty — Biblical teaching. 4. Church history — Primitive and early church,

     ca. 30-600. 5. Bible. N.T. Epistles of Paul — Criticism, interpretation, etc.   I. Title.

BV639.P6L66   2010

261.8′32509015 — dc22

                                   2010023293

www.eerdmans.com

For our son Torrin:
  May your life continue to be marked out
    by spirited generosity.

Contents

Preface

"Thank God it's them instead of you." These words from the British seasonal song "Do They Know It's Christmas Time" (1984) cynically express a prevalent (yet seldom articulated) sentiment of the affluent western world: thank God that desperate poverty engulfs others elsewhere in the world, not me, and not us.[1] But the song also expressed an optimism that the human spirit could move beyond self-interest to initiate practical projects on behalf of those in need — not least in the holiday season when friends and family are remembered with generous gifts. Might it be that the poor might also be included within our practical remembrances?

"Remembering" the poor in tangible ways forms a central focus of this book. The book's origins lie in a lecture series on Paul's letter to the Galatians that I delivered while teaching at the University of Cambridge in the mid- to late 1990s. In that context I noted in one of my lectures that the prevailing interpretation of the phrase "remember the poor" (Gal 2:10) is marked by a notable lacuna in its evidential base. Setting out to find the missing evidence in the years that followed, I came to the view that it is impossible to fill that evidential void, precisely because the interpretation of Gal 2:10 that predominates in the scholarly world is itself beset by an interpretative inaccuracy — an inaccuracy that has infected the scholarly genes for centuries, being passed unchecked from one generation to another.

What began as an exegetical curiosity soon came to take on larger pro-

1. "Do They Know It's Christmastime?" by Bob Geldof and Midge Ure, performed by Band Aid (1984).

portions, both historically and theologically. Increasingly I came to the view that this single exegetical inaccuracy has played a part in blinding us to a key dimension of the early Jesus-movement — a dimension that is critical to understanding the historical origins of that movement, and not least Paul's place within it. Further, this single exegetical inaccuracy may well have contributed to the neglect of an essential component of Christian identity and practice. This book sets out the basis for rethinking the place of "remembering the poor" in the early Jesus-movement of the Greco-Roman world. In addition, it may also contribute to rethinking the place of "remembering the poor" among groups of Jesus-followers today, for those who think that the theological convictions and practices of the early Jesus-movement may continue to have some relevance in a world so very different from that one long ago.

There are, I am quite sure, many weaknesses in the argumentation of this book, only some of which I am cognizant. No doubt others will be well placed to spot these weaknesses. Some academic friends have already helped me in thinking through issues, strengthening the argument and spotting weaknesses that, consequently, were ironed out prior to publication. Listing their names in the late stages of writing this book runs the risk of leaving some out unintentionally, and thereby incorporating further weaknesses. But the risk is worth taking, if only to signal my indebtedness to others. So I offer my thanks to the following friends and scholars: John Barclay, Richard Bauckham, Markus Bockmuehl, David Downs, James Dunn, Paul Foster, Steve Friesen, Simon Gathercole, Beverly Gaventa, Richard Hays, David Horrell, Larry Hurtado, Robert Jewett, Kelly Liebengood, Anneliese Parkin, Todd Still, Nicholas Taylor, Francis Watson, Dan Williams and Greg Woolf. Special thanks go to the students at Baylor University whose contributions in a doctoral course on "Paul, Poverty and the Greco-Roman World" have helped to hone the argumentation significantly. These include: Libby Ballard, David Beary, Tim Brookins, Lindsay Cleveland, Brian Gamel, Heather Gorman, Peter Rice, and Nick Zola. Special mention must be made of Tyler Davis, who assembled the bibliography, and especially of Nick Zola, who went far beyond the call of duty in helping to edit the whole of the manuscript and in compiling the indexes. The excellence of his editorial eye was surpassed only by the quality of his dedication to an otherwise thankless task.

Some of the chapters of this book have appeared in earlier form in other publishing venues, although revised here to one extent or another. Parts of chapter three and parts of Appendix 1 are based on my article "Exposing the Economic Middle: A Revised Economy Scale for the Study of Early Urban

Christianity," *JSNT* 31 (2009): 243-78. Parts of chapters five and six contain material from my article "Good News to the Poor: Jesus, Paul and Jerusalem," in Todd Still, ed., *Jesus and Paul Reconnected: Fresh Pathways to an Old Debate* (Grand Rapids: Eerdmans, 2007), pp. 37-65. The argument in some parts of chapter seven was first published in my "The Poor of Galatians 2:10: The Interpretative Paradigm of the First Centuries," in Bruce W. Longenecker and Kelly Liebengood, eds., *Engaging Economics: New Testament Scenarios and Early Christian Interpretations* (Grand Rapids: Eerdmans, 2009), pp. 205-21, although the argumentation presented here takes account of more data and, consequently, is both more accurate and more compelling than the earlier version. Sections of chapters ten and eleven are drawn from my article "Socio-Economic Profiling of the First Urban Christians," in Todd Still and David Horrell, eds., *After the First Urban Christians: The Socio-Historical Study of Pauline Christianity Twenty-Five Years Later* (London/New York: Continuum, 2009), pp. 36-59. I am grateful to the publishers for extending permission to reproduce the argument of these articles within the larger argument of this book. Abbreviations used in this book are standard, generally following the *SBL Handbook of Style*.

"I am not ashamed of the gospel"

Paul's Alleged Disregard for the Poor

When exploring economic dimensions of the early Jesus-movement, don't bother with Paul — the controversial follower of Jesus whose texts comprise roughly half of the New Testament. With regard to issues of poverty and wealth, Paul's theological deliberations are of very little relevance to either historical reconstruction or contemporary theological consideration.

This attitude predominates in both popular and academic circles. It is also wrong. I seek to demonstrate this claim within the pages of this book, where care for the poor is shown to be an integral part of the "good news" that Paul preached. For Paul, economic assistance of the poor was not sufficient in and of itself, nor was it exhaustive of the good news of Jesus; but neither was it supplemental or peripheral to that good news. Instead, falling within the essentials of the good news, care for the poor was thought by Paul to be a necessary hallmark of the corporate life of Jesus-followers who lived in conformity with the good news of the early Jesus-movement.

This claim is what sets this book apart from most others that deal with Paul. Influential books that dig deeply into Paul's theology and ethic are usually characterized by their lack of any real engagement with Paul's views and practices pertaining to poverty *per se*.[1] There is plenty of engagement with

---

1. Examples from among front-runners of Pauline study include: Victor Paul Furnish, *The Moral Teaching of Paul* (Nashville: Abingdon, 1979); James D. G. Dunn, *The Theology of Paul the Apostle* (Grand Rapids: Eerdmans, 1998); Udo Schnelle, *Apostle Paul: His Life and Theology* (Grand Rapids: Baker Academic, 2003). See also Richard B. Hays's very abbreviated discussion of the matter in his *The Moral Vision of the New Testament* (San Francisco: HarperCollins, 1996), p. 465, where discussion of "sharing possessions" in the early Jesus-

his views on the law, christology, soteriology, theology proper, ecclesiology, pneumatology, ethics, and the like. And the fun of exploring Pauline theology (or is it "theologizing"?) is not just in examining what he wrote but how his mind worked, and how (or whether) these things may have fit together comprehensively in his mind. But in these efforts at exegesis, historical reconstruction and theological exploration, the default setting is to imagine that the widespread poverty all around Paul had very little traction or significance in his theology, practice or writings. In fact, even crediting Paul with an "attitude" or a "view" on this matter might be thought of as going beyond the evidence, since his own writings show a general and monolithic paucity of concern about the poor of his own world — except as potential adherents to communities of Jesus-followers. Little wonder, then, that surveys of philanthropy at the turn of the common era regularly say little or nothing about Paul, even when written by those who survey the alleviation of poverty by Jews and Christians of the ancient world.[2]

This way of seeing things might seem commonsensical on first blush. But it is plagued by weaknesses, as will be demonstrated on a number of fronts within the covers of this book. A few scholars have registered dissatisfaction with the popular view of Paul and poverty, noting there to be "poverty" in this field of study.[3] Here I argue along similar lines, although my own case is markedly different and notably distinctive in a number of important respects.

Usually, however, on the few occasions when attention turns to Paul and poverty, the issue is dealt with in one of three ways: (1) it is excused as being inconsequential, usually on the basis that Paul had bigger fish to fry; (2) it is discussed in relation to Paul's efforts to raise a collection for the benefit of the "poor among the saints in Jerusalem" (Rom 15:26); and (3) grand claims are made about how Paul did, in fact, care about the poor and needy, but without much argumentative basis being offered for such claims.

---

movement runs aground in the Pauline letters, except to make a gesture to the collection for the Jerusalem community. Examples of the same tendency could be multiplied inordinately. Published one hundred years before this book, Adolf Deissmann's *Light from the Ancient East* (London: Hodder and Stoughton, 1910) included important challenges to Pauline scholarship on precisely this matter.

2. So, for instance, Robert H. Bremner, "Jewish, Christian and Islamic Texts on Giving and Charity," in his *Giving: Charity and Philanthropy in History* (London: Transaction Publishers, 1994), pp. 11-20.

3. See especially Justin J. Meggitt, *Paul, Poverty and Survival* (Edinburgh: T&T Clark, 1998); Steven J. Friesen, "Poverty in Pauline Studies: Beyond the So-called New Consensus," *JSNT* 26 (2004): 323-61.

The "bigger fish to fry" approach is exemplified in the following quotations from Leslie Hoppe and Peter Davids respectively. Hoppe writes:

> Paul's attitude toward the poor was probably colored by his expectations regarding the imminent return of Christ. The apostle's belief that Christ's return was near made dealing with socioeconomic problems at any great length unnecessary.[4]

Along the same lines, Davids writes:

> [W]hen Paul discusses wealth and charity . . . , [he] lacks the sharp note of prophetic denunciation [that characterizes other figures of the Jesus-movement]. . . . This may be due to the fact that . . . [his] imminent eschatology made social issues less important.[5]

What these estimates offer is, in a sense, an "apology" that seeks to explain, and evidently excuse, Paul's apparent lack of concern for the poor. Central to that apology is Paul's eschatological expectation: that is, if Jesus was thought to be returning soon, why worry about the poor, since they will be "blessed" when the kingdom is finally established once and for all in the very near future?[6] In the words of Barry Gordon, Paul "does not appear interested in ex-

---

4. L. J. Hoppe, *There Shall Be No Poor Among You: Poverty in the Bible* (Nashville: Abingdon, 2004), 158.

5. Peter H. Davids, "The Test of Wealth," in Bruce Chilton and Craig Evans, eds., *The Missions of James, Peter, and Paul: Tensions in Early Christianity* (Leiden: Brill, 2005), 355-84, p. 358. A similar estimate is offered by Ellen F. Davis, although in relation to the broader issues of "agrarian" responsibility. She writes (*Scripture, Culture, and Agriculture: An Agrarian Reading of the Bible* [Cambridge: Cambridge University Press, 2009], p. 7): "An agrarian reading of the New Testament is possible and necessary. Granted, the theme of land care is less pronounced there, likely because many of the writers expected an imminent end of the world as we know it."

6. Nils Dahl's comments (*Studies in Paul* [Philadelphia: Fortress Press, 1977], pp. 24-25) can be read along similar lines: "Paul was aware that he was living in the last days. He expected to see Jesus' return and the end of the world. . . . In this situation, property and money had little significance; they belonged to the age which was perishing. Paul uses phrases like 'material benefits' . . . and 'matters pertaining to this life' [to characterize economic matters]. The contrast is to the spiritual good, i.e., to matters that relate to God and to his kingdom. Economic affairs are trivial." But what Dahl intended to illustrate is that economic prosperity was not a part of Paul's own concerns; Dahl did not intend to suggest that Paul was unconcerned about the poor. So he notes (p. 26): "The congregation [of Jesus-followers] becomes the decisive social reality for the Christian way of life, and communal life by necessity involves the use of possessions."

horting his followers to pay attention to the progress of the world in which they live"; instead, Paul's writings "suggest a quietist, if not an outright retreatist attitude to economic engagements," precisely because Paul maintained that "the world as we know it is passing away" and "our time is growing short."[7]

Maintaining a view of this kind, Davids feels it justified to contrast Paul's view of "charity" with the view that emerges from the Letter of James. For the author of that letter (whether it be the brother of Jesus himself or someone writing in his name), charity is essential to a life of faithfulness before Israel's deity; for Paul, on the other hand, charity is simply a matter of one's own discretion. With Paul's instructions about his collection in 2 Corinthians 8–9 in view, Davids compares James and Paul in this way:

> For James charity . . . is not in any way optional. It is essential. Paul, in contrast, views charity as voluntary. It may show the reality of one's confession, but he never makes it essential. . . . Paul persuades, encourages, even manipulates with his rhetoric, but he does not command, for in the end the decision [to act charitably] is individual and voluntary. . . . James is not arguing with Paul. . . . [Instead] James is moving in a totally different conceptual world than Paul.[8]

Whereas James puts care for the economically needy at the very heart of (what might be called) Judeo-Christian identity (e.g., Jas 1:27), Paul simply does not. In this view of things, one might be tempted to revel in diversity of opinion within the early Jesus-movement, or we might be tempted to evaluate the positions of Paul and the author of James in terms of their theological attractions and practical relevance.

William Loader advocates a similar position. He notes a contrast between Paul and Jesus on the issue of the poor:

> None of his [Paul's] writings would lead one to understand that good news for the poor was a central feature in the message of Jesus, but then he says little if anything about Jesus' own teaching and preaching. The focus is rather on the reconciling effects of the cross for humanity alienated by sin.[9]

---

7. Barry Gordon, *Economic Analysis before Adam Smith* (New York: Harper & Row, 1975), p. 88.

8. Davids, "The Test of Wealth," pp. 369-70.

9. William Loader, "'Good News to the Poor' and Spirituality in the New Testament:

Loader bolsters the point by noting two instances illustrating how Paul, unlike Jesus, had no real concern about the needs of the poor in general. The first involves Paul's "confrontation [with] the more well-off in Corinth" regarding the Lord's Supper in 1 Corinthians 11. Whereas the issue that Paul addresses seems to have an economic dimension to it, Loader notes that Paul's real "concern is neglect of [the community's] members, not the needs of the poor in general." The second instance is Paul's collection for the poor in Jerusalem. Loader notes that Paul's motivations for undertaking the collection were primarily driven by "theologically political reasons," rather than a genuine concern to meet the needs of the poor as a result of the gospel of the Jesus-followers. In Loader's estimate, "Paul gives no indication that addressing human poverty . . . was central to the gospel message."

A slightly different tone might be thought to emerge from Loader's pen in another of his publications, however. When discussing the collection for the saints in Jerusalem Loader claims that Paul

> organized collections wherever his mission went. He appears to have laid great store on the collection as a sign of the Gentiles belonging to the people of God. . . . Gathering money for the needy belonged to his call.[10]

There is no contradiction in Loader's position, however. What Loader is outlining in his two publications is a distinction between Paul's perception of "the gospel message" and of his own apostolic responsibilities. If care for the poor has no foothold in the gospel message, it nonetheless had a foothold in his own apostolic commission, but only in terms of "gathering money for the needy" *in Jerusalem,* which as Loader says elsewhere, was a concern driven by "theologically political reasons"[11] rather than being driven by the gospel itself.

For Loader, because Paul extracted concern for the poor from his "gospel message," his theology was deficient when judged in light of the good news of Jesus of Nazareth. For Earle Ellis, however, the fact that Paul's gospel was not concerned about matters of poverty and other issues demonstrates

---

A Question of Survival," in Geoffrey D. Dunn, David Luckensmeyer, and Lawrence Cross, eds., *Poverty and Riches;* vol. 5, Prayer and Spirituality in the Early Church (Strathfield, NSW: St Paul's Publications, 2009), 3-35, p. 31. The quotations that appear in the following paragraph are taken from pp. 31-32.

10. W. Loader, *The New Testament with Imagination* (Grand Rapids: Eerdmans, 2007), p. 68.

11. Loader, "Good News to the Poor," p. 32.

precisely its theological robustness. Ellis maintains that "[l]ike Jesus and the New Testament writers generally, he [Paul] displayed no interest in using his ministry for broader humanitarian concerns" other than the release of individual souls "from the bondage of death." This lack of interest in humanitarian concern was "rooted in the Apostle's total theological outlook, which, like early Christianity generally, had more affinities with Epicurean withdrawal from society than with Stoic engagement with it."[12] According to Ellis, to interpret Paul as having "humanitarian concerns" is "to confuse Paul's doctrine of received 'righteousness' (δικαιοσύνη) imputed by God to the individual sinner in Christ with the teaching of a visionary social 'justice' to be achieved by Adamic man through Marxist revolution."[13] Such an approach to Paul displays "affinities . . . with traditional Roman Catholic theological sympathies for a salvation by human works or by a mixture of God's action and human endeavor."[14]

At times, however, scholarly opinion appears more generous and more promising with regard to concern for the poor. The classicist Peter Brown sketches Paul as one who was "deeply preoccupied by the problems and opportunities raised by the presence of wealth among the believers" and who "was convinced that the secret of the unity of believers lay in a steady circulation of goods among 'the brethren.'"[15] In this portrayal, Brown allows Paul to look like those other early followers of Jesus who "took for granted, as part of an inherited conglomerate of notions shared with Judaism, . . . that they were responsible for the care of the poor of their own community" — people not unlike the author of James and, of course, James's own brother, Jesus. But Brown's portrait of Paul is not as "promising" as it might initially appear, since his evidence is founded simply on the fact that Paul raised a collection for Jerusalem followers of Jesus. Based almost exclusively on Paul's collection efforts, Brown's grand claims look rather spurious.[16]

12. E. Earle Ellis, *Pauline Theology: Ministry and Society* (Grand Rapids: Eerdmans, 1989), p. 154 (main text and n. 157) and p. 155.

13. Ellis, *Pauline Theology,* p. 158.

14. Ellis, *Pauline Theology,* p. 158 n. 172. Ellis's position is, in my view, a disastrous misreading of Paul.

15. Peter Brown, *Poverty and Leadership in the Later Roman Empire* (Hanover, NH: University Press of New England, 2002), p. 18.

16. This is slightly unfair to Brown, who actually pluralizes the notion of Paul's collection for the poor in Jerusalem to include collections for the indigenous poor: "He wrote frequently in his letters about collections raised to support needy communities, and most especially to support 'the poor among the saints' in Jerusalem" (p. 18; compare p. 22). One fears, however, that Brown has generously taken Paul's multiple references to the Jerusalem collec-

Similarly, in his study of Paul's collection Keith F. Nickle argued that "charity" was "a natural consequence of Pauline theology."[17] He amplifies the claim in this way:

> Concern for the needs of the poor was one of the expressions of fellowship in Christ. Christian charity was motivated not by sympathy or self-righteousness but by Christian love which was the determinative force of that fellowship.[18]

In supporting the claim, however, Nickle draws his evidence almost exclusively from Paul's theological reflections on his collection efforts for "the poor among the saints in Jerusalem."[19] That the poor had any stronger foothold in Paul's theological concerns, other than by nature of their being within the network of Mediterranean Jesus-groups, is not evident from Nickle's reconstruction.

Along similar lines to those of Brown and Nickle, Dieter Georgi has eloquently argued that "Paul is very much aware of the urban fact that cash and creed are intimately interrelated." The point might sound refreshing, but once again it is driven only with reference to Paul's collection efforts: "This shows in [Paul's] treatment of the issue of the collection for Jerusalem," which was "interrelated with the major themes of his theology, especially with Christology and the concepts of trust, grace, and justification. They have to be rediscovered as being extremely concrete."[20] Judging by Paul's

---

tion and imagined them as being separate initiatives (i.e., "collections raised to support needy communities"). In this way, his conclusion about Paul's concern for the indigenous poor rests on unstable exegetical foundations, even if his conclusion might prove to be right on other exegetical grounds.

17. Keith F. Nickle, *The Collection: A Study in Paul's Strategy* (Naperville: Alec R. Allenson, 1966), p. 102.

18. Nickle, *The Collection*, p. 103.

19. Nickle, *The Collection*, pp. 104-111.

20. Dieter Georgi, *The City in the Valley: Biblical Interpretation and Urban Theology* (Atlanta: Society of Biblical Literature, 2005), p. 283. See also his elaboration of this point on pp. 296-98, which begins: "In the collection, a cycle of grace occurs in which money is the expression and means of a process that moves human hearts and draws people together.... The collection turns into a demonstration of this interplay of divine gift and human gratitude."

Much like Brown and Georgi, Gerhard Uhlhorn (*Christian Charity in the Ancient Church* [New York: Charles Scribner's Sons, 1883], p. 87) claimed of Paul that "[n]one of the other apostles ... has expressed himself so amply concerning alms and deeds of charity," although the evidence upon which this statement is made pertains almost exclusively to the collection.

comments in 2 Corinthians 8–9, it is certainly the case that Paul could adorn
the rationale for his collection efforts with deeply rooted theological convictions. But this is slightly different than saying that caring for the poor stands
front and center within Paul's theology. As David Downs notes, "given that
the collection for Jerusalem seems to have been a one-time caritative donation, we should not overstate the extent to which . . . charity was 'of the essence' in the Pauline churches."[21] Downs's point has merit, especially if we
assume that the evidence for generous initiatives towards the poor within
communities founded by Paul is limited to the collection initiative that Paul
undertook solely in the mid-50s CE.

At times, however, claims are registered that put care for the poor front
and center in Paul's project, even though those claims often lack a sufficient
exegetical base. In 1994, for instance, Neil Elliott produced a fresh interpretation of Paul that, at one point, established some "hunches" about Paul, including one that he calls "most provocative":

> Paul would have recognized what liberation theologians call "the prefer-
> ential option for the poor" as an authentic expression of Israel's faith and,
> consequently, of the gospel of Jesus Christ. . . . It would be extremely
> anachronistic . . . to expect Paul to think in terms of the sort of economic
> or political analysis that liberation theologians practice today. As to what
> informs and impels that analysis in liberation theology, on the other hand
> — [that is,] "a commitment to think for the sake of the poor and op-
> pressed people" and to consider the links between theology and praxis in
> terms of that commitment (Juan Luis Segundo) — there are indications
> in Paul's writings that he was no stranger to such a commitment.[22]

So Elliott makes his hunch explicit in this audacious claim that runs completely counter to those of, say, Hoppe and Davids noted above: "Any interpretation that excludes the possibility of Paul's awareness of the poor, and
his reflection on the situation of the poor in the light of the gospel he proclaimed, ought to be considered doubtful."[23] Elliott tells his reader that in a
later chapter of his book he will demonstrate "that Paul's apostolate embod-

---

21. David J. Downs, *The Offering of the Gentiles* (Tübingen: Mohr Siebeck, 2008), p. 110.

22. Neil Elliott, *Liberating Paul: The Justice of God and the Politics of the Apostle* (Maryknoll, NY: Orbis Books, 1994; repr. Sheffield: Sheffield Academic Press, 1995), p. 87, citing
J. L. Segundo, "Two Theologies of Liberation," in *Liberation Theology: A Documentary History* (Maryknoll, NY: Orbis Books, 1990), p. 356.

23. Elliott, *Liberating Paul*, p. 88.

ies the commitment to the poor."[24] That later chapter does, indeed, offer some resources toward that end — such as Paul's establishment of communities of peace and justice, and his critique of ideologies of privilege and power. Elliott virtually concludes his book on precisely this same note: "the world of privilege in which Paul moved" was "the world to which he spoke on behalf of the poor."[25] Nonetheless, Elliott's work falls short of constructing a case whereby Paul's own concern for the poor is presented in any extended fashion. While Elliott rightly highlights Paul's denigration of culturally determined definitions of honor and power, his case for Paul's own entrenched concern for the poor is relatively weak, except by extension from Paul's "countercultural" tendencies.

Along similar lines, Davina Lopez's post-colonial analysis approaches Paul's texts with fresh perspectives — a promising start if Paul is to be recharacterized with regard to his view of the poor. Much like Elliott, Lopez consistently characterizes Paul as one who occupied "a vulnerable, subversive social position of solidarity among others," who engaged in "subversive action among the defeated," who preached a gospel of "good news of and with the impoverished, the poor, and others" in his role as "an apostle to the marginalized through his mission to the defeated," thereby "linking Paul's mission to the nations with the preferential option for the poor and marginalized at the core of the Bible."[26] While Lopez's work is refreshing in many ways, its claims about Paul and the poor far outstrips its argumentation. There is really very little in Lopez's work that demonstrates the basis on which one can speak of Paul in relation to a biblical "preferential option for the poor," other than to say that "Paul consistently requests that the strong care for the weak (Rom 14 and 15), that the rich wait for the poor to start eating (1 Cor 11)."[27] But appealing to Paul's discussion of the weak and the strong in Romans 14–15 reveals a misunderstanding of what that passage is about, since the "weak" and "strong" are not primarily economic identifiers in that context.[28] And Lopez takes no account of the view of 1 Corinthians 11 represented by Loader, who sees it as having no relevance to a gospel that

24. Elliott, *Liberating Paul*, p. 88.

25. Elliott, *Liberating Paul*, p. 230.

26. Davina C. Lopez, *Apostle to the Conquered: Reimagining Paul's Mission* (Minneapolis: Fortress, 2008), pp. xii, xiv, xv, 22.

27. Lopez, *Apostle to the Conquered*, pp. 147-48.

28. On this, see especially John Barclay, "'Do We Undermine the Law?': A Study of Romans 14.1–15.6," in James D. G. Dunn, ed., *Paul and the Mosaic Law* (Tübingen: Mohr Siebeck, 1996), pp. 287-308.

links Paul's mission with the "preferential option for the poor and marginalized at the core of the Bible." Even if Lopez can be shown to be right in her conclusions, she offers little exegetical base for those conclusions.

John Howard Yoder's influential book *The Politics of Jesus* has much the same effect. Yoder notes the prevailing view that "the apparent social radicality of Jesus himself . . . was clarified and put in its place" by Paul, ensuring that "the person and character — and especially the career — of Jesus made no unique or determining contribution" to Christian ethics over the millennia. In this scenario, "there is in the midst of the [Christian] canon a chasm separating the ethic of Jesus from that of the apostolic church, of such a nature that one must choose between the two."[29] Against the backdrop of this distinction between Jesus and Paul, ecclesiastical interpretation has favored Paul over Jesus.[30] But is the distinction accurate? Yoder thinks not. Instead, he wants to reclaim in Paul "an ethic that is derived in its shape and in its meaning, and even in its language, from the novelty of the teaching and the work and the triumph of Jesus," precisely in the way that Paul "speaks to the relation of persons to each other within the most stable functions of society, [that is,] the family and the economy."[31] While the claim looks promising, it is based wholly on Yoder's interpretation of the *Haustafeln* or "household codes" of Col 3:18–4:1 and Eph 5:21–6:9. With regard to those passages, Yoder seeks to demonstrate that relationships between Jesus-followers are to be characterized by a kind of mutual subordination. This might set the stage for a further demonstration of Paul's concern for the poor, not least by linking Paul's theological ethic to Jesus' own proclamation of good news characterized by "social radicality." Ultimately, however, Yoder's analysis of Pauline texts is not articulated in terms of, nor deals with, Jesus' own proclamation of "good news to the poor."

More promising is Marcus Borg and John Dominic Crossan's book *The First Paul*.[32] Its subtitle, *Reclaiming the Radical Visionary behind the Church's*

---

29. John Howard Yoder, *The Politics of Jesus*, 2nd ed. (Grand Rapids: Eerdmans 1994 [1972]), pp. 10 and 168 respectively.

30. Yoder depicts the traditional tendencies of theologians in this way (*The Politics of Jesus*, p. 225): "Because Paul is different from Jesus or because justification is different from social ethics, therefore the way of Jesus, it was classically held, has lost its bindingness for our age."

31. Yoder, *The Politics of Jesus*, p. 179.

32. Marcus Borg and John Dominic Crossan, *The First Paul: Reclaiming the Radical Visionary behind the Church's Conservative Icon* (London: SPCK, 2009). Compare the estimate of Paul articulated by Martin Luther King Jr. (C. Carson, ed., *Symbol of the Movement*, vol. 4

Conservative Icon, might suggest that, if we were to look anywhere for a Paul whose gospel includes care for the poor, it would be this book, which demonstrates Paul to be "radical" in his vision of the gospel. And such a "radical" vision does have a foothold within its pages. In contrast to the impression given by Hoppe and Davids, Borg and Crossan assert that communities founded by Paul must have been "share communities," involving the "sharing of material as well as spiritual resources."[33] Their reasoning with regard to the sharing of material resources involves the following four points. First, the giving of bread was central to Jesus' ministry (as in the phrase "give us this day our daily bread"), and "[t]here is no reason to think that Paul dropped this emphasis."[34] Second, since Paul likened Jesus-followers to a "family," we should "imagine that the people in Paul's communities took care of each other," despite the economic fragility that would have marked out their ordinary existence.[35] Third, passages from 2 Thessalonians and 1 Timothy (both thought to be pseudonymous) illustrate that "freeloaders" were taking advantage of the internal mechanics of share-communities founded by Paul.[36] And fourth, Paul's stipulations concerning the Lord's Supper in 1 Cor 11:17-34 demonstrate that, for him, communities of Jesus-followers were those in which "[e]verybody gets enough" through the sharing of material resources.

Some of these points are stronger than others, and the stronger ones will reappear at a later point in this book. But even if Borg and Crossan are moving in the right direction with some of their claims, there is a sense in which their portrait of Paul's "radical" message about the sharing of material resources outstrips its exegetical foundations. This tendency is further evident in the concluding paragraph of their book, where they universalize the significance of Paul's collection efforts for "the poor among the saints in Jerusalem" so that the enduring feature of Paul's message ("then, now and always") is listed as being "about 'fair balance,' or a distributive justice, in which God's family all get an equitable share of God's world."[37]

of *The Papers of Martin Luther King, Jr.* [Berkeley: University of California Press, 2000], p. 187): "It has always been the responsibility of the Church to broaden horizons, challenge the status quo, and break the mores when necessary. Such was the role of Amos and Jeremiah, of Jesus and Paul."

33. Borg and Crossan, *The First Paul*, p. 188.
34. Borg and Crossan, *The First Paul*, p. 189.
35. Borg and Crossan, *The First Paul*, p. 189.
36. Borg and Crossan, *The First Paul*, pp. 189-90.
37. Borg and Crossan, *The First Paul*, p. 224.

In my estimate, there are better and more numerous data to be brought to the table than the ones suggested by Borg and Crossan (and without having to resort to universalizing Paul's Jerusalem collection) in order to catch a glimpse of the (so-called) "radical" Paul. In the chapters that follow, I will construct a case that demonstrates how care for the indigenous poor within the Greco-Roman world lay at the heart of Paul's understanding of the "good news" of the early Jesus-movement (although that good news is not in any way reducible simply to care for the poor). While the communities of Jesus-followers in Jerusalem became a specific focus of his attention from 53 through 57 CE, the collection that he undertook for them was merely one expression of an overarching principle about care for the poor that had long guided him when configuring the identity of Jesus-groups. Even if the theological vision outstripped practical realities, care for the poor was nonetheless firmly embedded within Paul's understanding of the internal matrices of the good news. As such, my case runs directly counter to that of, say, Barry Gordon, who interprets "the character of the economics of the Pauline epistles" in this way: "The communities for which he [Paul] feels responsible are not to make their incorporation in Christ an occasion for a plunge into experimentation with economic relationships."[38] While one might quibble with words like "plunge" and "experimentation," it is the simple word "not" that I find to be most misguided in Gordon's estimate.

The overarching argument of this book unfolds in the following fashion. The first part of the book examines "the poor in their ancient places" — that is, the historical and theological contexts that need to inform consideration of Paul and the poor. Chapters in this first main part of the book will:

- highlight elite acquisitiveness that so easily transpired in the advanced agrarianism of the ancient world (chapter 2);
- establish a multi-level "economy scale" that will assist in interpreting data with as much reliability and precision as possible throughout the course of this book (chapter 3);
- assess the extent to which charitable initiatives for the economically vulnerable were already present within non-Judeo-Christian sectors of the Greco-Roman world (chapter 4); and
- illustrate that care for the needy was integrally embedded within established theological traditions of Early Judaism, being noticeable not least

38. Barry Gordon, *The Economic Problem in Biblical and Patristic Thought* (Leiden: Brill, 1989), p. 78.

in the interests of Jesus, his early followers, and most likely his own influential brother, James (chapter 5).

The second part of the book examines "the poor in Pauline places" — that is, the place of the poor in Paul's theology and in communities that he founded. Chapters in this part of the book will:

- collect the evidence demonstrating that care for the poor was a vital part of Paul's theology and his expectations for communities of Jesus-followers (chapter 6);
- contrast the way that the phrase "remember the poor" of Gal 2:10 is interpreted in patristic documents and in contemporary scholarship (chapter 7);
- establish an exegetical basis for interpreting "remember the poor" in general alignment with the earliest patristic paradigm (chapter 8);
- demonstrate how this fresh exegesis enables the phrase "remember the poor" to resonate fully with the theological interests of the Galatian letter (chapter 9);
- offer economic profiles of Jesus-groups that Paul founded, and of certain figures within those groups (chapter 10);
- propose potential attractions of Jesus-groups for people of different economic levels in Greco-Roman urbanism (chapter 11); and
- assemble the data pertaining to economic relations within Jesus-communities and place them within a context of Paul's theology of gifting, difference and enhancement within groups of Jesus-followers (chapter 12).

The final chapter (chapter 13) will summarize the book's main argument, applying it to Paul's own socio-economic profile and his attitude to vulnerability.

Before all that, however, I need first to explain a few terminological, stylistic and conceptual choices that run throughout all the chapters of this book. First, much of this book will involve discussion of such things as "charitable initiatives" in the early Jesus-movement and the Greco-Roman world. Although the point will be made explicitly in one or two places, the issue of "charity" is controversial, not least in what it can all too easily signal about the giver (as superior) and the receiver (as inferior), as well as in what it can all too easily mask with regard to the need for structural configuration of economic systems. While we might hope that contemporary theological reasoning would take full account of such issues in our twenty-first-century world, a study of poverty alleviation in the ancient world is (I fear) far more restricted in its discursive parameters. Even if contemporary Christian discourse on poverty should go beyond the constraints imposed upon (much of the) ancient Christian discourse by its historical context, the study of poverty alleviation in the early Jesus-movement and its Greco-Roman context will generally be limited in both its terminology and conceptualization to "charitable initiatives" and the like.

Second, in what follows the term "Christian" is restricted to "Christian" phenomena of the second century CE and following, while terms like "the early Jesus-movement," "Jesus-followers," and "Jesus-groups" are used when discussing "Christian" phenomena of the first century CE. This is a judgment call that not all will agree with. But I do it for one main reason, itself both historical and theological. The terms "Christian" and "Christianity" have all too easily and too often implied to some that what Jesus began soon became something other than a form of Judaism. In its unnuanced form, this conceptualization is both historically and theologically problematic, at least with regard to the majority of the movement's first two generations or so. In any given instance, the relationship of early Jesus-followers to mainstream forms of Judaism will require careful articulation, which a term like "Jesus-followers" does not implicitly prejudice. And as this book itself hopes to show, the early Jesus-movement was itself a vibrant but variant form of Judaism with regard to concern for the poor. Rather than the term "Christian," others such as "Jesus-followers" and "Jesus-movement" help to avoid a potentially anti-Jewish skewing of the data, and permit a better nuancing of that movement's relationship to and/or within Judaism at any given point.

Third, in this project I refer to "God" with the terms "Israel's deity" or "the deity of Israel" (except in quotations from interpreters or from scriptural passages). I do this for reasons other than theological or ideological ones. Certain points in the argument of this book encroach upon the issue of the "marketplace of the deities" in the Greco-Roman world, in which case the depiction of one deity as "God" in contrast to others as "gods" ultimately runs against the historiographic grain.[39] Discourse that differentiates one "deity" from another (or from other "deities") replicates the historical context of the ancient world far better than discourse that implicitly prejudices

39. Not altogether dissimilarly, see N. T. Wright, *The New Testament and the People of God* (London: SPCK, 1992), pp. xiv-xv; since then, however, Wright has generally reverted to the more traditional stylistic choice.

its historical reconstruction with stylistic choices driven by a Judeo-Christian worldview. The mainstream Judeo-Christian worldview was a relatively rare one in the ancient world, and the Judeo-Christian conviction that "Israel's deity" is also the sovereign "God" of all creation who alone is worthy of worship and obedience would have been looked upon with suspicion by many in the ancient world. For them, the monotheistic worship of a single sovereign "God" would have seemed specious (since the deities were many)[40] and perilous (since the more deities you had in your pocket, the better your chances of survival and success). In historical reconstruction, discussing ancient deities without a "partisan" terminological bias does better justice to the worldviews that predominated in the Greco-Roman world, and drives the terminological preference for the noun "deity" that appears throughout this book.[41]

Fourth, and relatedly, there is the issue of how to employ gender-specific pronouns when discussing "Israel's deity." Is Israel's deity masculine, feminine, neither, both, or something altogether different? Again, for reasons other than theological, I err on the side of using masculine pronouns ("he," "his," "him") when pronouns are called for in this project. A pronoun of some kind is required stylistically in a sentence such as this one: "Israel's deity expected justice of his people but instead he saw bloodshed." To try to avoid traditional pronouns in favor of recently devised ones would simply make a sentence of that kind unworkable. To use "God-self" (with its uppercase "G") not only resorts to prioritizing of the Judeo-Christian deity but also is clumsy in the possessive case; to use "god-self" or "deity-self" is both stylistically clumsy and conceptually unworkable. Consequently, in view of our current language restrictions, a more traditional pronoun is required. While it is theologically problematic to restrict our conceptualization of the Judeo-Christian deity to any single gender, since a pronoun is stylistically necessary, I resort for merely historical reasons to the male pronouns, if only because this is the way that the ancient writers who devoted themselves to Israel's deity generally employed their pronouns.

Fifth, and less controversially, throughout this book I delineate its main sections through an uncomplicated numerical system. The four main parts of chapter 3, for instance, are delineated by a numerical differentiation: §3.1,

---

40. Note 1 Cor 8:5, with Paul's Judeo-Christian conviction taking over in 1 Cor 8:6.

41. This preference to avoid the "God/god" distinction in historical reconstruction has no necessary bearing on related theological issues about the nature of reality; the historian who writes about "Israel's deity" in the context of her historical investigations might well be seen offering praise in either a synagogue on the sabbath or in a church on Sunday.

§3.2, §3.3 and §3.4. This system allows for an ease of cross-referencing within the book, so that gestures can be made to argumentation registered earlier or later in the book. These gestures are delineated in ways such as: "see §3.3 above" or "as noted in §10.5 below." Moreover, those main sections are listed at the start of every chapter, in order to allow the reader to see in advance the argumentational flow that is to follow within that chapter. My aim in this is simply to assist the reader in the process of noting and assessing the argumentational foundations at key points.

Sixth, in this book English translations of the Bible are taken from the New Revised Standard Version (NRSV), except in a few instances where I have preferred to translate the passage alternatively. Wherever quotations of primary or secondary literature appear in the main body of the text in languages other than English, I have tried to ensure that (1) a translation can be found nearby, or (2) the quotation's content is obvious from my comments surrounding it.

And so we turn to the task of reconstructing the historical and theological contexts of poverty and care for the poor within the Greco-Roman world, against which Paul's own contribution to caring for the poor needs to be placed.

THE POOR IN THEIR ANCIENT PLACES

CHAPTER 2

"You have dishonored the poor man"

Advanced Agrarianism and Elite Acquisitiveness

2.1: Outlining Advanced Agrarian Cultures

2.2: Scriptural Denunciation of Elite Acquisitive Manipulation

In the 1970s Jesus-musical *Godspell,* the song "All for the Best" contrasts the disparities between the poor and the rich in the time of Jesus.[1] For the poor person, life is marked out by sadness, curses, the absence of any prospects, with creditors yapping at his heels. Although life for the poor man is little other than "crying, sighing and dying," he is assured that "when you go to heaven, you'll be blessed," and "yes, it's all for the best." Meanwhile, the rich live in leisure and luxury, "pulling pots of gold from thin air" and "making mountains of money." Controlling all the resources of the land, the rich are mimicked as saying, "Who is the land for? The sun and the sand for? You guessed! It's all for 'the best' [i.e., the rich]," while at the same time admitting that "Someone's got to be oppressed [i.e., the poor]."

Although playful, this little song puts its finger on the fundamental pulse of the harsh economic realities of the "advanced agrarian" cultures of the ancient world. In many agrarian societies, a large percentage of the population comprised primarily of peasant workers would have been cogs in a socio-economic machine that was largely controlled by only a small percentage of elite, who frequently ensured that they themselves were the primary beneficiaries of that socio-economic machinery. In such societies, the ten-

---

1. Lyrics by Stephen Schwartz, 1973.

dency is for those in control to imagine not only that "someone's got to be oppressed" but that, in fact, such a situation is all for "the best."

The world in which the early Jesus-movement took root was just such a world, a world in which Jesus is remembered to have said not only "blessed are the poor" (Luke 6:20; see also Matt 5:3) but also "woe to you who are rich . . . woe to you who are full now . . . woe to you who are laughing now" (Luke 6:24-25). The fundamental reason why such woes would have been spoken lies in the dynamics inherent within advanced agrarianism, as outlined in §2.1 below.

2.1: Outlining Advanced Agrarian Cultures

Macro-sociologists often distinguish between five forms of pre-industrial societies (as outlined below in the chart "Advanced Agrarian Societies in Developmental Context"):[2]

1. hunter-gatherer societies
2. simple horticultural
3. advanced horticultural
4. simple agrarian
5. advanced agrarian

Advanced Agrarian Societies in Developmental Context

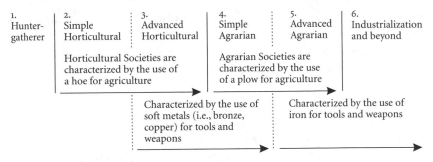

Although all five pre-industrial societies draw their primary resources from agricultural extraction, they are nonetheless configured differently. Moving from left to right on the chart involves moving from the nominal resources

2. The classic study is Gerhard E. Lenski, *Power and Privilege: A Theory of Social Stratification* (2nd ed.; Chapel Hill: University of North Carolina Press, 1984 [1966]).

of a hunter-gatherer's virtual hand-to-mouth and usually itinerant existence, through the hoe-based horticultural societies in which people-groups could settle in a single location and cultivate tracts of land, to the plow-based agrarian societies that saw arable land harvested extensively, with sizeable agricultural surpluses extracted from it.

Around the elevated agricultural yields of advanced agrarian cultures grew an administrative and economic infrastructure that had the potential to become highly imbalanced in terms of how those yields benefitted society. The most imbalanced advanced agrarian cultures heavily channeled resources from the peasants who worked the land "upwards" to the elite who controlled the economic and administrative mechanisms. Between the elite and the peasants grew up retainers who, receiving benefits from the elite, worked to the advantage of the elite in ensuring that as many resources as possible were put at their disposal. The distribution of the population within the most imbalanced advanced agrarian societies was close to being inversely proportional to the distribution of resources and power. When modeled, an advanced agrarian population is shown to be bottom-heavy, as evidenced in Gerhard Lenski's graph of advanced agrarianism (replicated on p. 22), which reveals the tremendous imbalance in societal power that could develop within advanced agrarian societies, to the benefit of the relatively few elite, through the assistance of their retainers.[3] In the Lenski graph, the amount of social power attributed to different sectors of society is represented by the vertical dimension, while the number of people at any level of social power is represented by the horizontal dimension. Certain qualifications might need to be applied to Lenski's graph when it is applied specifically to rural or to urban contexts, and some advanced agrarian cultures would have been more elongated than others. But in general, Lenski's graph has stood the test of time as a basic outline of population distribution within advanced agrarian society.[4]

Controlling the majority of the resources-that-mattered within advanced agrarian societies were the elite of various sorts (often headed by a ruler, as in Lenski's graph). Over against the masses, the elite controlled the mechanisms of resource distribution.[5] Inevitably, those mechanisms were

3. Lenski, *Power and Privilege,* p. 284; cf. also p. 82.

4. Complicating the Lenski model is the matter of the relationship of agrarian societies within larger agrarian empires. In such scenarios, indigenous authorities are underlings to the ruling authorities of the larger governing entity, often with conflicting interests. On this and other weaknesses in Lenski's model, see Richard A. Horsley, *Scribes, Visionaries, and the Politics of Second Temple Judea* (Louisville: Westminster John Knox Press, 2007), p. 61.

5. An obvious example is their ability to store grain supplies in storehouses until such a

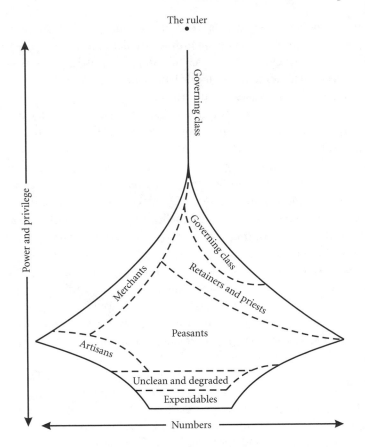

used to ensure the interests of the elite (although it was not always in the interests of the elite to override the interests of the peasantry).[6] Religious systems managed by priestly retainers usually bolstered the prospects of the elite, with the deities justifying the way things were and legitimating further

---

time as the grain prices increase — that is, "wealthy landowners [refuse] to sell their produce at reasonable prices because they are waiting for less bountiful harvests; . . . [they interfere] with the food supply and [enter] into partnership[s] in order to drive up the price of grain" (Justinian, *Dig.* 47.11.6; 48.12.2).

6. On elite self-restraints as themselves serving the interests of the elite, see especially L. de Ligt, "Restraining the Rich, Protecting the Poor: Symbolic Aspects of Roman Legislation," in W. Jongman and M. Kleijwegt, eds., *After the Past* (Leiden: Brill, 2002), 1-46. With regard to denunciations of elite acquisitiveness by authors within the Hebrew Bible, see Walter J. Houston, *Contending for Justice: Ideologies and Theologies of Social Justice in the Old Testament* (rev. ed.; London: T&T Clark, 2008).

initiatives to fortify the resources of the elite, usually at the expense of others. Legal systems tended to reflect elite interests, with justice often being determined on the basis of where people were placed in the system of power and resources.[7] The elite often devised opportunities to acquire land or other resources from others, usually through lightly disguised pilfering.[8] The plundering of land rights was often done through official confiscation and was legally rubber-stamped when an elite orchestrated acquisition of tracts of land held by non-elite. In this venture they proved to be enormously effective and successful.[9]

The majority of the non-elite were involved in manual labor of some kind, a form of existence that was generally despised among the elite. Most laborers earned whatever living they could make from some form of agricultural extraction. Some laborers were fortunate to own their own small farms. Significant numbers, however, were tenant farmers, who rented their farms from "absentee landlords" (customarily at exorbitant costs and for short periods of time), or were slave-tenants tasked with the responsibility of extracting the yields of the land for the landowner. Whether the landowner-tenant relationship "was more akin to partnership or to exploitation depended to a large degree on the bargaining power of the tenant,"[10]

7. On this, see de Ligt, "Restraining the Rich, Protecting the Poor," where he makes the point repeatedly at the start of his article (pp. 1-2), the first paragraph of which reads: "It has . . . become a banality in historical research that, far from representing a neutral force contributing to the orderly functioning of society, the judicial apparatus of the state has generally operated in the interests of the social group that controls it . . . [and] the Roman empire was no exception to this rule."

8. See *CIL* VIII 10570, 14464, where some tenants (describing themselves as "poor rustic people tolerating a livelihood gained from the work of our own hands") see themselves as "unfairly matched with a lessee" who himself was "most influential . . . because of his lavish gifts," and who had been raising the land rental on the tenants and requiring them to work more than they had been contracted to work. The case was decided in their favor in this instance, but it was likely to have been exceptional in this regard.

9. So Cyprian writes (*Don.* 12): The elite are those "who add forests to forests, and who, excluding the poor from their neighborhood, stretch out their fields far and wide into space without any limits, who possess immense heaps of silver and gold."

10. Dennis P. Kehoe, "Landlords and Tenants," in David S. Potter, ed., *A Companion to the Roman Empire* (Oxford: Blackwell, 2006), 298-311, p. 305. Kehoe had already noted, however, that "the relationship between landowner and slave was in essence one of exploitation, no matter how kind the landowner might seem" (p. 301). Kehoe's article is framed by this recognition at both the start and finish. At the start of the article, he notes that "agricultural wealth played a crucial role in the social and political structures of the Roman Empire" and that the "elite classes that ruled the empire . . . depended on the production of their estates

but a tenant's bargaining power was normally quite minimal.[11] Although some landowner-tenant relationships would have been "healthier" than others, the common denominator in them all was the financial gain that inevitably came to the elite landowner whenever surplus was involved, often at the expense of the tenant.[12]

Others also worked the land. Day laborers sought work in any capacity, but usually for only meager recompense. Except in cases of those who owned small farms, the harvests that workers extracted generated surpluses for urban elite landowners — many of whom had acquired the land through the beneficence of the ruler or through an acquisitive take-over that could not have been fought off in any court of "justice." The "courts of law" could barely pretend to be anything other than "instruments of social control . . . [and] one way in which superior social status was displayed and maintained" in the public arena.[13] Often tenant farmers had previously owned the very farm that they now rented from the elite, and the surpluses that they garnered from the land now went to the coffers of the urban elite.[14] And when workers were "a dime a dozen," there was little to prevent the urban

---

or the revenues that maintained their social and political privileges" (p. 298), while at the end of the article he notes that "the revenues that the state and the landowning elite derived from agriculture helped to sustain the magnificent urban culture of the Roman Empire, but these revenues depended on extracting surplus production from numerous small-scale tenants" (p. 311). In between, however, he at times avoids painting a harsh picture of the elite, noting occasions in which, despite their intentions of "living the evil life" (as in one complaint against them), they were not always permitted to get their own way without restraint (pp. 307-308), or another in which the landowner did not act with the severity that Roman law permitted him (pp. 309-310). At the same time, Kehoe notes that the profits of the elite "depended on maximizing the effort extracted from the slaves," who "represented a commodity" and who "might be worked to death" in the process of resource extraction (p. 301).

11. L. Foxhall, "The Dependent Tenant: Land Leasing and Labour in Italy and Greece," *JRS* 80 (1990): 97-114.

12. Compare Kehoe, "Landlords and Tenants," p. 306: "this form of tenancy seems well designed to serve the interests of the upper-class landowners seeking stable incomes from their farms." For an in-depth study of technology and agrarian change, see P. Horden and N. Purcell, *The Corrupting Sea: A Study of Mediterranean History* (Oxford: Oxford University Press, 2000), pp. 231-97.

13. John S. Kloppenborg, "Egalitarianism in the Myth and Rhetoric of Pauline Churches," in E. A. Castelli and T. Taussig, eds., *Reimagining Christian Origins* (Philadelphia: Trinity Press International, 1996), 247-63, pp. 255-56.

14. Cicero (*Fam.* 11.11.1; 13.7.1-2) makes the latter point when saying that the fortunes of the civic centers like Atella and Arinum are derived from the rent acquired by the elite from renting out the rural lands that they own.

elite from maximalizing the percentage of their "top-slice" by exploiting their rural workers, through the assistance of a business manager, and to the point of leaving them with nothing more than the bare resources needed for the most basic form of living — a case of "living just enough for the city."[15]

This is the knife-edge existence that characterized the lives of many peasants of the ancient world. For long stretches, some might have survived at subsistence level, at times getting the odd bit of good luck to provide them with a thin cushion against the harsh realities of life, and at other times dropping below subsistence levels temporarily, only to pull themselves out of what was all-too-often the inevitable end. Some who owned their own land will have been much more fortunate, in that the surpluses that they harvested were not automatically siphoned off and designated as the property of the elite. But many who did not own land were not so fortunate, having to resort to banditry, beggary, prostitution, and the like, in order to forgo the inescapable grip of poverty.

Manual laborers at the boundary of subsistence and destitution may have empathized with Homer's characterization of Sisyphus, "the craftiest of men" (*Il.* 6.154). In Homeric lore, Sisyphus was confined in Hades where he was forced to role a stone up a mountain to its summit. Each time, when it neared the summit, the stone would roll back down to the bottom of the mountain, with Sisyphus having to start the grueling process all over again — a process to be repeated throughout all of time. Unlike the promises held out by the infamous American Dream, the myth of Sisyphus spoke of the futility of human existence for those who expected there to be some correlation between the amount of effort one mustered and one's consequent achievements.

In many ways parasitic to the agricultural base of agrarian cultures, but also somewhat independent from its structures, were merchants, traders, artisans and shop or tavern owners. Many of them will have struggled at subsistence levels. The second-century rhetorician Lucian of Samosata (*c.* 125-80 CE) describes the life of an artisan as being "laborious and barely able to supply them [i.e., the artisans] with just enough."[16] For a great many, however,

---

15. Here I am borrowing a phrase, of course, from the Stevie Wonder song "Living for the City." Similar dynamics were in play for the fishing industry; see K. C. Hansen and Douglas E. Oakman, *Palestine in the Time of Jesus* (Minneapolis: Fortress, 1998), pp. 106-110.

16. Lucian, *Fugitivi* 12-13. Compare his depiction of Micyllus, a leather-working artisan, who depicts his own impending death as a time when he will never again "go hungry from morning to night or wander about in winter barefooted and half-naked, with my teeth chattering from cold" (Lucian, *Cataplus* 20).

even the harsh life of a struggling artisan might have seemed like comfort. These were the unskilled laborers who filled the cities, making themselves available for any form of menial work in order to survive. For them, life was nothing short of precarious. Their diet and living conditions often assured as much.[17] In short, for many "cities were death traps at the best of times."[18]

Some urbanites, however, will have managed to carve out a more economically secure existence. In the first two centuries of the common era, for instance, signs of modest economic growth within agrarian imperialism is largely to be attributed to commerce, trade and mining initiatives. Some of the luckier and/or better placed seem to have benefited from this growth in some economic sectors. (The impact of this on the population percentages will be discussed in chapter 3 and appendix 1 below.)

I have not attempted here to spell out a full economic description of advanced agrarian cultures, or to account for all of the economic dimensions of the ancient world. With regard to the Greco-Roman world, for instance, I have left to one side the role and placement of various features: education and literacy; militarization and warfare; scribalism; taxation systems; usury loans; patronage; honor systems; kinship; the perception of limited good; the advantages of cash crops over against subsistence crops; forms of resistance; slavery; debt and debt release; and monetization.

No attempt is made here to trace out the interrelated mechanisms contributing to economic well-being in the ancient world; instead, it is enough to highlight several features that have been adequately demonstrated by others, and which provide the backdrop against which the present study operates. Evident in the ancient record is a glaring difference in economic security between the elite few at the one end of the socio-economic spectrum and the many at subsistence level at the other end. There were middling groups (as will be shown in chapter 3 below), and some agrarian cultures fostered middling groups more than others, but there was nothing like the "middle class" that predominates in most western cultures today. There were not the kind of checks and balances placed on societal power that characterizes most democracies of the twenty-first century. In general, power was raw, and was often utilized brashly to redistribute resources upwards to those in

17. On the Greco-Roman urban context, see Justin J. Meggitt, *Paul, Poverty and Survival* (Edinburgh: T&T Clark, 1998), pp. 41-73. On housing in the city of Rome itself, see the evidence collected by Robert Jewett, *Romans* (Minneapolis: Fortress Press, 2007), pp. 53-55.

18. W. Jongman, "Beneficial Symbols: *Alimenta* and the Infantilization of the Roman Citizen," in W. Jongman and M. Kleijwegt, eds., *After the Past* (Leiden: Brill, 2002), 47-80, p. 70.

control in a brazenly acquisitive fashion. Those with power did everything to acquire more power, often in blatantly calculating and oppressive measures that compounded life's difficulties for those less secure than themselves. Nets of social security to catch those in need and buffer the ravages of hardship were (at best) few, far-between, and feeble. Those who lost out simply had to find a way of living in more precarious situations.

In this discussion I have erred on the side of avoiding historical anecdotes for the various features mentioned. This is because, for our purposes, the sole feature that needs to be highlighted is the acquisitive character of power in advanced agrarian cultures in general, with the elite being well-placed to use their power to acquire the resources of others. Passages from the Judeo-Christian scriptures will be used to illustrate the point in §2.2 below.

One other example is offered here, however, since it illustrates how those in power at times stopped at nothing in their efforts to extract even the smallest of resources out of the impoverished. In his *De specialibus legibus* 3:159-60, the first-century Alexandrian Jewish philosopher Philo gives an account of a tax collector, a retainer of the elite. The tax collector persecuted some of the families of those who, being unable to pay their taxes, had fled the region of the tax collector's authority. The tax collector is said to have

> carried off [the debtors'] wives, and their children, and their parents, and their whole families by force, beating and insulting them, and heaping every kind of insolent and ill treatment upon them, to make them either give information as to where the fugitives had concealed themselves, or pay the money instead of them, though they could not do either the one thing or the other.

Philo does not shy away from recounting the specifics of horrific torture that the tax collector inflicted on this family in his efforts to extract the relatively small amounts of tax owed:

> he tortured their bodies with racks and wheels, so as to kill them with newly invented kinds of death, fastening a basket full of sand to their necks with cords, and suspending it there as a very heavy weight, and then placing them in the open air in the middle of the market place, that some of them, being tortured and being overwhelmed by all these afflictions at once, the wind, and the sun, and the mockery of the passersby, and the shame, and the heavy burden attached to them, might faint miserably; and that the rest, being spectators, might be grieved and take warning by their punishment.

The portrait is hopefully a much exaggerated one. But even in its exaggerated form, it is indicative of how the retainers of the elite could be regarded as ruthless in their efforts to extract even small amounts of resources from the poor.

There would no doubt have been instances in which the relationship between the elites and their sub-retainer workforces was more symbiotic and healthy, and less disproportionate and exploitative.[19] And as will be argued in §4.3 and §4.4 below, instances of elite generosity to those in need are not at all absent from the ancient record. And for some enterprising elite, even generous initiatives to the needy could become instruments for the win-win of enhancing both societal health and (thereby) personal prestige. Nonetheless, agrarian societies were inevitably structured to benefit the elite (and their retainers), and often to the detriment of many of the sub-elite.[20] In general, agrarian societies fostered elite acquisitiveness, and agrarian elite were known to ensure that any restraints there might be against acquisitiveness were kept firmly in their own control, to their own advantage. Those who lost out were the numerous poor, many of whom faced a life of extreme poverty against the ravages of elite acquisitiveness. Although their voices have for the most part been omitted from the material record of agrarian societies, those voices can occasionally be heard in texts of critique against the elite.

This is perhaps nowhere more the case than in the literary records of the Judeo-Christian tradition.[21] The next section offers something of an inventory of Judeo-Christian voices against the acquisitiveness that could all too

19. See, for instance, the essays in H. M. Parkins, ed., *Roman Urbanism: Beyond the Consumer City* (London: Routledge, 1997). The balance between oppressive and symbiotic relations between the urban and rural areas is struck well by R. MacMullen (*Roman Social Relations: 50 BC to AD 284* [New Haven: Yale University Press, 1974], p. 55): "Town and country got along together . . . because they had to. Very different their needs, very unequal their resources, and of course very different their treatment of each other. If in the relationship the peasant seems most often the loser, that was simply his lot, to give and suffer, but to get something in return as well."

20. Richard S. Ascough (*Lydia: Paul's Cosmopolitan Hostess* [Collegeville, MN: Liturgical Press, 2009]) tries to do justice to both issues, noting first how rural and urban contexts "were mutually dependent for their survival" (p. 16), before concluding that "despite the mutual dependency of one on the other, the urban centers had both the physical and social advantages" (p. 17), not least because "land became concentrated in the hands of a few persons" located in the city, "where power and benefaction by the elite predominated" (p. 25).

21. I cannot enter into the discussion of whether the prophetic literature of the Jewish scriptures was composed by disenfranchised elites or relatively poor challengers of the system. On these matters, see Jon L. Berquist, *Judaism in Persia's Shadow: A Social and Historical Approach* (Minneapolis: Fortress Press, 1995), 184-85; Johannes Un-sok Ro, "Socio-Economic Context of Post-Exilic Community and Literacy," *ZAW* 120 (2008): 597-611.

easily tip the relationship of elite and sub-elite from being one of healthy symbiosis to one of unhealthy oppression and injustice.

2.2: Scriptural Denunciation of Elite Acquisitive Manipulation

Against the backdrop of elite acquisitiveness in advanced agrarian societies, the scriptural resources of the Judeo-Christian tradition stand out starkly. While some traditions depict wealth as the result of divine blessing on the virtuous,[22] there is nonetheless a fairly consistent "prophetic" voice denouncing the way in which the elite can all too easily work the socioeconomic machinery to acquire resources for themselves.[23] It is this acquisitive dimension of poverty and wealth that, when it appears on the scriptural radar, is denounced almost ubiquitously.

Glimpses of the acquisitive nature of advanced agrarian society are evident in 1 Sam 8:11-20. There the prophet Samuel warns the people of Israel of the implications of establishing an elongated agrarian society. The people were seeking to replace their structures of leadership (in which a group of elders shared authority) with another that designated a single figure, a ruler, at the top of the social structures, in order that the people of Israel might be "like other nations" (1 Sam 8:5, 20). Israel's deity instructs Samuel to warn them of the consequences, and so Samuel says the following words, to the effect that "absolute power will corrupt absolutely" (1 Sam 8:11-18):

> These will be the ways of the king who will reign over you: he will take your sons and appoint them to his chariots and to be his horsemen, and to run before his chariots; and he will appoint for himself commanders of thousands and commanders of fifties, and some to plow his ground and to reap his harvest, and to make his implements of war and the equipment of his chariots. He will take your daughters to be perfumers, cooks and bakers. He will take the best of your fields and vineyards and olive orchards and give them to his servants. He will take the tenth of your grain and of your vineyards and give it to his officers and to his servants. He will take your menservants and maidservants, and the best of your cattle and your asses, and put them to his work. He will take the tenth of your flocks, and you shall be his slaves. And in that day you will cry out because of

---

22. Compare Deut 8:17-18; Prov 22:2-4; 28:25.
23. Compare the prophetic critique of the oppressive elite in Amos; e.g., Amos 2:6-7; 3:15; 5:21-24.

your king, whom you have chosen for yourselves; but the LORD will not
answer you in that day.

This speech testifies to the acquisitive nature of advanced agrarian societies. Samuel's reconstruction of the implications of moving to a more elongated agrarian structure was intended to repulse the people from going
down that road. But the people insist, intent as they were to appoint a king
who could lead them into warfare (i.e., to acquire properties not currently
their own). But if it was intended as a repugnant portrait of the implications
of moving further into elongated agrarianism, it looks rather tame in relation to the elongation of the Greco-Roman world, where the power of the
elite outshone the power of the Israelite king depicted in 1 Samuel 8.

Similarly tame, but nonetheless illustrative, is the story of king Ahab's
acquisition of Naboth's vineyard in 1 Kings 21. King Ahab is said to want
Naboth's vineyard because it is next to his palace, and he offers Naboth its
value in money or an even better vineyard in exchange. Naboth refuses the
offer, because the vineyard was his ancestral inheritance. While Ahab sulks,
his wife Jezebel devises a plot to accomplish her husband's wishes. Before
long, Naboth's death is wickedly orchestrated, whereupon Ahab takes possession of Naboth's vineyard, which he had so desperately wanted. Unsur-
prisingly, the reader is told King Ahab did "what is evil in the sight of the
LORD" (1 Kings 21:20).

The prophets of Israel often denounced the excesses of agrarian acquisitiveness. Isaiah declares that Israel's deity "expected justice" of his people but
instead he "saw bloodshed"; he expected "righteousness, but heard a cry" (Isa
5:7) As Isaiah explains, the injustice and unrighteousness that Israel's deity
saw among his people pertain to the acquisitiveness of Israel's elite (Isa 5:8):
"You who join house to house, who add field to field, until there is room for
no one but you, and you are left to live alone in the midst of the land!"

Similarly the prophet Micah outlines the culture of elite acquisitiveness
in two simple verses (Mic 2:1-2):

Alas for those who devise wickedness and evil deeds on their beds! When
the morning dawns, they perform it, because it is in their power. They
covet fields, and seize them; houses, and take them away; they oppress
householder and house, people and their inheritance.

Seizing the possessions and resources of others is effortlessly done when it is
simply "in one's power" to do it, apart from moral or institutional deter-

rence. That the gain of the powerful is acquired through unjust means is outlined in the accusations against them, uttered on behalf of Israel's deity by Micah (Mic 6:9-12):

> The voice of the LORD cries to the city: . . . "Hear, O tribe and assembly of the city! Can I forget the treasures of wickedness in the house of the wicked, and the scant measure that is accursed? Can I tolerate wicked scales and a bag of dishonest weights? Your wealthy are full of violence; your inhabitants speak lies, with tongues of deceit in their mouths."

Unjust means of measurement (i.e., scant measures, wicked scales, dishonest weights) ensured that the elite's retainers received higher levels of repayment than those required by the terms of the agreement.[24] The "violence" of the wealthy here is not physical violence or warfare, but economic violence against the well-being of those insecurely placed on the economic structures of advanced agrarianism. So the prophetic speech against the elite likens their schemes to the shedding of "blood" through the corruption of the courts (7:2-3):

> They all lie in wait for blood, and they hunt each other with nets. Their hands are skilled to do evil; the official and the judge ask for a bribe, and the powerful dictate what they desire; thus they pervert justice.

This kind of acquisition at all costs (or better, acquisition at no cost, but simply through the manipulation of power) is frequently denounced in the Judeo-Christian scriptures. The prophet Amos, speaking on behalf of the deity of Israel, forewarns of the utter destruction of the acquisitive elite. Depicting Israel's deity as the one "who makes destruction flash out against the strong, so that destruction comes upon the fortress" (Amos 5:9), and depicting the strong as those who hate "the one who speaks the truth" to them prophetically at the city gates (5:10), the divine denunciation of elite acquisitiveness is articulated in the following fashion (Amos 5:11-12):

> Therefore because you trample on the poor and take from them levies of grain, you have built houses of hewn stone, but you shall not live in them;

---

24. For an exploration of this in relation to the "measure for measure" aphorism of the early Jesus tradition, see John S. Kloppenborg, "Agrarian Discourse and the Sayings of Jesus: 'Measure for Measure' in Gospel Traditions and Agricultural Practices," in Bruce W. Longenecker and Kelly Liebengood, eds., *Engaging Economics: New Testament Scenarios and Early Christian Reception* (Grand Rapids: Eerdmans, 2009), 104-128.

you have planted pleasant vineyards, but you shall not drink their wine. For I know how many are your transgressions, and how great are your sins — you who afflict the righteous, who take a bribe, and push aside the needy in the gate.

The elite have built their treasures from the resources extracted unjustly from the poor, and in the process their hearts are hardened against the very ones that the deity of Israel had committed himself to — i.e., "the needy at the gate."[25]

Through Micah, the deity of Israel announces that his wrath is already at work in punishing the acquisitive elite (Mic 6:13-16):

Therefore I have begun to strike you down, making you desolate because of your sins. You shall eat, but not be satisfied, and there shall be a gnawing hunger within you; you shall put away, but not save, and what you save, I will hand over to the sword. You shall sow, but not reap; you shall tread olives, but not anoint yourselves with oil; you shall tread grapes, but not drink wine. For you have kept the statutes of Omri and all the works of the house of Ahab, and you have followed their counsels. Therefore I will make you a desolation, and your inhabitants an object of hissing; so you shall bear the scorn of my people.

The hyperbole only accentuates the divine disapproval of the way that the elite have manipulated their positions in order to be "satisfied."

Towards its closure, the Isaianic corpus offers a vision of the "new heavens and a new earth" that the deity of Israel will create. In the short pseudo-apocalyptic text of Isa 65:17-22, Israel's deity describes the new creation as a place devoid of acquisitiveness and its side-effects:

Behold I will create new heavens and a new earth. The former things will not be remembered, nor will they come to mind. . . . I will rejoice over Jerusalem, . . . the sound of weeping and of crying will be heard in it no more. Never again will there be in it an infant that lives but a few days, or an old man who does not live out his years. . . . They will build houses and dwell in them; they will plant vineyards and eat their fruit. No longer will they build houses and others live in them, or plant and others eat.

---

25. On the historical context of Amos's critique, see Ellen F. Davis, *Scripture, Culture, and Agriculture: An Agrarian Reading of the Bible* (Cambridge: Cambridge University Press, 2009), pp. 123-25.

In this embodiment of the eschatological age, the corporate life of Israel will itself display the sovereignty and transforming power of Israel's deity. Thus, resources will not be siphoned off to benefit the few; instead, the agonies and tragedies experienced predominately by the poor will be replaced by equitable relationships of production, harvest and benefit.

It might be that we should hear Jesus' denunciation of scribes in Luke 20 against this backdrop. In Luke 20:46-47 (see also Mark 12:38-40), Jesus depicts the scribes (probably temple scribes) as those immersed in the honor code of the ancient Mediterranean world and, accordingly, as those who acquire the property of the vulnerable in order to enhance their own stature and status:

> Beware of the scribes, who like to walk around in long robes, and love to be greeted with respect in the marketplaces, and to have the best seats in the synagogues and places of honor at banquets. They devour widows' houses and for the sake of appearance say long prayers.

According to Jesus in that passage, people who act in the way of honor-through-acquisition are condemned.[26]

The most pronounced description of divine judgment against acquisitiveness of the elite and their retainers appears in the Johannine apocalypse. An extended snapshot of the unraveling of the acquisitiveness of advanced agrarianism is offered in Rev 18:9-19. Having depicted the destruction of the great whore (i.e., the city Babylon, a cipher for Rome), the narrative then shifts to focus on the reaction of the elite and those parasitic on the extreme excesses of acquisitive agrarianism, after the destruction of the system from which they have benefitted:

> And the kings of the earth, who committed fornication and were wanton with her, will weep and wail over her when they see the smoke of her burning; they will stand far off, in fear of her torment, and say, "Alas! alas! thou great city, thou mighty city, Babylon! In one hour has thy judgment come."

26. Compare *T. Mos.* 7:3-9: Those who rule in the Jerusalem temple after the time of Herod the Great will be "destructive and godless men, who represent themselves as being righteous, but . . . they will be deceitful men, pleasing only themselves, false in every way imaginable. . . . They consume the goods of the poor, saying their acts are according to justice, (while in fact they are simply) exterminators, deceitfully seeking to conceal themselves so that they will not be known as completely godless because of the criminal deeds (committed) all day long."

And the merchants of the earth weep and mourn for her, since no one buys their cargo any more, cargo of gold, silver, jewels and pearls, fine linen, purple, silk and scarlet, all kinds of scented wood, all articles of ivory, all articles of costly wood, bronze, iron and marble, cinnamon, spice, incense, myrrh, frankincense, wine, oil, fine flour and wheat, cattle and sheep, horses and chariots, and slaves, that is, human souls. "The fruit for which thy soul longed has gone from thee, and all thy dainties and thy splendor are lost to thee, never to be found again!"

The merchants of these wares, who gained wealth from her, will stand far off, in fear of her torment, weeping and mourning aloud, "Alas, alas, for the great city that was clothed in fine linen, in purple and scarlet, be-decked with gold, with jewels, and with pearls! In one hour all this wealth has been laid waste."

And all shipmasters and seafaring men, sailors and all whose trade is on the sea, stood far off and cried out as they saw the smoke of her burn-ing, "What city was like the great city?" And they threw dust on their heads, as they wept and mourned, crying out, "Alas, alas, for the great city where all who had ships at sea grew rich by her wealth! In one hour she has been laid waste."

At the center of this eulogy to agrarian acquisitiveness is the list of goods on which the massive surpluses of the elite and their retainers were founded. Starting with the most precious entries of "gold, silver, jewels and pearls," the list in Rev 18:12-13 outlines all sorts of other commodities, in descending or-der. At the bottom of the list, after the entries "wheat, cattle and sheep, horses and chariots," is found a sobering entry: "slaves, that is, human souls" (σωμάτων, καὶ ψυχὰς ἀνθρώπων).[27] The list ominously exposes the value-system of advanced agrarianism in which the elite and their retainers grow rich unrestrainedly, without concern for the "human souls" that they tram-ple in the process, or for the earth that they are destroying in their acquisitive quest (11:18).[28]

---

27. I take the καί to be epexegetical, unpacking something of the meaning of "slaves." Johannes P. Louw and Eugene A. Nida's entry for σῶμα in Rev 18:13 (*Greek-English Lexicon of the New Testament Based on Semantic Domains* [New York: United Bible Societies, 1988/89], §87.78) reads: "a slave as property to be sold, with the probable implication of commerce."

28. The Johannine apocalypse links all the economic developments of the first-century world to Rome (i.e., the harlot). A different view is propounded by David Mattingly ("The Imperial Economy," in David S. Potter, ed., *A Companion to the Roman Empire* [Oxford: Blackwell, 2006], 283-97, p. 296), who suggests that some economic sectors were indepen-dent of Rome's imperial economy: "free market trade flourished alongside the imperial

Judeo-Christian traditions frequently speak out against the acquisitiveness of the advanced agrarian elite, offsetting rampant avarice with vigorous prophetic calls for supporting the vulnerable and caring for the needy. As the next chapter demonstrates, the economically poor would have comprised at least half of the urban environment of Paul's mission.

---

economy, especially in the core provinces of the empire. This can be seen in part in the long-distance transport and wide distribution of many goods to centers other than the city of Rome and the main military frontiers." With this view of the flourishing of "free market trade," Mattingly introduces some of the issues to be addressed in chapter 3 below.

"The least of these"

Scaling Poverty in the Greco-Roman World

If the socio-economic structures of the ancient agrarian world differed from those of the modern western world, so too did the population distribution within the economic spectrum of Greco-Roman urbanism. Although the Jesus-movement had its earliest roots in the rural contexts of Galilee, urban centers quickly became the primary context for the expansion of the early Jesus-movement throughout the Mediterranean basin. Greco-Roman urbanism was the environment in which Paul's missionary efforts were concentrated. Consequently, in order to derive a clearer vision of Paul's ministry within the economic contours of the Greco-Roman world, it is important to outline the economic configuration of the urban population of the Greco-Roman world. That is what this chapter seeks to do, modeling an "economy scale" that will help to earth several important aspects of the argumentation of subsequent chapters of this book.

3.1: On Modeling Greco-Roman Poverty

Being pre-industrial and primarily agrarian, the Greco-Roman economic system was substantially different from economic systems that predominate in the developed and capitalist world of the twenty-first century. When this simple observation is lost from view, it is all too easy to read texts from the ancient world through the relatively comfortable lenses of contemporary middle-class affluence, and to be relatively numb to the economic dynamics that regimented ancient life to a considerable extent.

Analysis of economic realities of the Greco-Roman world have been high on the agenda of research over the past few decades, with significant developments in historical understanding having resulted especially from recent archaeological advances. Interdisciplinary dialogue between classicists and historians of the early Jesus-movement has been especially helpful in foregrounding the economic context in which that movement took root and expanded.

In fact, one particularly important development in this area has been the creation of heuristic scales or charts that offer economic profiling of the Greco-Roman world. In this chapter, I work towards establishing an economy scale, through which the data of successive chapters will be fed.

Why is an economy scale helpful — in fact, necessary? The answer lies in the very nature of the extant evidence from the Greco-Roman world. The literary remains of the Greco-Roman world show no standardization in their terminological usage with regard to economic stratification, not least with regard to levels of economic poverty. It is often postulated that in ancient literature the term πένης refers to one who has resources of some kind but struggles to survive through the harsh conditions of toil (i.e., owners of small farms, and the like), whereas the term πτωχός was used to signal the beggar without resources whatsoever (see Aristophanes, *Plut.* 552–54).[1] And Plato imagined the ideal republic to include the poor man who labors with his hands (the πένης) but to exclude the destitute man (the πτωχός), since such a person is the result of "a defective culture and bad breeding" (*Resp.* 552D; see also *Leg.* 11.936B, C). But if this distinction looks like the promising beginning of an economic stratification arising from the ancient data themselves, the promise is short-lived in relation to a broad cross-section of the data. The ancient record shows a fundamental instability regarding the terminology and the conceptualization of poverty. In his play *Dyskolos*, for instance, Menander applies the term πτωχός to the land-owning and slave-

---

1. So, J. P. Louw and E. A. Nida (*Greek-English Lexicon of the New Testament Based on Semantic Domains* [New York: United Bible Societies, 1988/1989], 57.50) define πένης as "a person who is poor and must live sparingly, but probably not as destitute as a person spoken of as πτωχός."

owning character Gorgias (ll. 284-86). Conversely, Philo uses the term πένης of destitute people without land (e.g., *Virt.* 90, 97; *Spec.* 2:85, 105; 3:159; *Legat.* 123). And in the *Clementine Homilies,* when Peter states that Jesus "pronounced the faithful poor to be blessed" because they were so poor as to have nothing at all, the term used is not πτωχός, as we might expect if the terminology were stable, but πένης (πιστοὺς πένητας ἐμακάρισεν, 15.10). As Robin Osborne notes, then, neither πένης nor πτωχός "was sufficiently laden with associations with a particular level of need to prevent its use in quite other circumstances."[2]

Relatedly, some ancient authors show a preference for using only one term to connote a spectrum of poverties, rather than dissecting poverty into various terminological compartments. Whereas the authors collected in the New Testament make far greater use of πτωχός than πένης, Josephus and Philo much prefer πένης and its cognates to πτωχός. So when Philo wants to speak of a poor man becoming destitute, he uses not πτωχός but the comparative form of πενιχρός to depict destitution (πενιχρότερον, *Spec.* 2:75; see also *Virt.* 84).

Moreover, while it is the case that ancient rhetoricians frequently collapsed non-elite status into one overarching economic category of poverty, at times they also relegated less-affluent elite to that same category. In the first century CE the poet Martial described Gaurus as poor (*Epigr.* 4.67), although Gaurus is said to have possessed 300,000 sesterces — hardly a trifling amount. In Marcian's *Novel* 4 (mid-5th century CE), a woman is depicted as a "pauper" who is also said to be worthy of marrying an elite senator. As Caroline Humfress suggests, this is "probably a woman of (what we might term) middling means, perhaps even a woman of high rank who had lost her family patrimony and had thereby become poor, or rather poorer. She was certainly not one of the destitute 'permanent poor.'"[3] Similarly Plutarch connects the "deprivation of wealth" with the loss of opportunities to demonstrate one's opulence, when he writes: "most people think themselves deprived of wealth if they are prevented from showing off; the display is made in the superfluities, not the essential of life" (*Cat. Maj.* 18). Further, according to Anneliese Parkin, when Seneca discusses giving assistance to the needy poor (a *pauper* or *egens*), he reduces the scope of the poor to "respectable citizens, and not

2. R. Osborne, "Roman Poverty in Context," in M. Atkins and R. Osborne, eds., *Poverty in the Roman World* (Cambridge: Cambridge University Press, 2006), 1-20, p. 11.

3. C. Humfress, "Poverty and Roman Law," in Atkins and Osborne, eds., *Poverty in the Roman World,* 188-203, p. 188.

the most desperate members of their society," so that Seneca "advocates giving to the poor man of *worth*," not the destitute.[4] By contrast, when Paul speaks about the poor and the needy, it is arguable that he imagines precisely the destitute and, perhaps, those living at subsistence levels.

Further still, in some rare instances the ancient elite found it to their own advantage to depict themselves as poor.[5] This rhetorical strategy is used by Philo in his discussion of the laws of Moses, when he lists himself as among the poor ("we poor men," οἱ πένητες ἡμεῖς, *Spec.* 2:20) — although clearly we should be wary of accepting this as an accurate description of his economic profile in absolute terms.

Accordingly, extant texts from antiquity demonstrate how relative and imprecise both the terminology and the conceptualization of poverty were, being "open for persuasive definition and ascription according to context, and even more open to remaining vague and ambiguous."[6] When dealing with data from the ancient world, the rule of thumb must be that "each reference to 'poverty' and 'the poor' . . . must be read in its particular case-specific context,"[7] precisely in view of ancient and modern "fuzziness of the language about and meanings of poverty."[8] Since ancient authors demon-

---

4. Anneliese Parkin, "'You do him no service': An Exploration of Pagan Almsgiving," in Atkins and Osborne, eds., *Poverty in the Roman World,* 60-82, p. 62. So, for instance, Seneca writes (*Ben.* 4.9): "We seek to do honourable acts, solely because they are honourable; yet even though we need think of nothing else, we consider to whom we shall do them, and when, and how; for in these points the act has its being. In like manner, when I choose upon whom I shall bestow a benefit, and when I aim at making it a benefit; because if it were bestowed upon a base person, it could neither be a benefit nor an honourable action." A similar sentiment may characterize Cicero's discussion; for fuller discussion, see §4.2 below.

5. On the rhetorical advantages of presenting oneself as poor, see G. Woolf, "Writing Poverty in Rome," in Atkins and Osborne, eds., *Poverty in the Roman World,* 83-99, pp. 97-99.

6. Osborne, "Roman Poverty in Context," p. 15. With regard to legal definitions of poverty in the Roman world, Humfress ("Poverty and Roman Law," p. 202) suggests that "there is no general or constant definition of poverty, rather the tacit recognition that the poor would *include* those lacking all property," even if non-propertied persons would not exhaust the category of the poor. Compare Koenraad Verboven (*The Economy of Friends: Economic Aspects of Amicitia and Patronage in the Late Republic* [Brussels: Latomus, 2002], p. 112): "The qualification 'poor' *(pauper)* was a very subjective and vague term that was used very loosely by Roman nobles to indicate almost anyone not belonging to at least the *prima classis.*"

7. Humfress, "Poverty and Roman Law," p. 203.

8. Denise Kimber Buel, "When Both Donors and Recipients Are Poor," in Susan R. Holman, ed., *Wealth and Poverty in Early Church and Society* (Grand Rapids: Baker Academic Press, 2008), 37-47, p. 39.

strate significant slippage in their use of terms pertaining to poverty, scholarly discourse needs to be extra vigilant in arriving at conceptual precision.

It is for this reason that the heuristic exercise of devising an economy scale pertaining to ancient data will prove to be helpful, even necessary, to assist in contemporary discourse about Greco-Roman economic stratification. Establishing a heuristic economic scale offers the potential of grounding scholarly discourse in a workable taxonomy from which to progress discussion and debate. In chapter 10 below, this will be shown to be especially helpful in getting beyond the moribund debates within New Testament scholarship about the social level of the earliest Jesus-followers. To a large extent, that debate is itself the result of a lack of conceptual clarity, as interpreters engage in argumentation without first having established a stable discursive context.

3.2: Binary Models of the Greco-Roman Economy

In recent years, historians have expended significant effort in defending various models of economic stratification of the ancient world. One such model is the binary model of economic differentiation, in which an extremely small group of elite is contrasted with a huge and undifferentiated majority struggling at subsistence level.[9] This binary model reflects the rhetorical differentiation that is common in Greco-Roman literature, in which the respectable elite are contrasted with the ordinary poor. Differentiations between the few *honestiores* and the huge majority of *humiliores* are numerous in elite Greco-Roman literature.[10] Generally speaking, among the Greco-Roman elite, the term "the poor" often referred to "anyone who was not of the ruling orders," and it is this contrast of the elite and the sub-elite that is "institutionalized . . . by the division between *honestiores* . . . and *humiliores*."[11]

---

9. Advocates of binary schemes include Geza Alföldy, *Die römische Sozialgeschichte* (3rd ed.; Wiesbaden: Steiner Franz Verlag, 1986), pp. 52-55; J. P. Toner, *Rethinking Roman History* (Cambridge, MA: Polity Press, 2002), pp. 50-51.

10. Some examples can be found in C. R. Whittaker, "The Poor in the City of Rome," in *Land, City and Trade in the Roman Empire* (Aldershot: Variorum Ashgate, 1993), article 7 [there is no sequential pagination throughout the book; internally the article's pagination is from 1-25], pp. 1-3; see also J. H. Hellerman, *Reconstructing Honor in Roman Philippi: Carmen Christi as cursus pudorum* (Cambridge: Cambridge University Press, 2005), pp. 6-8. Other examples could be added to his survey, such as Cicero *Mur.* 1; *Resp.* 2.40.

11. Whittaker, "The Poor in the City of Rome," p. 8.

But binary rhetorical constructs of this sort are not to be taken as economic descriptors of the Greco-Roman world. The point will be returned to below. For now, it is enough to note that binary modeling has a strong foothold in some sectors of New Testament studies. The most significant recent advocate of a binary model is Justin Meggitt. In his important book *Paul, Poverty and Survival*, Meggitt argues that Greco-Roman society "was split into two distinct groups, with a wide gulf separating them."[12] In his view, "the non-élite" who comprised "over 99% of the Empire's population, could expect little more from life than abject poverty"; an extremely "bleak material existence . . . was the lot of more than 99% of the inhabitants of the Empire."[13] These are bold claims, perhaps the starkest of claims by those who advocate binary forms of modeling the Greco-Roman economy.

Occasionally interpreters who advocate a binary model attempt to nuance their model somewhat, in an effort to take account of data that would otherwise compromise their model. But their attempts often reveal how tenuous their binary models can be. In his 2005 monograph, for instance, Joseph Hellerman recognizes that a two-strata perspective "blurs somewhat in real life," while at the same time awkwardly postulating that it possesses "the advantage of clarity."[14] This represents an odd historiography. Nor does Hellerman improve his case when noting that "for the purposes of macro-sociological analysis of ancient society, it is fair to retain a twofold division, since this is precisely the way in which the ancients themselves viewed their social world."[15] In this, Hellerman's interests in "macrosociology" have simply entangled him in the rhetorical constructs of the ancient elite, rather than coming to better grips with the *realia* of (what Hellerman calls) "real life."

Meggitt's own advocacy of a binary model is similarly curious. Meggitt frequently charges the proponents of the (so-called) "new consensus" (i.e., Wayne Meeks, Gerd Theissen and others who imagine that Jesus-groups es-

---

12. Justin J. Meggitt, *Paul, Poverty and Survival* (Edinburgh: T&T Clark, 1998), p. 50.

13. Meggitt, *Paul, Poverty and Survival*, pp. 50 and 99. William R. Herzog (*Parables as Subversive Speech: Jesus as Pedagogue of the Oppressed* [Louisville: Westminster John Knox Press, 1994], p. 63) is almost as blatant in his view that, apart from the few elite, "everyone else lived in subsistence poverty or worse," except for "a small portion of the merchant class." Compare Lester L. Grabbe (*A History of the Jews and Judaism in the Second Temple Period* [New York: T&T Clark, 2004], p. 193), who differentiates between the "vast numbers of the poor and the tiny few of the rich."

14. Hellerman, *Reconstructing Honor in Roman Philippi*, p. 168 n. 14.

15. Hellerman, *Reconstructing Honor in Roman Philippi*, p. 168 n. 14.

tablished by Paul had among their number some who were quite well-off economically) with reconstructing economic realities of the ancient world in conformity with the predominately elite bias of the ancient record.[16] But Meggitt's own advocacy of binary dichotomization is in full accord with the rhetorical construction of the elite. Furthermore, Meggitt himself notes that a binary model is not sufficiently nuanced, but he explains this away as being a necessary hostage to fortune in order to ground his thesis properly. The self-confessed precariousness of a binary construct is cited at the beginning of Meggitt's book, and needs to be cited at length here:

> Of course, there were significant differences between members of this group [i.e., the poor]. . . . Some would have lived more precarious lives than others. . . . But in order to emphasize the reality of the economic predicament that was shared by *all* members of this group, it is important that this term is used without lengthy qualifications, wherever applicable. As a consequence, I am aware that much of my subsequent analysis appears at times somewhat differentiated [i.e., binary] but this is, I feel, a necessary price to pay in order to bring out such an important and neglected aspect of the lives of the Pauline Christians.[17]

16. Justin J. Meggitt, "Sources: Use, Abuse, Neglect: The Importance of Ancient Popular Culture," in E. Adams and D. Horrell, eds., *Christianity at Corinth* (Louisville: Westminster John Knox Press, 2004), pp. 241-54. In the same volume, Bengt Holmberg labels Meggitt's interpretative lens "pauperistic" ("Methods of Historical Reconstruction," in Adams and Horrell, eds., *Christianity at Corinth*, 255-71, pp. 263-65): Meggitt "is determined to understand Paul and his Christian communities as really poor" and "dismisses everything that might point in other directions"; in Meggitt's work, the "alleged common economic predicament" of early Jesus-groups "overshadows, not to say obliterates, any differences as regards status indicators"; "Meggitt has closed his eyes to sociohistorical reality and simplified it beyond historical belief." See further his criticisms on pp. 266-67, and those of Peter Oakes, "Methodological Issues in Using Economic Evidence in Interpretation of Early Christian Texts," in Bruce W. Longenecker and Kelly D. Liebengood, eds., *Engaging Economics: New Testament Scenarios and Early Christian Reception* (Grand Rapids: Eerdmans, 2009), 9-34, pp. 28-29.

17. Meggitt, *Paul, Poverty and Survival*, p. 5. Nonetheless, at times even Meggitt breaks out of his own "pauperistic" frame of reference. Some of the poor whom Meggitt discusses are recognized not to be "facing an immediate subsistence crisis" (p. 117); some are said to have owned slaves and fed extra mouths (p. 131); some existed "just above subsistence level" (p. 132). At one point Meggitt speaks of not just "two classes" (i.e., the elite 1% and the 99% poor) but of "all classes" (p. 150). Further, Meggitt notes that the Pharisees comprised "a trans-class phenomenon" (p. 95), which is an odd reconstruction in a world of 1% elite and 99% impoverished. Further still, he notes the case of Lucian of Samosata (p. 24, n. 82), who early on had trained as a stonemason but then moved into legal training and ended up a

One gets the sense that, in order to prove that all urban Jesus-followers lived in squalid conditions, Meggitt first must excuse himself for taking liberties in his reconstruction of economic realities of the ancient world, not least with his claim that everyone except 1% lived in squalid conditions. If widespread and notable data need to be swept under the carpet in order to prove a thesis, it might be better to sweep the thesis under the carpet instead.

The distinction between the elite and the plebs that is so embedded within the rhetoric of Greco-Roman literature must be seen for what it is: a rhetorical construction that served to reinforce the binary values and worldview of the elite, legitimating the accumulation of power by the elite over and above the masses.[18] As Neville Morley notes, "elite sources often treat the rest of the population as an undifferentiated mass, and apply the vocabulary of poverty indiscriminately," with such rhetorical constructs being "deliberate attempts at constructing and promoting . . . an image of society for particular purposes" — i.e., to reinforce "the social structure that kept the masses in their place."[19] The point is made explicitly by Aelius Aristides in the second century CE: "the existence of inferiors is an advantage to superiors since they will be able to point out those over whom they are superior" (*Or.* 24.34). In short, it served elite purposes to relegate all who were not among the elite to the category of "the poor" indiscriminately.[20] Conse-

---

prominent sophist and rhetor, suggesting something of a gradation of upward mobility, despite Meggitt's yawning chasm between the elite and the impoverished. Compare Lionel Casson (*Travel in the Ancient World* [London: Allen and Unwin, 1974], p. 140): "Vedius Pollio, who started life as the son of ex-slaves and went from rags to riches, built himself a villa on a height between Naples and Puteoli which he called Pausilypon; so distinctive was it that it gave its name to the hill, Posillipo as it is known today, where his property once stood."

18. The fact that the same unrefined differentiation could be adopted by non-elite authors only testifies to the way in which the differentiation had entrenched itself in the rhetorical constructs of the ancient world.

19. N. Morley, "The Poor in the City of Rome," in Atkins and Osborne, eds., *Poverty in the Roman World*, pp. 29 and 26 respectively; see also p. 39. An exception to this rhetorical distinction is representing oneself as poor, despite one's elite status. This is evident in Martial, for instance, who describes himself as one "who will always be a poor man" (*Epigr.* 5.13), although in the same context he also crows about his equestrian rank and imperial patronage (5.17, 19). See n. 5 above.

20. The "tone" of this comment by A. Wallace-Hadrill (*Houses and Society in Pompeii and Herculaneum* [Princeton: Princeton University Press, 1994], p. 144) goes to the same conclusion: "the vast riches squandered by the elite of the late Republic and early Empire, and the contrast with the undoubted squalor experienced by the poor, tempt us into polarizing the culture of the elite and that of the masses. It is easy (and perhaps for us morally satisfying) to dramatize this contrast."

quently, rhetorical constructs of this kind are illegitimate economic indicators in the reconstruction of ancient economic situations. The ancient elite usually "collapse the categories [of non-elite economic status] into one," according to Greg Woolf, and thereby offer little sense of "the gradations of poverty" that characterized their world.[21]

3.3: Towards a Non-Binary Economy Scale for Greco-Roman Urbanism

If a rigid binary model is unhelpful for economic reconstructions of the Greco-Roman world, other models are far more promising. In this regard, work in the first decade of the twenty-first century has proved especially productive. At the forefront of this effort lies Steven Friesen's effort to craft out a "poverty scale" for Greco-Roman urbanism — precisely the context in which Jesus-groups founded by Paul were rooted. In his proposed poverty scale of 2004, Friesen set out seven economic categories of Greco-Roman urbanism — listed as "PS" or "poverty scale" entries, from PS1 (the most wealthy) through to PS7 (the most destitute). Friesen supplied estimated percentages for each of the seven levels, as indicated on page 45.[22]

As Friesen himself made clear, the outlining of an economic taxonomy for Greco-Roman urbanism is an enterprise that is fraught with difficulties, due to the many complexities that append themselves to any such effort. And the extent to which a taxonomy of this kind has constructive utility within study of the Jesus-movement has yet to be tested by a cohort of scholars. But in my view, Friesen's poverty scale offers a real step forward as a heu-

---

21. Woolf, "Writing Poverty in Rome," p. 94. He goes on to note: "Neither Juvenal nor Seneca have much to gain . . . from portraying a more gradated social hierarchy; elsewhere the condemnation that both show to social climbers implies forcefully that no unbreachable gulf existed between rich and poor."

22. Steven J. Friesen, "Poverty in Pauline Studies: Beyond the So-called New Consensus," *JSNT* 26 (2004): 323-61. See also Friesen, "Injustice or God's Will: Explanations of Poverty in Proto-Christian Communities," in Richard A. Horsley, ed., *Christian Origins*, vol. 1 of *A People's History of Christianity* (Minneapolis: Fortress Press, 2005), pp. 240-60; Friesen, "Injustice or God's Will: Early Christian Explanations of Poverty," in Susan R. Holman, ed., *Wealth and Poverty in Early Church and Society* (Grand Rapids: Baker Academic, 2008), 17-36. It is clear that, with this scale, Friesen means to include the whole urban population within his percentages. So when laying out his reasoning with regard to the scale's percentages, he speaks of the "inhabitants," "men, women and children," "families," "the population under Roman imperialism" and "city populations" (Friesen, "Poverty in Pauline Studies," pp. 340-43).

Scale	Description	Includes	%
PS1	Imperial elites	imperial dynasty, Roman senatorial families, a few retainers, local royalty, a few freedpersons	0.04
PS2	Regional or provincial elites	equestrian families, provincial officials, some retainers, some decurial families, some freedpersons, some retired military officers	1
PS3	Municipal elites	most decurial families, wealthy men and women who do not hold office, some freedpersons, some retainers, some veterans, some merchants	1.76
PS4	Moderate surplus	some merchants, some traders, some freedpersons, some artisans (especially those who employ others), and military veterans	7 (?)
PS5	Stable near subsistence level (with reasonable hope of remaining above the minimum level to sustain life)	many merchants and traders, regular wage earners, artisans, large shop owners, freedpersons, some farm families	22 (?)
PS6	At subsistence level (and often below minimum level to sustain life)	small farm families, laborers (skilled and unskilled), artisans (esp. those employed by others), wage earners, most merchants and traders, small shop/tavern owners	40
PS7	Below subsistence level	some farm families, unattached widows, orphans, beggars, disabled, unskilled day laborers, prisoners	28

ristic device for further analyses of Greco-Roman urbanism in general and the early Jesus-movement in particular. Ignoring Friesen's efforts is not a live option. With its seven-point scale and apportioned percentages, Friesen's poverty scale offers a nuanced tool for the analysis of economic stratification in urban contexts of the Greco-Roman world.

At this point, however, I need to register my own preference for speaking not of a "poverty scale" with corresponding "PS" levels, as Friesen did in 2004, but of an "economy scale" with corresponding "ES" levels. Consequently, I will abandon Friesen's terminology of "poverty scale" and "PS" levels from this point onwards.

In an article published in January 2009, I assessed Friesen's work and gave reason for reworking the percentages of his model somewhat. (Part of my argument appears in Appendix 1 below.) I argued that Friesen's percentages for economic stratification of the urban population of the Greco-Roman world should be adjusted to allow more "exposure" to the "middling groups." I was guided in these proposals by a number of factors, one being the argument of Walter Scheidel in an article published in 2006. There Scheidel argued that the middling groups would have comprised at least 20 to 25% of the Greco-Roman world.[23] I thought this was too high, and proposed dropping Scheidel's levels by roughly 5%, estimating that an appropriate middling-group number should increase from Friesen's 7% to something like 17%. In reworking Friesen's percentages, I proposed that Friesen's model should be adjusted along the following lines, when outlining the economic distribution of Greco-Roman urban contexts:

	Friesen's Percentages	My Reworked Percentages
ES1-ES3	3	3
ES4	7	17
ES5	22	25
ES6	40	30
ES7	28	25

Late in 2009, however, another article was published that set out different terms of reference. Entitled "The Distribution of Income in the Roman Empire," this article offered a studious analysis of "the probable size of the Roman economy and the distribution of income across its population."[24]

23. The following is an example of the way Walter Scheidel articulated his 2006 view ("Stratification, Deprivation and Quality of Life," in Atkins and Osborne, eds., *Poverty in the Roman World*, 40-59, pp. 54, 51-52): "[T]here is sufficient evidence in support of the notion of an economic continuum from a narrow elite to a steadily broadening middling group as we move down the resource ladder. Sources ranging from Republican Italy to imperial Egypt and Syria all point in the same direction. It is perfectly possible to reconcile the dominance of a disproportionately affluent elite with the presence of a substantial 'middle.' . . . Not necessarily formally beholden to landed elites as 'Mediterraneanist' clients, they [the middling groups] would have provided the backbone sorely lacking from a hypothetical, more extremely dichotomous society that pitted a few wealthy toffs with their entourage of slaves and freedmen against countless marginalized subsistence peasants and day-labourers."
24. Walter Scheidel and Steven J. Friesen, "The Size of the Economy and the Distribution of Income in the Roman Empire," *JRS* 99 (2009): 61-91.

This article evidenced ground-breaking erudition from start to finish, enabling even further refinement in the discussion of economic distribution.

The notable thing about this article, however, was that it was co-authored by Walter Scheidel and Steven Friesen — distinguished scholars who had already published vastly different estimates about the size of the Greco-Roman economic middling groups. Friesen had estimated their number at 7% in 2004, while Scheidel had proposed 20-25% in 2006. Then at the meeting of the Society of Biblical Literature in 2007, Scheidel participated alongside Friesen in a discussion of the Roman economy and became interested in Friesen's attempts to attribute levels to the overall imperial economy. A partnership transpired, and in the process, Scheidel adjusted his estimate for the middling groups significantly downwards.

One of the two main interests of the Scheidel and Friesen article is "to establish, through a variety of methods, a convergent range of estimates of the size of the economy (that is, the Gross Domestic Product) of the Roman Empire at the time of its putative demographic peak in the mid-second century C.E."[25] Scheidel and Friesen make use of three indicators in order to arrive at an estimate of the GDP of the Roman empire: consumption expenditure, aggregate income, and income ratios. Those indicators provide them with lower (pessimistic) and upper (optimistic) limits for the estimated GDP of the Roman empire. Noting "the broadly convergent nature" of their three estimates, they concluded that "the economic product of the Roman Empire at its peak approached . . . somewhat less that HS 20bn [i.e., 20 billion sesterces]."[26] The imperial GDP "is highly unlikely to have fallen short of or to have exceeded these figures by a margin of more than 20 per cent" of that amount,[27] with their preferred GDP estimate being "HS 17-19bn."[28]

With this GDP estimate in hand, Scheidel and Friesen move to their second specified interest:

> To ask who enjoyed the fruits of that economy by developing a model of income distribution and inequality, informed by our estimate of overall GDP. The answer to this question is vital for all Roman social history. Were there just a few super-wealthy surrounded by a mass of relatively

---

25. Scheidel and Friesen, "The Size of the Economy," p. 62.

26. Scheidel and Friesen, "The Size of the Economy," pp. 73-74. Compare their comments on p. 62: "We argue that the population of the Roman Empire generated a total income approaching . . . 20 billion sesterces per year."

27. Scheidel and Friesen, "The Size of the Economy," p. 74.

28. Scheidel and Friesen, "The Size of the Economy," pp. 73, 75.

undifferentiated poor? Or were there middling groups and a more finely gradated continuum from wealth to indigence?[29]

Since the GDP figure of 17 to 19 billion sesterces is fairly stable (despite a 20% margin up or down), if the contribution to the GDP is increased at one level, the contribution of another economic level must be decreased. Scheidel and Friesen begin their determination of income distribution by estimating the aggregate elite income, comprised of senatorial, equestrian, decurial and other elite incomes (i.e., the *Augustales*). Through various calculations, Scheidel and Friesen put the total elite income at between 3 and 5 billion sesterces (or between 16% and 29%) of the total GDP of 17 to 19 billion sesterces.[30] Since another billion sesterces would probably have been absorbed by state and community initiatives, this (they say) leaves approximately 11 to 14 billion sesterces of income for the sub-elite sectors of the Roman imperial economy ("non-élite civilians would have disposed of HS 11-14bn per year").[31] With this figure in hand, and with an estimate of what a middling income must have looked like (i.e., "2.4 times 'bare bones' gross subsistence"),[32] Scheidel and Friesen estimate that the middling groups would have comprised between 6% (the pessimistic estimate) and 12% (the optimistic estimate) of the Roman imperial population. The fact that the Scheidel-Friesen model is based on "zero-sum" principles (i.e., to raise something here requires lowering something there) restricts the possibilities to raise the percentage for the middling groups. In order to increase the middling groups to a percentage higher than 12%, one would need to make other adjustments within the model, such as raising the estimated GDP of the imperial economy or lowering the percentages or incomes of the elite.[33] Any

29. Scheidel and Friesen, "The Size of the Economy," p. 62.

30. Note their caution (Scheidel and Friesen, "The Size of the Economy," p. 81): "We propose a minimum total elite wealth of at least HS 3bn, a level that may well have been exceeded by one or two billion sesterces . . . illustrating the considerable margin of error."

31. Scheidel and Friesen, "The Size of the Economy," p. 82.

32. Scheidel and Friesen, "The Size of the Economy," p. 84.

33. In a 2009 SBL presentation at New Orleans, Friesen plugged the percentages that I proposed in my 2009 economy scale into the database that he and Scheidel currently employ, and demonstrated that my 2009 figures would result in an imperial GDP of 22 billion sesterces. This would equate to a GDP 16% larger than the upper end of their figure of 17 to 19 billion sesterces — although note that Scheidel and Friesen recognize that their estimated figure for the imperial GDP has a 20% margin of error ("The Size of the Economy," p. 74). Note also that Friesen's SBL calculations assumed that my 2009 figure of 17% for the middling groups could be applied to middling groups in both urban and rural contexts, where I

such adjustment, however, would render the Roman imperial economy "highly anomalous in world historical terms."[34] Accordingly, with regard to the middling groups, Scheidel and Friesen conclude that they were small in number, "accounting for not more than roughly one-tenth of the imperial population."[35]

It would be foolish to imagine that Scheidel and Friesen's robust calculations could be significantly overturned here. Their work represents a breakthrough in the economic analysis of the Greco-Roman world. One might, of course, query the legitimacy of certain of their decisions. For instance, it is arguable that the income of the *Augustales* should not be calculated as elite income, as in the Scheidel-Friesen model, but primarily as upper-level middling income. But even that would redistribute only half a percent or so from the elite to the middling groups. Consequently, I find myself content to operate within the general terms of reference of the Scheidel-Friesen model. Since in 2009 I cited reasons to adopt what Scheidel and Friesen term an "optimistic" position regarding the Greco-Roman economy, I find myself at the upper end of their estimate for middling groups in the Greco-Roman world — i.e., about 12% of the total Greco-Roman population.

But I must also demur from aligning myself with one or two other features of their work. Whereas the numbers that Friesen used for his 2004 "poverty scale" went from low enumerations (e.g., PS1) through to high enumerations (e.g., PS7) in identifying elite through to sub-subsistence levels, the Scheidel and Friesen scale of 2009 inverts that relationship, with low enumerations equating to the poorest members of imperial society (e.g., enumerated as 0.25 through to 1.39), slightly higher numbers identifying the middling groups (e.g., 1.40 through to 5), and the highest numbers identifying the elite (e.g., 6 through to 600+).[36] Whether low or high numbers should refer to elite members is of no real significance. The fact that the 2009 scale allows for much greater refinement at the upper end may mean that it has most utility when determining the economic profiles of the ancient elite. But when it comes to data from Paul's texts, such refinement is unnecessary, to the point of being awkward, and perhaps unworkable. The paucity of data

---

had only intended that percentage to be applicable to urban contexts. If rural contexts had a smaller population percentage than urban contexts (as I argue below), the figure of 22 billion that Friesen attributed to my 2009 percentages would need to be reduced.

34. Scheidel and Friesen, "The Size of the Economy," p. 88.

35. Scheidel and Friesen, "The Size of the Economy," p. 88.

36. See the Scheidel and Friesen model, "The Size of the Economy," p. 85, and definitions of that model throughout the article.

for reconstructing the economic profile of early Jesus-followers suggests that, rather than adopting a fabulously refined scale of the sort proposed by Scheidel and Friesen in 2009, we would be better to employ the broader, much less-refined economic levels first proposed by Friesen in 2004. It is hard to imagine much utility in crafting out more than four or five sub-elite economic levels — i.e., those outlined by the indicators ES4 (perhaps ES4a and ES4b) through ES7.

The Scheidel-Friesen model of 2009 runs along somewhat different lines to the Friesen model of 2004 in one very notable and important feature. Whereas in 2004 Friesen was concerned to estimate population percentages for *urban* contexts of the Greco-Roman world, in 2009 Scheidel and Friesen were concerned to estimate population percentages for the Roman imperial world *in total*. But this raises the question of whether we should imagine middling groups being embedded within rural contexts to the same extent as urban contexts. Scheidel and Friesen make the point this way:

> [Middling groups] need not have been evenly spread out across the Empire. The greater their spatial concentration, the larger the economic impact and social standing would have been. The "consumer-city" regime of the Roman world encourages speculation that civilian "middling"-income groups may have been disproportionately present in urban contexts, even if this idea ultimately defies empirical verification. For instance, if some 15 per cent of the total population resided in towns and [if] "middling" income households were twice as common there as in the countryside, anywhere from one-eighth [i.e., 12.5%] to one quarter [i.e., 25%] of the urban populace might have fallen in this "middling" category.[37]

The response that Scheidel and Friesen give to this prospect differs from mine, however. They claim that "a substantially higher degree of concentration [in urban contexts] would imply that rural areas were almost entirely populated by subsistence-level households, which seems unrealistic."[38] In a zero-sum game (i.e., with a ceiling of 17-19 billion sesterces for the imperial economy), increasing the numbers within the urban middling groups necessarily reduces the numbers elsewhere — i.e., within the rural middling groups. Scheidel and Friesen are hesitant to increase the percentage of urban middling groups for fear of wiping rural middling groups from our economic reconstruction of the Greco-Roman world. So, if 67% of the mid-

37. Scheidel and Friesen, "The Size of the Economy," p. 90.
38. Scheidel and Friesen, "The Size of the Economy," p. 90.

dling groups were placed in urban contexts (i.e., twice as many urban middlers as rural middlers), those groups could be thought to have comprised as much as 25% of the urban population in an optimistic scenario; but the knock-on effect would be to drastically reduce the middling-group percentage within Greco-Roman rural contexts.

While it is important to exercise caution on this matter, it seems unrealistic to imagine complete parity between urban and rural population percentages. For each of the five main groups that Friesen identifies as belonging to ES4 (i.e., "some merchants, some traders, some freedpersons, some artisans [especially those who employ others], and military veterans"), it was the urban context that would have offered the most attraction, over against the rural environment.[39] For the merchants, traders and artisans of ES4, the urban context offered considerably more opportunity to "capitalize" on their middling assets. Urban centers had enhanced access to land and sea routes, along with a concentrated local, immigrant and itinerant population that would constantly have required goods and services.[40] The freedpersons of ES4 would also have been likely to gravitate to urban contexts, not least to enhance the prospects of their sons, who (unlike their fathers) would have been eligible to enter the *ordo* of civic governance, if luck enhanced their wealth acquisition and their patronage connections.[41] And military veterans among ES4 may also have found added attraction in settling in urban as opposed to rural contexts. As John Patterson notes, "[t]he Augustan period and the years immediately following saw a significant number of army veterans becoming *decuriones*" of cities.[42] Whether hoping to imitate their veteran predecessors or to benefit through patronage or "friendship" connections with established

39. I do not build my case on Mary T. Boatwright's view (*Hadrian and the Cities of the Roman Empire* [Princeton: Princeton University Press, 2000]) that the urban context offered an improved quality of life, although that view is not inconsequential to the point.

40. John R. Patterson (*Landscapes and Cities: Rural Settlement and Civic Transformation in Early Imperial Italy* [Oxford: Oxford University Press, 2006], p. 238) notes that "a community with good communications and access to major local and external markets would have been more likely to be a destination of wealthy immigrants" than rural destinations. This is likely to have been the case not only for elite immigrants, but for ES4 immigrants as well. On p. 261, Patterson states that urban growth and prosperity "led to increasing profits for artisans and traders of the city . . . and [to] social groupings just below the traditional elite" — i.e., those within Friesen's ES4.

41. Tacitus has this to say about urban civic leaders whose background was rooted in servile origins: "Very many knights, and numerous senators, have such an origin" (*Ann.* 13.27). On this, see Patterson, *Landscapes and Cities,* pp. 236-39.

42. Patterson, *Landscapes and Cities,* p. 237.

decurial veterans, military veterans may well have imagined better prospects to wait for them in urban contexts than in rural ones.

Since there is reason to imagine a preference for urban settings among each of Friesen's five representatives of ES4, it runs against the grain of expectation to imagine percentage parity between urban and rural middling groups.[43] I propose, then, that we imagine the ES4 middling groups to have comprised about 15% of the urban population. Building on the proposals by Scheidel and Friesen, this proposal is informed by the following convictions:

1. an "optimistic" interpretation of the middling groups in the Roman economy is to be preferred over a "pessimistic" one (see Appendix 1 below);
2. the income of the *Augustales* needs to be attributed primarily to the middling groups rather than the elite (see Appendix 1 below); and
3. the urban environment had more attraction to middling group members than rural environments.

In light of these three factors, the optimistic 12% that the Scheidel-Friesen model permits with regard to the size of middling groups in the Roman economy as a whole should be raised to roughly 15% for the urban context in which the early Jesus-movement sprang up.

---

43. A related issue also needs to be considered in this regard — that is, precisely what we mean by "urban." Are Scheidel and Freisen right to locate only 15% of the Greco-Roman population in urban contexts, or is this percentage itself too low? In his 2004 reconstruction of Greco-Roman urbanism, Friesen focused on cities of 10,000 or more (estimated to have comprised 5% of the Greco-Roman population), but the judgment to restrict urbanism to that number is somewhat artificial. As Friesen notes, civic decurions were absent from only the smallest "urban centers," which he identifies as "small towns, villages, way stations etc.," all of which "were too small or had insufficient resources to be organized" in relation to a decurionate.

According to Gerd Theissen ("The Social Structure of Pauline Communities: Some Critical Comments on J. J. Meggitt, *Paul, Poverty and Survival*," *JSNT* 84 [2001]: 65-84, p. 72), centers with populations as small as 3,000 inhabitants would have been known as small urban cities in the ancient world, many of whose inhabitants earned their living by farming. In Mary T. Boatwright, Daniel J. Gargola and Richard J. A. Talbert, *The Romans, From Village to Empire* (Oxford: Oxford University Press, 2004), p. 343, the figure for urban centers falls between five and fifteen thousand people.

In this regard, it is interesting to consider the small city of Philippi. Wayne A. Meeks (*First Urban Christians: The Social World of the Apostle Paul* [New Haven: Yale University Press, 1983], pp. 49 and 46 respectively) identifies it as one of the "rather small towns" of the empire, "primarily an agricultural centre," and being comprised of "not more than six hundred to eight hundred meters from wall to wall along its east-west axis."

Much the same might be said for the urban elite. Although Scheidel and Friesen apportion the elite to only 1.2% of the total imperial population, the majority of them made their primary base in urban contexts. Consequently, the percentage of the elite within *urban* populations needs to be raised relative to the Scheidel and Friesen estimate for overall elite percentages. We might want to dispute whether the best percentage for the elite among urban populations is 2.5%, 3% or some other figure. But since these are merely estimates, I am content to err with the figure of 3% that Friesen originally proposed for urban contexts.[44]

Consequently, a revised economy scale for the study of the early urban Jesus-movement is outlined in the chart below, where Friesen's 2004 figures appear alongside my initial and successive adjustments to his seven-level scale:

	Friesen's 2004 Urban Percentages	My 2009 Urban Percentages	My Revised Urban Percentages
ES1-ES3	3	3	3
ES4	7	17	15
ES5	22	25	27
ES6	40	30	30
ES7	28	25	25

3.4: Elaborating the Economy Scale

Several points need to be registered in relation to this economy scale. First, it cannot be overemphasized that this economy scale is only a heuristic starting point for considering economic stratification in Greco-Roman urban contexts. Any model is an abstraction by necessity, and the percentage estimates of the economy scale are merely rough guides. Moreover, indigenous variations are bound to have occurred. Consequently, any application of the

44. There is much to be debated, however, even with regard to adjusting the elite presence in urban contexts by half a percentage point one way or another. Precisely because the elite commanded such enormous resources, adjusting their estimated urban population by half a percentage point has a significant knock-on effect in terms of the contributions of other economic levels to the Roman imperial GDP. While I stand to be corrected in sticking to a 3% figure for the urban elite, a half percentage refinement one way or another will not assist or affect the larger argument of this project.

urban economy scale will need to be attentive to the heuristic nature of the scale and responsive to indigenous differences.[45] Nonetheless, since heuristic constructs are required, and since unarticulated models are to be avoided, and since this economy scale commends itself as historically informed, it will be used as the interpretative filter through which to assess the data pertaining to the interests of this project.

Second, with the economy scale in place, we can now give greater definition to our conceptualization of "the poor." According to Peter Garnsey and Greg Woolf, the poor can be defined as "those living at or near subsistence level, whose prime concern it is to obtain the minimum food, shelter, and clothing necessary to sustain life, whose lives are dominated by the struggle for physical survival."[46] According to Friesen's descriptors, and without further qualification, this definition would seem to apply to economic levels ES7 and ES6 — i.e., something like 55% of the ancient world. If ES5 is closely related to these poverty levels, it is not characterized by their same precarious conditions, being associated with neither the poverty groups of ES6 and ES7 nor the middling groups of ES4; instead, it is comprised of groups modestly endowed (economically speaking) that fell between those economic levels.

Complicating this depiction, however, is the fact that many of those who fell within ES6 and ES7 also belonged to households and, consequently, were not exposed to the harsh realities of poverty to the same extent as those in ES6 and ES7 who lived beyond household structures. When considered apart from their role as household functionaries, the vast majority of slaves might well have conformed perfectly to the Garnsey and Woolf definition of "the poor." But as functionaries within a household, their "struggle for physical survival" and their concern "to obtain the minimum food, shelter and clothing necessary to sustain life" is less apparent than would have been the case for those beyond households.

Third, we need to guard against estimating that "for nearly everyone in

---

45. For an interesting case for the virtual absence of poverty in Roman Egypt, see D. W. Rathbone, "Poverty and Population in Roman Egypt," in Atkins and Osborne, eds., *Poverty in the Roman World*, 100-114.

46. Peter D. A. Garnsey and Greg Woolf, "Patronage of the Rural Poor in the Roman World," in Andrew Wallace-Hadrill, ed., *Patronage in Ancient Society* (London: Routledge, 1989), 153-70, p. 153. See also Woolf, "Food, Poverty and Patronage," *PBSR* 58 (1990): 205: "By 'the poor' I do not mean the entire population of the Roman empire excluding the aristocracy. I mean those who lived at or near subsistence level, and whose lives were dominated by the struggle for physical survival. Their resources to withstand crises, physical, agricultural and social, were virtually non-existent."

the Roman empire, poverty was a way of life."[47] With ES1 through ES4 comprising roughly 18% of the urban population, an estimate of that kind does not apply to one sixth of the Greco-Roman urban population. Even those at ES6 and ES7 who were embedded within households do not quite conform to the definition of poverty outlined by Garnsey and Woolf. Nor is it clear that the phrase "poverty was a way of life" is a justified description of the 27% of the population represented by ES5 (especially those within households). Those within ES5 would clearly have been conscious of their economic vulnerabilities and their proximity to poverty, but to lump them together with those in ES6 and ES7 is to overgeneralize. That poverty affected all three groups is clear, but it affected them in different ways. As John Barclay aptly notes, the difference between ES5 and ES7 is simple and stark: life versus death.[48] It might be "vulnerable life" versus "impending death," but the difference is notable nonetheless.

Fourth, as noted in Appendix 1 below, ES4 looks to be a significantly elongated category of wealth. Friesen's descriptor of ES4 as involving "moderate surplus" pertains to the lower levels of ES4 but fails to describe its upper levels adequately, where (for instance) the *apparitores* and the *Augustales* are most likely to be placed. For this reason, it might be appropriate to split ES4 into two separate levels, moving then from a seven-point scale to an eight-point scale. For present purposes, however, we will on occasion make a distinction between ES4a (the upper end of ES4) and ES4b (the lower end of ES4), thereby accounting for the fact that just below the decurial level of ES3, wealth could be amassed at relatively significant levels (rather than simply being "moderate").

Fifth, proposing a figure of 15% for ES4 should not be seen as reestablishing the notion of a "middle class" into our economic taxonomy of the ancient world. The claim is frequently made that there was no "middle class" in the ancient world. This assertion is rightly made, since the notion of "class" itself is a relatively modern construct, grounded in Marxist analysis — at least in the sense of a "class" consisting of an identifiable stratum of society with a relatively stable shared profile and common socio-economic interests in relation to wealth production. As Thomas Francis Carney notes well, the Roman world was generally founded on the principles of patronage, not class stratification:

---

47. Friesen, "Poverty in Pauline Studies," p. 358.

48. John M. G. Barclay, "Poverty in Pauline Studies: A Response to Steven Friesen," *JSNT* 26 (2004): 363-66, p. 366 n. 2.

[S]ociety resembled a mass of little pyramids of influence, each headed by a major family — or one giant pyramid headed by an autocrat — not the three-decker sandwich of upper, middle, and lower classes familiar to us from industrial society. . . . Patronage virtually precludes . . . the emergence of class consciousness. . . . Under the divisive local loyalties of patronage . . . , the latter [i.e., the sub-elite] were unaware of its class interests. . . . The client of a power wielder . . . becomes a powerful man and himself in turn attracts clients. Even those marginal hangers-on to power attract others, more disadvantageously placed, as their clients. . . . It is quite different from the three-layer sandwich of a class society.[49]

This portrait of ancient economic relationships serves rightly to warn against imagining the existence of a middle "class" in the Greco-Roman world.

But this exclusion of the middle "class" from the ancient world has sometimes been misconstrued to mean that, in the ancient world, the enormous gap between the elite and the poor was filled only by a significant vacuum. When P. A. Brunt wrote in 1970 that "There is no evidence for a middle class in the city intervening between them [the upper class] and the poor,"[50] he was as right as he was wrong (at least if by "the poor" he was envisioning those at the bottom end of the economy scale). There may have been no middle class, but there were middling groups. In this, two things are to be recognized simultaneously: (1) a substantial number of people comprised middling economic groups in Greco-Roman urbanism, and (2) the strategies for survival and security available to those middling groups were much different to the strategies open to the so-called "middle class" in industrial and post-industrial societies. Whenever the balance between these two is skewed, things tend to go wrong in one direction or another: either a modern economic theory is applied to the ancient world (i.e., "class") or a broad band disappears from the economic spectrum of the Greco-Roman world (i.e., "middling").[51]

49. T. F. Carney, *The Shape of the Past: Models and Antiquity* (Lawrence KA: Coronado Press, 1975), pp. 90, 94, 121 and 171. See also M. G. Smith, "Pre-Industrial Social Stratification Systems," in N. J. Smelser and S. M. Lipset, eds., *Social Structure and Mobility in Economic Development* (Chicago: Aldine Press, 1966), pp. 141-76.

50. P. A. Brunt, *Italian Manpower, 225 BC–AD 14* (London: Oxford University Press, 1971), p. 383.

51. For instance, D. Gill uses Garnsey and Saller's point about the absence of a "middle class" in the ancient world to criticize Wayne Meeks's view "that somehow Christians fall into a middle social group" ("Acts and the Urban Élites," in David W. J. Gill and Conrad Gempf, eds., *The Book of Acts in Its Graeco-Roman Setting*, vol. 2 of *The Book of Acts in Its First Century Setting* [Grand Rapids: Eerdmans, 1994], 105-118, p. 118, n. 79).

Sixth, the economy scale should not be seen as an attempt to peripheralize or trivialize the poignant issues pertaining to "structural" poverty in the ancient world. With a sizeable proportion of the Greco-Roman world skimming the surface of subsistence and occasionally dropping down below it (ES6 and ES7), and with another sizeable proportion living in a fragile suspension above subsistence level (ES5), studies of the early Jesus-movement cannot be immune to the pressing "realities of poverty" that affected the majority of the imperial world. The relative absence of nuanced discourse on poverty for its own sake within the literary remains of the ancient elite should not blind us to the realities of life that pressed down on vast swathes of the Greco-Roman population. Economic exploitation was inherent within the structures of Greco-Roman agrarianism, not least with regard to the potential for elite acquisitiveness (cf. chapter 2 above). This is where the economy scale for population percentages needs to be correlated with consideration of the socio-economic machinery that drove advanced agrarian systems and the matrices of socio-economic, religio-political status codes that animated most cultures of the ancient world. Consequently, in our imaging of urban Greco-Roman contexts at the time when the early Jesus-movement was finding its feet, squalid conditions affecting the lives of multitudes of people need to be placed front and center.[52]

Seventh, increasing the presence of middling groups within the Greco-Roman world in general does not necessarily lead to the conclusion that a similar percentage must be applied to middling groups within urban communities of Jesus-followers. It is unlikely, for instance, that, among urban Jesus-followers, the percentage for ES4 Jesus-followers would have risen much above 10% in comparison to the percentage of ES5 through ES7 Jesus-followers. Leaving ES1 through ES3 out of consideration, Friesen's original depiction of urban economic stratification in the Greco-Roman world was virtually replicated in his depiction of economic stratification in Jesus-groups founded by Paul, with a tiny percentage in ES4 and a huge percentage in ES5 through ES7. But this results in a rather monochrome comparison that dulls us to the potential differences between economic stratification in Greco-Roman urban contexts generally and in early communities of Jesus-followers particularly.[53] At stake, then, is the way we conceptualize the rela-

---

52. For a helpful catalogue of life at or near subsistence in the Greco-Roman world, see Meggitt, *Paul, Poverty and Survival*, pp. 53-73.

53. A monochrome analysis is even more evident in Meggitt's *Paul, Poverty and Survival*, with 99% of the Greco-Roman world's population being comprised of those in poverty, as compared, evidently, with 100% of Jesus-groups founded by Paul.

tionship of the early Jesus-movement to the society around it. Issues of this sort are addressed in chapters 10 through 12 below.

Finally, it would be instructive to test the heuristic viability of the economy scale in relation to (1) the interpretation of the available texts of the early Jesus-movement and (2) our conceptualization of the rise of that movement. Friesen himself has applied the model to texts beyond the Pauline corpus, such as the Johannine Apocalypse, the letter of James, the Acts of the Apostles, and the *Shepherd of Hermas*, and David Horrell has applied it to 1 Peter.[54] There may well be scope for applying the economy scale to other New Testament data as well. Nonetheless, in New Testament studies the economy scale is likely to be most constructive in relation to the Pauline corpus, not least because of the extent of that corpus. And in that regard, the urban economy scale proposed here has particular bearing on issues addressed elsewhere in this book, not least the following:

1. How are we to conceptualize the economic realities at play within Jesus-groups founded by Paul?
2. To what extent can an economic taxonomy help to ground our discussion of the economic level of particular individuals known to us from Paul's letters?
3. Do Paul's texts reveal him to imagine urban Jesus-groups to gravitate towards a particular economic level?
4. Might it be that many of the individuals named in Paul's texts belonged to ES4, even though Paul's advice about how to work and save for others is generally applicable to the unnamed of ES5?
5. To what extent were ES4 Jesus-followers offering financial support to Jesus-groups in a fashion that rendered them, in effect, benefactors of those communities?
6. To what extent would ES4 Jesus-followers have been civic-minded in their aspirations and thereby complicit with a pro-Roman civic ethos? And relatedly, to what extent might the presence and function of ES4 members have affected the way in which urban Jesus-groups appropriated the message of good news concerning their crucified Lord and Savior?
7. Are there indicators that urban Jesus-groups were comprised largely of people floundering around the subsistence levels of ES6 and ES7?

54. See Friesen, "Injustice or God's Will"; David Horrell, "Aliens and Strangers? The Socio-Economic Location of the Addressees of 1 Peter," in Bruce W. Longenecker and Kelly D. Liebengood, eds., *Engaging Economics: New Testament Scenarios and Early Christian Reception* (Grand Rapids: Eerdmans, 2009), pp. 176-202.

An economy scale, albeit merely a heuristic device, will not *answer* such questions for us, but it will enable our debates to be more focused than would otherwise be the case.[55]

In the chapters that follow, I will attempt to link my own discussions to this model wherever appropriate. Although this will pertain especially to the Pauline data, the model will also help to ground the discussion of the next chapter, when considering issues of charitable initiatives in the Greco-Roman world.

55. Similarly, a poverty scale will enable us better to register cases such as that of the fifth-century Christian Salvian, whose writings reveal a disconnection between a theological construction of radical poverty inherited from Christian discourse and his own experience of relative poverty. According to C. Grey ("Salvian and the Poor in Fifth-Century Gaul," in Atkins and Osborne, eds., *Poverty in the Roman World,* pp. 162-82), the kind of poverty that Salvian seems cognizant of in his vicinity is the poverty of the small landowner, or even "less wealthy members of local aristocracies" (p. 180), but not the poverty of utter destitution. Nonetheless, even if his own conceptualization of poverty gravitates towards ES5 or even possibly ES4, the rhetoric that he applies in his theological discourse gravitates towards ES7.

CHAPTER 4

"When did we see you hungry?"

Charitable Initiatives in the Greco-Roman World

4.1: Charitable Initiatives in the Greco-Roman World
4.2: Generous Initiatives That Do Not Qualify as Charitable
4.3: Generous Initiatives That Qualify as Charitable
4.4: Generous Initiatives That Defy Strict Categorization
4.5: Charitable Initiatives and the Deities
4.6: Conclusions

4.1: Charitable Initiatives in the Greco-Roman World

It is a common view that, apart from Jewish traditions and practices, care for the poor was virtually absent in the ancient world prior to the rise of Christianity. Care for the poor had very little foothold in the religious, moral and legal structures of ancient society prior to the Common Era.

In his standard study of Greek civilization, for instance, W. W. Tarn insisted that "[p]ity for the poor had little place in the normal Greek character."[1] John A. McGuckin depicts the Greco-Roman world as characterized by the conviction that the poor were not worthy of "attention, solace, or compassion,"[2] and that beggars were good-for-nothings who did little other than lie and cheat. But things began to change, the case goes, with the emergence

---

1. W. W. Tarn, *Hellenistic Civilization* (New York: Plume, 1974), p. 110.
2. John A. McGuckin, *The Westminster Handbook to Patristic Theology* (Louisville: Westminster John Knox Press, 2004), p. 359.

of Christianity in the second through fourth centuries, and beyond.[3] So the influential classicist Paul Veyne writes:

> Paganism was aware of the poor man only in his most commonplace shape, that of the beggar encountered in the street. . . . [It] had abandoned without much remorse the starving, the old and the sick. . . . All this changed with the coming of Christianity, in which almsgiving resulted from the new ethical religiosity. . . . Old people's homes, orphanages, hospitals and so on are institutions that appear only with the Christian epoch.[4]

There is relatively solid basis for such estimates, in that they correspond with the preponderance of ancient data. For instance, Polybius (203-120 BCE), a Greek historian of the Hellenistic period, characterized the Roman way as follows: "no one ever thinks of giving any of his private property to anyone if he can help it" (*The Histories*, 32.12). By contrast, in the second quarter of the second century CE, the philosopher and Christian apologist Aristides depicted Christian communities as being animated by a character of intense economic provision (*Apology*, 15):

> Kindliness is their nature. There is no falsehood among them. They love one another. They do not neglect widows. Orphans they rescue from those who are cruel to them. Every one of them who has anything gives ungrudgingly to the one who has nothing. If they see a travelling stranger they bring him under their roof. They rejoice over him as a real brother, for they do not call one another brothers after the flesh, but they know they are brothers in the Spirit and in God. If one of them sees that one of their poor must leave this world, he provides for his burial as well as he can. And if they hear that one of them is imprisoned or oppressed by their

3. See, for instance, M. Prell, *Sozialökonomische Untersuchungen zur Armut im antiken Rom: Von den Gracchen bis Kaiser Diokletian* (Stuttgart: Steiner Verlag, 1997), p. 268.

4. P. Veyne, *Bread and Circuses: Historical Sociology and Political Pluralism* (London: Penguin, 1990 [trans. of *Le Pain et le cirque* (Paris: Éditions du Seuil, 1976)]), pp. 31, 33. It is curious that Peter Brown accuses Veyne of overlooking Christian initiatives when explaining the rise of care for the poor in the early centuries of the Common Era (*Poverty and Leadership in the Later Roman Empire* [Hanover, NH: University Press of New England, 2002], pp. 6-9). In my view, this criticism is not well founded; it merely serves to open up some rhetorical space for Brown's own work. Better is Brown's charge against Veyne that "to have characterized an evolution is not the same thing as to have explained it," although, as this book on Paul and poverty seeks to demonstrate, Brown's own efforts place the origins of Christian care for the poor (1) far too late (i.e., his emphasis on second- through fourth-century initiatives) and (2) at far too elevated a social status (i.e., his emphasis on Christian bishops).

opponents for the sake of their Christ's name, all of them take care of all his needs. If possible they set him free. If anyone among them is poor or comes into want while they themselves have nothing to spare, they fast two or three days for him. In this way they can supply the poor man with the food he needs.

If Aristides' rhetoric is polemically self-serving in congratulating Christian communities of his day, it is not alone in testifying to the economic dimension of Christian communities in second-century literature. In the mid-second century CE Lucian of Samosata noted much the same as Aristides, although he (unlike Aristides) was no admirer of Christianity. He observed:

> The earnestness with which the people of this religion [i.e., Christianity] help one another in their need is incredible. They spare themselves nothing to this end. Apparently their first law-maker [i.e., Moses] has put it into their heads that they all somehow ought to be regarded as brethren [*Peregr.* 13].

Lucian sought also to demonstrate the naivety that operates within Christian communities on the basis of their familial care of others in need: "if any charlatan and trickster comes among them, he quickly acquires sudden wealth by imposing upon simple folk" (*Peregr.* 13).[5]

In the late second century CE Tertullian followed Aristides' lead by putting Christianity on the moral high ground, as demonstrated in the way that Christians care for the needy (*Apol.* 39):

> We have our treasure-chest. . . . On the monthly day, if he likes, each puts in a small donation; but only if it be his pleasure, and only if he be able: for there is no compulsion; all is voluntary. These gifts are, as it were, piety's deposit fund . . . to support and bury poor people, to supply the wants of boys and girls destitute of means and parents, and of old persons confined now to the house; such, too, as have suffered shipwreck.

It turns out, of course, that the primary beneficiaries are fellow Christians (i.e., those who have suffered "for nothing but their fidelity to the cause of God's Church"), so that the outsider to their communities say, "See how they love one another." Christian community involves practical mutuality in all but one respect: "One in mind and soul, we do not hesitate to share

5. According to the same passage, this is precisely what the wily cynic philosopher Peregrinus did, setting himself up as the "prophet, cult-leader, head" of one Christian community.

our earthly goods with one another. All things are common among us but our wives."[6]

The Roman emperor Julian (332-63 CE; emperor from 360 to 363), who in 361 declared himself a devotee of the pagan deities against the Christian deity, nonetheless testified to the respectability of Christian social action even as he sought to extract Christian influence from his empire. Noting the way in which the poor were "neglected and overlooked" by pagan sectors and the way that Christians (and Jews) "devoted themselves to benevolence," Julian also took note of the way that "the impious Galileans [i.e., Christians] support not only their poor, but ours as well," not least since "everyone can see that our people lack aid from us" (*Ep.* 22.430D).[7] These ancient evaluations are significant in noting a general lack of concern for the poor apart from Judeo-Christian strands of the ancient world.

Since the preponderance of data falls along these lines, historians have often arrived at conclusions such as these:

- "No Roman cult groups, not even those that were primarily mutual groups, are known to have looked after strangers and people in need. . . . Provision for the poor was not an ethical priority in Roman culture."[8]
- "What is remarkable is that the poor became a very important part of Christian thought and practice, in a world having little or no concern for them."[9]
- In the Greco-Roman world, "where[ver] the poor are prominent it is due to their peculiar moral valency in Christian . . . thought."[10]

6. For the benefit of his non-Christian reader Tertullian notes that "we are your brethren as well, by the law of our common mother nature," although because of persecution against Christians he adds "though you are hardly men, because brothers so unkind."

7. See also also the fifth-century Christian historian Sozomen, *Hist.* 5.16.5. See further P. Johnson, *A History of Christianity* (New York: Touchstone, Simon and Schuster, 1976), p. 75; D. Ayerst and A. S. T. Fischer, *Records of Christianity,* Vol. I: *The Church in the Roman Empire* (Oxford: Basil Blackwell, 1971), pp. 179-81.

8. Gillian Clark, *Christianity and Roman Society* (Cambridge: Cambridge University Press, 2004), pp. 23-24. See her fuller discussion on pp. 106-111, 115, where she writes: "[Some Christians] were making efforts to provide . . . food, clothing and care for all who needed it. . . . As always not enough [Christians] were doing this. . . . But at least they tried, and no one has yet shown that non-Christian Roman society made any such effort." So also Peter D. A. Garnsey and Caroline Humfress, *The Evolution of the Late Antique World* (Cambridge: Orchard Academic, 2001), pp. 107-31.

9. Gildas Hamel, *Poverty and Charity in Roman Palestine, The First Three Centuries* C.E. (Berkeley: University of California Press, 1990), p. 236.

10. Greg Woolf, "Writing Poverty in Rome," in M. Atkins and R. Osborne, eds., *Poverty*

- "The triumph of the Christian religion enabled a strong minority to make an entire society sensitive to poverty."[11]

Views of this sort are commonplace among classicists and historians of antiquity.

Moreover, on the basis of such evidence, historians have postulated that its notable social practice best explains the spread of Christianity throughout the Roman empire. So Henry Chadwick suggests that the "practical application of charity was probably the most potent single cause of Christian success."[12] Classicists have repeatedly made the point that care for the destitute among Jesus-followers was "a new form of charity" in the ancient world that "exercised a powerful attraction within the cities of the later Empire" and offers the historian "one explanation for the success of Christianity."[13]

Although estimates such as these do justice to the bulk of the evidence, it also needs to be noted that this scenario of charity-driven growth should not imply that charity was wholly absent from the Greco-Roman world until the emergence of Christianity. Two interconnected issues need to be flagged at this point. The first, which is addressed primarily in later chapters, concerns the dating and characterization of charitable efforts within communities of Jesus-followers. For instance, Veyne writes:

> From the second century at least, the Christian Church was to be no longer satisfied with urging the faithful to show beneficence privately but would institutionalize it, setting up a "chest" *(arca)* for aid to widows, or-

---

in the Roman World (Cambridge: Cambridge University Press, 2006), 83-99, p. 84. Woolf includes Jewish and Islamic thought too, but the latter is not pertinent to the Greco-Roman world being considered here. On care for the poor in the latter part of the second millennium, see Donald T. Critchlow and Charles H. Parker, eds., *With Us Always: A History of Private Charity and Public Welfare* (Oxford: Rowman & Littlefield Publishers, 1998); Robert H. Bremner, *Giving: Charity and Philanthropy in History* (London: Transaction Publishers, 1994).

11. Veyne, *Bread and Circuses,* 33. So too his comments on p. 30: "pity for the disinherited, that pity which is so natural a sentiment when felt, but which societies can endure for thousands of years without feeling, and which, in any case, they feel only when major interests allow this to happen."

12. H. Chadwick, *The Early Church* (Harmondsworth: Penguin, 1967), p. 56, with examples on pp. 56-58. On this, see especially Richard Finn, *Almsgiving in the Later Roman Empire: Christian Promotion and Practice, 313-450* (Oxford: Oxford University Press, 2006).

13. C. R. Whittaker, "The Poor in the City of Rome," in *Land, City and Trade in the Roman Empire* (Aldershot: Variorum Ashgate, 1993), article 7 (there is no sequential pagination throughout the book; internally the article's pagination is from 1-25), p. 4.

phans, the poor, the old, the sick and those in prison, under the control of the hierarchy.[14]

Similarly, Peter Brown lays out the rationale of his book on ancient poverty in this way:

> I wish to trace some of the steps by which the leaders of the Christian church, the bishops, actively engaged in forms of the exercise of power that helped to bring about that transition [i.e., from pre-Christian to Christian attitudes towards poverty]. . . . To put it bluntly: in a sense, it was the Christian bishops who invented the poor. They rose to leadership in late Roman society by bringing the poor into ever-sharper focus. They presented their actions as a response to the needs of an entire category of persons (the poor) on whose behalf they claimed to speak. It was these actions that contributed decisively to the change. . . . Step by step, they soaked significant areas of late antique society in the novel and distinctive dye of a notion of "love of the poor."[15]

These assessments are correct in so many ways that it seems almost counter-productive to nit-pick at them. Nonetheless, what needs to be shown is that, within Christianity, the setting up of initiatives to care for the needy was not a phenomenon that belonged to the second century and beyond (contra Veyne);[16] and it was not simply Christian bishops who "invented the poor" (contra Brown).[17] Instead, things such as caring for the poor of the Greco-Roman world lay at the very heart of the earliest movement of Jesus-followers. Chapters 6 through 13 below are dedicated to demonstrating the point.

The second issue concerns pre- and non-Christian charitable initiatives in the Greco-Roman world. With regard to favorable postures towards the poor in the ancient world, a stark contrast between the pre- and non-Christian world on the one hand and the communities of Jesus-followers on the other is not wholly sustainable. The view that charitable postures to-

14. Veyne, *Bread and Circuses*, 24.

15. Brown, *Poverty and Leadership*, pp. 8-9.

16. Since the initial clause in the quotation from Veyne includes a notable qualification (i.e., "From the second century at least"), his claim is buffered from extreme overstatement, even though it errs on the side of focusing attention beyond the first century CE.

17. Since Brown demonstrates that care for the poor was a characteristic of the earliest Jesus-movement (e.g., *Poverty and Leadership*, p. 19), the overstatement of his claim is evident from within his own work.

wards the poor emerged only as a result of the influence of Jesus-followers of the first and subsequent centuries is attractive for two reasons. First, the preponderance of evidence does, in fact, lie on this side of the balance. Second, the differentiation of non-Judeo-Christian and Judeo-Christian attitudes provides an eminently useable interpretative framework when laying out a rough overview of historical phenomena.

But apart from the majority of ancient data and the advantage of providing a "high-level" heuristic tool for historiography, the view that charitable initiatives for the poor resulted exclusively from Judeo-Christian theology is problematic in its lack of precision and nuancing. It is vulnerable to a slice of important evidence that undermines its stark formulation, thereby making it misleading for purposes of close historiography, and making it questionable if used as a basis for assessing the moral identity of ancient religious phenomena.[18] As will be shown below (§4.3 through §4.6), there were at least low-level forms of care for the poor in the ancient world.

Before moving to discuss ancient generous initiatives, it needs to be noted that our analysis will inevitably revolve around two primary issues. First, it will be considered whether instances of generosity in the Greco-Roman world would have benefitted "the poor" at economic levels ES6 and ES7, most of whom were trapped in what has been termed "structural" or "conjunctural" poverty. Second, for those initiatives that can be said to have benefitted the poor, scholars have regularly probed as to the motivation behind them, considering whether they include a notable humanitarian dimension or whether other interests take prominence, outstripping any humanitarian dimension. Of course, if the first issue is sometimes difficult to determine, the second is even more so. The issue of motivation is notoriously difficult to pin down, not only because the pertinent extant data are so slim, but also because initiatives are so often driven by a motivational mixture. Here more than anywhere, perhaps, historiography is far less a science than an art, and historians will craft their artistic depictions of the past in different ways. There will be occasion to say more about motivation in the

---

18. T. E. Woods ("How Catholic Charity Changed the World," in his *How the Catholic Church Built Western Civilization* [Washington, DC: Regnery Publishing, 2005], pp. 169-86) is sufficiently nuanced in recognizing some forms of charity outside of Judeo-Christian circles, while also giving preponderance to Judeo-Christian initiatives. Nonetheless, Woods's apologetic interests may have prevented him from demonstrating pre- and non-Christian charity in anything more than a sentence or two, just as his Catholic commitment enables him to claim for "Catholicism" what might be claimed instead for proto-orthodox Christianity (i.e., pertinent to both Catholicism and Protestantism).

following sections, but I raise the point here both to indicate how assessments will be made in the sections that follow (i.e., with regard to both the targeted beneficiaries and the possible motivations of the initiator), and to register up front the ofttimes fragile nature of those assessments.

4.2: Generous Initiatives That Do Not Qualify as Charitable

In order to assess the extent to which charitable initiatives for the poor had a foothold within the pre- and non-Judeo-Christian world, it is important that we exclude certain types of expenditures from consideration. These involve expenditures that do not conform to what we might reasonably call "care for the poor" — with "the poor" being defined (by Peter Garnsey and Greg Woolf, as noted in §3.4 above) as "those living at or near subsistence level, whose prime concern it is to obtain the minimum food, shelter, and clothing necessary to sustain life, whose lives are dominated by the struggle for physical survival."[19]

In this regard, it is important to note from the start that generosity abounded in the Greco-Roman world. Indeed it was one of the virtues of the honorable man to be generous with his resources.[20] Firmly embedded within ancient honor codes, generosity was a primary means of bolstering social prestige.[21] But generosity itself is not the issue at stake here. Pertinent to the interests of this project are the kinds of generosity that reached the poor of ES6 and ES7 levels. And in that regard, a number of forms of Greco-Roman generosity fail to qualify as charitable, since much of the generosity of the ancient world tended to be restricted to higher economic levels.[22]

19. Peter D. A. Garnsey and Greg Woolf, "Patronage of the Rural Poor in the Roman World," in Andrew Wallace-Hadrill, ed., *Patronage in Ancient Society* (London: Routledge, 1989), 153-70, p. 153.

20. See, for instance, Aristotle, *Eth. Nic.* 4.1.6; Isocrates, *Or.* 1.27.

21. Cf. Bruce J. Malina (*The New Testament World: Insights from Cultural Anthropology*, 3rd ed. [Louisville: Westminster John Knox Press, 2000], pp. 37-38): "Prestige derives from the domination of persons rather than things. Hence any concern people show for the acquisition of goods derives from the purpose of gaining honor through generously disposing of what one has acquired among equals or socially useful lower-status clients. In other words, honor is acquired through beneficence, not through the fact of possession and/or the keeping of what one has acquired."

22. A. R. Hands, *Charities and Social Aid in Greece and Rome* (Ithaca, NY: Cornell University Press, 1968), p. 61: "[T]he classical preoccupation with *philotimia* left little room for any mention of pity — or of 'the poor' as particularly deserving of such pity."

For instance, generosity was often expended when honoring office holders within associations. This sort of thing is evident from inscriptions showing how associations honored their treasurers. The Achaean inscription *IG* 112 1262 from Piraeus (300/299 BCE) reads as follows:

> Whereas the supervisors have faithfully and zealously executed their responsibilities, both in regard to the sacrifices and all the other affairs of the association, (it is resolved) to commend them and to crown them with olive wreaths and to provide for them at the association's expense a votive plaque in the amount of 20 drachmae, on which both the crowns and the decree are inscribed.

Expenditures made to honor an association's supervisors do not qualify as charitable initiatives, since the people who benefitted were clearly not in desperate economic need. Such initiatives were made to fortify the honor of the association's most prominent member in order subsequently to enhance the reputation of the association itself.[23]

The inscription cited above also raises the prospect of generosity within the general membership of an association. So, the bestowal of honors upon the association's supervisors served an additional function of demonstrating to all outsiders of the association "that the association renders appropriate thanks to those who are zealous toward (the members) in acts of benefaction." Benefaction for association members has parallels in some ways to care for the poor within communities of Jesus-followers. But it also has significant differences. As will be shown in chapter 11 below, the predominant profile of members within associations gravitates towards the middling groups of ES4 and possibly ES5; by contrast, the predominant profile of members within communities of Jesus-followers in the first century CE gravitates towards ES5 and below. Intra-association generosity and benefaction, then, hardly qualifies as care for "the poor," at least if by that term we mean those at ES6 and below. Instead, it would have consisted of goodwill gestures that improved the prospects of predominantly middling-level adherents.[24]

Of course, members of Greco-Roman associations were often known to provide for other members of the association at times of hardship — i.e.,

---

23. In this regard, see especially *IG* 112 1261 [C].

24. Moreover, benevolent gestures within associations would have helped "to establish social superiority inside the group"; on this, see O. M. van Nijf, "*Collegia* and Civic Guards: Two Chapters in the History of Sociability," in W. Jongman and M. Kleijwegt, eds., *After the Past* (Leiden: Brill, 2002), 305-340, pp. 329-30.

when "unjust trials" came their way (*P.Cairo. dem.* 30606.23-24, from Tebtynis, 158/7 BCE) or when they had been considered negligent in repaying a loan (*P.Mich.Tebt.* V 243.9; from Tebtynis in the first century CE).[25] David Downs has argued that generosity of associations toward their own needy members implies "that pagan associations did occasionally adopt economic practices . . . intended to provide financial assistance for those in material need."[26] The claim has merit, but is somewhat overstated. There is generosity in such initiatives, of course, but it is not clear that care for association members who had come upon hard times squares wholly with care for the indigenous needy in general. Downs notes rightly that "[m]ost pagan voluntary associations were composed of those of middling status and wealth," and that "the utterly destitute may have been prevented from joining some associations by the relatively high cost of membership fees and banquets."[27] So the poor person worthy of economic support from other members of the association would have originally enjoyed an economic profile of ES4 or ES5. If an association member had dropped as far as ES6, say, he would qualify as "poor" within the terms set out by Garnsey and Woolf. But this is generosity of associations toward their own members who experienced economic misfortune. While this is, of course, highly laudable, never is the association expected to recruit members from among the poor in order to alleviate their poverty, and never is its charity depicted as having the potential to flow to the needy beyond the boundaries of the association. The generosity advertised by ancient associations is solely and exclusively intra-association generosity undertaken in (what was hoped to be) a *temporary* situation for those who have stumbled upon misfortune. If an association's members remained in their positions of "middling status and wealth," there would be no need for them to exercise charitable generosity, despite the vast numbers of desti-

25. I am grateful to John Kloppenborg for showing me an early draft of his compilation of these and other Achaean inscriptions, where he makes these points; the volume in which his contribution is to appear is provisionally entitled *Collegia, Cult Groups, and Guilds: Associations in the Ancient World* (forthcoming).

26. David Downs, *The Offering of the Gentiles* (Tübingen: Mohr Siebeck, 2008), p. 108. A somewhat similar position was adopted by Gerhard Uhlhorn, *Christian Charity in the Ancient Church* (New York: Charles Scribner's Sons, 1883), pp. 21-28. Uhlhorn saw in Greco-Roman associations "a shadow of love and charity" that was to blossom in Christian churches, arguing that "it is in the guilds that we find in heathenism for the first time anything approaching to the life of a Christian community" (p. 28). Nonetheless, Uhlhorn also stated that "there is nothing in the guilds which reaches to the height of actual charity, and this is a sure sign of how far distant that was from the ideas of the heathen world" (p. 23).

27. Downs, *The Offering of the Gentiles,* pp. 110 and 107-108 respectively.

tute all around them. The vision is restricted to the association, and ultimately to the honor of the association alone. The vast majority of the destitute could not have pinned the slightest hope on the generosity of
associations, simply because that generosity only flowed to "the poor"
among them who had once been economically secure enough to join an association in the first place, and who were probably expected to rise up to
their previous economic levels in due course.[28]

Hospitality, another common form of ancient generosity, was a practice
deeply entrenched in most parts of the Greco-Roman world. It involved a
host providing resources for travelers passing through his/her region. The
host might have offered baths, meals, clothes, entertainment, worship of the
deities, lodging and protection. There were various motivations for such acts
of generosity. These included: the attempt to disarm the stranger's potential
ill will (and the ill will of his deities) against the local people; the attempt to
earn the favor of those deities;[29] the host's attempt to bolster his own stand-

---

28. The same is likely to apply to what Downs calls "the most important literary testimony to the practice of care for the poor among pagan associations" (*The Offering of the
Gentiles*, p. 105) — that is, the letters exchanged between Pliny and the emperor Trajan in the
early second century CE. In one letter, the emperor Trajan instructs Pliny to allow the "benefit societies" (ἐράνους) to assemble in the city of Amisus, as long as the funds they collect are
not used to undermine social cohesion but "to relieve causes of hardship among the poor"
(*ad sustinendam tenuiorum inopiam utuntur*) (*Ep.* 10.93). But it is not at all clear that this is a
reference to poverty relief among the general populace. More than two hundred years ago
William Melmoth (*Letters of Pliny the Consul* [Boston: Larkin, 1809], p. 253) appended this
explanatory comment to Trajan's instruction: "[T]here were at Athens, and other cities of
Greece, certain fraternities, which paid into a common chest a monthly contribution towards the support of such of their members who had fallen into misfortunes; upon condition that if they ever arrived at more prosperous circumstances, they should repay into the
general fund the money so advanced." Despite the passing of the centuries, Melmoth's point
is likely to be on target. Trajan's instructions are less likely to pertain to care for those at or
below subsistence levels in general and more likely to pertain to the practice of giving a temporary "advance" to an association affiliate of formerly "middling" economic status, prior to
the affiliate's expected economic recovery. The scenario accords with Downs's observation
(p. 108) that "[s]ince the authors of the petition passed from Pliny to the emperor appear to
have been citizens of Amisus, with the term *tenuiores* Trajan may, in fact, be referring to
members of . . . 'the middling classes.'"

29. In this regard, Greco-Roman hospitality might be seen as a small-scale version of
the generous benefactions towards cults and temples, sponsored by the elite throughout
the Mediterranean basin. Making gestures of good-will to deities, their temples and their
devotees would have helped to enhance the regional prosperity. See Beate Dignas, *Economy
of the Sacred in Hellenistic and Roman Asia Minor* (Oxford: Oxford University Press, 2002),
pp. 38-39.

ing and reputation among his community, by showcasing his opulence, his influence, and/or his character; and simple altruistic interest.[30] But there is little in the material record to suggest that hospitality was regularly extended to the poor. If this was entertained in theory, it seems unlikely to have been put into practice.[31] The very ones targeted for hospitality were not normally in great economic need. Indeed, hospitality "often involved the giving of gifts between the two parties or at least an act of reciprocity."[32] Those who might enjoy hospitality in their travels were usually travelers from, at the lowest end, ES5 and upward.[33] Hospitality was not an ancient mechanism for giving assistance to the poor.

Another form of benefaction within Greco-Roman society is euergetism, the doing of "good deeds" within the civic arena. Euergetistic initiatives involved someone donating significant amounts of one's own money in order to resource civic provisions: roads, banquets, gladiatorial games, monuments, baths, theatres, pavements, temples, warships, and the like. The benefactors in virtually all of these initiatives were those within the civic elite — ES1 through ES3, although those at ES4 occasionally undertook some similar initiatives, sometimes by banding together to pool their resources.

Although euergetism was intended to benefit society, it should probably not be listed as an expression of concern for the well-being of the destitute directly. Euergetism was not a phenomenon of the "moral realm," since it was driven "not so much by natural inclination as by reason of the lure of

30. For more on motivational bases behind Greco-Roman hospitality, see Ladislaus J. Bolchazy, *Hospitality in Antiquity: Livy's Concept of Its Humanizing Force* (Chicago: Ares, 1977), pp. 1-20. Bolchazy differentiates between five different kinds of hospitality. In this, he errs on the side of constructing pure types and blurring the significant overlap among them.

31. The theory is narrated by Homer (*Od.* 17.219-22). But it ran counter to another narrative strand pertaining to hospitality, in which the higher the traveller's social status, the greater the hospitality he enjoyed. On this, see H. van Wees, "Greed, Generosity and Gift-Exchange in Early Greece and the Western Pacific," in W. Jongman and M. Kleijwegt, eds., *After the Past* (Leiden: Brill, 2002), 341-78, pp. 369-70.

32. Andrew Arterbury, *Entertaining Angels: Early Christian Hospitality in Its Mediterranean Setting* (Sheffield: Sheffield Phoenix Press, 2005), p. 115.

33. Because of its intra-ethnic dimension, Jewish hospitality towards other Jews might have dipped below ES5 levels. If, for the sake of argument, we imagine Jesus' mother Mary as being at ES6 (although this seems rather arbitrary), then the account of her being shown hospitality by Elizabeth in Luke 1:39-56 shows how intra-ethnic and intra-familial hospitality could function at lower economic levels. On the intra-ethnic dimension of Jewish generosity, see Hamel, *Poverty and Charity in Roman Palestine*, p. 218: "The basic rule was that one's own poor came before any others. The poor within the family, the village, the town, or the Jewish poor, had precedence."

honor" (Cicero, *Off.* 1.44). Quite simply, whatever benefits they may have contributed, euergetistic initiatives by the elite were primarily an essential mechanism in the inexhaustible quest for status capture. Pliny the Younger says it this way: "The boast of their good deed is considered to be the motive, not the consequence" (*Ep.* 1.8.15). The point has been made, for instance, by Paul Veyne, when noting how euergetism differs from charitable work for the poor "in ideology, in beneficiaries and in agents, in the motivations of agents and in their behaviour."[34] With regard to the motivation of euergetistic agents, Veyne claims that in most cases of public euergetism "what mattered was the point of honour — that is, the quest for honours."[35] Those who loved their city assisted their city, but "never the poor."[36] As Peter Brown notes:

> If some of them [i.e., the beneficiaries] were occasionally spoken of as "poor," it was because they were citizens perceived to be in danger of impoverishment, of coming down in the world, not because they already lay at the very bottom of society. There was little room in such a model for the true urban "poor," many of whom would, in fact, have been impoverished immigrants, noncitizens, living on the margins of the community.[37]

Consequently, although the poor would be among those who benefitted from euergetism, euergetistic initiatives were not aimed at relieving the hardships of the destitute, not least because the destitute had little to offer the elite in return.[38] In its most usual form, euergetism was a means of providing "edifices and pleasures to the citizens rather than alms to the poor."[39] As Lucy Grig states, "the traditional rules of civic euergetism . . . determined

---

34. Veyne, *Bread and Circuses*, p. 19.

35. Veyne, *Bread and Circuses*, p. 233. Early on in his book (p. 5), Veyne claims that euergetism would have arisen "from a wide variety of motives: careerism, paternalism, kingly style, corruption, conspicuous consumption, local patriotism, desire to emulate, concern to uphold one's rank, obedience to public opinion, fear of hostile demonstrations, generosity, belief in ideals." Of this list of a dozen possible motives, the first ten are, to varying degrees, immersed in the competition for public honor; only the final two come close to what might be called "moral warrants."

36. Brown, *Poverty and Leadership*, p. 5.

37. Brown, *Poverty and Leadership*, p. 5.

38. Whittaker, "The Poor in the City of Rome," p. 24: "Widows, orphans, migrants and the sick, whom the Church tended, were those whom Roman euergetism almost ignored. They were not the 'deserving poor.'"

39. Veyne, *Bread and Circuses*, p. 20.

that the generosity of the rich was not supposed to be aimed at those who truly required it."[40] That euergetistic initiatives were primarily motivated by honor-capture (as Veyne claims) is evidenced, for instance, by the frequency with which such initiatives coincided with the timing of elections to the municipal magistracies. Accordingly, Veyne considers there to have been a significant difference "between civic assistance in pagan antiquity and . . . charity to the poor."[41]

Patronage was widespread in the ancient world, and provided a mechanism whereby people of lesser socio-economic status could benefit by being clients to patrons of higher socio-economic status. The patron provided certain resources (e.g., financial initiatives, business contacts) to enhance the client's prospects for advancement. But patronage of this kind usually distinguished it from charitable initiatives to care for the poor. Those that benefitted from a patron's initiatives did not include those in the lower economic levels — the destitute of ES6 and ES7 especially. As Koenraad Verboven notes, "the poorest in Roman society rarely — if ever — enjoyed the benefits of patronage, because they rarely — if ever — had anything to offer in return."[42]

Having surveyed various forms of ancient generosity, it is evident that none of the phenomena cited qualifies as a *bona fide* effort to care for the destitute, because none of them were targeted to offset the needs of those who had for long been enmeshed within economic levels ES6 and ES7 specifically — i.e., those subject to the harsh conditions of "conjunctural pov-

---

40. L. Grig, "Throwing Parties for the Poor: Poverty and Splendour in the Late Antique Church," in Atkins and Osborne, eds., *Poverty in the Roman World*, 145-61, p. 158.

41. Veyne, *Bread and Circuses*, 30. The final clause reads "Christian charity to the poor." But since this is based on Veyne's general view that, for the most part, there was no "charity to the poor" in the pre- and non-Christian world, and since this view is shown in §4.3 below to be slightly problematic, I have chosen to remove the adjective "Christian" and apply his statement more generally. Veyne himself notes at times that there were pre- and non-Christian forms of charity, so I doubt he would mind the omission, not least since it does not change the force of his general claim.

42. Koenraad Verboven, *The Economy of Friends: Economic Aspects of Amicitia and Patronage in the Late Republic* (Brussels: Latomus, 2002), p. 113. So too Roman Garrison, *Redemptive Almsgiving in Early Christianity* (Sheffield: Sheffield Academic Press, 1993), p. 41: "the prevailing Graeco-Roman attitude was that benefits should be given exclusively to those who were regarded as worthy. . . . In general, those who were considered deserving of benevolence were one's social peers, fellow-citizens, family members and friends." Moreover, some Hellenistic-Jewish writers and Greco-Roman moralists attacked the values of benefaction as formulaic, sterile and calculating, rather than being founded on moral warrants.

erty." If these are not the places to look for instances of Greco-Roman care for the poor, there are other phenomena of the ancient world that might hold more promise, as noted in the following sections.

4.3: Generous Initiatives That Qualify as Charitable

The poor were everywhere in the ancient world, and almost nobody could avoid encountering them. But what attitudes and responses did such encounters transpire in those higher up the economy scale? The view that has predominated among historians has already been outlined in §4.1 above: namely, the poor were not worthy of attention, solace, or compassion. But this view is also in need of some qualification, with notable counter-instances needing to be registered, lest we wrongly imagine that the ancient world was virtually devoid of charitable initiatives for the poor.

The very fact that there were ES7 beggars on the street should cause us to recognize the existence of almsgiving in the Greco-Roman world. If no one ever tossed a coin to a needy person on the street, the phenomenon of begging would never have arisen. And the fact that some despicable characters went to great lengths to "cash in" on begging demonstrates that the "market" for beggars was not insignificant. This is evident in the Elder Seneca's *Controversiae* (10.4), which records how one loathsome man made his living by collecting exposed children who had been left for dead along the roadside and then mutilating their bodies (i.e., slicing off their tongues, chopping off their limbs, etc.) in order to augment the pity of passers-by and to increase his income through their alms.[43] Such a thing would not have happened in a world devoid of charitable initiatives and concern for the needy.[44]

---

43. The strategy has a foothold even within the twenty-first century, as depicted in the 2008 film *Slumdog Millionaire*. A different strategy for profiting from children in the ancient world is evident in a first-century inscription from Ephesus, authorized by the local Roman governor (*IEphesos* Iz, no. 18c, ll. 18-22): "It is my wish that the public slaves, who are said to buy infants for a trifling sum and dedicate them to [the deity] Artemis so that their own slaves are raised by her revenues, provide nourishment for their own slaves."

44. Compare Anneliese Parkin, "'You do him no service': An Exploration of Pagan Almsgiving," in Atkins and Osborne, eds., *Poverty in the Roman World*, 60-82, pp. 70-71: "One thing that is highly suggestive of the likelihood that disabled people were pitied is the custom of faking injuries or disabilities, for which a little evidence for this period survives. . . . Faking illness or disability is a common strategem if sick and disabled people are very successful in soliciting alms."

If almsgiving had a foothold in Greco-Roman societies, we can consider its character in relation to four facets: (a) the problem of pity; (b) initiatives undertaken by the sub-elite; (c) initiatives undertaken by the elite; and (d) motivations underlying generous initiatives.

4.3.1 The Problem of Pity

It is often maintained that a distaste for the emotion of pity prevented charitable initiatives from getting a foothold in the Greco-Roman world. The view is flawed. Some ancient Stoics did, of course, despise pity, seeing it as an illness of the soul that would upset one's inner balance. So Seneca called pity an "error of a weak soul, which is brought low by the sight of a stranger's misery" (*Clem.* 2.5.1; scc also 2.6.4). This was "error" because it involved putting one's self into the shoes of another, feeling his pain and being moved to act solely on the basis of an emotional twinge. Emotional involvement of this kind was thought to contradict the archetype of independent self-sufficiency (αὐτάρκεια) — i.e., the state of being content with one's own circumstances in life without being disturbed by emotion. And in this way, the emotion of pity ran contrary to the ideal of self-sufficiency.

But it is also important to note what else Seneca has to say about pity. For while he cautions against the emotion of pity, he does not caution against charitable action itself: "The wise man does not allow himself to experience this weakness of soul, but instead simply gives alms to the anonymous poor in the street, being as ready to give as someone who does feel pity" (*Clem.* 2.5.4).[45] As Anneliese Parkin has well noted, Seneca's statement is significant for several reasons. First, it suggests a distinction between emotional and non-emotional initiative — with only initiatives based on emotion being seen as problematic. In this, Seneca differentiates between the emotion of "pity" *(misericordia)* and the act of "mercy" *(clementia).* Second, Seneca's statement acts as a window onto the existence of charitable acts in

---

45. Arthur R. Hands (*Charities and Social Aid in Greece and Rome* [Ithaca, NY: Cornell University Press, 1968], p. 84) thinks that this must refer to alms for the elite who have fallen on hard times, but he is being unnecessarily suspicious here. See Cicero, *Tusc.* 4.43-57; *Acad.* 2.44.135; Seneca, *Ira* 1.9.2. So too, the Elder Seneca (*Controv.* 1.1.14) notes that reaching out a hand to give to the lowest in need is a common right among humanity. As Parkin notes ("Pagan Almsgiving," p. 65): "Stoicism, the philosophy most antagonistic to *feeling* pity, nonetheless advocates — in our parlance — *taking* pity. Pity *(misericordia)* is incompatible with *apatheia*, but mercy *(clementia)* is laudable."

the ancient world. The phrase "being as ready to give as someone who does feel pity" speaks volumes in this regard. As Parkin notes, "[n]ot only does Seneca by implication advocate almsgiving whilst rejecting that such acts must necessarily be the consequence of pity, but he also implies that other, less enlightened, people do give to beggars out of pity."[46]

Moreover, throughout his *De beneficiis* (written in the late 50s or early 60s CE), Seneca was intent to undermine the view that one gave to another simply in order to receive something back (i.e., generosity channeled through patronage systems); instead, for Seneca, giving to another is its own reward, regardless of whether one receives something back in return. Setting himself up as an example, Seneca says that helping paupers gives him great satisfaction, and he does not expect anything other than gratitude in return (e.g., *Ben.* 3.8.3).[47]

Furthermore, it needs to be noted that, even if some Stoics held a harsh line against the emotion of pity, it is not at all obvious that their position was representative of the majority of people in the ancient world.[48] The whims of certain philosophers often did not permeate the populace. And even among philosophers, many did not disdain the emotion of pity. This is true even of Stoics (e.g., Musonius Rufus) and Epicureans (see Diog. Laert. *Vit. Philosoph.* 10.118). Moreover, the rhetorical and tragic traditions of the Greco-Roman world "actively sought to arouse pity in the audience," as did

---

46. Parkin, "Pagan Almsgiving," p. 63.

47. At times Seneca puts restrictions on who qualifies as the needy person worthy of assistance (e.g., *Ben.* 1.1.2; 4.11.1). In Parkin's estimate, such qualifications cast a shadow over the whole of Seneca's discussion of giving to those in need: "it quickly becomes clear that the 'needy' in question . . . are respectable citizens, and not the most desperate members of their society. Seneca advocates giving to the poor man of *worth*. . . . This is the semiotics of patronage" ("You do him no service," p. 62). According to Parkin, when discussing the phenomenon of economic generosity, both Seneca and Cicero slip into models of patronage; "most of their thought on giving dwells on *beneficentia*, on the assessment of a good risk for a return of honour" (p. 62). If she is right, those "of worth" would not include those in the lower economic levels — the destitute of ES6 and ES7 especially. On the other hand, so much of Seneca's discussion is unencumbered by consideration of the "poor man of worth" that Parkin's estimate itself appears devoid of generosity at times. The issue cannot be adjudicated here, but would involve fuller consideration of Seneca's cosmopolitan view of humanity (*Ep.* 44.2; 47.10; 110.10), and his view of benevolence in relation to imitation of the deities (or nature) (*Ep.* 95.50; 104.23; see also §4.5 below). My thanks to Tim Brookins for engaging discussions on these issues.

48. It is possible that Seneca is attempting to do two things simultaneously: (1) maintain a Stoic emphasis on the importance of avoiding pity, and (2) improve the reputation of Stoicism among the (more charitable) populace.

"early imperial historians" who generally viewed pity to be "a desirable response to misfortune, provided its objects have not authored their own fates."[49]

In sum, then, there is no reason to believe that ancient attitudes to charitable giving were held captive to one strand of Stoic conviction. Any disdain of emotional pity among some Stoic philosophers would not necessarily have dictated the attitudes and behaviors of the populace to the extent of completely denuding society of charitable initiatives. And even those like Seneca who disavowed the emotion of pity were not opposed to charitable initiatives that were stripped of emotional involvement.

4.3.2 Charitable Initiatives among the Sub-Elite

There is an old adage that goes something like this: "If you are in need, borrow money from a poor man."[50] The poor, in this view of things, are more willing to give to the poor, and are more willing to give with fewer (or no) strings attached.

Was this the case in the Greco-Roman world? The problem, of course, is that we simply do not have data sufficient enough to reconstruct sub-elite attitudes and behavior with any real certainty. Seneca's statement about "being as ready to give as someone who does feel pity" might be taken, for instance, to reveal something of the sentiment of the sub-elite world, although that is not wholly clear. Nonetheless, Parkin seems to be generally correct when, after triangulating ancient sources, she concludes the following:

> Most gifts to the destitute [in the Greco-Roman world] must have come from non-elites. . . . It has been claimed that Christians were the first people for whom pity was the deciding factor in almsgiving, but we cannot be certain of this. . . . There is a grave deficit of sources which represent the

---

49. Parkin, "Pagan Almsgiving," p. 63 n. 10. On the imperial historians, see D. S. Levene, "Pity, Fear and the Historical Audience: Tacitus on the Fall of Vitellius," in S. Morton Braund and C. Gill, eds., *The Passions in Roman Thought and Literature* (Cambridge: Cambridge University Press, 1997), pp. 128-49.

50. In his novel about Jesus (*The Book of Witnesses* [London: Collins, 1971], pp. 115-16), David Kassoff makes this point by means of the character nicknamed "Kwuz," a beggar: "You'd think people with a lot of blessings to be thankful for would give the most, wouldn't you? I mean, it follows, doesn't it? Rich people, big givers. Like hell. The givers are the poor people. Always have been."

views and habits of those belonging to the lower strata of Graeco-Roman society, but such texts as can be gathered suggest quite the opposite of this claim.[51]

In Parkin's estimate, "from the primary evidence available for almsgiving among the lower strata, it appears to have been common, normal, although not compulsory, to give to the destitute when they presented themselves."[52]

One further phenomenon needs to be noted here. According to the Elder Seneca, it was commonly known that women who had previously exposed a child, leaving it outside to die or to be picked up by someone else, often gave alms to beggars. A woman would do this evidently on the off-chance that the beggar was her son abandoned long ago, or in the hope that if she gave alms to someone else's son, perhaps someone would also be giving alms to her abandoned son (*Controv.* 10.4.19-20). Such women were unlikely to be elite. Here was a common but low-level form of generosity towards the poor that, were it not for the remarks of the Elder Seneca, would otherwise have gone unrecorded in the annals of history.

Notably, however, Seneca's observation meshes with one other piece of ancient evidence, and a very significant one, which comes not from ancient

51. Parkin, "Pagan Almsgiving," pp. 69-70. See also Hans-Joachim Degenhardt, *Lukas, Evangelist der Armen* (Stuttgart: Verlag Katholisches Bibelwerk, 1983), pp. 180-81; H. Bolkestein, *Wohltätigkeit und Armenpflege im vorchristlichen Altertum* (Utrecht: A. Oosthoek Verlag, 1939), pp. 94-95. M. R. P. McGuire seeks to show that three pieces of Bolkestein's evidence for low-level pagan charity in the western empire actually testify to oriental influence through the transportation of slaves from east to west; see his "Epigraphical Evidence for Social Charity in the Roman West," *AJP* 67 (1946): 129-50.

52. Parkin, "Pagan Almsgiving," p. 73. Here we might also mention the case mentioned by Thucydides, the Athenian historian of the fifth century BCE who is often credited with having a thoroughly pessimistic view of human nature. Nonetheless, he notes how the people of Athens acted during a plague in 430 BCE. As G. Herman recounts ("Reciprocity, Altruism, and the Prisoner's Dilemma: The Special Case of Classical Athens," in C. Gill, N. Postlethwaite and R. Seaford, eds., *Reciprocity in Ancient Greece* [Oxford: Oxford University Press, 1998], 199-226, p. 218), according to Thucydides "most of the people who died had caught the disease while nursing the sick. . . . As soon as this became known, people faced a dilemma: should they yield to their instincts and avoid the sick, or comply with the social norms and visit them? Either alternative was unattractive: in the first case, they risked not being looked after if they themselves fell ill, in the second, they risked contracting the disease at once. Nevertheless, writes Thucydides, there were people who chose to visit and nurse the sick because 'they made it a point of honour to act properly,' and 'felt ashamed to think of their own safety.' To put it another way, some people, acting under the constraint of social norms, took a course of action which ran contrary to the desire for self-preservation, their wish to act in the interests of society outweighing even the fear of death."

literary texts but from the ruins of Pompeii. With the eruption of Mount Vesuvius in 79 CE, the cities of Pompeii and Herculaneum were buried under 60 feet of ash and pumice, in effect encasing their urban life in a time-capsule that archaeological excavation has been uncovering with ever-increasing efforts. Within its finds lies the Estate of Junia Felix. Although she was likely to have been born into a family of freedmen, Junia Felix seems to have inherited vast amounts of wealth, and is probably to be placed in the ES3 economic level at least. Mary Beard describes her estate in this way:

> At the time of the eruption, this large property with its imposing entrance . . . covered the whole of what had once been two city blocks not far from the Amphitheatre. It included a number of different units: a privately run, commercial bathing establishment, a number of rental apartments, shops, bars and dining rooms, a large orchard and a medium-sized private house.[53]

One of the rooms within this vast villa had a frieze painted onto it, depicting various life scenes from the forum of Pompeii. The scenes may not be "strictly realistic" depictions of Pompeian life, portraying "a Pompeian street scene in the mind's eye of a Pompeian painter." But even if they are "an imaginative re-creation," the scenes "offer as vivid a picture as we could hope to have of life on the Pompeian streets."[54]

The frieze depicts snapshots of daily life not so much among the elite but primarily among the sub-elite — ironmongers; salesmen; fast-food vendors; men and ladies bartering over cloth, shoes, baskets and pans; children playing between the columns of a building; and the like. And taking prominence in one scene is a well-dressed woman who, accompanied by a twelve-year-old youth (or so), is handing a coin to a destitute, poorly clad beggar (perhaps only a few years older than the child who accompanies the woman). The scene has been preserved in an eighteenth-century engraving of the now-faded original, as in illustration 1 on page 80.

It is not altogether clear whether the philanthropic woman belongs to the sub-elite or the elite, but the likelihood is that she is sub-elite. Most, and

---

53. Mary Beard, *Pompeii: The Life of a Roman Town* (London: Profile Books, 2008), p. 72. The earthquake of 62 CE seems to have destroyed much of her property, although her rental income from the various components of her *domus* would have assisted her in restoring the property, prior to the fateful eruption of 79.

54. Beard, *Pompeii*, p. 73.

Illustration 1: An eighteenth-century sketch of one of the panels of the frieze at the villa of Junia Felix (from Beard, *Pompeii*, p. 74; *Antichità di Ercolano*, vol. 3, plate 43).

perhaps all, of the other scenes depict sub-elite figures,[55] and instead of the woman being surrounded by an entourage, she is followed by a single youth. So although she is indeed "an elegant lady,"[56] she is unlikely to be a member of the elite. Perhaps we should place her somewhere within the elongated category of ES4.

Here then is an artistic impression of the sort of thing that happened on the streets of Pompeii. In an ordinary Pompeian day, along with children playing, youth being taught, and adults bartering, one might also catch a glimpse of one of the urban poor being given a coin by a sub-elite woman.

4.3.3 Charitable Initiatives Undertaken by the Elite

According to Paul Veyne, the Greco-Roman elite would not have worried about the state of the poor, leaving that instead to the lower social orders.[57] According to Parkin, "the rich did not in fact often give to the destitute: they will have been largely protected from the attentions of beggars in public by their servants, clients or lectors, and many entrenched in the doctrine of euergetism or *beneficentia* may genuinely have believed that it was

55. In one scene, the local elite are depicted only in the background (Beard, *Pompeii*, p. 73). In another, men sit to adjudicate a legal case (Beard, *Pompeii*, p. 75), but they appear to be retainers adjudicating a trivial case rather than the civic elite.

56. Beard, *Pompeii*, p. 76.

57. Veyne, *Bread and Circuses*, p. 20.

money not well used."[58] Moreover, the elite sources from the early imperial period "show a general lack of understanding of the realities of conjunctural poverty and underemployment, and a marked mistrust of the apparently idle unemployed, loitering in the streets."[59] This blind-spot in the discourse of the elite is taken for granted (probably in exaggerated fashion) in Jesus' parable of the rich man and Lazarus, as in these words from Luke 16:19-21:

> There was a rich man who was dressed in purple and fine linen and who feasted sumptuously every day. And at his gate lay a poor man named Lazarus, covered with sores, who longed to satisfy his hunger with what fell from the rich man's table; even the dogs would come and lick his sores.

Lazarus failed to register on the rich man's radar, with the rich man being unaware of or unconcerned about Lazarus's plight. Jesus' parable sets out a scenario in which the "realities of conjunctural poverty" were of no impact upon the cocooned world of the rich man.

We should be careful, however, not to paint too monolithic and extreme a picture of the Greco-Roman elite. If being ignorant or uncaring about the needs of the poor around them was a propensity of the ancient elite, it is also important to note that there were exceptions that stand out starkly against this general backdrop. Parkin entertains the possibility in this way:

> We can fight too hard to argue away every possible reference to almsgiving [by the elite]. . . . It is surely right to say that the elite were more likely to help their own peers fallen on hard times, but this is not to say that they never helped anyone else. Granted, pity was traditionally and ideologically felt for those who might be in a position to return it . . . , but we must be open to [other] possibilities in social practice."[60]

---

58. Parkin, "Pagan Almsgiving," p. 68. Even if the elite did, at times, find the poor within their sights, it is not clear that the poor would have wanted it that way. See Carlin A. Barton (*Roman Honor: The Fire in the Bones* [Berkeley: University of California, 2001], p. 225): "In Plautus's *Asinaria* the poor man is not only embarrassed but deeply suspicious of the kindly and equal treatment afforded him by his rich neighbor. We might describe the poor man's anxiety as fear of being patronized. The respect shown him by his rich neighbor threatens to make him even more hopelessly in debt to, and so more vulnerable to, an already more powerful man."

59. Parkin, "Pagan Almsgiving," p. 77. On this, see G. Woolf, "Writing Poverty in Rome," in Atkins and Osborne, eds., *Poverty in the Roman World*, pp. 83-99.

60. Parkin, "Pagan Almsgiving," p. 65.

Perhaps the frieze in the Pompeian villa of Junia Felix helps to make Parkin's point. Although the altruistic woman in the frieze is probably sub-elite, she stands prominently in the villa of an elite woman, advertising and embodying a form of generosity that might have been esteemed by Junia Felix herself.

Or we might consider the case of Publilius, an elite man of the first century BCE. He was known to have been "much interested in gift-giving and says several times that it is good to give, to have pity on those in need and to give without moralizing about it."[61] We might be suspicious about whom Publilius imagined to be "in need." Would such people have been restricted to his peers who had fallen on hard times, or would they have been the poor entrenched in conjunctural poverty — that is, those whose lives were normally marked out by ES6 or ES7 levels?

It seems, then, that Parkin's caution about fighting "too hard to argue away every possible reference to almsgiving" by the elite is apt. Not least, unless the data present reason to do otherwise, we might err on the side of generosity when reading inscriptions such as the one made in 86 BCE in honor of Damidas, who served for two years as the city doctor of Dytheion (located in the south of Laconia). It speaks of him as one who "lack[ed] nothing in zeal and love of honor," and who thereby "did what was just for those who had need (τοῖς χρείαν ἔχουσιν), so that there might be equality to all, both poor and rich (κα[ὶ πένησι καὶ] πλουσίοις), slave and free" (*IG* V/1 1145, lines 17-21). Here, notably, the quest for honor is bound up with caring for the needy and the poor. In fact, as the inscription goes on to demonstrate, Damidas offered his medical services to the city free of charge at a time when the civic finances were quite restricted (lines 45-47). Among those from the ancient record who might qualify as good-hearted elite men, Damidas would be a likely candidate.[62]According to Morgan, the generous among the elite were known even to have invented reasons for making gifts to the needy, a view that is not out of line with the description of Damidas in this first-century inscription.[63]

61. Teresa Morgan, *Popular Morality in the Early Roman Empire* (Cambridge: Cambridge University Press, 2007), p. 93.

62. So Downs (*The Offering of the Gentiles*, p. 105): The inscription indicates "that 'civic' euergetism could occasionally extend beyond the bounds of citizens of the *polis*, and that poverty and lack of social status were not necessarily barriers to medical care (and other forms of assistance?) in certain contexts."

63. Morgan, *Popular Morality*, p. 93 and passages cited from Publilius Syrus's *Sententiae* in Morgan's footnote 55. For Hellenistic examples, see Herman, "Reciprocity, Altruism, and the Prisoner's Dilemma," pp. 217-20. This would have been part and parcel of their attempts to outdo each other in public benefaction in general. On this impulse in classical Athens, see

Generosity toward the economically needy of ES6 and ES7 was not necessarily at odds with the profile of the economically elite; at times, it might itself have coincided with, and been an expression of, their social prestige.[64]

Or there is the famous case of Musonius Rufus (c. 30-100 CE). Born into the equestrian order (i.e., ES2), Musonius had already become a notable figure in Rome by the time of Nero, and was twice banished from Rome (by the emperors Nero and Vespasian).[65] A popular Stoic philosopher, he taught Epictetus (55-135 CE) and influenced a great many others, advocating a liberal Stoicism that emphasized the importance not of learning philosophical theory but of living ethically.[66] Most importantly, this involved showing benevolence to others, even to the point of denouncing excessive acquisition of possessions. While there is no indisputable evidence that Musonius Rufus advocated benevolence to the poor of ES6 and ES7, pointers in that direction do exist (see below). And such a practice would not be out of alignment with Musonius Rufus's strenuous advocacy of benevolence within society, and his eschewal of hoarding possessions in ever-greater amounts instead of using them benignly for others. His stance on these matters was not simply that of an elite who advocated civic euergetism, although it would no doubt have

---

especially Paul Millett, "The Rhetoric of Reciprocity in Classical Athens," in Gill et al., *Reciprocity in Ancient Greece*, pp. 227-53.

64. Karl Polanyi makes the point in exaggerated fashion (*The Great Transformation* [Boston: Beacon Press, 1957], p. 46): "the premium set on generosity is so great [in primitive societies] when measured in terms of social prestige as to make any behaviour other than that of utter self-forgetfulness simply not pay. Personal character has little to do with the matter." So too Thomas Hobbes (*Leviathan*, 1.15): "No man giveth, but with intention of Good to himselfe." So too A. B. Weiner (*Women of Value, Men of Renown: New Perspectives in Trobriand Exchange* [Austin: University of Texas Press, 1976], p. 221; cf. pp. 76-77) concluded from an anthropological survey that those indigenous people who claimed that their charitable initiatives were motivated only by "love" and "generosity" were "following a myth that serves in their society to hide a reality of self-interest." Compare also M. Mauss (*The Gift: Forms and Functions of Exchange in Archaic Societies* [trans. I. Cunnison; London: Routledge & Kegan Paul, 1954 (1925)], p. 1): in archaic exchange relationships, gifts are paraded as being motivated by voluntary, disinterested and spontaneous generosity, "but the accompanying behaviour is formal pretence and social deception, while the transaction itself is based on obligation and economic self-interest."

65. So too C. E. Lutz, "Musonius Rufus, 'the Roman Socrates,'" *YCS* 10 (1947): 3-147, p. 24: "His very prominence in public life, his active concern with the problems of his day, and his keen sense of duty to society necessarily made him an object of Nero's persecution."

66. For example, see Musonius Rufus, "That There Is No Need of Giving Many Proofs for One Problem" (Lutz, "Musonius Rufus," p. 36, lines 10-12): "For only in this way will philosophy be of profit to anyone, if to sound doctrine he adds conduct in harmony with it."

included that.[67] He advocates "do[ing] good to many people through public and private charity" (δημοσίᾳ καὶ ἰδίᾳ πολλοὺς ἀνθρώπους εὐεργετῆσαι, 19.25-26), by "help[ing] people" in need (εἰς ἀνθρώπους ἀναλίσκειν, 19.28) and "by cheerfully doing good" (τῷ προθύμως εὐεργετοῦντι, 19.30).[68] The despicable person is one who can help others but chooses not to.[69]

In the estimate of Cora Lutz, what is most notable about Musonius is his "active concern for his fellow-men," to the extent that she says this of him:

> Indeed, Musonius' contribution to ethical philosophy . . . lies in the new spirit which he infused into the old Stoic concept of "humanitas." In his own personal relations, he reveals kindliness and warm human sympathy for human kind. In his teachings he emphasizes the necessity for sympathetic understanding in all human relationships [including those pertaining to slaves and women]. He is one of the first to advocate contributing to the common good by devoting one's resources to charity. . . . The high idealism, combined with the noble humanitarianism of his teachings, represents the greatest height Stoicism ever reached.[70]

Against the backdrop of his writings, it would seem churlish to deny that a historical core resides within the following tradition about Musonius Rufus:

> Musonius ordered a thousand sesterces to be given to a beggar . . . who was pretending to be a philosopher. When several people told him that the rascal was a bad and vicious fellow, deserving of nothing good, Musonius . . . answered with a smile, "Well then, he is worthy of money (ἄξιος οὖν ἐστιν ἀργυρίου)."[71]

---

67. Compare Musonius Rufus, "On Clothing and Shelter" (Lutz, "Musonius Rufus," p. 123, lines 25-26): A large and beautiful house is of little value compared with the benefits of blessing "the city and fellow-citizens from his own resources" (πόλει καὶ πολίταις ἐκ τῶν ἑαυτοῦ).

68. So too Musonius Rufus, "Must One Obey One's Parents under All Circumstances?" where all humanity is required by Zeus to be "just, honest, beneficent" (δίκαιον, χρηστόν, εὐεργετικόν [Lutz, "Musonius Rufus," p. 104, line 33]), among other things. See also his "That Kings Should Study Philosophy" (Lutz, "Musonius Rufus," p. 66, line 11): εὐεργετικός, χρηστός, φιλάνθρωπος.

69. This is the spirit of a saying found in Lutz, "Musonius Rufus," p. 137, line 26: The despicable man is recognized "by his inability [i.e., unwillingness] to be helpful" (κατὰ τὸ ἀδύνατον εἶναι ὠφελεῖν) [my translation].

70. Lutz, "Musonius Rufus," pp. 29-30.

71. The translation is that of Lutz ("Musonius Rufus," pp. 143, 145), except for the final phrase, which is my own.

The tradition locates the generosity of the elite Musonius Rufus even as far down the economy scale as ES7.

Or there is the example of the people of Rhodes. The first-century CE geographer Strabo made note of elite charitable initiatives on the island of Rhodes (the name shared by its capital city) in this way (*Geogr.* 14.2.5):

> The Rhodians are concerned for the people in general, although their rule is not democratic; still they wish to take care of their multitude of poor people (συνέχειν δ᾽ ὅμως βουλόμενοι τὸ τῶν πενήτων πλῆθος). Accordingly, the people are supplied with provisions and the needy are supported by the well-to-do (οἱ εὔποροι τοὺς ἐνδεεῖς ὑπολαμβάνουσιν ἔθει τινὶ πατρίῳ); and there are certain liturgies that supply provisions, so that at the same time the poor man receives his sustenance (τόν τε πένητα ἔχειν τὴν διατροφήν) and the city does not run short of useful men.

The claim that "certain liturgies" accompanied the giving of resources to the poor signals that these were occasions of public honor. This is reinforced by the observation that through these "liturgies" of honor there is no shortage of "useful men." Honor-capture is clearly involved here. But there is no indication in any of this that the poor who benefit are anything other than those at the lowest end of the economy scale — i.e., those who required assistance even to have "sustenance." Strabo's focus is on the populace in general (not simply those worthy of attention) and, within their number, the economically "needy." The Rhodians certainly caught Strabo's eye as being notable with regard to elite charitable initiatives for the benefit of the poor, but we might be cautious about concluding that they were singular in this practice throughout the Mediterranean basin. The ancient database includes examples of similar practices of care for the destitute sponsored by the elite.[72]

The material record of the ancient world does not allow us to reconstruct what elite care for the poor might have looked like in any great detail, or how often it was undertaken. Low-level forms of that phenomenon inevitably lie beyond our historical grasp. We might tend to think that the elite involved themselves in generous ventures that generally bypassed caring for the poor. But it would be unwise to conclude that charitable gestures and/or initiatives were wholly restricted to sub-elite levels; to maintain such a view is to run contrary to the best historical evidence.

---

72. For descriptions of similar situations, see Lysias 24; Aristotle, *Ath. Pol.* 6.5 and 49.4.

4.3.4 Motivations Underlying Generous Initiatives

If we can never be sure why ancients did what they did, charitable gestures are certainly no exception. Nonetheless, certain clues allow us to survey a spectrum of motivational bases that might have been in play at any given time.

Parkin finds that the material record suggests a variety of motivations for giving to the needy in different situations. For some, to give to someone in need (and to give without emotional involvement) helped to reinforce their sense of superiority.[73] Some may have tossed a coin to a beggar after having him perform demeaning acts (i.e., acting like a dog, etc.). At times, beggars would be paid money simply to stop them heckling, robbing carriages, bullying shops and stalls, and the like. And at times the elite may even have initiated schemes to assist the poor in order to heighten their own public honor (see especially §4.4 below).

But despite a spectrum of motivations such as these, it would be crass to rule out one of the simplest explanations for charitable initiatives in the Greco-Roman world — i.e., genuine humanitarian concern. To suggest this is not simply wishful thinking. Neither is it a form of anachronistic ethnocentrism in which contemporary values are imported back into the ancient world. Instead, this explanation must be included within the historian's explanatory toolbox in her efforts to interpret the past in its full dimensions.

The point is made, for instance, when considering how the ancients explain the rise of the early Jesus-movement. As will be shown in chapter 5 below, the Lukan account of this rise implies that the explosion in the membership of the early Jerusalem community was, in part, the result of the community's provision of resources for those in need (Acts 2:44-47; 4:32-37). The fact that care for the needy is used to endear the movement to Lukan audiences beyond an exclusively Jewish one may indicate that such values commanded respect within the Greco-Roman world, regardless of the extent to which they were acted upon. The same is true for the Lukan author's depiction of Cornelius as a devout man who "gave alms generously to the people" and who consequently was spoken well of by the whole Jewish nation and whose prayer was heard by Israel's deity (Acts 10:2, 22, 31).

---

73. See Parkin, "Pagan Almsgiving," 79. See also Jesus' words in Matt 6:2: "Whenever you give alms, do not sound a trumpet before you, as the hypocrites do in the synagogues and in the streets, so that they may be praised by others. Truly I tell you, they have received their reward."

Perhaps such generosity would have been appreciated by more than simply "the whole Jewish nation," however. In *Contra Apionem* 2.283, for instance, Josephus notes how all the nations "seek to imitate" (μιμεῖσθαι δὲ πειρῶνται) the Jewish people for "the charitable distribution of our goods" (τὴν τῶν ὄντων ἀνάδοσιν). That the point is exaggerated is clear from the other things that Josephus lists as being universally lauded by the gentile nations about the Jews (i.e., Sabbath observances; fasts; festivals; food laws; concord; work ethic; persistence under persecution). But even if it is hyperbolic, it is nonetheless indicative that the "charitable distribution of possessions" (i.e., caring for the needy) could be listed as commendable among the non-Jewish peoples. If Josephus is attempting to credit charitable initiatives within the Greco-Roman world to the influence of Judaism, he could only do that if charitable initiatives towards the poor were already known to be practiced, at least to a limited degree, within non-Jewish sectors of the ancient world, even if such practices were not defining characteristics of that world.

In this regard, we need to recall once again the famous comment attributed to the emperor Julian — that opponent of Christianity who sought to outdo it in morally-inspired generosity. Noting the way in which the poor were "neglected and overlooked" by non-Christians and the way that Christians "devoted themselves to benevolence," Julian also took note of the way that "the impious Galileans [Christians] support not only their poor, but ours as well," not least since "everyone can see that our people lack aid from us." Like much of the data of this chapter, this piece of information has a double edge. In one regard, it testifies to a general lack of morally-inspired initiatives for the poor within the Greco-Roman world, at least when compared to the frequency and quality of those initiatives within Christian churches. But it also testifies to an unspoken recognition that such things are inherently good and, moreover, that even those who may have failed to put them into practice will have recognized that.

In canvassing possible motivations for charitable initiatives in the ancient world, motivational multiplicity must be registered, but not at the expense of wholly excluding good-natured generosity for those in need. And as will be shown in §4.5 below, there is every reason to think that, on occasion, such initiatives may well have been undergirded by a "theological" conviction about the character and expectation of the deities themselves.

4.4: Generous Initiatives That Defy Strict Categorization

In §4.2 we saw various forms of generosity that should not be factored into a taxonomy of care for the poor in the ancient world, no matter how noble and well-meaning those generous initiatives might have been in other regards. And in §4.3 we have seen forms of generosity that, in all likelihood, should be factored into a taxonomy of care for the poor in the ancient world. At this point, two specific forms of generosity are featured whose position with regard to the issue of ancient care for the poor is debated.

The first of these is the act of providing grain to the poorer inhabitants of Rome by Roman emperors. According to Moses Finley, although the state did not show much concern for the poor in the ancient world, the grain dole sponsored by Roman emperors was "the famous exception" to that rule.[74] It was Augustus who first supervised the grain dole of Rome (probably between 22 and 18 BCE), and who established the pattern for succeeding emperors to emulate.

While there can be no doubting that the provision of grain for the poor in Rome "represented exceptional generosity on the part of Roman emperors,"[75] the grain dole is nonetheless difficult to assess in terms of whether it qualifies as care for the ancient poor, since the beneficiaries of the initiative were quite restricted in profile. The poor that were targeted were not the poor in general; instead, they were those based in the city of Rome who were Roman citizens and who could testify to the fact by producing a specific token when required to prove their right to the grain. If the beneficiaries of this initiative did, in fact, include the poor of ES6 and ES7, the poor who were targeted were restricted to the poor who resided within the capital city alone and who were citizens of that city.

But it is not even clear that these "poor" citizens based in Rome were

74. Moses I. Finley, *The Ancient Economy* (London: Chatto & Windus, 1975), p. 40. There Finley also listed state-sponsored alimentary schemes as another "famous exception."

75. W. Jongman, "Beneficial Symbols: *Alimenta* and the Infantilization of the Roman Citizen," in W. Jongman and M. Kleijwegt, eds., *After the Past* (Leiden: Brill, 2002), 47-80, p. 48. But note also Brown's point (*Poverty and Leadership*, p. 4): "The emphasis on the personal generosity of the emperor Augustus and his successors toward the *plebs* of Rome . . . was a statement that veiled, in acceptable classical form, their overpowering authority as emperors." The other grain dole that we know of is that of Oxyrhynchus, in which members of the elite were the beneficiaries. See especially Peter D. A. Garnsey, *Famine and Food Supply in the Graeco-Roman World: Responses to Risk and Crisis* (Cambridge: Cambridge University Press, 1988), pp. 265-66.

among the ES6 and ES7 levels. Greg Woolf notes that the recipients of food distributions were "frequently drawn from a privileged group somewhere near the top of the huge middle bracket between paupers and nobles," identifying these middling recipients as "[f]reeborn mostly, urban probably, outside the municipal nobility, but maybe only just."[76] While the grain dole in Rome may have included those further down the economy scale, it may well have been intended more to prevent economic slippage of the middling groups than to foster economic well-being of the poor.[77] On balance, then, the grain dole in the city of Rome is unlikely to qualify as a *bona fide* ancient form of charity for benefit of the truly poor.

A second form of generosity that might qualify as care for the poor are the alimentary schemes that some of the elite established in order to support children.[78] Such schemes became widespread in imperial Italy of the late first and early second century CE, when they were adopted as imperial strategies. But before the initiation of imperial alimentary initiatives, private alimentary initiatives already had currency both within and beyond Italy, although it is impossible to reconstruct how many alimentary schemes were established throughout the Mediterranean basin.[79]

That there was a difference between imperial and private alimentary schemes needs to be kept firmly in view, as will become evident in the following paragraphs. For now, it is important to note that, unlike private schemes, the imperial schemes were funded through the direct involvement of the Roman emperor himself. Willem Jongman outlines the two kinds of schemes in this way:

In the private schemes, an elite benefactor donated an estate, or its income, to a city for the support of children. The emperor's scheme worked

76. Greg Woolf, "Food, Poverty and Patronage: The Significance of the Epigraphy of the Roman Alimentary Schemes in Early Imperial Italy," in *PBSR* 58 (1990): 197-228, p. 205.

77. Furthermore, the initiative was undertaken only by a single figure (i.e. the emperor), acting in his official capacity. It is not an initiative undertaken by the general populace or a sector within it, nor was it intended as a model to be imitated by others on a less impressive scale.

78. On alimentary schemes, see Peter D. A. Garnsey and Greg Woolf, "Patronage of the Rural Poor in the Roman World," in A. Wallace-Hadrill, ed., *Patronage in Ancient Society* (London: Routledge, 1989), 153-70, p. 161; R. P. Duncan-Jones, *The Economy of the Roman Empire: Quantitative Studies* (2nd ed.; Cambridge: Cambridge University Press, 1982), pp. 288-319; John R. Patterson, "Crisis: What Crisis? Rural Change and Urban Development in Imperial Appennine Italy," *PBSR* 55 (1987): 115-46; and especially Jongman, "Beneficial Symbols."

79. The first private alimentary scheme that we know of (from Pliny, *Ep.* 7.18) was that of T. Helvius Basila, in the third quarter of the first century CE.

similarly: the subsidies for the children were not paid directly, but came from the interest on loans by the emperor (from his personal patrimony) to local landowners. This interest was to be paid by the landowners to the city for the purpose of the *alimenta*.[80]

In the case of private schemes, the city managed the resources on behalf of the individual, who was named and honored on inscriptions and, no doubt, in ceremonial recognition. In the case of imperial schemes, the emperor himself would have been included in any inscriptional and ceremonial honors.

The inscriptional data give glimpses into these schemes. We know, for instance, of a Neratius Corellius who endowed 22,000 sesterces to benefit children locally at Ligures Baebiani in Italy (*CIL* 9.1455, 2.14). Similarly, Menodora, an elite woman of the first-century CE from Galatian Pisidia, having regularly distributed wheat and money throughout her city, also established an endowment of 300,000 denarii in order to provide for local children, in memory of her own deceased son.[81] The number of children supported through alimentary schemes usually extended into the hundreds.[82] Alimentary schemes normally prioritized funding for boys — either in the number of boys supported or the amount of money awarded to them.[83]

In the late first century and early second century CE, the first government-sponsored alimentary schemes become evident. Modeled on private alimentary schemes already in existence,[84] these imperial schemes were the initiatives of the emperors Nerva (96-98 CE) and Trajan (98-117 CE; see *ILS* 6509 + 6675), although they carried on for a century or so after them. Pre-

80. Jongman, "Beneficial Symbols," pp. 51-52.

81. See R. van Bremen, "Women and Wealth," in A. Cameron and A. Kuhrt, eds., *Images of Women in Antiquity* (Detroit: Wayne State University Press, 1983), 223-42, p. 223 for the inscriptional data.

82. See for instance, R. P. Duncan-Jones, "Human Numbers in Towns and Town-Organisations of the Roman Empire: The Evidence of Gifts," *Historia* 13 (1964): 199-208, pp. 205-206; Sarah B. Pomeroy, *Goddesses, Whores, Wives, and Slaves: Women in Classical Antiquity* (New York: Schocken, 1975), pp. 203-204, whose main point is that the primary beneficiaries were male rather than female.

83. In this regard, it is especially interesting to note the provision of an alimentary scheme for children by an unnamed woman from a ranking senatorial family in Hispalis (i.e., Seville) in the mid-first century CE (see Duncan-Jones, "Human Numbers," pp. 206-208). Two alimentary schemes had already been established by a husband and wife team whose endowment had been providing resources for about 175 local boys and girls. But the unnamed woman from the senatorial family donated an additional endowment to support the children further — especially the girls, to whom a larger amount of funding was allocated. Compare also the alimentary scheme that benefited only girls, as recorded by *CIL* XIV 4450.

84. So Woolf, "Food, Poverty and Patronage," p. 208.

sumably as a demonstration of his devotion to the emperor Trajan, Pliny the Younger initiated an alimentary scheme of his own at Comum. At a capital of 500,000 sesterces and with annual revenues of 30,000 sesterces, the scheme benefitted about 175 boys and girls.

These alimentary schemes have occasionally been cited as instances of generous initiatives by the elite to offset poverty in the ancient world, although debate continues as to whether concern for the poor had anything to do with the imperial initiatives. The debate can be characterized in relation to the positions taken by John Patterson on the one hand and R. P. Duncan-Jones on the other. Patterson claims that "the emperor and private benefactors are unlikely to have spent large sums on supporting poor children if this was not in fact necessary or desirable."[85] According to him, imperial alimentary schemes were necessary and desirable precisely in order "to help poor children in Italy." Moreover, the imperial schemes were motivated by double concern on the part of Roman emperors. First, the emperors wanted "to demonstrate their generosity and emphasize imperial concern for Italy as a whole," and second, the emperors "also seem to have been concerned to target problems relating to poverty."[86] The motivations intermingle, of course, but seem also to be distinguishable in Patterson's view. In this, Patterson is much like Moses Finley, who thought of imperial alimentary schemes as extremely exceptional cases of ancient "concern for the poor" by the state, albeit in a short-lived and ineffectual fashion.[87]

On the other hand, Duncan-Jones sees little other than imperial interests at work in alimentary schemes. He estimates that the imperial alimentary schemes were motivated primarily "to encourage a rise in the birthrate" by sponsoring fertile couples in their child-rearing years, in order thereby to augment the workforce and offset economic stagnation.[88] In his view, the imperial schemes kept poorer children alive by providing them with the basic elements of subsistence, in the hope of enhancing the imperial coffers in due course.[89]

85. Patterson, "Crisis: What Crisis?" p. 129.

86. John R. Patterson, *Landscape and Cities: Rural Settlement and Civic Transformation in Early Imperial Italy* (Oxford: Oxford University Press, 2006), p. 51.

87. Finley, *Ancient Economy,* p. 40.

88. Duncan-Jones, *The Economy of the Roman Empire,* p. 295.

89. Duncan-Jones, *The Economy of the Roman Empire,* pp. 300, 303: "The only beneficiaries appear to have been the children whose subsistence the [schemes] guaranteed. . . . [M]odern views that depict the Italian *alimenta* as not directed towards the poor are probably misleading," precisely because the "low rate of benefit suggests that the Trajanic grants

If the thorny issue of motivation is problematic, the same is true with regard to whether the children supported through such schemes were, in fact, "poor," being part of impoverished families. The only explicit evidence from the ancient world to support such a view comes from the anonymous author Pseudo–Aurelius Victor. He claimed towards the end of the fourth century CE (long after alimentary schemes had ceased to exist) that emperor Nerva "ordered that girls and boys born of needy *(egestosis)* parents in the towns of Italy should be fed at public expense" (*Epitome de Caesaribus* 12.4). Nothing is said of non-imperial schemes, but the imperial targeting of "girls and boys of needy parents" is likely to be indicative of the beneficiaries of non-imperial schemes as well. The question is, however, whether this assessment of the beneficiaries as "needy" is indebted to an awareness of first-century phenomena or to the Christian values and initiatives of the fourth-century world. Greg Woolf makes the point:

> Christian emperors, and senators, *were* concerned for the poor. Constantine, the first Christian emperor (307-37) issued two edicts . . . instructing imperial officers in Italy and in the province to provide for the newborn children of the poor, in an attempt to limit infanticide and the selling of children. Perhaps [Pseudo–Aurelius Victor] . . . interpreted the *beneficia* of Nerva . . . in a "modern" light.[90]

If we suspect Pseudo–Aurelius Victor to "have imputed an anachronistic kind of virtue" on Nerva, as Woolf suggests, then there is nothing in the ancient record to indicate that the beneficiaries of alimentary schemes were destitute children. Woolf writes:

> The epigraphy of the private schemes is not informative about the economic conditions of their intended recipients. On the other hand they do take care to define other criteria of eligibility based on age, gender, legitimacy, free birth and occasionally local citizenship. No mention is made of poverty or need.[91]

---

were intended for poor families." Contrast Jongman ("Beneficial Symbols," p. 63), who argues that "the allowances were generous."

90. Woolf, "Food, Poverty, and Patronage," pp. 204-205.

91. Woolf, "Food, Poverty, and Patronage," p. 209. The same view is held by E. G. Turner, "Oxyrhynchus and Rome," *Harvard Studies in Classical Philology* 79 (1975): 16-23, and J. Carrie, "Les distributions alimentaires dans les cités de l'Empire romain tardif," in D. Vera, ed., *Demografia, Sistemi Agrari, Regimi Alimentari nel Mondo Antico* (Bari: Edipuglia, 1999), 273-88.

Woolf believes that the beneficiaries of alimentary schemes were probably "a random selection of the citizenry, including some individuals of slender means certainly, but not biased in their favor."[92]

Consequently, in Woolf's view the purpose of alimentary schemes was solely to heighten the status of those elite involved in setting up and operating the alimentary schemes. Alimentary schemes were based on the principle "of reciprocity, not of altruism: in return for his *beneficia* the benefactor wins status and *gratia*."[93] As "symbols of acquired prestige," alimentary schemes were nothing more than "theatre, drama played by the emperors to the people with the imperial and local aristocracies taking bit parts."[94] Woolf concludes:

> Poverty undoubtedly existed in Trajanic Italy, but the imperial alimentary schemes were not a response to it. They did not constitute the one exception to the rule that the Roman world had little compassion for the poor or that no ancient government ever regarded them as their responsibility.[95]

Jongman's view is not altogether different from Woolf's, although he keeps the emperor himself much more to the fore in his explanation of what alimentary schemes were meant to accomplish.[96] According to Jongman, "the focus on children as recipients of imperial benevolence served no practical social policy, but reflected the new and more hierarchical relationship between emperors and subjects." Imperial alimentary schemes were "loaded with symbolism" in both registering the social hierarchy of emperor, civic elite and ordinary citizens on the one hand, and at the same time reinforcing imperial oversight as itself paternally beneficial. In this way, imperial alimentary schemes "combined group identity, magisterial authority and benefits into a highly socializing mixture," as if the whole of the empire were within the emperor's benevolent grasp, like "the emperor's children."[97] Or in the words of Richard Gordon:

92. Woolf, "Food, Poverty, and Patronage," p. 211.

93. Woolf, "Food, Poverty, and Patronage," p. 217.

94. Woolf, "Food, Poverty, and Patronage," pp. 218 and 227 respectively.

95. Woolf, "Food, Poverty, and Patronage," p. 227. Woolf is right to articulate his conclusions in terms of "imperial alimentary schemes," since his analysis focuses primarily on state-sponsored alimentary schemes, whose motivational base might differ somewhat from that of private alimentary schemes, despite their overlap with regard to honor-capture.

96. And in this regard Jongman has to emphasize that imperial alimentary schemes were both much more widespread and much more generous than has usually been thought: "I . . . argue that it [i.e., the imperial alimentary initiative] was generous, that many of a town's children received support, and that many towns had *alimenta*" (p. 53).

97. The quotations are taken from Jongman, "Beneficial Symbols," pp. 54, 63, 75.

It is evident that the major purpose of this philanthropy is not to relieve poverty. Part of the function of philanthropic gestures is to register and naturalize the inequalities of the social system in each community, just as the emperor's patronage and generosity marshals and orchestrates the overall hierarchy of the system as a whole. The gifts objectify the relations of respect, dependence, authority and power upon which the entire euergetic system rests.[98]

In short, according to Jongman, the imperial alimentary initiative "uses the children as a metaphor for the new and more hierarchical relation between ruler and ruled."[99]

With regard to the beneficiaries of imperial alimentary schemes, Jongman strikes a healthy balance: The schemes "were not poor relief in the sense that they were only aimed at the poor, but they surely relieved the poor. . . . There were so many beneficiaries that the poor must have constituted the majority of the recipients."[100] One might go so far as to suggest that, if the imperial alimentary schemes failed to care for the poor to any large extent, the symbolic value of those schemes about the beneficence of the emperor in relation to the whole of his empire would have been seriously undermined.

With this overview in mind, there remain significant questions pertaining to both the motivation behind the imperial alimentary schemes and the extent to which the beneficiaries of those schemes included the truly poor.

But there is a danger in letting the extensive discussion about imperial schemes run roughshod over our understanding of the private schemes. The financing of the two differed, in that the private schemes (especially those that preceded the imperial schemes) did not include the emperor in their financial configuration and, consequently, might not have carried the same imperial symbolism or political goals.[101] If we exclude care for the poor from the scope of their motivation, the motivation behind private alimentary schemes might seem solely to be those identified by Woolf — i.e.,

---

98. R. Gordon, "The Veil of Power: Emperors, Sacrificers and Benefactors," in M. Beard and J. North, eds., *Pagan Priests: Religion and Power in the Ancient World* (Ithaca: Cornell University Press, 1990), 199-231, p. 229.

99. Jongman, "Beneficial Symbols," p. 50.

100. Jongman, "Beneficial Symbols," n. 100 on pp. 72 and 71 respectively.

101. I imagine a scenario in which private alimentary schemes caught the attention of the emperor who, for politically-motivated reasons, imitated and implemented similar schemes on a grander scale.

honor-capture by the elite who benefitted from the public proclamation of their efforts.[102]

The ancient honor-quest may not have full explanatory power, however, with regard to private alimentary schemes. Whereas Woolf errs on the side of distinguishing between honor-capture initiatives on the one hand and benefitting the poor on the other, the two need not necessarily be disentangled. The case of the people of Rhodes, noted by Strabo (in §4.3.3 above), is a case in point, in which the elite found ways to capture honor and to benefit the poor simultaneously, in gestures of offsetting poverty within their society.[103] Even those among the synagogue community who excelled in charitable initiatives were not immune to extending generosity to others in order to enjoy special honors within that community (e.g., the awarding of special seats in the synagogue).[104] Caring for the poor is not necessarily incompatible with the quest for honor, and vice versa.[105]

Determining whether private alimentary schemes may be cases in which honor and care for the poor coincide depends on how closely we relate the motivations of private and imperial schemes. If we imagine that the interests of the imperial schemes overlapped significantly with those of private schemes, then the likelihood that private schemes demonstrate humanitarian concern decreases. If we apply to private schemes Jongman's view of the highly symbolic significance of imperial schemes, then we arrive at a motivation for private schemes in which alimentary benefactors generously gave of their resources in order to reinforce a vision of the imperial order as inaugurating a time of plenty for all within the empire. The poor are beneficia-

---

102. Compare 1 Cor 13:3, where Paul entertains the notion of giving away all of one's possessions without genuine care for the poor.

103. It might be, then, that in rightly calling us away from seeing alimentary schemes (especially imperial ones) as merely altruistic, Woolf himself has fallen victim to an unnecessary dichotomizing of "altruism" and "self-interest," which he of course knows are not necessarily to be set in opposition. A helpful attempt to balance the two can be found in C. Gill, "Altruism or Reciprocity in Greek Ethical Philosophy?" in Gill et al., eds., *Reciprocity in Ancient Greece*, pp. 303-328.

104. Lee I. Levine, *The Ancient Synagogue: The First Thousand Years* (New Haven: Yale University Press, 2000), p. 373. See also Luke 20:46-47; Mark 12:38-40. And the same was true with the great advent of care for the poor within the Christian churches of the second century and beyond, in which almsgiving provided a strong foundation upon which one's reputation could be built.

105. Herman urges historians to get beyond either-or questions such as "Is this or that act in itself 'good'?" and "Is this or that virtue competitive or collaborative?"; see his "Reciprocity, Altruism, and the Prisoner's Dilemma," p. 201.

ries, and the concern is altruistic, but in this scenario the humanitarian concern is subordinate to imperial interests.

Alternatively, if we imagine that the interests of the imperial schemes had little to do with those of private schemes, then the likelihood that private schemes demonstrate humanitarian concern increases. As Gerhard Uhlhorn suggested long ago, "that the [alimentary] endowments were not due to political motives entirely, but spring in some measure from motives of humanity as well, is shown . . . by the fact that a great many of them were deeds of private individuals."[106] In conjunction with the example of the first-century people of Rhodes, we might imagine that private alimentary schemes were set up to benefit the civic order (and thereby to gain personal honor for their benefactors) in a fashion that included the altruistic motivation of wanting to assist many among or including the truly poor.[107]

It is clear that, even in the case of alimentary schemes, elite generosity rarely existed without a healthy dose of self-interest mixed in with it. What is much less clear is whether private alimentary schemes were (rare?) instances of elite altruism to benefit the sub-elite, not least the poor. In my estimate, private alimentary schemes should probably be included in a taxonomy of ancient charitable initiatives for the poor of ES6 and ES7, even if imperial alimentary schemes and the Roman grain dole are much less likely to be eligible for that taxonomy.

4.5: Charitable Initiatives and the Deities

When discussing charitable initiatives for the poor in the Greco-Roman world, it is not unusual to hear that "almsgiving was not sanctioned by any prevalent form of morality in the Greco-Roman period."[108] Instead, accord-

---

106. Uhlhorn, *Christian Charity in the Ancient Church*, p. 20.

107. Even in this scenario, private alimentary schemes might not have benefitted the poor alone, but instead a broader cross-section of beneficiaries (compare Jongman's claim above, that the schemes "were not poor relief in the sense that they were only aimed at the poor, but they surely relieved the poor"). Nonetheless, it might be argued that the poverty of the alimentary beneficiaries goes unmentioned on alimentary inscriptions since the beneficiaries' status in poverty could simply be assumed. If this were the case, the challenge in executing an alimentary scheme was not in deciding whether the beneficiaries should be poor or not; the challenge was in determining who among the poor should benefit.

108. Justin J. Meggitt, *Paul, Poverty and Survival* (Edinburgh: T&T Clark, 1998), p. 166. Cf. Uhlhorn, *Christian Charity in the Ancient Church*, p. 30: Worship of the pagan gods "afforded no opportunity for or inducement to charity. The giving of alms is no part of it."

ing to a commonplace view, the fact that care for the poor became so widespread in Christian sectors of the Greco-Roman world is to be credited to the Judeo-Christian theology that undergirded those sectors.

Even those who recognize that charitable initiatives were not absent from the ancient world often argue that such initiatives were unconnected to a conviction about the expectations of the pagan deities. So Rodney Stark says: "It was not that the Romans knew nothing of charity, but [Roman charity] was not based on service to the gods," precisely because "there were no doctrinal bases or traditional practices for them [the Romans] to build upon."[109] Parkin, one of the strongest advocates for the existence of pre-Christian Greco-Roman almsgiving, also advocates this view. According to her, the fact that beggars converged in high proportion in temples ("beggars haunting Roman temples") is a "rather mysterious phenomenon" because there is no "evident religious connection to be made between mainstream Graeco-Roman religion and almsgiving."[110] Since a religious platform is absent from Greco-Roman almsgiving, Parkin has little recourse for explaining why the ancient poor gathered at local temples other than to propose that

109. Rodney Stark, *Rise of Christianity* (Princeton: Princeton University Press, 1996), p. 88. Later Stark writes (p. 211): "The simple phrase 'For God so loved the world . . .' would have puzzled an educated pagan. And the notion that the gods care how we treat one another would have been dismissed as patently absurd." Stark's point is highly exaggerated, as evidenced by Greco-Roman codes of hospitality, for instance, where it is clear that the gods did, in fact, care how humans treat each other.

110. Parkin, "Pagan Almsgiving," p. 66. Compare the case of an old man begging for food around the temple of Minerva and the temple of Augustus on the Palatine; Martial, *Epigr.* 4.53. So too Dio Chrysostom, *Or.* 32.9. Notice also Tertullian's polemic against non-Christian charity in temples: "our [Christian] compassion spends more in the streets than yours does in the temples" (*Apol.* 42). Even if Tertullian downgrades charity in temples in comparison to Christian charity in the street, his polemic only works if there was at least a low-grade form of charity within pagan temples.

It is also significant that the widespread and multifaceted Magna Mater cult was associated with a form of almsgiving. "Missionary-beggars" or "cult performers" beat drums and played flutes in the temples to the great Mother deity, after which they took up a collection for their efforts. This was likely to have been (and been perceived as) a fund-raising exercise for the cult temples; so Lucian (*Cronosolon* 12) depicts such people as "those who would beg for the Mother [deity]." But no doubt others took up their place as temple beggars as a means of offsetting their poverty. So the historian Claudius Aelianus (c. 175-235 CE) recounts how an elite ruler fell into abject poverty and became "a Mother's beggar" (μηταγύρτης), beating drums and playing the flute in a temple to earn a living for himself (*Var. hist.* 9.8). On begging in the temples of the Mother of the deities, see especially S. Elliott, *Cutting Too Close for Comfort: Paul's Letter to the Galatians in Its Anatolian Cultic Context* (London: T&T Clark, 2003), pp. 202-205.

the answer must only lie in basic human concern for those in need (referring to the Elder Seneca's *Controversiae* 1.1.14).

It is best, however, to avoid a complete partitioning of low-level almsgiving and religion in the ancient world. While pagan deities were not thought of as "loving" humanity in the way that the Judeo-Christian deity was, this does not necessarily mean that they were thought to be morally indifferent. Some ancient philosophical traditions depict the deities as being concerned about how humans treat one another.

The point can be made by pressing Parkin's view of why the poor converged in high percentages in temples. Attempting to explain that phenomenon, Parkin excludes a theological rationale, repeating the estimate that in the pre-Christian world no theological rationale existed to support the caring for the poor. At no point does she allow herself to consider what might otherwise look like an explanation to be revisited, and one involving theological dimensions. Perhaps the poor converged on temples in their efforts to make themselves visible to those who had just paid honor to a deity in those very temples. Perhaps it was not exceptional for the veneration of a deity to be preceded or followed by a gesture of goodwill to the needy as a precursor to or consequence of that veneration.

A variety of ancient data lend some assistance to this assumption, all of which depict the deities as having been regarded as appreciative of generosity, benevolence and good will among the populace. Some ancient inscriptions testify to this. In *IG* II 1275 from Achaia, for instance, support for others in need (albeit those others being members of the association) is listed as a demonstration of personal piety and of divine blessing.[111] The relevant section reads:

> And if a member should be wronged, they [i.e., the association's members] . . . shall come to his assistance, so that everyone might know that *we show piety to the gods* and to our friends. To those who do these things, *(may) many blessings come upon them, their descendants and their ancestors.*

As John Kloppenborg notes, this inscription "suggests that service rendered to members . . . constitutes a display of piety (ll. 9-10) and that such acts will be rewarded" by the deities.[112] While this is unlikely to qualify as care for the

---

111. See John S. Kloppenborg, "Associations in the Ancient World," in Amy-Jill Levine, Dale C. Allison Jr., and John Dominic Crossan, eds., *The Historical Jesus in Context* (Princeton: Princeton University Press, 2006), pp. 329-30.

112. Cited from John S. Kloppenborg's collection of Achaean inscriptions, to appear in

poor, it is nonetheless an instance of giving a theological justification and rationale to the giving of assistance to those who require it (or are worthy of requiring it).

New Testament data itself assumes that the Greco-Roman world was not wholly devoid of appreciation for those who offered alms for the poor, perhaps even being religiously motivated in this regard. The Acts of the Apostles depicts care for the needy as one of the means whereby the early community of Jesus-followers in Jerusalem bolstered its membership (e.g., 4:32-37, discussed further in chapter 5 below). Having already noted that this assumes a Greco-Roman readership that is respectful of such initiatives,[113] it needs also to be noted here that this same narrative feature links those initiatives to a religious motivation. The Jerusalem Jesus-followers were respecting their deity through those initiatives. A narrative of this kind would not have been rhetorically effective in non-Jewish sectors of the Greco-Roman world if care for the poor was not already appreciated in that larger context, not least in relation to prospects of divine retribution or divine blessing. Despite its hyperbole, Josephus's claim that all the nations "seek to imitate" the Jewish people for "the charitable distribution of our goods" (*C. Ap.* 2.283) underlines the point.

It is important also to register here a different but related conviction about the deities in the Greco-Roman world. The "Hippocratic" text *De morbo sacro ("On the Sacred Disease")*, which predates the common era by several centuries and had some currency in the ancient world, was written by one who sought to correct certain mistaken beliefs that had taken hold about the nature of the deities. He sought to demonstrate that diseases of the body are not manufactured by malicious divinities or suprahuman agents, precisely because such beings are devoid of malevolent intent. Dale Martin makes the point well:

---

a volume provisionally entitled *Collegia, Cult Groups, and Guilds: Associations in the Ancient World* (forthcoming). In that same work, Kloppenborg writes: "The motif of divine blessings as rewards for piety and cultic service appears in other inscriptions: *IG* II2 4547-4548 A 6-7 (Phaleron, 400 BCE); *LSCGSup* 72 B 2-5 (Thasos, I BCE); *Syll*3 985.60-62 (Philadelphia [Lydia], I BCE); *Syll*3 997.11-16 (Smyrna, I BCE)."

113. The Lukan Gospel most likely was written to be distributed as widely as possible, and probably through the initiative of Theophilus, who himself was likely to have been Luke's patron. On this, see especially Loveday Alexander, *The Preface to Luke's Gospel: Literary Convention and Social Context in Luke 1.1-4* (Cambridge: Cambridge University Press, 1993), pp. 187-200; and Alexander, "Ancient Book Production and the Circulation of the Gospels," in Richard Bauckham, ed., *The Gospels for All Christians: Rethinking the Gospel Audiences* (Grand Rapids: Eerdmans, 1998), pp. 71-111.

> The Hippocratic author . . . rejects the idea that any particular disease is due to a personal, direct attack by a god bent on expressing anger or on harming particular persons. The gods . . . do not personally or directly cause particular diseases in particular people. . . . The gods purify; they do not pollute.[114]

This Hippocratic author counters the view that the deities are uncaring at best and sinister at worst. That view was widespread, as testified to by inscriptions about the deities who, in the instance of one woman, "put her in a punishment from which she did not escape"; likewise her son "died of the punishment [by the deities] that same day."[115] Similarly, readers of the popular *Iliad* by Homer would have encountered the idea that "the sorrowless gods have so spun the thread that wretched mortals live in pain" (*Il.* 24.525). This view of the deities was popular in the Greco-Roman world. Superstitions about deities who inflict horrendous injuries on humans when perturbed circulated widely among the populace. The author of this influential Hippocratic text, however, offered a much more benign interpretation of the relation between the deities and the wellbeing of humanity. For him, the deities have the best interests of humanity "at heart."

He was not alone in this regard. According to Plutarch (46-125 CE), the view that the deities are characterized by "goodness, magnanimity, kindness and helpfulness" has been taught to the populace by many "philosophers and political leaders" before him (*Superst.* 167E). Among them were such eminent philosophers as Plato (*c.* 429-347 BCE), Aristotle (384-322 BCE) and Theophrastus (*c.* 370-287 BCE).[116] For philosophers such as these, the hierarchy of being was interweaved with a hierarchy of goodness, so that superior beings were *de facto* characterized by superior goodness and benevolence.

Little wonder, then, that those of the ancient world who needed healing inevitably flocked to temples — not least to temples dedicated to Asclepius, the god of healing.[117] Those eager for healing may not have been convinced

---

114. Dale Martin, *Inventing Superstition: From the Hippocratics to the Christians* (Cambridge/London: Harvard University Press, 2004), p. 43. See further pp. 41-45.

115. *EA* 22, no. 69 (156-57 CE). The translation is from Elliott, *Cutting Too Close for Comfort*, p. 70. See her fuller discussion on pp. 62-88.

116. On this, see Dale Martin, *Inventing Superstition*, pp. 21-78.

117. See Emma J. Edelstein and Ludwig Edelstein, *Asclepius: Collection and Interpretation of the Testimonies* (Baltimore: Johns Hopkins University Press, 1998). Compare also the practice of abandoning sick and elderly slaves at temples to Asclepius. Veyne claims (*Bread and Circuses,* p. 33) that the ancients "did this mainly in order to get rid of them in a decent manner, by entrusting their fate to the gods."

by the philosophers' assurances about the benevolence of the deities, but they would have wanted to pursue all strategies in order to offset their situation. Accordingly, the purported benevolence of the deities might have inspired hopes for healing, not least at the temples of those very deities.

Relatedly, it probably should not surprise us that the poor (when differentiated from the ill) can also be found begging at ancient temples. Stories abounded in Greco-Roman society about the deities being benevolent and compassionate towards humanity. This was largely (but not exclusively) rooted in stories of deities who sponsor hospitality and goodness towards strangers. One common myth was recounted by Ovid (43 BCE–18 CE) in his popular work *Metamorphoses* (8.626-724; see also 1.125-215, 231-44). In this story, the two deities Zeus (= Zeus Xenios, the deity of hospitality and the friend of strangers) and Atlas come to earth in the form of human beings and wander through a neighborhood, expecting to have hospitality extended to them, but none is offered. The only ones to extend hospitality are the very ones that are least expected to perform this function — that is, an elderly and relatively poor couple, Philemon and Baucis. Because they share their meager resources with the disguised deities, they are rewarded with ascribed honor, while the rest of the populace were chastised for their inhospitable failures.

Other popular stories circulated along similar lines and to similar effect.[118] In them, the deities are depicted as approving, appreciating and rewarding hospitality.[119] And while hospitality is not to be confused with care

118. So also Homer *Od.* 6.119-21; 8.573-76; 9.175-76, 270-71; 13.200-202; 14.56-58, 283-84, 389; 17.457-87. See Amy L. Wordelman, "Cultural Divides and Dual Realities," in Todd Penner and Caroline Vander Stichele, eds., *Contextualizing Acts: Lukan Narrative and Greco-Roman Discourse* (Atlanta: Society of Biblical Literature, 2003), especially pp. 219-23; Arterbury, *Entertaining Angels*, pp. 25-26.

119. The story of Zeus and Atlas had widespread and long-term currency in the ancient world. This is suggested by four converging indicators. First, the saga is included in Ovid's *Metamorphoses*, itself being widely read in the Greco-Roman world. Second, the Lukan evangelist seems to have expected his story about Paul and Barnabas's entry into Lystra (with Paul thought to be the deity Hermes in human form and Barnabas thought to be Zeus in human form) in Acts 14:8-18 to be heard by many of his contemporaries against the backdrop of this story of pagan deities (see Hans-Joseph Klauck, *Magic and Paganism in Early Christianity* [Edinburgh: T&T Clark, 2000], pp. 58-59). Third, the pagan story is likely to be important also for understanding Paul's description in Gal 4:12-15 of his initial entry into Galatian territory (see chapter 12 below), just as the Lukan evangelist expected that the pagan story might also enhance his account of Paul (and Barnabas) entering Galatian Lystra. (Compare also Jesus' saying in Matt 25:40. The same identification of the needy as the embodiment of the deity/deities is evident in both Jesus' saying [metaphorically] and the pagan myth [literally].) And fourth, in the story's earliest version, the two deities were the local de-

for the poor (as noted above), such stories would have contributed to the depiction of the deities as predominately benevolent and kindly (despite the theme of judgment against those who fail to replicate these attributes) — precisely the kind of attributes that might have inspired glimmers of hope for the poor assembled at the temples of the deities.[120] The words of a third-century inscription (209-211 CE) from the Temple to Asclepius at Lambaesis (Africa) might suggest as much: "Enter a good man, leave a better one."[121] If Asclepius is not averse to healing "poor people" (τινὰ τῶν ἀπόρων ἰάσαιτο)[122] and is one who "has chosen to be men's benefactor in every respect" (εὐεργετεῖν προείλετο τοὺς ἀνθρώπους ἑκάστῳ),[123] perhaps his devotees will themselves find their way to toss a coin to a struggling beggar on the steps of the local temple dedicated to him. This is economic "trickle-down" theory driven by religious interest.

Even Seneca commended those who make good use of their resources by "look[ing] graciously upon the unfortunate," describing such people as being "like a god" (*deorum, Clem.* 2.6.3).[124] Seneca focuses on the "vast generosity of the deities" (*Ben.* 4.4), depicting them as those who "bestow upon us the countless blessings which they pour upon us unceasingly by night and by day" (*Ben.* 4.3), and as bestowing "upon us very many and very great benefits without hope of receiving any return" (*Ben.* 4.9). For Seneca, the whole world shares in "the bounty of heaven," which he depicts as "that most gracious fount" (*Ben.* 4.4; see 4.4-6). Consequently, he claims that "to help, to be

---

ities Tarchunt and Runt, whose identities were later updated to Atlas and Zeus, to be even later updated to Jupiter and Mercury. Stretching out over at least five centuries, the longevity of this basic saga and its enlargement of the deities from indigenous to empire-wide deities add further evidence to the prospect that this story had a widespread currency in the first century CE.

120. On the deity Asclepius's "beneficence to humanity" (φιλανθρώπευμα), see Julian, *Ep.* 78.419B; on his "kindness and love of humanity" (πραότητι καὶ φιλανθρωπίᾳ), see Aristides, *Or.* 73.24 [also 42.12]; see Edelstein and Edelstein, *Asclepius,* vol. 1, pp. 158, 164-65. In his Christian polemic against this extremely popular deity of healing, Tertullian (*Nat.* 2.14) gives a different portrait of him, as one full of "avarice" and the "love of gain," and who sought to "bring the living to their death"; see Edelstein and Edelstein, *Asclepius,* vol. 1, pp. 51-52.

121. *CIL* VIII, 1, no. 2584, recounted in Edelstein and Edelstein, *Asclepius,* vol. 1, p. 164.

122. Aelianus, *Fragmenta,* 100; see Edelstein and Edelstein, *Asclepius,* vol. 1, pp. 164, 204.

123. Aristides, *Or.* 5.

124. That Seneca restricts the use of resources to assisting "all the worthy" (*omnibus dignis*) does not negate the theological dimension of his comments. Note too that Seneca says that even the worthy might appear like the destitute ("emaciated and in rags"), perhaps implying that the destitute might hope that they are mistaken by a generous giver for one who has only tumbled into destitution temporarily.

of service, is the part of a generous and noble mind; he who gives acts like a god, [but] he who demands repayment acts like a money-lender" (*Ben.* 3.15). It comes as no surprise, then, when Seneca depicts the ungrateful person as one who is fearful of the gods, precisely because the gods are "the witnesses of all ingratitude" (*Ben.* 3.17).

Similarly Musonius Rufus claimed that Zeus himself requires all humanity to be "just, honest, beneficent" (δίκαιον, χρηστόν, εὐεργετικόν).[125] For Musonius Rufus, it is because of benevolent virtues that humanity resembles the divine. All people should be "high-minded, benevolent, and philanthropic" (μεγαλόφρων . . . καὶ εὐεργετικὸς καὶ φιλάνθρωπος) precisely because "this is how we conceptualize the divine" (τοιοῦτον γὰρ ἐπινοοῦμεν τὸν θεόν).[126]

It is probably not too much of a stretch, then, to imagine low-grade forms of almsgiving in the ancient world as having been linked to a religious motivation, at least on occasion. It may be that many of the populace in the Greco-Roman world "did not expect *gods* [themselves] to be merciful."[127] Nonetheless, even if compassion was not thought of as an attribute of the deities themselves, some ancients seem to have imagined that the deities expected human beings to show generosity towards each other, including the economically needy. The view that the Greco-Roman world had no religious traditions underpinning (low-grade forms of?) charitable initiatives for the poor is flawed.[128] Whatever charity there might have been in the Greco-Roman world may well have been underpinned at times by religious convictions about the deities.[129]

125. Lutz, "Musonius Rufus," p. 104, line 33.

126. Lutz, "Musonius Rufus," p. 108, lines 14-15, my translation. The passage is full of reflections on how such actions are θείους καὶ θεοειδεῖς ("godly and godlike," so Lutz). On Musonius' interest in imitating the deity Zeus, see also Lutz, "Musonius Rufus," p. 134, lines 18-21.

127. Kenneth Dover, *Greek Popular Morality in the Time of Plato and Aristotle* (Indianapolis: Hackett Publishing Company, 1994 [1974]), p. 156, emphasis added.

128. Wordelman, "Cultural Divides," pp. 219-23; Morgan, *Popular Morality;* David Konstan, *Pity Transformed* (London: Duckworth, 2001), especially chapter 4, "Divine Pity."

129. This is not necessarily to deny claims like those of Veyne (*Bread and Circuses,* p. 19): "The very word 'religion' differs in meaning when applied to pagan ritualism or to an ethical religiosity like Christianity." Veyne supposes that pagan "religion" was deficient in terms of morality. In hindsight, when judged by the moral standards of religions that were soon to emerge on the stage of world history, Veyne's claim is comparatively true, but it is in danger of emptying Greco-Roman religions of the diminished amount of moral features that they might nonetheless have had. The same is true of this claim by Michael Gorman

Traditions of religiously-motivated gestures for the needy are found within the extant data of the Greco-Roman world, to an extent that problematize unnuanced statements to the contrary. Those traditions about compassion for the needy were not necessarily embedded in "theologies" about the generous and gracious nature of the deities (although some philosophers characterized them in terms not unlike those). Clearly, charitable initiatives for the poor may not have been prominent in Greco-Roman societies, and even when they were undertaken they may often have transpired from "non-religious" motivations. Nonetheless, a tide of tradition (whose dimensions are difficult to determine) is evident in some extant sources and demonstrates that, at times, charitable initiatives were probably undergirded by a religious dimension in relation to the deities.

4.6: Conclusions

In this chapter I have attempted to construct a finely-balanced position. On the one hand, I have no intention here of dismantling the general consensus that, with the arrival of Christianity, charitable initiatives for the poor became evident to an unprecedented degree within the Greco-Roman world. To argue against this general commonplace would be to argue against the preponderance of the data. Both Christianity's casual observers (i.e., Lucian of Samosata) and its fiercest critics (i.e., the emperor Julian) seem to differentiate the practices of Christians from those of their non-Judeo-Christian contemporaries.

On the other hand, seeking to do justice to the full spectrum of data requires us to be quite nuanced when recounting ancient attitudes towards the poor and needy. The temptation is to do historiography in stark black-and-white terms, setting in complete opposition non-Judeo-Christian and Judeo-Christian values and practices. This would facilitate a much easier historical construct from which to mount a clean and tidy argument. But such a scenario would be historically misleading. A realistic portrait involves introducing some grays among the black and white strokes in our portraiture of the ancient world.

If this balancing act is a difficult one to pull off, it is not unprecedented

---

(*Apostle of the Crucified Lord: A Theological Introduction to Paul and His Letters* [Grand Rapids: Eerdmans, 2004], p. 29, emphasis original): "The deities . . . required satisfaction through perpetual sacrifices, but they seldom made ethical demands on their adherents. Their relationship with humans was more *contractual* and focused on proper *ritual*, rather than *covenantal* and focused on proper *ethical behavior* (as in Judaism).""

for historians to attempt it. The work of Gerhard Uhlhorn in the late nine-teenth century offers a case in point. In attempting to maintain a balanced view, however, Uhlhorn at times appears rather schizophrenic. One moment he claims that the Greco-Roman world "had not charity," not least because the constitution of "the Roman" included "a certain sort of meanness, not to say avarice," and because in general the Greco-Roman world was "a world without love."[130] In other moments, however, Uhlhorn claims that "there was at all times a gift ready for the beggar. . . . In Rome and in the other great towns, numerous beggars were to be found . . . and the passers-by readily threw them some small coin."[131] When this charitable dimension of things is in his view, Uhlhorn can speak of a new charitable consciousness "beginning to make itself felt even within the confines of heathenism itself."[132] Conse-quently, Uhlhorn envisions "heathen influence paving the way of the ad-vancing Christianity" with regard to charitable initiatives,[133] and likens the Greco-Roman world as "stretch[ing] forth in this respect towards Christian-ity," even though that world "could not of itself produce what Christianity brings."[134] In his best moments of doing justice to both sides of the balance, Uhlhorn's most lasting contribution might be his depiction of non-Christian charity and Christian charity in these terms:

> [In Greco-Roman charity] we may recognise traces of that current which flowed out from the midst of heathenism to meet the advancing tide of Christianity, . . . that current flowing out from the midst of heathendom towards the advancing flood of Christendom. . . . [In charitable initiatives of the Common Era] the Christian influence meets with a current of hea-then opinion already flowing partly in its own direction.[135]

130. Uhlhorn, *Christian Charity in the Ancient Church*, pp. 15, 9, 38, and 43 respectively.

131. Uhlhorn, *Christian Charity in the Ancient Church*, p. 4.

132. Uhlhorn, *Christian Charity in the Ancient Church*, p. 13.

133. Uhlhorn, *Christian Charity in the Ancient Church*, p. 42.

134. Uhlhorn, *Christian Charity in the Ancient Church*, p. 43. One reason why Chris-tianity brings charity to the world in an unprecedented way is, according to Uhlhorn, that women gain more prominence in Christian circles than in ordinary Greco-Roman society. He writes: charity "only becomes a possibility by the service of that [female] sex specially created and provided for the ministry of the distressed" (p. 40). More than a century later, the view has a curious air of inverted prejudice about it.

135. Uhlhorn, *Christian Charity in the Ancient Church*, pp. 28, 21 and 41 respectively. Bolkestein is usually cited as the scholar who championed this kind of position in his *Wohltätigkeit und Armenpflege im vorchristlichen Altertum*, but Bolkestein's 1939 work has clear precedents in Uhlhorn's work of 1883.

The same kind of balance is struck by Paul Veyne. Although Veyne occasionally errs towards constructing a black-and-white differentiation of the non-charitable Greco-Roman world and the charitable initiatives of the Christian churches, in other places he manages to pull off the balancing act, as in the following instance:

> The fact is that paganism helped some of the poor. . . . But there were also many poor whom paganism did not help at all. On the whole, paganism showed itself much less charitable in deeds than Christianity was to be, even if it *was* charitable to a small extent. . . . The attitude of charity, though greatly developed by certain religions, was not invented by them.[136]

Those who want clean, sharp and packaged historiography should avoid involving themselves in the data of ancient attitudes towards the poor, as Veyne's comment demonstrates.

Two observations need to be made here. First, it is arguable that the interpretative default of starkly differentiating ancient Judaeo-Christian traditions from non-Judaeo-Christian traditions with regard to care for the poor has resulted in an interpretative blind-spot as to a potential attraction of the early Jesus-movement. The point will be entertained in chapter 12 below. There it will be suggested, against the backdrop of the data presented in this chapter, that the early Jesus-movement would have had (previously unrecognized) attractions for those whose own sentiments included a concern about the well-being of the poor.

Second, in contemporary discussions of economic strategies, charity has become an easy target to denigrate as superficial and to dismiss as ineffectual. It is sometimes argued that charitable initiatives do nothing towards rectifying economic imbalance; countering poverty requires measures that operate at the level of deep cultural structures rather than at the surface level. Charity can even be depicted as a strategy of the pseudo-satanic, because it has the potential to leave the benefactor feeling justified while the fundamental problem goes unaddressed. Charity cannot plumb the depths of economic injustice, but it can mask it. Instead, only structural reconfiguration has any real hope of introducing equity into economic social relations.[137]

---

136. Veyne, *Bread and Circuses*, pp. 30-31.

137. Along similar lines, see William Easterly, *The White Man's Burden: Why the West's Efforts to Aid the Rest Have Done So Much Ill and So Little Good* (Oxford: Oxford University Press, 2007); or earlier, Graham Hancock, *Lords of Poverty: The Power, Prestige, and Corruption of the International Aid Business* (New York: Atlantic Monthly Press, 1989).

Clearly there is quite a lot to this. And it is not only modern wisdom, but ancient wisdom as well, precisely as recounted in the words "You do no service to a beggar by giving him food or drink, for two reasons: you lose what you give him, and you prolong his life for misery" (Plautus, *Trin.* 339, paraphrased). The primary disservice against the poor man arises from the fact that nothing of significance has really happened in this imagined gesture of care; instead, the poor man continues to be poor, and is perpetuated in his situation of poverty. It is of course the case that entrenched poverty cannot be rectified without structural change that transcends simple forms of charity.

But it also needs to be recognized that anything that might qualify as a structural strategy for offsetting poverty in the ancient world was out of reach of all but the tiniest minority of people in the ES1 through ES3 economic levels — i.e., those who controlled economic structures (to the extent that those structures could be controlled). If evidence of structural reform in the ancient world were to be forthcoming from the material record, by the very nature of things that evidence would emerge from efforts of the elite alone. Structural reform could not have emerged from the 97% of the ancient urban population that fell below ES3, simply because of the realities of ancient power. And of course, the examples of elite attempts at structural change are exceedingly few and far between.[138] For the most part, the elite were generally not involved in efforts to offset poverty, at least at the deep levels of economic configuration. Even generous alimentary schemes, if we wish to include them in a list of charitable initiatives, would seem to have left structural factors intact.

It is probably for this reason that Jesus makes his sobering statement that captures the realities of charity's effectiveness: "the poor you will have with you always" (Mark 14:7; Matt 26:11; John 12:8). If the elite were not going to change the structures, the sub-elite certainly could not. It was simply not feasible for those at lower economic structures to even contemplate anything more than a charitable posture towards the needy. But this in no way renders charitable acts of the Greco-Roman world as part of the problem of ancient economic injustice. Instead, charitable initiatives must have been seen (and probably should still be seen) as laudable, honorable acts that were worthy of commendation.

138. One such case might be that of Tiberius Gracchus, who in 133 BCE tried to put through land reforms so that the rich could not simply assimilate the lands of the poor.

CHAPTER 5

"Good news to the poor"

Judeo-Christian Theological Traditions

5.1: The Poor Remembered in Jewish Tradition
5.2: Preliminary Observations on Jesus Remembered
5.3: Jesus Remembered
5.4: The Early Jesus-movement Remembered
5.5: James the Brother of Jesus Remembered

When speaking of the exhortation to care for the poor that is so firmly embedded within the Jesus tradition, Paul Veyne noted that "[g]ospel morality is both popular and Jewish."[1] In this way, he triangulated a defining characteristic of the early Jesus-movement with both Jewish traditions on the one hand and, on the other, with the low-level forms of charitable initiatives in the Greco-Roman world that were noted in chapter 4 above. At this point, it is necessary to elaborate the "Jewish morality" and "gospel morality" to which Veyne tips his hat in his discussion of care for the poor in the ancient world.

---

1. Paul Veyne, *Bread and Circuses* (London: Penguin, 1990), p. 21. Compare his comments on p. 19: "Here we see three things converging: [1] a virtue that was dear to the Jewish people, loving-kindness, which . . . makes almsgiving a duty; [2] popular pagan morality, to which this loving-kindness, so natural to all humble people in every clime, was not alien either; and, finally, [3] the solidarity that bound together the members of the Christian sect."

5.1: The Poor Remembered in Jewish Tradition

It was briefly noted in §4.3 above that women were occasionally depicted as primary initiators of charitable initiatives in the ancient world. In examining the place of care for the poor within first-century Judaism, the story of one woman speaks loudly and clearly, since she has been immortalized for her charitable initiatives. The Jewish historian Josephus tells us of the initiatives of Helena, the queen of Adiabene, who in the late 40s CE went to Jerusalem "in order to worship at that temple of God (which was so very famous among all men) and to offer her thank offerings there" (*Antiq.* 20.49). The story Josephus tells continues in this way (*Antiq.* 20.51-53):

> Her coming was of very great advantage to the people of Jerusalem; for whereas a famine did oppress them at that time, and many people died for want of what was necessary to procure food withal, queen Helena sent some of her servants to Alexandria with money to buy a great quantity of corn, and others of them to Cyprus, to bring a cargo of dried figs; and as soon as they were come back, and brought those provisions, which was done very quickly, she distributed food to those that were in want of it,[2] and left a most excellent memorial behind her of this benefaction, which she bestowed on our whole nation; and when her son Izates was informed of this famine, he [also] sent great sums of money to the principal men in Jerusalem.

We might want to characterize these gestures of benevolence as mere political machinations on the part of Helena and Izates, not least when Josephus speaks of Helena's initiatives as a "most excellent memorial" to herself and of Izates dispensing money "to the principal men in Jerusalem." With regard to the generous initiatives that they established on behalf of the needy, however, Josephus's account suggests that Helena and Izates were motivated by their piety rather than any other factor. He repeatedly makes clear that they were intent to live honorably before the deity of the Jewish people (*Antiq.* 20.17, 34-35, 38) — with Izates himself seeking to live in conformity with the Jewish scriptures (*Antiq.* 20.38-48) and sending his five sons to Jerusalem to receive a Judean education (*Antiq.* 20.71). It is in relation to this intention of living honorably before Israel's deity that the charitable initiatives of Helena and Izates should be seen. And in the case of Helena, in both *Antiq.* 20.51-53 and in 20.101 Josephus highlights that her initiatives were for

---

2. Literally: τοῖς ἀπορουμένοις, "to those anxious" (about their food).

the benefit of those who were utterly anxious about their supply of food (τοῖς ἀπορουμένοις), which would have included those in ES6 and ES7. The point cannot be over-emphasized: when gentiles showed interest in honoring the deity of Israel and in living in conformity with his requirements, one of the things that emerged from them was a generosity towards others, including and/or especially the needy.

Another story, itself extremely popular in the first century CE, makes precisely the same point in repeated and poignant fashion. In the book of Tobit from the second-century BCE, the character that supplies the text with its name introduces himself in the third verse of the text, showcasing his Jewish identity and highlighting his honorable status with these words: "I, Tobit, have walked all the days of my life in the way of truth and justice, and I did many alms-deeds to my brethren, and my nation" (Tob 1:3). In offering his calling card at the very start of the text, the protagonist highlights his care for the poor as the most obvious mark of his Jewishness. If care for the poor is how Tobit registers his moral character, it is also the first moral component of instruction that he offers to his son Tobias. Those who would "revere the Lord" and "live uprightly" are, he says to Tobias, to "give alms from [their] possessions." That this is not just good advice is made clear by rooting it in the very character and intentions of the deity of Israel (4:7, 10-11):

> Do not turn your face away from anyone who is poor, and the face of God will not be turned away from you. . . . For almsgiving delivers from death and keeps you from going into the Darkness. Indeed, almsgiving, for all who practice it, is an excellent offering in the presence of the Most High.

The same point is registered by other characters in the story. Raphael says to Tobit and Tobias (12:8-10):

> Prayer with fasting is good, but better than both is almsgiving with righteousness. . . . It is better to give alms than to lay up gold. For almsgiving saves from death and purges away every sin. Those who give alms will enjoy a full life, but those who commit sin and do wrong are their own worst enemies.

Not surprising, then, is the fact that Tobit's deathbed speech to his sons and grandsons ends with Tobit telling a story about how almsgiving works to one's benefit before Israel's deity (14:10-11). Having made the point, Tobit utters his last ("But now my breath fails me") and dies. The storyteller has en-

sured that Tobit did not die until the exhortation to almsgiving was registered, as the capstone of Tobit's life of goodness and faithfulness before the
deity of Israel.

This emphasis on almsgiving should not be surprising, against the backdrop of Jewish conviction, tradition and scripture. When Philo summarizes
the attractions of the Mosaic law for his Hellenistic audience, it is precisely
this feature of generosity that he highlights as most laudable (*Spec.* 2:107):

> Is it not then fit to love these laws which are full of such abundant human-
> ity? By them the rich men are taught to share the blessings which they
> have and to communicate them to others; and the poor are comforted,
> not being for ever compelled to frequent the houses of the indigent to
> supply the deficiencies by which they themselves are oppressed.

In view of his attempt to wed the Jewish "philosophy" with the best of
Greco-Roman wisdom, it is not surprising that Philo also saw this principle
of caring for the poor as a simple principle of common sense. In advice to
the well-off, Philo states (*Ios.* 144): "Have you great abundance? Share it with
others; for the beauty of riches is not in the purse, but in the power it gives
one to succor those who are in need." This is Philo's way of endearing a Hellenistic readership to a principle firmly rooted in the Jewish scriptures.

In his tractate *Quod omnis probus liber sit*, Philo lauds "the sacred volumes" of Jewish scripture for a variety of virtues that they inspire by embedding virtues within their narrative of Israel's deity.[3] Philo offers a list of
various moral attributes that the Jewish scriptures awaken in people of character. The one that he saves for last is "the love of humanity, goodwill, equality beyond all power of description, and fellowship" (*Prob.* 84). This is the
last entry in his list not because it is the least important, but because it is the
capstone of what the Jewish scriptures inspire in those who live by them.
And so he notes that it is good "to say a few words" about this crowning feature of the Mosaic law. In that regard, Philo showcases the economic initiatives towards the poor by members of Essene communities (*Prob.* 85–87).

3. To miss this aspect of Philo's outlook is to neglect one of his most fundamental concerns with regard to the law. Unlike other law givers, who "bury the truth under a heap of
fabulous inventions" and stipulations, Moses put his laws in a larger, admirable context, says
Philo — one of narrative. He did this since he saw the need "to mould beforehand the dispo-
sitions of those who were to use his laws" (*Opif.* 1–2), rather than simply to say "do this" and
"don't do that." To offer mere stipulations is not to enhance "morality"; but to place stipulations in a broader context of the shaping of character is precisely what makes Moses's stipulations laudable.

That other great people of character arise from other nations feeds Philo's point about the relatedness of the Jewish scriptures with the best of the non-Jewish world (*Prob.* 93ff), but this should not detract from Philo's conviction that the Jewish scriptures augment a generosity of spirit toward the needy — as exemplified most fully in the practices of the Essenes.

The *Damascus Document,* found in the caves near the Qumran community on the shores of the Dead Sea, testifies to precisely this same conviction. It expects the people of Israel's deity "to separate from corrupt people and to avoid filthy wicked lucre" that is gained by various means, including "robbing the poor . . . , making widow's wealth their booty [through property seizures?] and killing orphans"; instead, the text calls on the people of Israel "to love each his brother as himself," which involves grasping "the hand of the poor and needy and alien, and to seek each the welfare of his fellow" (CD 6:14–7:1). For those who live in these and other ways, "God's covenant stands firm to give them life for thousands of generations" (CD 7:5-6).

Along the same lines, in the Egyptian *Sibylline Oracles,* the section of the text that most securely predates the Common Era (i.e., 3.97ff) includes a eulogy on what righteousness looks like in practice (3.211-94).[4] Included in that essay on what might today be called "Jewish identity" (i.e., this "race of most righteous men") are the following lines dedicated to concern for the poor (3:119-38):

> There is a city . . . in the land of Ur of the Chaldeans, from where there comes a race of most righteous men. They are always concerned with good counsel and noble works. . . . They care for righteousness and virtue and not love of money, which begets innumerable evils for mortal men: war and limitless famine. They have just measurements in fields and cities and they do not carry out robberies at night against each other nor drive off herds of oxen, sheep or goats, nor does neighbor move the boundaries of neighbor, nor does a very rich man grieve a lesser man nor oppress widows in any respect, but rather helps them, always going to their aid with corn, wine, and oil. Always a prosperous man among the people gives a share of the harvest to those who have nothing, but are poor, ful-

---

4. There is no serious dispute to the view that book 3 is "the oldest part of the Jewish and Christian corpus" (John J. Collins, *The Sibylline Oracles of Egyptian Judaism* [Missoula: Scholars Press, 1972/1974], p. 21). John Barclay identifies this section as offering "important evidence of the social and political attitudes of certain Egyptian Jews" just prior to the Common Era (*Jews in the Mediterranean Diaspora from Alexander to Trajan [323 BCE–117 CE]* [Edinburgh: T&T Clark, 1996], p. 219).

filling the word of the great God, the hymn of the law, for the Heavenly
one gave the earth in common to all.

The picture is one of utopian existence, of the "most righteous" kind of living. It is a world of equity (although not equality) and justice, in which the
rich assist the needy rather than taking initiatives to acquire their resources.
This, it is said, fulfills "the word of the great God," being poetically described
as "the hymn of the law."

Demonstrating that care for the poor was ingrained within the strongest
theological traditions of Early Judaism could take us far and wide in a survey
of the relevant data. We could record an extensive series of extracts from influential texts, each demonstrating how care for the poor was firmly embedded within Jewish traditions. For instance, *The Wisdom of Ben Sira* (or
Ecclesiasticus), a popular and influential book dating to the second century
BCE, repeatedly gives advice about the prudence of almsgiving:

3:30   As water extinguishes a blazing fire, so almsgiving atones for
        sin.

7:10   Do not grow weary when you pray; do not neglect to give
        alms.

12:3   Nothing good comes to one who persists in evil, or to one
        who does not give alms.

29:8   Be patient with someone in humble circumstances, and do not
        keep him waiting for your alms.

29:12   Store up almsgiving in your treasury, and it will rescue you
        from every disaster.

35:2   The one who gives alms sacrifices a thank offering.

40:24   Kindred and helpers are for a time of trouble, but almsgiving
        rescues better than either.

But such text-proofing would not merely be laborious to read; it is,
more importantly, unnecessary to the argument of this book. There are no
real detractors to the view that the undertaking of charitable initiatives for
those in need is deeply embedded within every main portion of the Jewish
scriptures (e.g., Deut 10:17-19; 24:10-22; Psa 146:7-9; Isa 10:2; 58:5-6; 61:8; Jer
7:6; Amos 8:4-6; Mal 3:5; etc.). There is little debate that "almsgiving was
widely understood within Judaism as a central and crucial expression of covenant righteousness," to the extent that the terms "almsgiving" and "righ-

teousness" were closely related and, at times, "could be regarded as synonymous."[5] And no one doubts that care for the needy continued to be a vibrant concern among Jews of Paul's day.[6] The point is recognized even in the New Testament itself (e.g., Matt 6:2; see also 25:31-45). Jewish synagogues throughout the Mediterranean basin performed many functions, but one function of the first-century synagogue was the collection of donations and resources to be used for charitable purposes, primarily through the donating of food and clothing to the poor and to orphans.[7] The emperor Julian, observing care of the poor by Christians of the third century CE, noted too that "no Jew ever has to beg" (*Ep.* 22.430D), since Jews cared for the poor and needy among their own ethnic group.

We need not be detained any longer, then, in demonstrating the point that is so evident within ancient Jewish texts: within Early Judaism, concern for the economically insecure is strongly attested as integral to Jewish identity, precisely because it is integral to the concerns of Israel's deity.[8] The Roman historian Tacitus characterizes the Jewish people as being "inflexibly honest and ever ready to show compassion" (*Hist.* 5.5.1); if there is exaggeration in Tacitus's comments, there is little reason to think it extravagant. James Dunn makes the point this way: "One of the most impressive features of Judaism past and present is the major emphasis it places on provision for the poor and disadvantaged — classically the widow, orphan and stranger";

5. James D. G. Dunn, *Beginning from Jerusalem; Christianity in the Making*, vol. 2 (Grand Rapids: Eerdmans, 2009), p. 459. See especially Roman Garrison, *Redemptive Almsgiving in Early Christianity* (Sheffield: Sheffield Academic Press, 1993), pp. 46-59.

6. Overviews of Jewish scripture and traditions to this effect are abundant. See, for instance, H. Bolkestein, *Wohltätigkeit und Armenpflege im vorchristlichen Altertum* (Utrecht: A. Oosthoek Verlag, 1939), pp. 34-66, 401-417; K. Berger, "Almosen für Israel: Zum historischen Kontext der paulinischen Kollekte," *NTS* 23 (1976-77): 180-204, particularly pp. 183-92; See especially Walter J. Houston, *Contending for Justice: Ideologies and Theologies of Social Justice in the Old Testament*, rev. ed. (London: T&T Clark, 2008). William Domeris gives his survey of the unjust causes of poverty within ancient Israel the title *Touching the Heart of God* (London: T&T Clark, 2007).

7. See, for instance, Lee I. Levine, *The Ancient Synagogue: The First Thousand Years* (New Haven: Yale University Press, 2000), pp. 3, 27, 69, 372; for evidence of later centuries, see pp. 271-72, 308, 366, 372-74. See also John M. G. Barclay, "Money and Meetings: Group Formation among Diaspora Jews and Early Christians," in A. Gutsfeld and D.-A. Koch, eds., *Vereine, Synagogen und Gemeinden im kaiserzeitlichen Kleinasien* (Tübingen: Mohr Siebeck, 2006), 113-27, p. 118.

8. The danger of this section is that it features the interest in almsgiving that is demonstrable in the literature of Early Judaism. Arguably, the prophetic vision of the Hebrew scriptures involves a much more "structural" analysis of the situation and its remedy.

as Dunn notes, charitable initiatives towards those in need was "a principal act of religious responsibility" for the pious within Early Judaism.[9] So too, Gildas Hamel contrasts Jewish traditions about the poor with the traditions that predominated within the Greco-Roman world:

> Jewish texts leave one with the impression of a greater respect for the poor. The reason for this . . . is that God stood out most clearly in the Hebrew Scriptures as the protector of the poor. . . . Century after century, Israelites were reminded that it was incumbent upon them to take care of widows, orphans and people fallen into poverty; that one is not to cheat, grab property, abuse slaves, hoard grain, tamper with weights and measures.[10]

Nicholas Wolterstorff says it this way: "Israel's religion was a religion of salvation, not of contemplation — that is what accounts for the mantra of the widows, the orphans, the aliens, and the poor. Not a religion of salvation *from this earthly existence* but a religion of salvation *from injustice* in this earthly existence."[11] Or as Pope Benedict XVI suggests, the fundamental theological tendencies within the Judeo-Christian scriptures (or their "metanorms") "reflect God's option to defend the poor, who are easily deprived of justice and cannot procure it for themselves."[12] This utterance by an early twenty-first-century Catholic Pope would have been heartily lauded by one first-century Jew, Jesus of Nazareth.

5.2: Preliminary Observations on Jesus Remembered

Care for the poor was integral to Jesus' proclamation, and presumably to his own activities and those of his entourage.[13] This claim will be defended in

9. Dunn, *Beginning From Jerusalem*, p. 391, n. 50.

10. Gildas Hamel, *Poverty and Charity in Roman Palestine, First Three Centuries* C.E. (Berkeley: University of California Press, 1990), pp. 201, 213-14.

11. Nicholas Wolterstorff, *Justice: Rights and Wrongs* (Princeton: Princeton University Press, 2008), p. 79.

12. Joseph Ratzinger (Pope Benedict XVI), *Jesus of Nazareth: From the Baptism in the Jordan to the Transfiguration* (trans. Adrian J. Walker; New York: Doubleday, 2007), p. 125; see his fuller discussion on pp. 120-27.

13. On the poor being supported by benefactors through the common purse of Jesus' entourage of disciples, see Brian Capper, "Jesus, Virtuoso Religion, and the Community of Goods," in Bruce W. Longenecker and Kelly Liebengood, eds., *Engaging Economics: New Testament Scenarios and Early Christian Reception* [Grand Rapids: Eerdmans, 2009], 60-80, pp. 74-75.

§5.3 below, although there will be no attempt there to relate Jesus' concern for the poor to other theological and practical dimensions of his goals or to the socio-religious context of first-century Palestine. That task has been valiantly carried out by others, and is not central to the thesis of this project. Consequently, only a general overview of pertinent data will be offered.

With that said, however, two things need to be noted initially. First, although a description of ancient agrarianism has been presented in some detail in chapter 2 above, it needs to be registered here that the economic context of first-century Judea and Galilee falls in line with that portrait of agrarianism in general, involving general hardship for the majority. Some in Judea and Galilee managed to live in relative comfort and security (with "relative" being key to this claim), and a few even enjoyed a "middling" existence that put them way above most others. Nonetheless, for the most part, subsistence living was the factor that united most of Judeans and Galileans in the early first century CE, with some above that line, and with some falling below that line at times, often with disastrous consequences. Although economic portraits of Jesus' historical context vary, many analyses are centered around a depiction of a region enmeshed in structural poverty to one extent or another. A recent study, for instance, places first-century Palestine in a situation of "province-wide depression."[14] It is against this backdrop that Jesus' proclamation of "good news to the poor" is most likely to be placed.

Second, the data assembled here have little to do with Jesus' own economic profile. There is debate about the extent to which poverty marks out Jesus' own existence. John Dominic Crossan, for instance, puts Jesus bordering on destitution. His argument runs as follows: Jesus belonged to a family headed (originally) by a τέκτων, a craftsman dedicated to the crafting of stone and/or wood; accordingly, this would have put Jesus' family in an extremely precarious economic situation — i.e., sandwiched between the peasants in their already insecure situation on the one hand and the expendables on the other, who were soon to depart this world.[15]

Crossan's modeling is very blunt. It is not the case that being a craftsman would necessarily have put Jesus in the grip of destitution, since craftsmen and artisans fell into various economic categories. Consequently, and on the basis of indicators specific to Jesus and his family, Craig Evans advises

---

14. Jane DeRose Evans, *The Coins and the Hellenistic, Roman and Byzantine Economy of Palestine* (Boston: American Schools of Oriental Research, 2006), p. 38.

15. John Dominic Crossan, *Jesus: A Revolutionary Biography* (San Francisco: HarperSanFrancisco, 1994), pp. 24-25.

that "it should not be assumed that Jesus or his family were poor, or that he was a peasant."[16] For Evans, Jesus should be placed in a position more economically secure than Crossan's portrait.

It might be beneficial to adjudicate the debate in relation to the ES categories of the economy scale set out in chapter 3 above. Although the percentages and descriptors applied there pertain to urban contexts, the lower-end categories of ES5 through ES7 might add precision to the discussion even here. The ES7 category would have engulfed the "expendables" that Crossan puts Jesus in close proximity to, while ES5 might well approximate the kind of economic profile applicable to Evans's view of Jesus. My own inclination is to see Jesus (prior to his emergence) towards the lower end of ES5, with "the poor" that his good news showcased falling into ES6 and ES7 — i.e., those who continually negotiated subsistence-level existence, either precariously above it or teetering below it (either temporarily or with terminal results).[17]

This venture into Jesus' own economic profile is something of an indulgence. It is not of central interest or consequence to the more pressing matter of the place of the poor within Jesus' own proclamation of the divine empire, as outlined below.

5.3: Jesus Remembered

One of the most historically secure traditions regarding Jesus of Nazareth is contained in both Matt 11:2-6 and Luke 7:18-23 — passages that recount one of the most critically defining moments in Jesus' public career. In the Matthean account, for instance, the imprisoned John the Baptist sends a query to Jesus: "Are you he who is to come, or shall we look for another?" (11:3). Jesus' reply in 11:4-5 outlines his actions already recounted in Matthew 8–9, with six entries listed as his credentials:

> "Go and tell John what you hear and see:
> 1. the blind receive their sight,

16. Craig A. Evans, "Context, Family and Formation," in Markus Bockmuehl, ed., *The Cambridge Companion to Jesus* (Cambridge: Cambridge University Press, 2001), 11-24, p. 14.

17. The tradition concerning Jesus' surviving family members meeting with Emperor Domitian in 90 CE places them above ES7 (Eusebius, *Hist. eccl.* 3.20.1-3), but it is unclear as to whether that tradition depicts them in the equivalent of ES5 or ES6. The Lukan story of Jesus' parents offering a sacrifice in the temple after Jesus' birth suggests that they could afford only a poor person's sacrifice (Luke 2:24; cf. Lev 12:8), denoting an economic level of ES6 at that stage of his life.

2. the lame walk,
3. lepers are cleansed,
4. the deaf hear,
5. the dead are raised up,
6. the poor have good news preached to them."

John the Baptist seems to have expected "the coming one" to bring the fire of judgment down from heaven against a wicked world (see Matt 3:7-12). Instead, what he found in Jesus was one who ate with tax collectors and sinners (see Mark 2:18-20; Matt 11:18-19; Luke 7:33-34), associating intimately with those that "the coming one" might have been expected to condemn.

Most of the components of Jesus' response to the Baptist's query resonate with Isaianic depictions of the acts of eschatological liberation performed by Israel's deity:

1. the healing of the blind in Isa 29:18, 35:5, 42:7 and 61:1;
2. the curing of the lame in Isa 35:6;
3. the restoration of the deaf in Isa 29:18 and 35:5;
4. the raising of the dead in Isa 26:19 and 29:18-19;
5. and the good news being preached to the poor in Isa 61:1.

Jesus' reply to John, then, seems to enlist in subtle fashion the Isaianic narrative of divine triumph and places Jesus and his actions centrally within that divine narrative.[18]

So much is standard interpretation. But what is somewhat more contro-

---

18. The exception to this is the reference to the healing of lepers. Note James D. G. Dunn's comment (*Jesus Remembered; Christianity in the Making,* vol. 1 [Grand Rapids: Eerdmans, 2003], p. 450): "There is nothing in Isaiah which might have inspired the inclusion of that item. Nor . . . is there any record of leprosy/skin diseases being healed in the records of the earliest churches. The item can be here only because it was generally believed (by Jesus too!) that he had also cleansed lepers."

Similarly, Jesus' reply is fashioned to do more than simply assure John of Jesus' messianic identity. It challenges the ideological basis on which John's query was founded. The very passages that act as Isaianic precursors to Jesus' list of activity occasionally contain references to divine judgment (29:20-21; 35:4; 61:2). But this feature is not mentioned in Jesus' overview of the main contours of his ministry. Instead, each aspect of Jesus' overview highlights the merciful and restorative power of Israel's deity at work in Jesus, rather than highlighting any judgmental dimension (although Jesus retained a place for that as well). So in this case, at least, the reply is both an assurance of Jesus' messianic identity and a corrective to John's understanding of that identity.

versial is the interpretation of the phrase that closes Jesus' reply to John the Baptist: "and the poor have good news preached to them." Why is preaching to the poor placed in a list of what otherwise consists wholly of dramatic miracles? And why is it placed in the final position of the list?

Its position as the final entry in Jesus' overview of his ministry (following a list of miracles) might appear to be anticlimactic, leaving the list awkwardly constructed. Perhaps it is for this reason that the term "the poor" (πτωχοί) is often interpreted as depicting not a deprived economic group but, instead, "those who are completely dependent upon God for help."[19] Support for this interpretation of "the poor" can be mustered from the term "the poor in spirit" of Matt 5:3. Against that backdrop, the term "the poor" might not signify material deprivation, but instead might signify those who have needs of a variety of kinds, irrespective of economic factors. While this interpretation has some attraction, the terms "the poor in spirit" of 5:3 and "the poor" of 11:5 are not synonymous and should not be conflated: "the poor in spirit" has a broader reference than simply economic depravity, while "the poor" generally has an economic reference as its primary reference, unless the context suggests otherwise.[20] And in this case the context is such that a non-economic reading of "the poor" is difficult to sustain. This is because, as we have seen, Jesus' words seem intended to resonate with the Isaianic narrative of divine triumph, and in Isa 61:1 "the poor" (עֲנָוִים; LXX πτωχοί) are most likely the economically deprived, and perhaps even the economically "oppressed" (so NRSV; cf. also Isa 61:6-9).[21]

It seems, then, that the term "the poor" has an economic meaning

19. David E. Garland, *Reading Matthew: A Literary and Theological Commentary on the First Gospel* (London: SPCK, 1993), p. 125.

20. The converse strategy is to read the "poor in spirit" of 5:3 in relation to the materially poor; e.g., Warren Carter, *Matthew and the Margins: A Socio-Political and Religious Reading* (Sheffield: Sheffield Academic Press, 2000), p. 131: "The poor in spirit . . . are those who are economically poor and whose spirits or being are crushed by economic injustice." But while the terms "poor in spirit" of Matt 5:3 and "poor" of Matt 11:5 overlap, they nonetheless have distinct referents.

21. With regard to Isaiah 61, William Loader ("'Good News to the Poor' and Spirituality in the New Testament: A Question of Survival," in Geoffrey D. Dunn, David Luckensmeyer, and Lawrence Cross, eds., *Poverty and Riches*, vol. 5 of *Prayer and Spirituality in the Early Church* [Strathfield, NSW: St Paul's Publications, 2009], 3-35, p. 6) notes that the term "the poor" in Isa 61:1 "could encompass a range of elements associated with being poor, including hunger, thirst, lack of shelter, subject to abuse and injustice, and longing for a change from tyranny. The immediate context of the word in Isa 61:1-2 supports this, since it associates the poor with the broken-hearted, the captives, and the blind, and looks to a day of release."

when Jesus uses it in the list that he compiles to outline his credentials to an uncertain John the Baptist (who himself is depicted, in the Lukan Gospel alone, as being concerned for the poor; Luke 3:11-14). The preaching of good news to the economically insecure should not, however, be seen as an anticlimax in a list that otherwise features dramatic miracles of divine power. It is the culmination of Jesus' list, not as an exception to what the others are about but as their capstone.[22] Jesus' reply depicts a world in which healing blindness, curing disease, restoring hearing and raising the dead were as exceptional as encouraging the poor. The astonishment that would have attended Jesus' miracles of power is, we are led to think, comparable to the astonishment that would have attended Jesus' pronouncement of blessing to the poor.

In the agrarian context of first-century Judea and Galilee, this is not wholly surprising. In that context, economic systems were configured in ways that generally promoted the interests of the elite and secure, often to the ensuing disadvantage of the poor and economically insecure. The system was so entrenched that Jesus himself is remembered to have said "the poor you will have with you always" (Mark 14:7; Matt 26:11; John 12:8). The point has already been demonstrated in more detail in chapter 2 above. So here it is enough to record James Dunn's estimate of Jesus' historical context:[23]

> Poverty . . . was a social condition, with social causes, often the result of greed and manipulation on the part of others. The poor were vulnerable before those members of society who controlled economic and political power, and who were willing to use that power ruthlessly. Consequently, the poor were also the downtrodden and oppressed, often pushed by circumstances to the margin of society.

Accordingly, Jesus' reply to John the Baptist seems to take full account of the force of the systemic injustice that was broadly inherent within the economic structures of his day. As evidence of his place within the narrative of divine triumph, Jesus highlighted not only pyrotechnic displays of divine power (i.e., miracles benefiting the blind, the lame, the deaf and even the dead) but also, and especially, the blessing of those who are economically "downtrodden and oppressed" — i.e., the poor. If structures leading to phys-

---

22. So too James D. G. Dunn (*Jesus and the Spirit* [London: SCM Press, 1975], pp. 60-61): The proclamation of the good news to the poor is "[m]ore important as an indication of the eschatological Now" than "the miracle of resurrection."

23. Dunn, *Jesus Remembered*, p. 518.

ical disease and death are prone to transformation before the invading power of Israel's deity, Jesus imagined the same power to threaten the otherwise unshakable economic structures that had embedded themselves within the agrarian systems of his day. The empire of Israel's deity offered to the poor the opposite of what the empires of the world offered, precisely because that empire is one of justice and mercy, as indicated within Isaiah 61 itself: "For I the LORD love justice, I hate robbery and wrongdoing" (61:8).

In this way, Jesus seems to have understood the encouragement of the poor as part and parcel of the unleashing of eschatological divine power against which no worldly structures could stand. Just as his miraculous healings were signs that the house of Satan was being plundered, the encouragement of the poor was also meant to be an indication of the way in which Israel's deity was overthrowing the economic exploitation that is systemically built into the very structures of this world. Clearly this is good news for those who found themselves to be despised within the ancient system of honor and shame that had entrenched much of the Greco-Roman world, including much of life within Palestine. As a consequence of Jesus' Spirit-filled ministry, however, those who were thought to be deficient in honor were becoming honorable citizens of the sovereign and eternal empire of Israel's deity, whatever their standing might be within the empires of this world.

This general interpretation of Jesus' words coincides wholly with the Lukan interpretation of the significance of Jesus' ministry found in the account of Jesus' preaching at Nazareth (Luke 4:17-21), as we will see momentarily. But it also coheres perfectly with Jesus' pronouncement of blessings, or "beatitudes," as recounted in Matt 5:3-12 and Luke 6:20-23. These accounts of Jesus' blessings have probably been refracted through the theological lenses of the Matthean and Lukan evangelists somewhat. So, for instance, twice we see the Matthean interest in the notion of "righteousness" reflected in the Matthean beatitudes (5:6, 10), without correspondence in the Lukan Gospel; and in the Lukan Gospel the pronouncement of four-fold blessings correspond with the pronouncement of four-fold curses (Luke 6:24-26), without correspondence in the Matthean Gospel. But, nonetheless, the pronouncement of such eschatological blessings is most likely to be traced back to Jesus himself in some form. This is especially the case with Jesus' blessings on the "poor,"[24] on those that "weep" and on those that "mourn."[25] And it is

---

24. πτωχοί, Luke 6:20; Matt 5:3 ("poor in spirit").
25. Those that "weep," κλαίοντες, Luke 6:21; those that "mourn," πενθοῦντες, Matt 5:4.

precisely these groups who are highlighted in Isaiah 61: the poor (LXX πτωχοί, 61:1), those who are broken-hearted (LXX τοὺς συντετριμμένους τῇ καρδίᾳ, 61:1), and those who mourn (LXX ποὺς πενθοῦντας/τοῖς πενθοῦσιν, 61:2-3). These beatitudes, then, add to the pool of evidence suggesting that Jesus saw his ministry as falling within the narrative of divine sovereignty and triumph, as highlighted in Isaiah 61. And furthermore, they testify to Jesus' conviction that the needy and down-trodden are primary targets of blessing within the empire of Israel's deity that was being made manifest in Jesus' own ministry.

It may well be significant that the first public words of Jesus in the Matthean narrative include words indebted to the narrative of Isaiah 61 (i.e., the beatitudes of Matt 5:3-12), especially since the same is true for the Lukan narrative, as is evident from Luke 4:17-21. That episode contains the first public words of Jesus in the Lukan Gospel, and there Jesus is shown to read the outline of his ministry right off the pages of Isaiah 61. Having been given the scroll of Isaiah to read before the synagogue, Jesus "found the place where it is written" in Isaiah:

> The Spirit of the Lord is upon me, because he has anointed me to bring good news to the poor. He has sent me to proclaim release to the captives and recovery of sight to the blind, to let the oppressed go free, to proclaim the year of the Lord's favor.

The Lukan author tells us that Jesus then said to those in the synagogue: "Today this scripture has been fulfilled even as you heard it being read." The fulfillment of scripture lies in Jesus' proclamation and enactment of merciful divine favor — including as the starting point of this list the proclamation of good news to the poor.

The Nazareth incident is depicted in the Lukan Gospel as a defining moment of Jesus' mission. In his story of the activity of Israel's deity in Jesus' ministry, the Lukan evangelist has moved the incident from the middle of Jesus' public ministry, where it falls in the Markan and Matthean Gospels (see Mark 6:1-6; Matt 13:53-58), to the beginning of Jesus' public ministry, taking place immediately after the account of Jesus' temptation. In the Lukan Gospel, this episode informs the audience about the essential features of Jesus' identity and mission, serving as the frontispiece to the narrative that follows. Like the other maiden speeches in the Lukan narratives, this one is likely to function as a kind of "speech in character," indicating the sort of thing Jesus would generally have said in a variety of situations.[26] And there, the proclamation of good news to the poor takes central position.

It needs to be recognized, of course, that the depiction of the Nazareth incident in Luke 4 is frequently considered to be a largely Lukan construct, at least in terms of the specific content of Jesus' words in that episode. This issue need not detain us here, since the Lukan version of the Nazareth incident falls well within the boundaries of Jesus tradition as we know it from other sources, not least the more secure traditions regarding (1) John the Baptist's questioning of Jesus, and (2) Jesus' pronouncement of blessings in the beatitude traditions.[27] In each of these traditions, as in the narrative of Luke 4, the Isaianic narrative of divine triumph (particularly as articulated in Isa 61) serves as the foundation for Jesus' pronouncement of good news and blessings to the poor.

So too, with Isaiah 61 serving as its narrative substructure, the poor referred to in the Nazareth incident of Luke 4 are those who were insecurely placed within the severe socio-economic systems of Jesus' day. Although the term "the poor" may take on broader connotations than straightforward economic ones in Lukan perspective,[28] the material sense of the term nonetheless maintains a high profile throughout the Lukan narrative.

That the Lukan evangelist has his eye on the materially impoverished is clear from the manner in which he highlights their plight repeatedly,

26. Compare Paul's speech in Acts 13. On this, see Bruce W. Longenecker, "Moral Character and Divine Generosity: Acts 13:13-52 and the Narrative Dynamics of Luke-Acts," in A. M. Donaldson and T. B. Sailors, eds., *New Testament Greek and Exegesis: A Festschrift for Gerald F. Hawthorne* (Grand Rapids: Eerdmans, 2003), pp. 141-64.

27. See, for instance, Dunn, *Jesus Remembered*, pp. 447-48, a position defended at length in his *Jesus and the Spirit*, pp. 54-60. There he concludes (p. 60): "[John's] question and [Jesus'] answer fit so neatly within the life-situation of Jesus and lack coherence if either or both were first prompted by a post-Easter situation, that the substance . . . of the account must be regarded as historical." See also Graham N. Stanton, *Jesus and Gospel* (Cambridge: Cambridge University Press, 2004), pp. 13-18.

28. The Lukan author occasionally seems to understand "the poor" in relation to wider categories than economic ones. He seems to include in their number not only those who had been overcome by the severity of the economic system but also those with illness and physical disabilities, those who had entered into despised professions, those excluded from the normal definition of the "people of Israel's deity," those possessed by evil spirits, and any others that found themselves marginalized, the object of derision or simply in need (not least, needing forgiveness). They are among those that the author considered "poor," the blessed ones to whom the empire of Israel's deity belongs (6:20). So Joel B. Green, "Good News to Whom? Jesus and the 'Poor' in the Gospel of Luke," in Joel B. Green and Max Turner, eds., *Jesus of Nazareth: Lord and Christ* (Carlisle: Paternoster Press, 1994), pp. 59-74.

through Jesus' words about them and his interaction with them. From the Lukan Gospel alone, such features would include:

1. Jesus' parable of the Samaritan (and the inn-keeper), who cared for a stranger from his own resources despite significant inconvenience and danger to himself (Luke 10:25-37);[29]
2. the Lukan version of the Lord's Prayer, with its petition that the Father "keep giving" (δίδου) the necessity of bread on a daily basis (Luke 11:3);
3. Jesus' parable of the rich fool, who hoards his possessions, rather than sharing them with those in need (so the implication seems to be; Luke 12:13-21);
4. Jesus' command to the rich man, "Sell your possessions and give to the poor [δότε ἐλεημοσύνην]" (Luke 12:33);
5. Jesus' parable of the Great Banquet, in which the invited guests include "the poor, the maimed, the blind and the lame" (Luke 14:15-24);
6. Jesus' parable of the rich man and Lazarus, in which the rich man finds himself in Hades as a consequence (it seems) of his failure to recognize the needy around him (Luke 16:19-31). In this parable, Jesus even intimates that "Moses and the prophets" are properly interpreted in contexts where the needs of the poor are not overlooked (16:29);
7. Jesus' words to the elite ruler of Luke 18, who is commanded to "sell all that you have and distribute it to the poor" (18:22); and
8. Zacchaeus' act of obedience to Jesus in giving half of his goods to the poor and ensuring that the rest of his resources could be claimed by those whom he had defrauded, to which Jesus responds, "Today salvation has come to this house" (Luke 19:8-9).

In light of such overall evidence, it seems fair to say that the materially poor and vulnerable were of special significance and concern to Jesus. Although the data for this conclusion come predominately from the Lukan Gospel, there are solid bases for it from the Matthean and Markan Gospels as well, to the extent that concern for the poor must have been high on Jesus' agenda in his proclamation of the coming of the "empire of God."[30]

---

29. I prefer to call this a story of the Samaritan and the inn-keeper; see Bruce W. Longenecker, "The Story of the Samaritan and the Inn-Keeper (Luke 10:30-35): A Study in Character Rehabilitation," *Bib Int* 17 (2009): 422-47.

30. This conclusion has a foothold even in the *Gospel of Thomas*. Although Logion 14 seems to repudiate almsgiving, in Logion 95 Jesus says: "If you have money, do not lend it at interest, but give to one from whom you will not get it back" — i.e., someone in ES7.

Much more would need to be said in a full exploration of this "economic" dimension of Jesus' ministry in all its permutations — not least in relation to (1) a theology of Jubilee,[31] and (2) Jesus' clash with the "middling rich" in Jewish Palestine.[32] But for our purposes it is enough to concur with the likes of others who have stressed the centrality of care for the poor within Jesus' teaching and practices. As Dunn writes: "For whom did Jesus intend his message? At or near the top of any list which Jesus himself might have drawn up were clearly 'the poor.'"[33] Or as Joel Green suggests, it is likely that Jesus imagined "the new world, the kingdom of God, as a place where poverty is absent."[34] It is little wonder, then, that as part of his proclamation of the kingdom or empire of Israel's deity, Jesus is remembered as saying "Blessed are the poor." Even if low-level forms of charitable initiatives are evident in the Greco-Roman world of Jesus' day, Moses Finley is probably right in his estimate that this sentiment of the poor being *blessed* "was not within the Graeco-Roman world of ideas, and its appearance in the Gospels . . . points to another world and another set of [Judeo-Christian] values."[35]

31. Some postulate, with good reason, that Jesus' pronouncements about the poor emerge from a much broader notion of the in-breaking of an eschatological Jubilee. See, for instance, Sean Freyne, *Jesus, a Jewish Galilean: A New Reading of the Jesus-Story* (London: T&T Clark, 2004), pp. 32, 47-48, 118-19; Marcus J. Borg, *Jesus: A New Vision* (San Francisco: HarperSanFrancisco, 1987), pp. 135-37; Richard A. Horsley, *Jesus and the Spiral of Violence: Popular Jewish Resistance in Roman Palestine* (San Francisco: HarperSanFrancisco, 1987), pp. 248-55.

32. See, for instance, John S. Kloppenborg, *The Tenants in the Vineyard: Ideology, Economics, and Agrarian Conflict in Jewish Palestine* (Tübingen: Mohr Siebeck, 2006); Philip Goodchild, *Theology of Money* (Durham, NC: Duke University Press, 2009), pp. 1-6, 201-203.

33. Dunn, *Jesus Remembered*, 517. It strikes me as bordering on the irresponsible to depict the "picture of Jesus as the watchdog of the poor and oppressed rural peasants" as a "traditional warm and fuzzy picture" (so Adele Reinhartz, "Crucifying Caiaphas: Hellenism and the High Priesthood in Life of Jesus Narratives," in F. E. Udoh et al., eds., *Redefining First-Century Jewish and Christian Identities* [Notre Dame: University of Notre Dame Press, 2008], 227-45, p. 241). The problem with this statement is its ambiguity. It is hard to know whether the implicit criticism of that characterization is directed towards Jesus-researchers or Jesus-followers, or perhaps something other altogether. In the end, however, to suggest as much runs the risk of trivializing the realities of poverty that affected so many in the ancient world, or of trivializing the efforts of so many who have compromised a "warm and fuzzy" lifestyle in order to assist the poor and oppressed in the name of Jesus over the years. The characterization may be required for strategic effectiveness in contemporary debate about historiography, but if so, it ironically would seem more indebted to the enormously "comfortable" world of the modern academic than to the ancient world itself, to which proper historiography should be sensitizing us.

34. Joel Green, *Luke*, p. 266.

35. Moses I. Finley, *The Ancient Economy* (London: Chatto & Windus, 1975), p. 38.

5.4: The Early Jesus-movement Remembered

If concern for the poor was a key component of Jesus' concerns, the same concern is evident in the earliest days of the Jesus-movement in Jerusalem, at least as the Lukan evangelist portrays those days. So the early chapters of Acts depict the earliest community of followers of the resurrected Jesus to be concerned with the material well-being of their members. The Lukan author tells of individuals making substantial donations to a common fund that was used to offset people's needs. So we read in Acts 2:44-47:

> All who believed were together and had all things in common; they would sell their possessions and goods and distribute the proceeds to all, as any had need. Day by day . . . they broke bread from house to house and ate their food with glad and generous hearts, praising God and having the goodwill of all the people.

To this the author adds the note, "And day by day the Lord added to their number those who were being saved" (2:47).

In his telling of these accounts, the Lukan author might be implying that the explosion in the community's membership (as described in 2:47) was a direct consequence of the community's provision of resources for those in need (as described in 2:44-47). This, at least, is the implication of his account in Acts 4:32-37. There the author notes that the early Jesus-followers did not make any personal claims to their possessions but shared everything between themselves. So in Acts 4:32 we read: "everything they owned was held in common." This point is then extensively elaborated in 4:34-37, being punctuated by claims such as "there was not a needy person among them" (4:34), and the common fund "was distributed to each as any had need" (4:35). But between the introduction of this scenario in 4:32 and its lengthy elaboration in 4:34-37 we find in 4:33 what might appear to be a stray comment: "With great power the apostles gave their testimony to the resurrection of the Lord Jesus, and great grace was upon them all." The observation about the outpouring of divine grace upon the community is not, in fact, structurally out of place. Instead, readers are to imagine that the evangelistic power of the apostles corresponded to, or was in direct relationship with, the integrity of the community to which the apostles belonged, being a community in which care for the needy was a marker of corporate identity.

Of course, some interpreters suspect that the Lukan author has painted a somewhat idealized portrait of communal sharing among the earliest Jerusalem Jesus-followers.[36] The notion of a perfectly functioning community that had no semblance of need within it was a Hellenistic ideal that a Greco-Roman reader of Acts might well have seen glimpses of in the Lukan characterization of the early followers of Jesus in Jerusalem — not unlike the way that the Jewish *Sibylline Oracles* depicts the community of the "most righteous men" who live in their own Edenic environment in "a city in the land of Ur of the Chaldeans" (noted in §5.1 above). But even if there is some stylization going on in the Lukan portrait, there is no reason to imagine simply on that basis that a historical underpinning is absent from that portrait.[37] The Lukan author is probably drawing on generally reliable traditions that demonstrated the practice of radical discipleship in the earliest stratum of the Jesus-movement in Jerusalem.

As in other eras in the church's history, caring for the needy evidently proved to be a powerful component of evangelistic activity for the earliest Jesus-followers. This interrelationship of social concern and evangelistic respectability leads to the consideration of one further figure in particular. As the recognized leader of the Jerusalem communities of Jesus-followers from the early 40s[38] to his death in 62 CE, it was probably James the brother of Je-

36. The author's own narrative suggests that there is some hyperbole in his depiction of the earliest Jerusalem Jesus-groups. In Acts 21:16, for instance, we hear of Mnason of Cyprus offering hospitality to other Jesus-followers within his own home. Mnason is depicted as "a disciple from the beginning" (ἀρχαίῳ μαθητῇ, trans. mine), and this early disciple continued to own his own home well in the late 50s, when the account of Acts 21 took place. Here, then, is one who seems not to have contributed (the whole of) his resources to the communities of Jesus-followers in Jerusalem but retained (a significant portion of) his material resources within his own control. And here, then, is a Lukan exception to the Lukan claim that "as many as were possessors of lands or houses sold them, and brought the proceeds of what was sold and laid it at the apostles' feet" (4:34-35).

37. On this, note Capper's point ("Jesus, Virtuoso Religion, and the Community of Goods," p. 77): "'Utopian' stylizing of these passages in phrases such as holding 'all things common' and calling 'nothing one's own' is clearly present, but does not undermine the historical value of the accounts. Philo and Josephus stylize their accounts of Essene virtuosi with a wide variety of motifs drawn from philosophical reflection on the ideal society, but since the discovery of the *Rule of the Community* from Qumran, such stylizing is no longer taken as a sound argument against the existence of Essene communities which fully shared their property. In Acts too, stylizing after the model of high Greek ideals of sharing cannot disprove the essential historicity of the original formal community of goods of the earliest post-Easter followers of Jesus in Jerusalem."

38. This is implied, for instance, (1) in the order of apostolic names in Gal 2:9, with James in the place of precedence, (2) in the term "men from James" in Gal 2:12, and (3) in the Lukan record of events in the second half of the Acts narrative, where James is clearly the fig-

sus who initiated the stipulation of Gal 2:10 that Paul (and communities founded by him) should remember the poor as part of the spreading of the good news. And so our focus shifts to James.

5.5: James the Brother of Jesus Remembered

Just as the poor held a central place in Jesus' proclamation and embodiment of the empire of Israel's deity, so the poor seem also to have held a central place in the concerns of Jesus' brother, James. The Letter of James demonstrates a "deep concern for and sympathy with the poor and persecuted."[39] Of course, the authorship of the Jacobite letter is disputed, with some thinking it to have been written by James himself from Jerusalem sometime in the 40s or 50s and others thinking it to have been written by an unknown author who deemed it best to attribute the text to James, probably within a relatively short period after James's death. The issue is of no real significance for our purposes. Even if the Letter of James is pseudonymous, it is significant that the unknown author thought the letter to be representative of the kind of things that concerned James the brother of Jesus. So the issue of actual authorship need not detain us further.[40]

What is significant is that this "letter" attributed to James has the poor and oppressed in the forefront of its interests repeatedly. One commentator puts the point well:

> No NT document — not even Luke-Acts . . . — has such a socially sensitized conscience and so explicitly champions the cause of the economically disadvantaged, the victims of oppression or unjust wage agreements, and the poor who are seen in the widows and orphans who have no legal defender to speak up for their rights. . . . In a day when economic and social wrongs cried out for redress, James directed attention to ways in which the poor and victimized could be helped . . . as a sign of a living faith.[41]

---

ure of primary authority in Jerusalem. So, in Acts 15, he speaks last in order to summarize the discussion and to point the way forward.

39. R. P. Martin, *James* (Waco: Word Books, 1988), p. lxvii, where this concern and sympathy are cited as "the chief theme" of the letter.

40. I am tempted to adopt the position of Dunn (*Beginning From Jerusalem,* pp. 1122-29, 1141), who thinks that while the letter may not have been composed by James himself, it nonetheless sets out his views, perhaps posthumously, but probably prior to the fall of Jerusalem in 70 CE.

41. Martin, *James,* pp. lxvii-lxviii.

The evidence for this view hardly needs reviewing. It is there in living color in Jas 1:22–2:26, for instance. An outline of that passage demonstrates how the author's discussion of the law, of faith, and of action combine to focus on the issue of the poor on three occasions — i.e., 1:27, 2:5 and 2:14-17, as noted in italics in the outline on page 130.

The same concern for the poor is obvious in Jas 5:1-6, with its rigorous denunciation of the rich (see also 1:9-11) — a denunciation that seemingly arises in view of their virtually inevitable oppression of the poor. We need not make a detour into the issue of whether the author imagines that one could be a follower of Jesus and simultaneously be economically well-off.[42] But it is nonetheless clear that, for the author of the Letter of James, one could not be an economically well-off follower of Jesus without caring for the poor and needy.

In light of this, we need to take note of the dynamics surrounding the death of James, the brother of Jesus. We learn from Josephus (*Antiq.* 20.200-202) that James was stoned to death as a law-breaker after an unjust trial had been rigged by the high priest Ananas (c. 62 CE). Moreover, Josephus tells us that Ananas's actions offended "those in the city who were most fair-minded." Sometimes it is deduced that "those who were most fair-minded" must have been opposed to Ananas's view that James had transgressed the law. But Josephus does not explicitly say that much. Instead, he focuses on Ananas's *trial procedures* as the point objected to by the "fair-minded" (i.e., it was not lawful for Ananas to assemble a Sanhedrin without the consent of King Agrippa). Josephus does not explicitly say that the fair-minded opposed the view that James was a transgressor, simply that they opposed the rigged trial procedures. Nonetheless, it is not too much to think that "fair-minded" opposition to Ananas's procedures was, in fact, driven by a sympathy for James and opposition to Ananas's negative view of James (compare the depiction of Joseph of Arimathea in Luke 23:50-54). The "fair-minded" point of view probably contended that James was a righteous man, rather than being a transgressor of the law, and that a properly orchestrated trial would have revealed that.

Why then would Ananas have needed to rig James's trial? The best solutions to this conundrum place James's situation within the context of

---

42. Mariam Kammel argues effectively that the author of James does imagine something of the sort to be possible; see her "The Economics of Humility: The Rich and the Humble in James," in Bruce W. Longenecker and Kelly Liebengood, eds., *Engaging Economics: New Testament Scenarios and Early Christian Reception* (Grand Rapids: Eerdmans, 2009), pp. 157-75.

THE STRUCTURE OF JAMES 1:22–2:24

I. The Principle of Hearing and Acting

1. The foolish hear but do not act on what they hear (1:22-24)
2. Blessed are those who act, in accord with "the perfect law" of liberty (1:25)

   a. There is no blessing for those who fail to act (1:26)

   b. *There is blessing for those who act to the benefit of the needy* (1:27)

II. Common Sense about Favoritism

Favoritism is out of kilter with the blessedness of acting for the needy (2:1)

Example: Showing preference to the rich (2:2-4)

   a. *This is foolish, because God has chosen the poor* (2:5)

   b. This is foolish, because the rich oppress you (2:6)

   c. This is foolish, because they blaspheme God by oppressing the poor (2:7)

III. Countering Favoritism That Runs Contrary to the "Perfect Law"

1. The law is to be understood in relation to the rule of loving one's neighbor (2:8)
2. Showing favoritism runs contrary to this understanding of the law (2:9); to succeed in every other aspect of the law is not good enough (2:10-11)
3. Live, therefore, in a way conscious of the law's essence, which opposes favoritism (2:12-13)

IV. Examples of Faith in Action

1. *Failing to care for the needy is the opposite of faith (and therefore runs contrary to the law)* (2:14-17)
2. Abraham and Rahab put their faith into practice, in holistic righteousness (2:18-24)

Ananas's larger power struggle, positioning James as a potential threat to Ananas's authority in some manner. The most plausible reconstructions of events leading up to James's death envisage James as highly critical of Ananas and some of the powerful Jewish aristocracy in Jerusalem. Ralph Martin, for instance, argues that James was probably disparaging of "Sadducean priests and their associates who despised and exploited the poor," with Ananas "react[ing] violently to James' eschatological denunciations of the rich and influential."[43] Similarly, P.-A. Bernheim suggests that "James criticized the greed of the priestly aristocracy, thus drawing its wrath upon himself."[44] If there is a primary reason for Ananas's animosity against James, it might well be found in the same concern for the poor and chastisement of the rich that we find enunciated in the letter bearing James's name.

James the brother of Jesus is an important figure in the story of how the riches of Jewish tradition regarding care for the poor were bequeathed to the world through the early Jesus-movement. He is also one of the Jerusalem apostles who, according to Gal 2:10, stipulated that Paul and Barnabas's mission to the gentile world should "remember the poor." It is to the place of the poor within Paul's theology, mission and communities that our focus now turns.

---

43. Martin, *James*, p. lxix.

44. P.-A. Bernheim, *James, Brother of Jesus* (London: SCM Press, 1997), p. 252. Note also the argument by D. Seccombe ("Was There Organised Charity in Jerusalem before the Christians?" *JTS* 29 [1978]: 140-43), undermining the view of Joachim Jeremias that the Jewish leaders in Jerusalem organized relief efforts for the poor at the time of Jesus.

THE POOR IN PAULINE PLACES

CHAPTER 6

"Do good to all"

Care for the Poor in Paul's Communities

6.1: Paul among His Judeo-Christian Predecessors and Successors
6.2: Care for the Poor within Paul's Communities
6.3: Conclusions

6.1: Paul among His Judeo-Christian Predecessors and Successors

It has been noted above that the practice of caring for the poor was deeply embedded in the Jewish scriptures and traditions and (therefore) in the proclamation and practices of Jesus and his earliest followers, especially those based in Jerusalem (i.e., the Jerusalem church and its figure-head, James the brother of Jesus). In developments beyond the first century CE, care for the poor would go on to become a hallmark of the proto-orthodox church in the second through fourth centuries CE (even if that phenomenon can be interpreted in relation to diverse motivational bases). Regarding care for the poor, then, lines of connection can be drawn from the scriptures and traditions of Judaism, to Jesus, to the Jesus-movement based in Jerusalem, and on to the proto-orthodox churches of the second through fourth centuries CE.

There might, of course, be weak links in this monolithic chain connecting Jewish scripture to the proto-orthodox church. And one prime suspect in this regard is Paul. Although this was noted already in chapter 1 above, the point deserves amplification here.

The view that the poor were peripheral to Paul's main theological concerns and outside the primary parameters of his gospel might seem to set Paul in contrast to Jesus. In fact, books and articles that compare Jesus and Paul almost always focus on matters other than the poor. At the heart of comparisons of Jesus and Paul are interests pertaining to: christology, soteriology, theology, Israel, the temple, the law, ethical particulars (e.g., divorce, loving others, taking oaths), women, the coming of the Lord, and the extent to which Paul was familiar with Jesus tradition (e.g., sayings, infancy narratives, etc.).[1] But rarely have the economically vulnerable, who took pride of place in Jesus' ministry, been used as a point of comparison between Jesus and Paul.

To illustrate the point, consider Paul Barnett's book *Paul: Missionary of Jesus.* Barnett sets for himself the task of determining whether Paul was "the real founder of Christianity." He focuses his study in these terms:

> Was Paul a true missionary of Jesus? Embedded in that question are others. Did Paul know about Jesus' life and teaching? Did Paul preach Jesus' message? Was Paul true to Jesus' intentions? Did Paul continue in the trajectory begun by Jesus?[2]

Barnett answers these questions affirmatively. According to Barnett, Paul had a solid awareness of the main concerns of the Jesus presented to us in the canonical Gospels. Comparing the teaching of Jesus with that of Paul, Barnett imagines that Paul, rather than striking out on his own and setting up a religion at some distance from that of Jesus, extended the message of Jesus. The claim is simple: "Paul's mission . . . is nothing less than the outworking of Jesus' own mission."[3] There is, however, nothing in Barnett's work to suggest that Jesus' concern for the poor was itself a part of Paul's mission. This problematizes Barnett's claim about Paul being "a true missionary of Jesus" who "[knew] about Jesus' life and teaching," who "[preached] Jesus' message," who "[w]as true to Jesus' intentions," and who "[continued] in the trajectory

---

1. See, for instance, Victor Paul Furnish's overview of scholarly interest in Jesus and Paul in previous generations, "The Jesus-Paul Debate: From Baur to Bultmann," in A. J. M. Wedderburn, ed., *Paul and Jesus: Collected Essays* (Sheffield: Sheffield Academic Press, 1989), pp. 17-50. His overview reveals (by default) that "the poor" is a neglected topic in the early debate, and the same could be shown in the debates of successive generations.

2. Paul Barnett, *Paul: Missionary of Jesus* (Grand Rapids: Eerdmans, 2008), p. 2.

3. Barnett, *Paul,* p. 99; here Barnett quotes J. R. Wagner, "The Heralds of Isaiah and the Mission of Paul: An Investigation of Paul's Use of Isaiah 51-55 in Romans," in W. H. Bellinger and W. R. Farmer, eds., *Jesus and the Suffering Servant: Isaiah 53 and Christian Origins* (Harrisburg: Trinity Press International, 1998), 193-222, p. 198.

begun by Jesus." If concern for the poor was central to Jesus' mission, and if Paul did not share that central concern, claims about Paul having extended the mission of Jesus look optimistically thin.

Similar in this regard is David Wenham's extensive attempt to demonstrate the common interests of Jesus and Paul, again in an attempt to discredit the view that Paul and Jesus were involved in fundamentally different theological programs. But notable is Wenham's struggle to make a significant connection between Jesus and Paul on the matter of a declared concern for the poor. The best Wenham is able to suggest is that Jesus' command in Matt 19:21 to "sell your possessions and give to the poor" compares favorably to Paul's statement in 1 Cor 13:3: "If I give away all my possessions . . . but do not have love, I gain nothing." Since the Greek expression for "possessions" is the same in each text (τὰ ὑπάρχοντα), Wenham makes the proposal that "this difficult teaching of Jesus was well known in the church, including Pauline circles."[4] But the conclusion optimistically overreaches its evidential base in an effort to establish a link between Jesus and Paul.[5] It may well be, of course, that Jesus' teaching about caring for the poor was, in fact, remembered in communities founded by Paul, but 1 Cor 13:3 provides no evidence of that.[6]

But perhaps we should not expect Jesus and Paul to have common interests regarding the poor. As was shown in chapter 1, the case is sometimes made that the poor were not a feature of Paul's mission because Paul expected the eschatological age to be established fully in the very near future. Leslie Hoppe says it this way:

> Paul's attitude toward the poor was probably colored by his expectations regarding the imminent return of Christ. The apostle's belief that Christ's

4. David Wenham, *Paul: Follower of Jesus or Founder of Christianity?* (Grand Rapids: Eerdmans, 1995), p. 84. Wenham is clearly a "maximalist" in finding as many bridges between Jesus and Paul as possible, sometimes at the expense of persuasive force, as in this case. In his little booklet on the subject (*Paul and the Historical Jesus* [Cambridge: Grove Books, 1998]), Wenham discusses Paul's theology and ethics, but never discusses the issue of "the poor." Under ethics, he focuses simply on matters of "divorce" and "women."

5. Not least, only the Matthean Gospel includes τὰ ὑπάρχοντα. In their versions of the saying (Mark 10:21; Luke 18:22), neither the Markan nor the Lukan Gospel includes this expression. So even if Wenham is right to think that the saying circulated widely, it is far from evident that the pertinent term itself ever circulated widely or that it had currency prior to the mid-80s, when Matthew's Gospel seems to have been completed. Attempts to establish parallels between Matt 19:21 and 1 Cor 13:3 inevitably are unsuccessful.

6. A better starting place would be Acts 20:35, discussed below.

return was near made dealing with socioeconomic problems at any great length unnecessary.[7]

Peter Davids says it this way: Paul's "imminent eschatology made social issues less important."[8]

But arguably just the opposite conclusion could be drawn. If Paul imagined that Jesus would soon return in eschatological glory, we might also imagine Paul wanting to establish communities that resembled the eschatological age in as many respects as possible. Paul was seeking to do precisely this in other respects, not least with regard to the unity of Jew and gentile in Christ. So why should concern for the poor have been any different? Moreover, Jesus too seems to have had expected the eschatological age to be fully implemented imminently (e.g., Mark 9:1; Matt 16:28; Luke 9:27),[9] and yet concern for the poor was part and parcel of his mission. Attempts to let Paul "off the hook" (in a sense) by appealing to his "imminent eschatology" ultimately do not get us very far. This is all the more true when keeping in mind Paul's claims that Jesus-followers had already been "delivered from the present evil age" (Gal 1:4), and had received "the Spirit of [God's] Son" (Gal 4:6) as the first fruit and guarantee of their salvation (see 1 Cor 10:11; 2 Cor 1:21-22; 5:5, 17; 4:4-6; 6:15; Rom 8:9-17; 13:11-13). Davids's claim might be adjusted along the following lines: Paul's emphasis on followers of Jesus having already enjoyed a transfer of lordships and being enlivened by the Spirit of God's Son makes social issues all the more important.

Quite simply, if Paul had an under-developed sense of concern for the poor, then his attitude simply must be contrasted with the great traditions of Judaism, with the attitude of Jesus, and with the practices of the Jerusalem-based Jesus-movement.[10] Perhaps such a scenario would cause us to conclude that the revelation of the resurrected Jesus to Paul on the Damascus Road had the effect of denuding Paul of any concern for the poor that he

---

7. Leslie J. Hoppe, *There Shall Be No Poor among You: Poverty in the Bible* (Nashville: Abingdon, 2004), p. 158.

8. Peter H. Davids, "The Test of Wealth," in Bruce Chilton and Craig Evans, eds., *The Missions of James, Peter, and Paul: Tensions in Early Christianity* (Leiden: Brill, 2005), 355-84, p. 358.

9. See the overview of the issue in James D. G. Dunn, *Jesus Remembered; Christianity in the Making*, vol. 1 (Grand Rapids: Eerdmans, 2003), pp. 431-37.

10. This is the inadvertent impression left by Pamela Eisenbaum, whose book *Paul Was Not a Christian: The Original Message of a Misunderstood Apostle* (New York: HarperOne, 2009) leaves plenty of scope for exploring Paul's Jewish identity in relation to care for the poor, but completely fails to consider the matter.

might have had prior to that christophany. When Paul claims that Israel's deity had revealed-and-apocalypsed his son "in me" (ἐν ἐμοί, Gal 1:16) and that Christ now lives "in me" (ἐν ἐμοὶ, Gal 2:20), it must be a different Jesus that resided in Paul than the one who is shown to have placed care for the poor at the forefront of his ministry and message. Here we are reminded of William Loader's poignant observation that "[n]one of his [Paul's] writings would lead one to understand that good news for the poor was a central feature in the message of Jesus."[11]

One way to remove the sting of such a conclusion would be to broaden our categories of comparison somewhat and to analyze Jesus and Paul in terms of their shared interest in reaching out to those usually thought to be beyond significance.

1. So, for Jesus, the grace and sovereignty of the deity of Israel broke down the deeply engrained structures of honor and shame that permeated and were perpetuated by many cultures throughout the ancient Mediterranean basin, and for Jesus this resulted in good news for the frequently despised poor.
2. Similarly, for Paul, the grace and sovereignty of the deity of Israel broke down the deeply engrained structures of ethnocentric covenantalism that permeated and were perpetuated by many Jewish communities throughout the Mediterranean basin, and for Paul this resulted in good news for the frequently despised gentiles.

In this broader context of comparison, a common pattern would seem to be shared by Jesus and Paul, even if differences are perceptible in Jesus' and Paul's application of that pattern.

But while such a comparison might be of some theological profit, it

11. William Loader, "'Good News to the Poor' and Spirituality in the New Testament: A Question of Survival," in Geoffrey D. Dunn, David Luckensmeyer, and Lawrence Cross, eds., *Poverty and Riches,* vol. 5 of *Prayer and Spirituality in the Early Church* (Strathfield, NSW: St Paul's Publications, 2009), 3-35, p. 31. Compare Orlando Patterson (*Rituals of Blood: Consequences of Slavery in Two American Centuries* [Washington, DC: Civitas Counterpoint, 1998], p. 229): "There are really two religions lurking in the bosom of the Christian church. One is the largely neglected religion that Jesus himself preached. . . . This religion, though, was largely discarded in one of the greatest distortions and misappropriations in the history of the world. In the [Christianity] that emerged after Jesus' execution, the focus of the young religion shifted completely. . . . This was all an invention after his death, an invention attributable, above all, to Paul, who became a virtual second founder and who, in his many writings . . . contemptuously neglected the actual sayings of Christ."

would also mask a more direct line of favorable historical comparison. For when comparing Jesus and Paul on the matter of "the poor," a mutual concern *is* in fact evident, although it has for too long been neglected in comparisons of the two figures. Significant data within the Pauline corpus testify to the fact that such care was a well-established practice within communities founded by Paul.

6.2: Care for the Poor within Paul's Communities

In his influential book *Chapters in a Life of Paul*, John Knox registered the view that there is "plenty of evidence in Paul's letters that the churches were expected to care for their poor."[12] Knox's claim, however, is overstated. The evidence might be strong, but there is not necessarily "plenty" of it. Although Paul could depict himself as one who had himself many times been "hungry and thirsty, often without food, cold and naked" (2 Cor 11:27), concern for the poor is not a primary feature of Paul's explicit rhetoric in his letters.

More significant than statistical counts of situational letters, however, is the way that consistent traces of "theological DNA" show Paul to have been uncompromising in promoting care for the poor as integral to the practice and theology engendered within Jesus-groups. The claim that Paul was uncompromising in promoting care for the poor can be demonstrated in relation to various data: (1) letters written by Paul for communities founded by him; (2) a letter written by Paul for communities founded by others; and (3) the earliest reminiscences about Paul from the first century CE. Moreover, (4) in one instance when an economic virus had infected communities founded by him, Paul mounts one of his most perplexed and vigorous challenges against the perpetrators of the problem, charging that they had emasculated the "good news" by compromising the "economic" dimension of their corporate gatherings. These four data converge to indicate that care for the poor ranked among one of the features that Paul hoped to foster within communities of Jesus-followers.

The first data-set comes from three letters written by Paul for guidance within his own communities: 1 Thessalonians, Galatians, and 2 Corinthians. Especially noteworthy is the rather ancillary but nonetheless extremely illustrative comment that Paul makes in 2 Cor 9:13. Towards the end of an ex-

---

12. John Knox, *Chapters in a Life of Paul*, rev. ed. (London: SCM Press, 1989), p. 38.

tended discussion about his collection for the poor among Jerusalem Jesus-followers (2 Cor 8–9), Paul broadens the frame of reference to speak not only of the Corinthians' generosity towards the Jerusalem Jesus-followers, as evidenced by their collection efforts, but also of their generosity towards all others: "by the generosity of your contribution for them [i.e., Jerusalem Jesus-followers] and for all [others]" (ἁπλότητι τῆς κοινωνίας εἰς αὐτοὺς καὶ εἰς πάντας). When considering Paul's attitude towards poverty, this simple phrase is far from being a casual throw-away line. It is indicative of a person whose concern for one particular subset of people arises from a more general concern for those in material need. In Paul's view, the generosity of the Corinthians towards other Jesus-followers in Jerusalem did not comprise a circumstantial and isolated event that, once completed, fulfilled and concluded their obligations to the economically disadvantaged. Neither was their generosity to the Jerusalem Jesus followers expected to derail all other forms of generosity while the collection was in progress. Instead, for Paul, Corinthian generosity represented an instantiation of a general practice of generosity that was to characterize the on-going corporate life of Jesus-groups "for all" of the needy.

The point is made also in Paul's Galatian letter (which will be given full "economic" consideration in chapter 9 below). At the very close of his letter to the Galatian communities, and just prior to picking up the "pen" himself in 6:11-18 to write his concluding summary, Paul dictates in 6:9-10: "Let us not grow weary in doing good. . . . Therefore, then, as often as God gives the opportunity, let us work the good for all people,[13] especially for those of the household of faith." While the intended targets of "doing the good" will be discussed in chapter 12 below, here it is important to note how the double particle "therefore then" at the beginning of 6:10 (ἄρα οὖν) draws special attention to the point that is being made, as if to signal that the flow of Paul's thought is coming to a culminating point.[14] According to Hans Dieter Betz, Gal 6:10 "summarizes and concludes the parenetical section" of Galatians, and as such "sums up in a general way, and in the form of a final appeal, what the Apostle regards as the ethical task of the Christian community.

13. NRSV: "Let us work for the good of all"; Greek: ἐργαζώμεθα τὸ ἀγαθὸν πρὸς πάντας.

14. ἄρα οὖν can serve as a relatively weak particle combination at places in Paul's letters (e.g., Rom 5:18; 8:12; 9:16; 14:19; 1 Thess 5:6; Eph 2:19). At times where it falls near the end of a self-contained section, however, it carries much stronger structural significance, as an indicator of a summarizing point (e.g., Rom 7:25; 2 Thess 2:15; cf. perhaps Rom 7:3; 9:18). In structural terms, Gal 6:10 has more in common with the latter case than the former case.

Hence, it serves also as a definition of Christian ethics."[15] And that "definition of Christian ethics" is framed in terms of "doing the good" (τὸ καλὸν
ποιοῦντες) and "work[ing] the good" (ἐργαζώμεθα τὸ ἀγαθόν) on behalf of
others.[16] This includes the notion of supporting those in need with material
aid — the needy within communities of Jesus-followers especially, but not
exclusively so. The point is hardly disputed. So much so that one commentator can state boldly and starkly that Paul's exhortation in this ethical summary "would surely at the very least include charitable works toward the
needy and poor."[17] And the view is strengthened by Bruce Winter's observation that the phrase "to do the good" (ἐργαζώμεθα τὸ ἀγαθόν) that appears
in 6:10 is (virtually) technical terminology in the ancient world for bestowing material benefits on others.[18] As Tom Wright notes, the phrase "to do the
good" was "in regular use in Paul's world, referring to financial contributions in civic and community life."[19] Prior to Paul's own summarizing conclusion in Gal 6:11-18, then, Gal 6:9-10 holds a key structural position in the
unfolding of Paul's Galatian letter, representing the end result or ultimate
outcome of his theological reflections. It is as if Paul does not allow his theological discourse to end without first registering its practical application in
strong and recognizable tones (i.e., "therefore then"!). And central to that
practical application is an admonition to care for others, among whom the
economically insecure (i.e., "the poor") would have taken pride of place.[20]

15. Hans Dieter Betz, *Galatians* (Philadelphia: Fortress Press, 1979), p. 310. Cf. Richard N.
Longenecker (*Galatians* [Dallas: Word Books, 1990], p. 282): The particle ἄρα οὖν "signal[s]
the conclusion or main point of a discussion. . . . Here it sets off the exhortation of this verse
as the conclusion and main point not only of the directives given in 6:1-10 but also of all that
has been said in 5:13–6:10. In effect, the exhortations of 5:13, 'through love serve one another,'
and 6:10, 'do good to all people,' function as an *inclusio* for all that Paul says . . . in 5:13–6:10." In
chapter 9 below, I attempt to demonstrate that 6:10 resonates as far back as Gal 2:10.

16. So Betz, *Galatians*, p. 309: "τὸ καλόν and τὸ ἀγαθόν mean the same thing ('the
good')."

17. Ben Witherington, *Grace in Galatia: A Commentary on Paul's Letter to the Galatians*
(Edinburgh: T&T Clark, 1998), p. 434. This resonates with the economic dimension of "the
good" that Paul has already introduced in Gal 6:6, when exhorting those who are taught to
"share all good things" (κοινωνείτω . . . ἐν πᾶσιν ἀγαθοῖς) with their teachers — i.e., support
their teachers financially.

18. Bruce W. Winter, *Seek the Welfare of the City: Christians as Benefactors and Citizens*
(Grand Rapids: Eerdmans, 1994), pp. 11-40.

19. N. T. Wright, *Paul for Everyone: Galatians and Thessalonians* (London: SPCK, 2002),
p. 79. The book is, of course, written for a "popular" audience, but the point is not compromised for that reason.

20. Justin J. Meggitt (*Paul, Poverty and Survival* [Edinburgh: T&T Clark, 1996], p. 156)

A similar privileging of key structural terrain for the admonition to care for others is found in a letter that Paul wrote to the Thessalonian Jesus-followers. Just prior to registering his final farewells in 1 Thess 5:23-28, Paul includes a list of admonitions in 5:12-22. Included within that list is the charge to "encourage the faint-hearted, help the weak (ἀντέχεσθε τῶν ἀσθενῶν), be patient with all of them" (5:14). The term the "weak" should probably be seen to include those who were economically vulnerable.[21] While the word "weak" has a wide semantic domain in Paul, it can at times include an economic dimension. This is especially evident in 1 Cor 1:26-29, where "the weak things of the world" (τὰ ἀσθενῆ τοῦ κόσμου) stand in contrast with "the strong things" (τὰ ἰσχυρά), in a context where the "strong" are defined as those who are wise, powerful and well-bred (σοφοί, δυνατοί, εὐγενεῖς). Moreover, according to one popular reconstruction of the Corinthian situation, "the weak" of 1 Corinthians 8 may well have had concerns about food because of their low socio-economic location.[22] Despite one's view of that matter, Paul uses the same term in the next chapter to speak of his own ministry: "To the weak I became weak, in order that I might win the weak" (ἐγενόμην τοῖς ἀσθενέσιν ἀσθενής, ἵνα τοὺς ἀσθενεῖς κερδήσω, 9:22). Here Paul is using the term "weak" to describe his self-imposed economic vulnerability, through which he hopes to enhance his apostolic ministry (cf. 9:12, 15-18), despite his rights to economic assistance (9:1-14; compare also 1 Thess 5:12-13, the verses immediately preceding Paul's reference to "the weak" in 1 Thess 5:14). In a parenetic passage like 1 Thess 5:14, the term "the weak" is likely to have similar economic resonances.[23] This view is shared by

---

identifies these verses as "clear evidence that almsgiving was practised (or at least prescribed) in the Pauline communities."

21. This seems far more likely than to take the weak as being those who are "morally" weak, with Paul involved in the act of psychagogy. For this reading, see Abraham J. Malherbe, *The Letters to the Thessalonians* (New York: Doubleday, 2000), pp. 318-20. Malherbe lists other possibilities as well, and rightly rejects them (p. 318), but never explores the option of the weak being those who are economically insecure, due perhaps to actual physical weaknesses and vulnerabilities.

22. Gerd Theissen, *The Social Setting of Pauline Christianity* (Philadelphia: Fortress Press, 1982), especially ch. 3, "The Strong and the Weak in Corinth: A Sociological Analysis of a Theological Quarrel."

23. Compare Greg K. Beale, *1-2 Thessalonians* (Downers Grove: InterVarsity Press, 2003), p. 166: "[T]he weak seem mainly to be those who lack in some physical manner in comparison to others, the sick, lame, blind or even economically destitute." It is the economically destitute that Beale goes on to foreground in his discussion. "Neglect of such disenfranchised people can lead to divisions and discord, as at Corinth when the well-to-do ate as

the author of Acts who, as will be discussed further below, attributes the term to Paul in a parenetic context towards the end of a discourse (Acts 20:35), precisely what we find in 1 Thessalonians. Immersed in a culture that proclaimed all to be well and plentiful under Rome's oversight,[24] the Thessalonian communities of Jesus-followers were not to lose sight of the poor who continued to populate their city and its neighboring countryside. Instead, they were to work for the establishment of the "good news" of peace and security in communities empowered by the divine Spirit in order to off-set the needs of the faint-hearted and weak. Just as in Gal 6:10 (see 1 Tim 6:18), so also in 1 Thess 5:15, when Paul comes to the letter's final exhorta-tions he focuses on "pursu[ing] the good" (τὸ ἀγαθὸν διώκετε), both in rela-tion to the corporate community (εἰς ἀλλήλους) and broader society in gen-eral (εἰς πάντας), with the poor and needy having a high profile in both categories.

If care for the poor was an integral part of Paul's instructions to several of the communities of Jesus-followers that he founded, his letter to the fol-lowers of Jesus in Rome indicates how he employed this same kind of struc-tural procedure when addressing Jesus-followers in communities founded by others — and significantly, when introducing himself and his gospel to those communities. So, in Rom 12:13 Paul encourages the Roman Jesus-followers, whose communities he had never visited, to offset "the needs [χρείαις] of the saints." While some have understood the word "needs" to have a non-material point of reference, Douglas Moo maintains that the "needs" mentioned here "are material ones: food, clothing, and shelter."[25] This is the most natural reading, since the term χρεῖαι frequently connotes material needs in Pauline texts (cf. Phil 2:25; 4:16, 19; Eph 4:28), and beyond. Here, then, Paul is exhorting Roman Jesus-followers to ensure that they make provision for others — "widows, orphans, strangers, and the commu-nity's poor in general."[26] This is highlighted again in Rom 12:16, where Paul

---

much as they wanted at the Lord's Supper while poorer church members had nothing to eat and went hungry (1 Cor 11:18-34)."

24. On imperial Golden Age ideology, see L. de Ligt, "Restraining the Rich, Protecting the Poor: Symbolic Aspects of Roman Legislation," in W. Jongman and M. Kleijwegt, eds., *After the Past* (Leiden: Brill, 2002), 1-46, pp. 23-25.

25. Douglas J. Moo, *The Epistle to the Romans* (Grand Rapids: Eerdmans, 1996), p. 779. So too James D. G. Dunn, *Romans* (Dallas: Word Publishers, 1988), p. 743: "here personal difficulties, particularly financial and daily necessities are probably in view."

26. Dunn, *Romans*, p. 743. So too Moo, *Romans*, pp. 779-80: "Therefore the fellowship we are called to here is the sharing of our material goods with Christians who are less well-

concludes his instruction about intra-corporate concerns, and where his final exhortation is to forsake pride and conceit by "associating with the lowly" (τοῖς ταπεινοῖς συναπαγόμενοι). Since the lowly of 12:16 must correspond in general measure to the needy of 12:13, the verb "associate" in 12:16 must connote an initiative that is demonstrably practical, being virtually tautologous with Paul's encouragement to offset "the practical needs" of others in 12:13.

As with his Galatian and Thessalonian letters, so too in his Roman letter Paul gives this instruction a key structural position. Romans 12:10-21 is comprised of two interlocking "essays" that offer depictions of genuine "love" — a notion introduced at the start of the section in Rom 12:9: "Let love be genuine" (ἡ ἀγάπη ἀνυπόκριτος). The two essays interlock at 12:14-16, with the first essay being comprised of 12:10-13, 15-16 (with regard to love within the communities of Jesus-followers) and the second being comprised of 12:14, 17-21 (with regard to love for those beyond those communal boundaries).[27] Notable about this structural interlock is the way that Paul highlights caring for the needy at either side of the interlocked material, both at 12:13 (i.e., before the interlock begins) and at 12:16 (i.e., at the end of the interlock). And that interlocked material itself amplifies the character of ἀγάπη, love.[28] Accordingly, in a letter that outlines something of Paul's good news to Jesus-followers in Rome, care for the needy is given a prominent foothold at a significant structural junction in a theological essay on how "love" is (to be) put into practical effect within communities of Jesus-followers.

This may be significant in relation to Paul's purpose for writing Romans. Among the various reasons why Paul might have written to Roman Jesus-followers is the possibility that the letter may have helped to alleviate their concerns about controversial dimensions of Paul's gospel and, thereby,

---

off." Moo continues, rightly in my view: "Some scholars think that Paul might be thinking specifically of the Jewish Christians in Jerusalem (cf. 15:25, 26) to whom Paul was bringing money collected from the Gentile churches (cf. 15:30-33). But, while we should not of course exclude these Christians from Paul's reference, there is nothing to suggest that he has them particularly in mind here."

27. I have argued for this interlocking pattern in my *Rhetoric at the Boundaries: The Art and Theology of New Testament Chain-Link Transitions* (Waco: Baylor University Press, 2005), pp. 95-99.

28. Roman Garrison, *Redemptive Almsgiving in Early Christianity* (Sheffield: Sheffield Academic Press, 1993), p. 31: "The letter to the Romans establishes for that community the high priority of ἀγάπη as the standard of Christian behaviour. Hospitality, humility and mutual respect for others, as well as generosity to the poor, are to be essential features of that love."

to endear his intended Spanish ministry to them.[29] Paul's purposes for writing to Roman Jesus-followers may well have included the hope that he could thereafter enlist their support (including, and especially, financial support) for his proposed proclamation of the good news in Spain (especially 15:24). By the twelfth chapter of his letter, Paul's Roman audiences are to get the strong impression that care for the needy was an essential ingredient of corporate "love" within communities of Jesus-followers that Paul established. In this way of looking at things, towards the very start of the predominately "paraenetic" section of Romans, Jesus-followers in Rome are helped to imagine how their financial support of Paul's Spanish ministry would result in the spreading of good things among the local populations of Spain through the care of needy people there.

Consequently, four of the seven undisputed texts of the Pauline corpus (i.e., 1 Thessalonians, 2 Corinthians, Galatians, and Romans) demonstrate that Paul included instruction concerning care for the poor in a completely natural and unforced manner within the rhetorical flow of his theological discourse. In fact, in his letter to the Galatian followers of Jesus, Paul seems to go out of his way to make the point that care for the needy is the culminating point in the full course of his theological deliberations (6:9-10). And in Romans, the same emphasis stands in structural pride of place, perhaps in relation to one of Paul's overarching motivations for writing the letter.

If such endorsements of care for the poor emerge from Paul as naturally as his most pronounced theological articulations, the same is true of four texts often thought to have been authored pseudonymously in Paul's name: 2 Thessalonians, 1 Timothy, Titus and Ephesians — to be considered presently. It needs to be noted, however, that the main argument here is not dependent on one's view of the authorship of these letters — a point to which we will return below.[30]

It is hard to pin down with any precision the situation that Paul's advice in 2 Thess 3:6-12 addresses with regard to the "idleness" of some Thessalonian Jesus-followers (a situation already foreshadowed in 1 Thess 5:14). What is clearer, however, is the corporate configuration out of which that situation must have emerged. Certain of the community's members seem to have taken it for granted that the Thessalonian communities of

---

29. No one defends the case more vigorously than Robert Jewett, *Romans* (Minneapolis: Fortress Press, 2007), especially pp. 74-91.

30. I think it likely that Paul himself authored 2 Thessalonians, even if I find it harder to say the same for Ephesians, 1 Timothy, or Titus.

Jesus-followers would offer them economic support despite their idleness. This presumption on the part of the "idle" members was realized when they became recipients of subsistence supplies from other Jesus-followers, probably as an expression of their corporate identity, itself undergirded by a consciousness of an eschatological influx of *agapē* self-giving. As Abraham Malherbe notes: "It is impossible to know with certainty how [those whom Paul calls 'idle'] justified their decision [to become idle]. It is quite possible, perhaps even likely, that they presumed on the extraordinary love of the Christian community for their support."[31]

At the bedrock of the corporate identity of the Thessalonian followers of Jesus, then, was a theological configuration that included a pronounced economic component. Again it is instructive to recall Malherbe's view of the situation:

> In early Christian paraenesis, *philadelphia* and *agapē* are expected to be expressed in a practical manner. . . . Given the importance of hospitality in the life of the house churches Paul and others established, the practice could easily become burdensome, especially to a church as remarkable for its love as the Thessalonian church was. It would be natural, even for this church, after extending hospitality for some months after its foundation, to inquire of Paul whether brotherly love obligated them to give material aid without regard to a person's ability to secure his own livelihood.[32]

In the context of a community struggling to interpret the precise nature of its economic responsibilities, Paul's commands in 2 Thess 3:6-12 are intended to preserve the viability of a community that serves the weak as an

31. Abraham J. Malherbe, *The Letters to the Thessalonians* (New York: Doubleday, 2000), p. 456. Winter's proposal regarding the situation behind 2 Thess 3:6-13 (*Seek the Welfare of the City*, pp. 41-60) builds too much on a fragile claim that being a "busybody" equated to entering into a patron-client relationship. Consequently, Winter's portrait of the Thessalonian situation has the needy Thessalonian Jesus-followers (who would not have been among the urban poor prior to a famine of 51 CE) running to the support of patrons. In my view, this skews the more likely scenario, as noted by Malherbe, that some Thessalonians were seeking the welfare on offer from within Thessalonian Jesus-groups, and that those seeking this welfare were precisely among the urban poor.

32. Malherbe, *Thessalonians*, pp. 255-56. A situation of this sort might well fit with Thessalonian fascination with the Cabirus myth, in which a dead but resurrected god will return to benefit the Thessalonian poor. On this, see especially, Robert Jewett, *The Thessalonian Correspondence* (Philadelphia: Fortress Press, 1986), pp. 127-32; Jerome Murphy-O'Connor, *Paul: A Critical Life* (Oxford: Oxford University Press, 1996), p. 118; Christoph vom Brocke, *Thessaloniki: Stadt des Kassander und Gemeinde des Paulus* (Tübingen: Mohr Siebeck, 2001).

expression of its love (see 1 Thess 1:3; 4:9-10). Paul's instructions are given in order to ensure that the resources of that community are not squandered in needless ways. But if by these instructions Paul sought to demarcate the truly needy from others who were benefitting from the community's generosity, he was also seeking thereby to preserve a demeanor of generosity and care among Thessalonian Jesus-groups. According to John Barclay,

> there is good reason to think that the ethic of generosity (Rom 12.8-10) was a significant feature of communities of "brothers" [i.e., Jesus-followers]. The fact that [in his Thessalonian letters] Paul has to turn his commendation of φιλαδελφία into a warning not to depend *overmuch* on other believers for financial support . . . indicates a general presumption that "brothers" will look out for one another (the label connoted in antiquity the sharing of resources, not equality).[33]

Marcus Borg and John Dominic Crossan crystallize the point in this way: "The need for such a command [i.e., the idle among you should 'earn their own living,' 2 Thess 3:12] demonstrates that these were in fact share communities."[34] This perception is reinforced in the very next verse, where Paul exhorts the Thessalonians: "Do not be weary in doing the good" (ὑμεῖς δέ, ἀδελφοί, μὴ ἐγκακήσητε καλοποιοῦντες, 2 Thess 3:13). As Malherbe notes, in its context this exhortation must refer "to the material support the church had given to their fellow members in need."[35] Even in contexts where the corporate generosity practiced within Jesus-groups has been taken advantage of by some Jesus-followers, Paul still upholds the principle of caring for those who were truly in need. And it is precisely on this note that the letter ends, prior to the final prayer (3:16), greeting (3:17) and benediction (3:18) that form the letter's conclusion.

Virtually the same situation is envisioned in 1 Tim 5:3-16. In the author's view, the community's support of needy widows was being abused by some who should not have been eligible for support of this kind.[36] In that context,

---

33. John G. M. Barclay, "Money and Meetings: Group Formation among Diaspora Jews and Early Christians," in A. Gutsfeld and D.-A. Koch, eds., *Vereine, Synagogen und Gemeinden im kaiserzeitlichen Kleinasien* (Tübingen: Mohr Siebeck, 2006), 113-27, pp. 120-21.

34. Marcus Borg and John Dominic Crossan, *The First Paul: Reclaiming the Radical Visionary behind the Church's Conservative Icon* (London: SPCK, 2009), p. 190.

35. Malherbe, *Thessalonians*, p. 458.

36. For more on this, see especially Winter, *Seek the Welfare of the City*, pp. 62-78. That similar situations marked out later periods of Christian history is suggested by the fact that Ambrose has to address an almost identical situation (*Off.* 2.76). Differentiations between

the author's first and final instructions indicate his position: "Honor widows who are real widows. . . . Let the church not be burdened, so that it can assist those who are real widows" (1 Tim 5:3, 16). If corporate funds are to be used for the needy, the community must exercise discretion in determining who the truly needy are. In this way, the fundamental character of generosity within the community will not be compromised, but preserved. Notably, then, much like Galatians, 1 Thessalonians, and 2 Thessalonians, the text of 1 Timothy comes to a close with an emphasis on doing good works. Those who are able are instructed "to do good, to be rich in good works, to be generous, and ready to share" (ἀγαθοεργεῖν, πλουτεῖν ἐν ἔργοις καλοῖς, εὐμεταδότους εἶναι, κοινωνικούς, 1 Tim. 6:18). In these exhortations, an economic dimension predominates. As William Mounce notes, the author "starts with the general 'do good' and moves to the more specific 'be rich in good deeds,' and then clarifies that by 'good deeds' he means sharing generously with others . . . [so that to] be truly rich is to give." Mounce concludes by noting that, while the final item in the list (κοινωνικούς, "ready to share") might refer to "sharing on a much broader plane" than simply economic support, it nonetheless acts in relation to the notion of "generosity" that precedes it (εὐμεταδότους εἶναι, "to be generous"), so that "both convey the common idea in Paul that the rich should share with the poor."[37] All this stands in sharp contrast to the portrait in 1 Tim 6:9-10 of those who are rich, whose love of money causes them to destroy others. Precisely the same emphasis prefaces the sentence just prior to 1 Tim 6:18, where the author instructs the economically rich to be of a different mindset than those who seek to capture honor through their riches (1 Tim 6:17). It would be perverse, then, if an economic dimension were not to be found in the author's instructions about good works, generosity, and sharing in 6:18. As Frances Young states, according to the author of 1 Timothy the "good works which result from salvation are certainly the practice of charity and what we might call welfare support."[38]

Along with 1 Timothy, the letter to Titus shares precisely the same struc-

---

the deserving and undeserving poor are also evident in legal stipulations in the early centuries CE; see *CTh* 14.18.1; *CJ* 11.26.1; *Nov. Iust.* 80.5.1. Compare also synagogual attempts to determine who among the Jewish community was worthy of charitable support; see Gildas Hamel, *Poverty and Charity in Roman Palestine* (Berkeley: University of California Press, 1990), p. 218 n. 42.

37. William Mounce, *The Pastoral Epistles* (Nashville: Thomas Nelson Publishers, 2000), p. 367.

38. Frances Young, *The Theology of the Pastoral Epistles* (Cambridge: Cambridge University Press, 1994), p. 31.

tural feature, with the letter's closing verses including an emphasis on the doing good to those in need: "And let people learn to devote themselves to good works in order to meet urgent needs [καλῶν ἔργων προΐστασθαι εἰς τὰς ἀναγκαίας χρείας], so that they may not be unproductive." Situated at Titus 3:14, this verse includes the author's concluding instructions, before a verse of final greetings. And they are instructions that "emphasize the theme of the epistle one last time" — that is, that Jesus-followers should be devoted to living in practical ways (cf. Tit 3:8).[39] The practical dimension that the author chooses to highlight is the offsetting of the needs of others. That an economic dimension is included in the author's instruction is further evidenced by the phrase τὰς ἀναγκαίας χρείας, which (as noted above) commonly denotes the critical necessities of life.

Similarly in Ephesians, the author lists the kinds of actions that demonstrate that Jesus-followers are "no longer liv[ing] as the gentiles live" (Eph 4:17; cf. 4:17-24). The third entry in the catalogue outlines how thieves are to give up stealing and, working honestly, are to "share with the needy" (ἵνα ἔχῃ μεταδιδόναι τῷ χρείαν ἔχοντι, 4:28). It is unlikely that the author imagined that only Jesus-followers who formerly were thieves would be sharing with the needy. More likely he imagined that they would join with other Jesus-followers in sharing with the needy, and in that way would serve as visible demonstrations of the claim that members of Jesus-groups were "no longer living as the gentiles live." Accordingly, the text is highly suggestive of the author's expectation that Jesus-groups will be marked out by caring for the needy, as testified to by the fact that even former thieves will be transformed, becoming participants in the corporate expression of divine grace given to them (ὁ θεὸς ἐν Χριστῷ ἐχαρίσατο ὑμῖν, 4:32).[40] As Ernest Best has noted, this verse "provides some evidence for the continuance of communal sharing of possessions among the early Christians."[41]

These instructions about caring for the needy from 2 Thessalonians, 1 Timothy, Titus and Ephesians are not to be seen as incidental add-ons that simply and feebly fill the rhetorical space of the Pauline letter; they are better

---

39. Mounce, *The Pastoral Epistles,* p. 458. Mounce reinforces the point (p. 459): Paul "wants to drive home the central thrust of the epistle: the practical necessity of good works (cf. Titus 1:16; 2:7, 14; 3:8)."

40. Cf. Ben Witherington, *The Letters to Philemon, the Colossians, and the Ephesians: A Socio-Rhetorical Commentary on the Captivity Epistles* (Grand Rapids: Eerdmans, 2007), p. 300: "What this verse suggests is that the Christian community was supposed to take care of their own, as Acts 2, 4, and 6 suggest."

41. Ernest Best, *Ephesians* (Edinburgh: T&T Clark, 1998), p. 455.

seen as standard features of Pauline exhortation. If these four texts were all written by Paul, they then provide a significant point of triangulation for the reconstruction of Paul's own theology and expectations. All four suggest that Paul supposed that urban Jesus-groups would care for the poor and needy (even if qualifications were at times required to ensure that Jesus-communities could continue to express generosity without unnecessarily draining their resources). If any of these letters were written pseudonymously, however, that would be even more significant, since those pseudonymous letters would then demonstrate the way that later authors (at least one, and perhaps as many as four), seeking to apply Paul's voice in new situations, simply presumed that care for the genuinely needy was (to be) a hallmark of communities that he had founded.[42]

A similar picture emerges in the depiction of Paul in the Acts of the Apostles (written about 95 CE), again demonstrating the extent to which Paul's own concern for the poor was deeply ingrained and was to be replicated in the corporate lives of Jesus-followers.[43] In Acts 20:18-35, Paul gives what are essentially his final words to the "gathered church" of communities that he has founded (represented by the entourage from Ephesus who had joined Paul in Miletus).[44] That farewell speech of exhortation closes with the words: "We must support the weak (δεῖ ἀντιλαμβάνεσθαι τῶν ἀσθενούντων), remembering the words of the Lord Jesus, for he himself said, 'It is more blessed to give than to receive'" (20:35). As noted above, the term "the weak" identifies those who are poor and economically vulnerable. Moreover, "supporting the weak" is not meant to involve simply praying for them or wishing them well. For the Paul of Acts 20, supporting the weak involves using material resources to offset the economic needs of others (see 20:33-34, where Paul himself appears as an example of precisely this behavior). Consequently, three things can be said of the Paul of Acts 20:

---

42. This is true even if one imagines the allegedly pseudonymous author of 2 Thessalonians to have simply copied the structure of 1 Thess when writing 2 Thessalonians. The fact remains that the pseudonymous author nonetheless kept the "care for the poor" clause in his letter on the assumption that this is what one does when writing in Paul's name. In my view, however, 2 Thessalonians is unlikely to be pseudonymous.

43. The Lukan portrait of Paul has at times been subject to criticism by interpreters who imagine that the author completely misrepresented Paul's theology and mission. Although there is reason to be cautious about some aspects of Lukan portraits in Acts, extreme versions of this view arise more from scholarly exaggeration and/or carelessness than Lukan exaggeration and/or carelessness.

44. So Acts 20:25: "And now I know that none of you, among whom I have gone about proclaiming the kingdom, will ever see my face again."

1. he includes exhortations about the necessity of caring for the poor within the speech that serves as his farewell speech to the communities of Jesus-followers that he founded and towards which had felt parental responsibility;[45]

2. he highlights concern for the poor and needy at the point of culmination in his words of exhortation; and

3. he embeds "support for the weak" firmly within his talk about "the message of his [God's] grace which is able to build you up and to give you an inheritance among all those that are sanctified" (20:32).

Although the Lukan author has not recounted Paul's precise words in Acts 20:18-35, he has nonetheless sought to reconstruct the sort of thing that Paul might have said on just such an occasion.[46] Orators, historians, and storytellers of the ancient world were trained in precisely this skill of reconstructing a person's "speech in character" in a manner appropriate to the context. Consequently, it is significant that the Lukan author thought that this speech was precisely the sort of thing that Paul would have said on an occasion like this. The Lukan author "remembers" Paul as one whose own practice and exhortation showcased concern for the poor towards the end of, but as an essential part of, his reflections on the good news that he proclaimed.[47] And in this regard, the author's attempt at "speech in character" in Acts 20:18-35 offers a highly significant glimpse on the portraiture of Paul in the last decade of the first century CE, and one that corresponds wholly with data from Paul's undisputed letters (i.e., Romans, Galatians, 1 Thessalonians, 2 Corinthians) and disputed letters (i.e., 2 Thessalonians, 1 Timothy, Titus, Ephesians).

In the Lukan depiction of the origins of the Jesus-movement, Paul as much as Barnabas has a claim to be devoted to initiating care for the poor. If Barnabas sold a field in order to help ensure that "no one among them

---

45. Beverly Gaventa (*Acts* [Nashville: Abingdon Press, 2003], p. 283) rightly notes: "As the book's most extended speech for those who are already Christian (cf. 11:5-17; 15:7-11, 13-21) and the last speech prior to Paul's captivity, this address occupies an important place in the book as a whole."

46. So Mikeal Parsons, *Acts* (Grand Rapids: Baker Academic, 2008), p. 290.

47. This may be all the more significant in view of the fact that the Lukan author has chosen not to recount the delivery of Paul's collection "for the poor among the saints in Jerusalem" (in Paul's words of Rom 15:26) in the narrative of Paul's final trip to Jerusalem (Acts 20–21). If the author omitted reference to the Pauline collection because the collection was not favorably received, as most think, he seems constrained nonetheless to document Paul's deeply-ingrained concern for the poor in other ways, taking opportunity to emphasize the point in Acts 20:35.

might be in need" (Acts 4:34-36), Paul preaches concern for the needy as an essential feature of his gospel about "his [God's] grace which is able to build you up and to give you an inheritance among all those that are sanctified" (20:32). In this way, the Lukan author remembers Paul's gospel of grace to include concern for the poor in much the same way as he remembers Jesus' proclamation of the kingdom to include the same concern.

In light of these data, it is not surprising that the narrative of the apocryphal *Acts of Paul and Thecla* (a second-century CE text) depicts Paul as one who distributes goods to the poor.[48] One "rich woman named Queen Tryphaena" (§27) is said to have given up "much clothing and gold so that she could leave many things to Paul for the service of the poor" (§41). There is little reason to think that the incident was historical. But it is notable nonetheless that Paul could be depicted a century or so after his death as one through whom the resources of the rich could reliably be channeled to the poor in an effort to offset their need. And little wonder, since this is the same Paul who is depicted within the narrative as selling his own cloak in order to buy food for starving children (§23).

There is still more to the picture, however — not the least of which is Paul's handling of an irritating Corinthian problem that included an economic dimension within its configuration. Having instructed the Corinthian Jesus-followers in 1 Cor 10:24 not to "seek your own advantage but that of the other," in the next chapter Paul speaks harsh words to them for failing to regard "the other" at all in their observance of the Lord's Supper. It is a commonplace to understand the problem behind 1 Cor 11:17-34 as involving a socio-economic dimension. Evidently some of those who were economically insecure were consequently being disadvantaged in the corporate gatherings of the community.[49]

Against this backdrop, Paul's discourse in 1 Cor 11:17-34 reveals Paul's extreme indignation at a situation in which economic factors of corporate identity were being overlooked by some Jesus-followers. In Paul's view, if the poor are disadvantaged, the power dimension of the Lord's Supper is short-

---

48. The following citations are from J. K. Elliott, *The Apocryphal New Testament: A Collection of Apocryphal Christian Literature in an English Translation* (Oxford: Clarendon Press, 1993).

49. A precise reconstruction of the situation in 1 Cor 11 need not be entertained here. Even when the specifics of their situational reconstruction vary, most scholars recognize an economic dimension to be involved. For a basic reconstruction, see James D. G. Dunn, *Beginning from Jerusalem; Christianity in the Making*, vol. 2 (Grand Rapids: Eerdmans, 2009), pp. 814-16.

circuited. Much like a true prophet of Israel, Paul links the serious offences against the poor within Corinthian communities to the harsh realities of divine judgment, noting: "For this reason [i.e., offending the Lord's Supper in your treatment of the poor], many of you are weak and ill, and some have died" (1 Cor 11:30). Paul pulls no punches in his assessment that real spiritual forces are at work in the way that the economic dimension of the good news had been compromised in Corinth. The equitable treatment of the poor at the Lord's Supper is required if communities of Jesus-followers hope to articulate and enact the eschatological renewal of all things through what the deity of Israel has done in Christ.

To counter this disregard of the needy among the Corinthians, Paul simply reintroduced the narrative of the self-giving Jesus into their consciousness, expecting them to follow in the narrative's wake. Jesus' command to "do this in remembrance of me" (11:24-25) is rightly glossed as, "Do this community meal in such a way that you really become a community that supports one another,"[50] or as, "Do this, that is, give yourselves (and your resources) up for others, just as I am doing for you."[51] In doing precisely that (i.e., giving of themselves and their resources) and in rectifying the (unintentional) Corinthian abuse of the poor, the Lord's Supper will again be eaten in a manner that "proclaims the Lord's death until he comes" (τὸν θάνατον τοῦ κυρίου καταγγέλλετε ἄχρι οὗ ἔλθῃ, 1 Cor 11:26).[52]

It is little wonder, then, that Paul's ire towards Corinthian abuse of the poor spills so boldly onto the pages of 1 Corinthians 11. For Paul, caring for the poor lies at the heart of the identity of Jesus-followers, because it lies at

---

50. Terrence J. Rynne, *Gandhi and Jesus: The Saving Power of Nonviolence* (Maryknoll, NY: Orbis Books, 2008), p. 186.

51. Suzanne Watts Henderson, "'If Anyone Hungers . . .': An Integrated Reading of 1 Cor 11.17-34," *NTS* 48 (2002): 195-208, p. 202. Her attractive proposal that the phrase εἴ τις πεινᾷ, ἐν οἴκῳ ἐσθιέτω in 11:34 means not "let the one (i.e, the rich person) who is hungry eat at home (before/after coming to the community meal)" but instead means "let the one (i.e., the poor person) who is hungry eat in the house (of Christian gathering)" unfortunately has too many exegetical obstacles to be ultimately convincing.

52. Cf. David J. Downs, "Is God Paul's Patron? The Economy of Patronage in Pauline Theology," in Bruce W. Longenecker and Kelly Liebengood, eds., *Engaging Economics: New Testament Scenarios and Early Christian Reception* (Grand Rapids: Eerdmans, 2009), 129-56, p. 151: Paul "encourages the Corinthians to recognize that unless the community embodies a concern for others, particularly the poor, modeled on the self-giving love of Jesus Christ, it cannot rightly proclaim the Lord's death." See also the extended theological analysis of the passage enunciated by Luise Schottroff, "Holiness and Justice: Exegetical Comments on 1 Corinthians 11.17-34," *JSNT* 79 (2000): 51-60.

the heart of the story of the Jesus who is proclaimed as Lord and at the heart of the story of the sovereign deity who judges all. For Paul, remembering the poor was to lie at the heart of the eschatological identity of communities he had founded, and was itself a practice integral to an embodied proclamation of the good news. In contrast to the claims of Hoppe and Davids, for instance, caring for the poor was not something that could wait until the eschatological age was fully implemented by Israel's deity; instead, it was something that Paul expected Jesus-groups to be doing already, as they experienced something of the eschatological age within their midst "until he comes."

6.3: Conclusions

The view that Paul was relatively unconcerned about the poor involves serious miscalculations. Even leaving to one side second-century depictions of Paul like the *Acts of Paul and Thecla*, other data consistently and uniformly suggest otherwise, including five of the undisputed letters of Paul (1 Thessalonians, 1 Corinthians, 2 Corinthians, Galatians and Romans), four of the disputed Pauline letters (2 Thessalonians, Ephesians, 1 Timothy, and Titus) and the Lukan depiction of Paul in Acts. Interweaving the evidence from these ten New Testament documents gives the lie to the view that care for the economically needy played no part in Paul's gospel. Instead, it is best to believe that Paul expected concern for the indigenous (and deserving) poor to be a hallmark of Jesus-groups that he founded throughout the Mediterranean basin — no doubt as an outworking of the story of Israel's deity of justice, refracted now through the story of the Galilean Jew who stood alongside the poor in the promise of divine blessing.

Accordingly, the fact that Paul does not devote whole chapters of his extant letters to the issue of care for the poor does not mean that he had no such concerns. Paul's letters dealt with matters that were situationally urgent; if those letters are silent with regard to care for the poor, we still need to ask whether that is a reflection on Paul's own theology or whether, in fact, care for the poor was being observed without compromise in the Jesus-communities that his extant letters addressed. The better view is the latter. Various factors are in its favor. We have noted a fairly consistent structural patterning across a variety of Paul's texts; we have noted how Paul imagined the gospel itself to be compromised when economic relationships were skewed in unhealthy configurations; and we have noted that the socio-rhetorical situation for Paul's Thessalonian letter/letters is one in which care for the needy was assumed to be a fundamental feature of the very character of that community, whose practical "love" (i.e., burden bearing) was proclaimed throughout the region (1 Thess 1:2-10). These data suggest that care for the poor was, in fact, deeply embedded within Paul's theological concerns. The fact that his letters usually do not explicitly address those issues demonstrates that the same concern for the poor must have been shared by the communities he had founded and that their practices were not (usually) negligible in that regard.

Paul expected urban Jesus-followers to seek the welfare of their city by "doing good," not least through "sharing self-generated financial resources" with the needy.[53] It is time, then, to call a moratorium on the ill-considered view that Paul thought it unnecessary to "[deal] with socioeconomic problems at any great length." It is also time to reconsider the meaning of the phrase "remember the poor" in Gal 2:10, as in chapters 7 through 9 below.

53. Winter, *Seek the Welfare of the City*, p. 58.

CHAPTER 7

"Remember the poor"

Interpretive Paradigms in Conflict

7.1: Earliest Interpretations of Galatians 2:10
7.2: The Poor of Galatians 2:10 and the Ebionite Connection
7.3: The Ebionite Basis of the Contemporary Consensus
7.4: Argumentational Adjustment within the Contemporary Consensus
7.5: Conclusions

Not infrequently, interpreters see Paul's mention of "the poor" in Gal 2:10 as peripheral and secondary to the main issues of the Jerusalem meeting, out-lined by Paul in 2:1-10. That is the impression, for instance, given by one of the most influential interpreters of Galatians in the late twentieth century, Hans Dieter Betz. He depicts the instruction articulated by the Jerusalem leadership to "remember the poor" as an "additional request" that was "supplementary" and "unrelated to the main points of the debate" in Jerusalem. In Betz's view, "what had been requested and granted was a kind of philanthropic gesture."[1]

Betz and others who hold this view do not see this "philanthropic gesture" as simply a piece of good advice about how Jesus-followers should live in general. If "remember the poor" is simply good advice, Paul should also

---

1. Hans Dieter Betz, *Galatians* (Philadelphia: Fortress Press, 1979), p. 101. Cf. Larry Hurtado ("The Jerusalem Collection and the Book of Galatians," *JSNT* 5 [1979]: 46-62, p. 51): "It is often thought that [the phrase 'remember the poor'] is of no real significance, and only serves to give an unimportant detail of the agreement with Jerusalem."

have listed other pieces of good advice that the Jerusalem apostles might have mentioned in their meeting (which must have lasted several days). But Paul lists no such advice when recalling his discussions with Jerusalem leaders about the essentials of the gospel. Why then did he mention the admonition to remember the poor?[2]

The answer that has pervaded New Testament scholarship is that the admonition to "remember the poor" fell into a distinct category, being neither "gospel" (as outlined in Gal 2:1-9) nor general halakhic advice about lifestyle. Instead, the admonition to "remember the poor" is thought to fall within the category of what Betz calls "church politics," either as a solitary gesture or as an initiative bound by certain conditions pertaining only to the earliest Jesus-movement.[3]

This view is ultimately based on the estimate that, in one way or another, the term "the poor" identifies members of the Jesus-movement *in Jerusalem,* either collectively or in part. This view is well expressed in Louw and Nida's amplification of Paul's words in Gal 2:10: "all they asked was that we should remember the needy *of their group.*"[4] Lou Martyn's commentary is standard in this regard: "by mentioning 'the poor,' the Jerusalem leaders refer to their own church, or to a circle of persons within that church."[5] Michael Goulder claims that "the poor" is "the name by which the pillars spoke of their movement," so that the term "means the churches of Jerusalem and Judea."[6] Reading Gal 2:10 against the backdrop of Rom 15:25-26, Richard Horsley makes the point this way:

> it is clear that ["the poor"] meant those in the Jerusalem community who were literally poor, probably because they had no means of self-support. The limited resources they had pooled were hardly sufficient to sustain them long-range. Thus other nascent assemblies of Christ were to send economic assistance to the poor in Jerusalem.[7]

---

2. Sam K. Williams (*Galatians* [Nashville: Abingdon Press, 1997], p. 55) raises the question this way: "In light of the numerous details about the Jerusalem conference that are missing in Gal 2:1-10, why does Paul include this one, the request to remember the poor?"

3. Betz, *Galatians,* p. 99.

4. Johannes P. Louw and Eugene A. Nida, *Greek-English Lexicon of the New Testament Based on Semantic Domains* (New York: United Bible Society, 1988, 1989), §29.16, emphasis added.

5. J. Louis Martyn, *Galatians* (New York: Doubleday, 1997), p. 207.

6. Michael Goulder, "A Poor Man's Christology," *NTS* 45 (1999): 332-48, p. 333.

7. Richard A. Horsley, *Covenant Economics: A Biblical Vision of Justice for All* (Louisville: Westminster John Knox Press, 2009), p. 144.

Bengt Holmberg calls this interpretation of the phrase "an *undisputed fact*."[8] Ben Witherington calls it "quite clear."[9] And in his discussion of Galatians 2, Richard Longenecker claims: "All that can be said *with certainty* is that here in v 10 the Jewish Christians *of Jerusalem* are principally in view."[10] This "certain," "clear" and "undisputed" interpretation is so entrenched that it is legitimate to identify it as commanding the firm consensus within the guild of New Testament scholarship, with practically no voices of dissent.[11]

Curiously, however, while the phrase "remember the poor" is understood as a reference to Jesus-followers in Jerusalem as early as the late fourth century CE, the same cannot be claimed for interpretations of Gal 2:10 prior to that time. While the current consensus can hail a Jerusalem reference to be a "certainty" and "an undisputed fact" when discussing "the poor" of Gal 2:10, that "fact" has no foothold in the earliest interpretations of Gal 2:10 in the second through mid-fourth centuries CE.

The goals of this chapter are to register the two competing interpretations of the phrase "remember the poor" of Gal 2:10, and to test their legitimacy through some initial explorations. Towards that end, §7.1 through §7.3 assess the data from the patristic era,[12] while §7.4 and §7.5 assess forms of argumentation that have predominated in recent scholarship.

7.1: Earliest Interpretations of Galatians 2:10

With regard to "the poor" of Gal 2:10, the "undisputed" consensus of today corresponds with what might have been a consensus as far back as the late

---

8. Bengt Holmberg, *Paul and Power: The Structure of Authority in the Primitive Church as Reflected in the Pauline Epistles* (Philadelphia: Fortress Press, 1980), p. 35.

9. Ben Witherington, *Grace in Galatians: A Commentary on St Paul's Letter to the Galatians* (Edinburgh: T&T Clark, 1998), p. 144.

10. Richard N. Longenecker, *Galatians* (Dallas: Word Books, 1990), p. 60, emphasis added.

11. The notable voice of dissension goes back to the late nineteenth century; see V. Bartlet, "'Only Let Us Be Mindful of the Poor': Gal. 2.10," *The Expositor* 9 (1899): 218-55. James D. G. Dunn comes the closest in breaking out of the consensus (e.g., *The Epistle to the Galatians* [London: A&C Black, 1993], pp. 112-14), but still gives a full explanation as to why "the poor" refers "particularly [to] those at Jerusalem itself (cf. Rom. xv.26)" (p. 112).

12. Not discussed here are citations of Gal 2:9-10 in the Church Fathers that have no relevance to the issue of the identity of "the poor" (e.g., Augustine, *Op. Mon.* 24; *Tract. Ev. Jo.* 109.5; John Chrysostom, *Hom. Act.* 33, 37; *Hom. 1 Cor.* 39; *Hom. Eph.* 10; Jerome, *Helv.* 15; Gregory Nazianzen, *Or. Bas.* 2.51).

fourth century CE. This is illustrated from Ephrem the Syrian (306-73), Jerome (329-420 CE), and John Chrysostom (347-407 CE).

When interpreting Gal 2:10 in his commentary on the Pauline epistles in the second half of the fourth century, Ephrem speaks of the poor who were in Jerusalem *(qui erant Jerosolymis)*. In the same way, in his commentary on Galatians (387 CE) Jerome identifies "the poor" of 2:10 as "believers from the Jews" *(ex Judaeis credentes)*, whose desperate situation has resulted from the fact that they had laid their possessions at the feet of the apostles (cf. Acts 4:32-37) or from the fact that other Judean Jews are persecuting them for their abandonment of the law (*Comm. Gal.* 337D). With this identification of "the poor" established, Jerome goes on to link the phrase "remember the poor" with Paul's later collection efforts, on behalf of "the poor among the saints" of the Jerusalem community (338A).[13]

Much the same is evident in Chrysostom's more elaborate handling of the verse. When amplifying Gal 2:10 in his *Homiliae in epistulam ad Galatas commentarius* (written in or after 395 CE), Chrysostom writes: "Who were these poor persons? Many of the believing Jews in Palestine had been de-prived of all their goods." Chrysostom makes the point that Paul's efforts on behalf of "the believing Jews in Palestine" were intended precisely to demon-strate the unity within the missions to "the circumcised" and "the uncircumcised." Using Paul's voice, Chrysostom elaborates the verse in this way: "to the sustenance of the poor among the Jews I also contributed my share, which, had there been any dissension between us, they would not have accepted." Like Jerome, Chrysostom imagines that Gal 2:10 relates directly to Paul's collection efforts of his later ministry. In contrast to many today, Chrysostom is of the opinion that Paul's collection for "the poor" (i.e., "the believing Jews in Palestine") was warmly accepted, and he amplifies the point in this way:

> Wherefore he exercises much zeal, as appears in the Epistles to the Romans and Corinthians, that these persons should meet with much at-tention; and Paul not only collects money for them, but himself conveys it, as he says, "But now I go unto Jerusalem ministering unto the saints," for they were without the necessities of life. And he here shows that in this instance having resolved to assist them, he had undertaken and would not abandon it [*ad loc.*].

---

13. My thanks go to Lindsay Cleveland for bringing Jerome's *Commentariorum in Epistulam ad Galatas* to my attention.

Precisely the same interpretation of Gal 2:10 is evident in Chrysostom's *Homiliae in epistulam ad Hebraeos,* published after his death in 407 CE.[14] In each of these two cases, Chrysostom links Gal 2:10 with Paul's collection for the poor among the saints in Jerusalem.

If Ephrem, Jerome and Chrysostom offer late-fourth- and early-fifth-century precedents to the contemporary consensus on Gal 2:10, it is notable that earlier interpretations of the verse show no cognizance of a geographic restriction. This is evident from Tertullian's early-third-century engagement with the views propounded by Marcion in the middle of the second century. Paragraph 3 of Tertullian's fifth book in *Adversus Marcionem* (207-8 CE) discusses Gal 2:9-10. There he writes:

> Rightly, then, did Peter and James and John give their right hand of fellowship to Paul, and agree on such a division of their work, as that Paul should go to the heathen, and themselves to the circumcision. Their agreement, also, "to remember the poor" was in complete conformity with the law of the Creator, which cherished the poor and needy.

No mention is made here of the agreement being established in order to relieve the hardships of poor Jesus-followers *in Jerusalem.* Tertullian takes the agreement of Gal 2:10 to indicate that both the Jerusalem apostles and Paul unanimously agreed in upholding (a part of) the law given by the sovereign creator deity to the Jewish people long ago. So the excerpt already cited above from *Adversus Marcionem* 5.3 continues in this way: "It is thus certain that the question was one which simply regarded the law, while at the same time it is apparent what portion of the law it was convenient to have observed." With this claim, Tertullian is attempting to undermine Marcion's charge that the Christian deity is wholly different from (and superior to) the deity of creation who bound himself to Israel. And Tertullian's efforts in this regard gain force from a point that he sought to establish earlier in his text. In *Adversus Marcionem* 4.14, Tertullian argued at length that the sovereign creator expressed his great concern for the poor in order that he might be recognized as the same deity that is proclaimed by Jesus and the apostles. Just as the first recorded word of the creator was a "very good" word, so the first recorded words of Jesus in the Sermon on the Mount are also words of goodness: "Blessed are the needy [*sic*] . . . because theirs is the kingdom of heaven."[15] In this way, says Tertullian, the "principle of the New Testament"

---

14. Chrysostom, *Hom. Heb.* 2 ("Argument and Summary of the Epistle").

15. Tertullian is clearly aware of the interpretive issue at stake when translating oi

is initiated "after the example of the Old." Citing eight passages from the Old Testament that demonstrate how entrenched care for the poor and needy is within the heart of the creator, Tertullian addresses Marcion directly with these words:

> For even if you suppose that the promises of the Creator were earthly, but that Christ's are heavenly, it is quite clear that heaven has been as yet the property of no other God whatever than Him who owns the earth also; it is quite clear that the Creator has given even the lesser promises (of earthly blessing) in order that I may more readily believe Him concerning His greater promises (of heavenly blessings) also [*Marc.* 4.14].

According to Tertullian, the creator "specially designed that the promise of a similar blessing should serve as a preparation for the gospel, that so men might know it to be His." The implication is that the only deity who is concerned so specifically with the poor and needy is the creator who revealed himself to Israel. Tertullian charges that Marcion's own deity "has never given proof of his liberality by any preceding bestowal of minor blessings." This, says Tertullian, is in complete contrast to the only true deity, the creator who has revealed himself both in the Old Testament and in the Christ, and who in each case has revealed himself to be concerned for the poor.

Moreover, Tertullian suggests that it is this concern for the poor that causes the gentile nations to be attracted to Christianity. He finds this demonstrated in passages from Isaiah, who spoke about the gentiles when he wrote, "Behold, they shall come swiftly with speed." And their swift approach to the creator is in the knowledge, according to Tertullian, that "'they shall neither hunger nor thirst. Therefore they shall be filled' — a promise which is made to none but those who hunger and thirst." In this way, says Tertullian, "the promise of fullness to the hungry is a provision of God the Creator." Tertullian imagines Isaiah to have prophesied about the offsetting of material poverty within the Christian church for the benefit of the poor of the gentile nations, not simply for Jewish Jesus-followers in Jerusalem. For Tertullian, this is a concrete expression that the deity who is operating in the church is one and the same as the creator who revealed himself in scripture.

It is this theological construct that Tertullian draws on when concluding that the agreement to "remember the poor" in Gal 2:10 is about how the law

---

πτωχοὶ τῷ πνεύματι in Matt 5:2 as "needy," writing in parenthetical tone: "for no less than this is required for interpreting the word in the Greek."

of the creator is to be apportioned within Christianity. For Tertullian, Paul and the Jerusalem leaders agreed (1) that circumcision is a part of the creator's law that *is not essential* to Christian observance, and (2) that cherishing the poor and needy is a part of the creator's law that *continues to be essential* to Christian practice. Tertullian gives the impression that the charge to "remember the poor" is one mutually agreed upon by Paul and the Jerusalem leaders (i.e., "their agreement"), as if the two ministries were linked in a single effort for the poor in different sectors, without any single point of focus or restriction.

If Tertullian asserts that care for the poor fulfills the law of the creator (contra Marcion), it is equally important to note what he *fails* to give consideration to. There are no hints whatsoever that Tertullian considered "the poor" to be a geographically-restricted term; in fact, just the opposite is the case. Tertullian's argument presumes that "the poor" of Gal 2:10 are not simply Jerusalem Jesus-followers. Had there been common knowledge that "the poor" of that verse were solely Jesus-followers in Jerusalem, Tertullian would be leaving his argument about fulfilling the law of the Creator open to dispute. Had he known of a Jerusalem-centric interpretation of "the poor," Tertullian would have needed to demonstrate that, although the agreement to "remember the poor" was initially a matter of benefiting a particular group of people (i.e., Jewish Jesus-followers in Jerusalem), the initiative on behalf of the poor in Jerusalem was itself a particular concretization of a more fundamental principle about care for the poor, a principle rooted in the law of the creator. But Tertullian does not argue in such a way. The best explanation for this rhetorical road-not-taken is that Tertullian was unaware of a view that considered "the poor" to be based in Jerusalem alone.

Even more to the point, it should be noted that a Jerusalem referent for "the poor" in Gal 2:10 would have suited Tertullian's refutation of Marcion perfectly, since Marcion had sought to polarize Paul and the Jerusalem community within the early Jesus-movement. Countering Marcion's dichotomizing historiography would have been all the easier if Tertullian could have registered the simple observation that Paul had agreed with the Jerusalem leadership that the Jesus-groups he founded would send money to support the Jerusalem poor. What better way to counter Marcion's partitioning of Paul and the Jerusalem followers of Jesus than to point out the common knowledge that "the poor" of Gal 2:10 were, in fact, based in Jerusalem. But Tertullian does not avail himself of this kind of reasoning. The best conclusion to draw from this road-not-taken is that a Jerusalem-centric interpretation of "the poor" of Gal 2:10 was simply unknown to Tertullian. Could it be that Gal 2:10 was interpreted without reference to Jerusalem Jesus-followers up to the beginning of the third century of the common era?

This hypothesis gains support from the works of the other two figures who engage with Gal 2:10 prior to the fifth-century CE: Origen (185-254 CE) and Athanasius (293-373). In his allegorical exegesis of Matthew's Gospel (*Commentarium in evangelium Matthaei*, probably dating from the second quarter of the third century), Origen refers to Gal 2:10 in his imaginative reconstruction of a hypothetical discussion among Jesus' disciples about the way that masters should treat slaves (16.8.165-180). The principle articulated in Eph 6:9 is affirmed, with the heavenly Lord teaching "that masters should cease from threatening [slaves] throughout their households" (ἀνιέναι τὴν ἀπειλὴν τοὺς δεσπότας κατὰ τῶν οἰκετῶν). But the point is also made that this principle is not being practiced effectively, through "sinful motives" and "by treating the poor with contempt" (ὁτὲ μὲν προφάσει ἁμαρτίας, ὁτὲ δὲ τῷ καταφρονεῖν τῶν πτωχῶν). It is at this point that Origen cites Gal 2:9-10 directly, prefacing it with the note that such disdainful behavior runs "contrary to the apostolic word" (παρὰ τὸν ἀποστολικὸν λόγον), as testified to by the citation from Gal 2:9-10: "They extended to me and Barnabas the right hand of fellowship, in order that we might go to the nations, and they to the circumcised, only in order that we might remember the poor" (δεξιὰς ἔδωκαν ἐμοὶ καὶ Βαρναβᾷ κοινωνίας, ἵνα ἡμεῖς εἰς τὰ ἔθνη, αὐτοὶ δὲ εἰς τὴν περιτομήν· μόνον τῶν πτωχῶν ἵνα μνημονεύωμεν).[16] In this context, there is no indication that Origen imagined the "apostolic word" to operate as anything other than a general maxim for those who would be disciples of the "heavenly Lord" (κύριον ἐν οὐρανῷ). Like Tertullian before him, Origen's discourse seems unrestricted by any sense that "the poor" of Gal 2:10 might be Jerusalem Jesus-followers. And as with Tertullian, so Origen's presentation might also have been weakened had it been the case that "the poor" of Gal 2:10 was commonly known in his day to refer to Jesus-followers in Jerusalem.[17]

Jumping to the next patristic citation of Gal 2:10, the phrase "remember the poor" appears on three occasions in the extant texts of Athanasius's fourth-century literary corpus. In Athanasius's *Historia Arianorum* 61.1.3, written in 358 CE, we read:

16. The view that μόνον τῶν πτωχῶν ἵνα μνημονεύωμεν in Gal 2:10 modifies Gal 2:9 will be considered in chapter 8 below. See especially n. 22 in chapter 8.

17. Having been based in Alexandria and Caesarea, Origen himself would have been familiar with Christian communities and traditions in Judea during the second century.

For the Lord gave the command to remember the poor [ὁ μὲν γὰρ κύριος ἐνετείλατο τῶν πτωχῶν μνημονεύειν]; He said, "Sell what you have, and give alms" [Luke 18:22] and "I was hungry and you gave me something to eat, I was thirsty and you gave me something to drink. For as much as you did this to one of the least of these, you did it to me" [Matt 25:35, 40].

Athanasius show no cognizance that the phrase "remember the poor" pertained in the first instance to Jerusalem Christians. In Athanasius's hands, the phrase becomes uprooted from its epistolary and historical contexts, having become almost like a floating logion of Jesus, one of the gnomic commands of Jesus that (like those of Matt 25:35, 40 and Luke 18:22 [slightly reworded]) is applicable to anyone and everyone who would be his disciple.[18]

It is little wonder, then, that the phrase "remember the poor" appears in two of Athanasius's undated works in lists of general admonitions. In Athanasius's *Homilia in illud: Ite in castellum* 7.7.2, the phrase appears alongside three other simple exhortations from the NT:

Let us cease from sinning (τοῦ ἁμαρτάνειν παυσώμεθα [cf. 1 Pet 4:1]). Let us remember the poor (τῶν πτωχῶν μνημονεύσωμεν [cf. Gal 2:10]). Let brotherly love continue (ἡ φιλαδελφία μενέτω [Heb 13:1]). Do not neglect to show hospitality to strangers (τῆς φιλοξενίας μὴ ἐπιλανθάνεσθε [Heb 13:2]).

Athanasius's *Homilia in illud: Euntem autem illo* 10.8.3 illustrates much the same approach to Gal 2:10, placing the phrase within the context of general maxims of Christian lifestyle:

Let us strive for excellence, beloved, and let us willingly look forward to the sufferings that result as a consequence (ἀρετὴν προτιμήσωμεν, ἀγαπητοί, καὶ τοὺς ὑπὲρ ταύτης πόνους ἑκουσίως ἀσπασώμεθα); let us do our best to exercise self-control (ἐγκράτειαν ἀσκήσωμεν [cf. Gal 5:23; 2 Pet 1:6]); let us remember the poor (τῶν πτωχῶν μνημονεύσωμεν [cf. Gal 2:10]).

Consequently, in these three extant texts from Athanasius, the phrase "remember the poor" is presented without geographical restriction, as a part

18. That the phrase could be uprooted from its epistolary context to form a general maxim of lifestyle may also be evident from the way the phrase morphs into "only remember the bread of the poor" (μνημονεύσῃς τῆς τῶν πτωχῶν μόνον διατροφῆς) in Georgius Syceota's mid-fourth-century work *Vita sancti Theodori Syceotae* (here 54.17).

and parcel of what it means to live a life of Christian "excellence" in any place and time.

A final example of interpreting Gal 2:10 without reference to the collection or the Jerusalem poor occurs in the early-fourth-century Syriac author Aphrahat, the "Persian Sage" (died c. 350 CE). His *De Sustentatione egenorum* [*Dem.* 20], written about 343/44, is an entire treatise devoted to the biblical mandate (from both the Jewish scriptures and the New Testament) of caring for the poor. Among his numerous examples, Aphrahat quotes Gal 2:10 nearly verbatim at the end of *Dem.* 20.16, making the point that the apostles who preceded Paul asked only that Paul do exactly what he was already eager to do: remember the poor.[19] The citation is directly framed by references to Jesus' teachings on poverty from the Sermon on the Mount, firmly squaring the Galatian reference in a context of caring for the poor in general, not merely for the poor in Jerusalem.

One further thing needs to be noted from the extant literature up to the late fourth century — that is, the tendency to interpret Gal 2:10 as articulating a principle of (what might today be called) Judeo-Christian identity even among ancient interpreters who imagined that "the poor" of that verse were specifically Jesus-followers based in Jerusalem. We have seen, for instance, that Chrysostom interprets Gal 2:10 as referring to the poor in Jerusalem in his *Homiliae in epistulam ad Galatas commentarius*. But it is also important to note that this interpretation is not exhaustive of Chrysostom's handling of the verse. On occasion, Chrysostom uses that verse to encourage almsgiving within the Christian church in general. Although Chrysostom imagined Gal 2:10 to make historical reference to the impoverished Jesus-followers of Jerusalem, he is eager to extend the sense of the verse so that it applies to his own audience, being a feature of Christian living in general. So, in Homily 25 of Chrysostom's *Homiliae in Acta apostolorum*, the text of Gal 2:9-10 is cited on three occasions. In the first, the phrase "remember the poor" is used to amplify the point that almsgiving and concern for the poor were markers of what it meant to be a follower of Jesus in the apostolic period, even in times of hardship.[20] In the second, the almsgiving of gentile Jesus-followers to the benefit of Judean churches is used by Chrysostom to indicate how the church universal offsets affliction and difficulty by nature

19. Joannes Parisot, *Aphraatis Sapientis Persiae: Demonstrationes,* vol. 1 (Paris: Firmin-Didot, 1894), pp. 921-22 (Syriac edition with Latin translation). I am indebted to Nick Zola for pointing me to Aphrahat's use of Gal 2:10.

20. Chrysostom: "Mark how the famine becomes to them the means of salvation, an occasion of alms-giving, a harbinger of many blessings."

of its essential "fellowship." In the third, Chrysostom highlights various forms of almsgiving as being essential to proper discipleship. Setting out the example of Zacchaeus as one for whom salvation involved giving away one's goods, and showing that a purse was carried among Jesus and his disciples in order to help the poor that they met along the way, and before showing how this concern for the poor coheres with Old Testament scripture, Chrysostom simply inserts the example of Paul to demonstrate the point: "And Paul also says, 'Only that we remember the poor.'"

In these cases, Chrysostom does not balk at imagining "the poor" of Gal 2:10 to have been "the poor in Judea," but it is notable that in each case the geographical location of the beneficiaries is a secondary matter, overshadowed by the passage's pertinence in relation to care for the poor in general. In this way we see that Gal 2:10 was used by Chrysostom as an example not simply of a particular ecclesial polity or "church politics" (so Betz), restricted to gentile efforts on behalf of Jewish Jesus-followers in Jerusalem. Instead, for Chrysostom it came closer to being a feature of Christian identity.[21]

This is especially evident in Homily 4 of Chrysostom's *Homiliae in epistulam ad Philippenses*. There, Chrysostom gives no indication whatsoever that he understood "the poor" of Gal 2:10 to have referred in the first instance to Judean Jesus-followers in Paul's day. Instead, extolling the virtue of almsgiving as "a great, marvelous light," he says simply: "Much mention doth Paul, too, make of this mercy. In one place, hear him say, 'Only that we should remember the poor.'" Chrysostom adds two other passages from "Paul" to make the point: "And again, 'And let our people also learn to maintain good works' [Tit 3:14]. And again, 'These things are good and profitable unto men' [Tit 3:8]." In this context, Chrysostom shows how mercy, which

21. It is also important to note Chrysostom's assumption that the early Jesus-movement was united in its commitment to "remember the poor." In his *Hom. Act.* 14, when discussing the appointment of the deacons in Acts 6, Chrysostom notes that seven deacons were needed to take in the great sums of money that came to the community. The motivation for the money coming from within the community's own resources is found in Gal 2:10: "Only," it is said, "that we should remember the poor." In Chrysostom's view, remembrance of the poor is something that the Jerusalem community first bound itself to before binding Paul to the same (not surprisingly, in view of the narrative of Acts 2 and 4). This is clear from the sentence that follows immediately, which explains the manner of fund raising: "And how did they bring these [funds] forward? They fasted." Chrysostom does not say, "they charged the Apostle Paul to do it." Even in Chrysostom's reading of Gal 2:10, then, there is the recognition that the two missions are being yoked together in a common cause, even if the common cause included the poor among the Jesus-groups of Jerusalem in the first instance.

results in almsgiving, is an expression of the identity of true humanity and lies at the very heart of reality, the very heart of the creator: "For this is the true character of humanity, to be merciful, yea rather the character of God, to show mercy. . . . If you ask why such and such things are, you will always find your answer in Goodness." However he might have imagined the geographical specificity of "the poor" of Gal 2:10 in some of his other writings, in this Homily he links the passage to a more general principle of Christian lifestyle, using it to laud the virtue of Christian almsgiving in general. Here again we witness Chrysostom's departure from seeing Gal 2:10 as testifying simply to an incident of "church politics"; for Chrysostom, it seems more the case that concern for the communities of Jesus-followers in Jerusalem was a specific application of an essential feature of Christian character.

Much the same is evident also in Jerome's handling of Gal 2:10 outside of his commentary of Galatians. So in his letter "To Salvina" (*Epist.* 79; written c. 400 CE), Jerome discusses the advice of the author of 1 Tim 5:9-10 concerning care for widows under sixty years of age, where the advice is that young widows should not receive care from treasuries for the poor within communities of Jesus-followers but should, instead, seek to remarry. Fearful that the reader of that passage might find Paul to despise youth, Jerome points out two things: (1) elsewhere Paul is shown to treasure youth; and (2) in this particular passage, Paul is simply wanting the church to support those in real and poignant need, as opposed to less-pressing need. In making this second point, Jerome wants his audience to know that Paul had an entrenched concern for the poor in general. So he sets out an interpretation in which Paul's advice about widows in 1 Tim 5:9-10 is interpreted in relation to Paul's concern for the poor in general, as found in Gal 2:9-10. According to Jerome, Paul was intent on "making provision for people of all stations but especially for the poor, the charge of whom had been committed to himself and Barnabas." In this way, Jerome characterizes the phrase "remembering the poor" in Gal 2:10 as a general overarching principle that is shown to have particular and concrete expression in 1 Timothy in terms of care for widows within communities of Jesus-followers. Evidently Jerome did not think it to be a stretch of the imagination to characterize Paul and Barnabas as those who trained gentile churches to make "provision for people of all stations but especially for the poor."

While these observations are significant, they also might have the potential to undermine the case made above with regard to Tertullian, Origen, Athanasius and Aphrahat. If Jerome and Chrysostom thought that "remember the poor" of Gal 2:10 had a geographically-restricted referent in its first instance but also that it had a more general and universal applicability, perhaps the same was also true of Tertullian, Origen, Athanasius and Aphrahat. Perhaps what we observe in their handling of Gal 2:10 is simply the general or universal application of a text that they knew to be more restricted in its primary referent.

This possibility cannot be ruled out, but neither does it strike me as being probable, for several reasons. Tertullian's handling of Gal 2:10, for instance, appears in a highly polemical piece of writing, the fundamental issue being about whose reading of scripture (Tertullian's or Marcion's) is more legitimate. If a geographically-specific interpretation of Gal 2:10 was widespread in Tertullian's day, he would have known his case to be somewhat vulnerable since it bypasses the primary referent of Gal 2:10 — i.e., the Jerusalem church of the first generation of the Jesus-movement. To offset this vulnerability, Tertullian would have needed to register his interpretative reasoning more effectively, especially because his rhetorical situation is one of *denouncing* another person's view on the grounds of inadequate understanding of the biblical texts. In that rhetorical context, neglecting a primary meaning of Gal 2:10 would have weakened the effectiveness of his case considerably. That Tertullian makes no effort to discuss a Jerusalem-centric interpretation of Gal 2:10, then, suggests that Chrysostom and Jerome's "two-dimensional" interpretation of Gal 2:10 was not a rhetorical option for Tertullian. A Jerusalem-centric reading of Gal 2:10 must have been unknown to Tertullian and to his early third-century audience.

Moreover, as noted above, a Jerusalem referent for "the poor" in Gal 2:10 would have suited Tertullian's refutation of Marcion perfectly, since it would have been an easy rhetorical route whereby to eliminate Marcion's differentiation of Jerusalem and Paul. That Tertullian did not go down this route is not an indication of a missed opportunity on his part. Instead, we must surmise that Tertullian did not avail himself of this relatively unassailable strategy simply because it was not a live option for him; the view that "the poor" pertained in some manner to Jerusalem Jesus-followers was nonexistent in his day.

Further, if Gal 2:10 was known to include a reference to Jerusalem Jesus-followers in the third through mid-fourth centuries, it is somewhat curious that the six extant references to that verse during that time (once by Tertullian; once by Origen; three times by Athanasius; once by Aphrahat) fail to make reference to that fact.

A further factor that makes it unlikely that a Jerusalem referent is to be found in the phrase "the poor" is outlined in §7.2 below, where it will be argued that, in the second through mid-fourth centuries, the term "the poor (ones)" was never understood as a technical term that identified the Jerusalem-based Jesus-movement.

7.2: The Poor of Galatians 2:10 and the Ebionite Connection

We have seen that the earliest extant Christian literature is suggestive that "the poor" of Gal 2:10 was not thought to refer to Jerusalem Jesus-followers. This coheres perfectly with the data assembled by others with regard to how the term "the poor" was used in Christian discourse in the early centuries. In two major articles of the mid-1960s, for instance, Leander Keck forcefully combated a deep-seated view with regard to the Ebionites — i.e., Jewish Christians who came to bear the name "the poor ones" (Aramaic: אביוניא; Hebrew: האביונים), and who had a visible presence within the spectrum of Christianity from the second through the fourth centuries CE, dropping out of our view by the middle of the fifth century.[22] Prior to Keck's work, it was commonly asserted that these Jewish-Christian Ebionites or "poor ones" had consciously retained the self-designation of the earliest Jerusalem-based Jewish Christianity (or Christian Judaism). But Keck established that this view is fundamentally flawed. In a compelling argument, he demonstrates the following:

> [T]here is insufficient reason for thinking that the Ebionite literature, insofar as it is recoverable, reflects the continuous line between the Ebionites and the hypothetical group calling itself "the Poor" in primitive Christianity. . . . The link with the practice of the primitive church in sharing wealth came much later as an apologetic device and cannot be taken at face value.[23]

In 2003, Richard Bauckham confirmed Keck's earlier work, demonstrating that the claim to inherit the name of early Jerusalem Christianity (i.e.,

22. Leander E. Keck, "The Poor among the Saints in the New Testament," *ZNW* 56 (1965): 100-129; Keck, "The Poor among the Saints in Jewish Christianity and Qumran," *ZNW* 57 (1966): 54-78.

23. Keck, "The Poor among the Saints in Jewish Christianity and Qumran," pp. 64-66. The quotation continues: "Even if we were to follow Schoeps in saying that these Ebionites are the biological (!) [*sic*] descendants of the radical right wing of Jewish Christianity which Paul opposed, we need not say that their subsequent self-justification has historical merit or that their practices and theories represent the church before 70 A.D."

"the poor ones") may have been made by "later Ebionites" but it "was not the original significance of their name."[24] Bauckham and Keck argue persuasively that the origins of the name "Ebionite" lie in post-70 CE developments, involving "a sectarian, etiological exegesis of Acts promoted by the Ebionites in defense against the imperial church."[25] Consequently, the self-designation of the Ebionites has little value in determining the technical terms of the Jesus-movement in its first generation.[26]

Moreover, as Keck shows, of all the ancient historians of earliest Christianity, only Epiphanius of Salamis (d. 403), writing his *Panarion (Adversus haereses)* in 374-77 CE, suggests that the Ebionites explicitly claimed to be the inheritors of the name of the earliest Jesus-movement in Jerusalem (*Panar.* 30.17). The usual view within the literature of the early church fathers is that the Ebionites were the followers of a heretic named Ebion. The linking of the Ebionite name to Jerusalem Jesus-followers has no precedent in the extant discussion of the early Jesus-movement prior to Epiphanius, even when we would expect it to have arisen in the discourse of second- and third-century discussion of the early Jesus-movement and/or the Ebionites. So, for instance, in his account of the history of the Jerusalem church, the second-century historian Hegesippus (writing *c.* 165-75) never uses any special designation such as "the poor" when referring to the Jerusalem church, even when it would have perfectly fit his rhetorical purposes to do so.[27] The same is the case for

24. Richard J. Bauckham, "The Origin of the Ebionites," in Peter J. Tomson and Doris Lambers-Petry, eds., *The Image of the Judaeo-Christians in Ancient Jewish and Christian Literature* (Tübingen: Mohr Siebeck, 2003), pp. 162-81, especially p. 178.

25. Keck, "The Poor among the Saints in Jewish Christianity and Qumran," 59; Bauckham, "Origin of the Ebionites," pp. 178-81. So too Gildas Hamel, *Poverty and Charity in Roman Palestine, First Three Centuries C.E.* (Berkeley: University of California Press, 1990), p. 191: "There are problems with identifying these Ebionites with the πτωχοί of Rom 15.26 and Gal 2:10"; see further p. 191 n. 157.

26. Moreover, in his article "The Poor among the Saints in Jewish Christianity and Qumran," Keck demonstrated the extent to which religio-historical parallels have been overdrawn in relation to the early Jesus-groups in Jerusalem on the one hand and the Dead Sea community (and *Psalms of Solomon*; cf. Pss Sol 69:32; 72:2) on the other hand, so that the circumlocutionary use of "the poor" in first-century religious communities has been significantly overplayed in scholarship. The point continues to be overlooked; see, e.g., James D. G. Dunn, *Beginning from Jerusalem: Christianity in the Making*, vol. 2 (Grand Rapids: Eerdmans, 2009), p. 13, and p. 13 n. 54. But see Horsley, *Covenant Economics*, p. 144.

27. As Keck notes ("The Poor among the Saints in Jewish Christianity and Qumran," pp. 56-57): "[I]n the story of Domitian's interrogating the descendents of Jesus' family, Hegesippus refers to their extremely limited means: about 9,000 denarii in the land which they worked themselves (Euseb. *H.E.* III 20). Here would have been an obvious occasion to

figures like Justin Martyr (100-165), Irenaeus (130-202), Origen (185-254), and Eusebius (275-339), whose texts provide occasional counter-evidence to the view that Jerusalem Jesus-followers were known as "the poor."[28]

The findings of Keck and Bauckham provide the larger context into which can be fit the data assembled above regarding the interpretation of Gal 2:10 up to the late fourth century CE. That interpretations of Gal 2:10 in the earliest centuries CE show no trace of restricting "the poor" to Jerusalem Jesus-followers dovetails perfectly with the fact that the early church fathers never designated Jerusalem Jesus-followers as "the poor ones" prior to the late fourth century.

But this data establishes more than just an overarching context into which our findings on Gal 2:10 fit; it also helps to explain how late fourth- and early-fifth-century readers came to interpret "the poor" as having reference to the earliest Jesus-followers in Jerusalem. It is noteworthy, and arguably more than a simple coincidence, that the earliest extant identification of "the poor" of Gal 2:10 with Jerusalem Jesus-followers arises only in the second half of the fourth century and the early fifth century (in the works of Ephrem, Jerome and Chrysostom), who were writing in the wake of the spurious linking of Ebionism with early Jewish Jesus-followers in Jerusalem. While Epiphanius happened to articulate the link sometime between 374 and 377 CE (and it may have predated his articulation by a few decades), Jerome's Galatian commentary was written in 387 or so, Chrysostom's commentary was written no earlier than 395 CE, and his *Homilies on the Epistle to the Hebrews* were written late in his life and published only after his death in 407 CE. It is not difficult to imagine that the spurious linking of the Ebionite "poor ones" and the early Jesus-movement in Jerusalem arose in the middle of the fourth century or so,[29] and that once the link had been made, it then

---

say something about 'the Poor' or the Ebionites. Yet, there is no reference to either the idea or the practice of 'the Poor.' Instead, he reports that the family owned the land on which they paid taxes. Furthermore, when Hegesippus lists the seven heresies of the church, he does not include the Ebionites . . . , nor does he include them in his list of Jewish sects (*H.E.* IV 22). It appears, therefore, that . . . the silence of Hegesippus is not accidental: he does not know of any group which called itself 'the Poor' or 'the Ebionites.'"

28. So, for instance, Origen consistently claims that the name of the Ebionites denoted their *theological* poverty, due to their continuing observance of the law and their low view of Christ. Never does he entertain the notion that the Ebionites claimed that their name was inherited from the first Jerusalem Jesus-followers.

29. Whether or not this link was first made by Epiphanius is of no concern for our purposes. The point is that it is first testified to in the late fourth century in Epiphanius' work, and not before that date.

influenced Ephrem, Jerome and Chrysostom as they read Gal 2:10. Otherwise we must imagine it to be a mere coincidence that the six extant texts that deal with Gal 2:10 prior to the mid-fourth century show no cognizance of "the poor" being based in Jerusalem,[30] while the authors writing after the mid-fourth century imagine precisely that. In my estimate, the coincidence is less than likely.

7.3: The Ebionite Basis of the Contemporary Consensus

That "the poor" was considered to have a non-specific referent at least until the middle of the fourth century CE sets those early centuries in sharp contrast not only with interpreters like Ephrem, Jerome and Chrysostom, but also with the preponderance of historical-critical scholarship since the nineteenth century.[31] The view that "the poor" equals "the Jerusalem poor" is so entrenched in contemporary interpretation that it embodies the scholarly consensus — the interpretative paradigm that informs the discourse of the academic guild.

The long-standing basis on which this paradigm has been founded within New Testament scholarship is, arguably, the equation of the Ebionite name with that of the first followers of Jesus in Jerusalem. While other data are often presented in support of the "paradigmatic" consensus of modern New Testament scholarship, over the years the Ebionite argument has provided the primary foundation for that consensus. A quotation from the renowned historian Henry Chadwick shows how easily the equation can be asserted:

> The Jewish Christians [of the second through fourth centuries CE] called themselves Ebionites, a name derived from the Hebrew word meaning "the poor"; it was probably a conscious reminiscence of a very early term

---

30. Other than the texts examined here, there are no others that are relevant to the issue. This estimate is based on the data from two TLG searches, one in which πτωχός and μνημονεύω appear within five words of one another, and one in which μόνον, πτωχός and μνημονεύω appear within five words of one another. My thanks to David Beary for collecting the search data. Not relevant to our discussion are occurrences of πτωχός and μνημονεύω in fifth-century literature and beyond, and in texts that pre-date the fifth century in which close occurrences of πτωχός and μνημονεύω do not pertain to Gal 2:10. These include Eusebius, *Comm. Ps.* 23.809.24; Didymus Caecus, *Fr. Ps.* 62.13; Georgius Syceota, *Vita sancti Theodori Syceotae* 54.17 (although see n. 18 above).

31. I make no claims to the predominant form of interpretation in the years between Chrysostom and the rise of the historical-critical method.

which is attested by St Paul's letters as an almost technical name for the Christians in Jerusalem and Judea.[32]

Chadwick works from the supposition that the Ebionites are the inheritors and perpetuators of the self-designation or "technical name" of the earliest Jerusalem-based Jesus-followers.

This single supposition is frequently amplified in the works of New Testament scholars in any number of ways. The prolific and distinguished Martin Hengel articulates a common version of the basic paradigm when he interprets Gal 2:10 in this way:

> According to Paul, the only real "obligation" imposed by the Jerusalem community was that the two missionaries to the Gentiles should arrange a collection for the "poor" in Judaea among their mission communities. As there was a severe famine in Palestine in AD 47-49, we can see why this collection should be particularly necessary. However, . . . the "poor" are not simply the materially poor; what we have here is a religious title which the earliest community adopted and which is preserved in the later designation of the Palestinian Jewish Christians as "Ebionites."[33]

While this version of the paradigm is frequently replicated within the guild of New Testament scholarship, variations exist. Some would make adjustments to Hengel's formulation to take account of data in slightly different ways. But for those who might demur from the odd point here or there, there is no compelling need to abandon the general paradigm or interpretative network that Hengel articulates, only to tweak its application in subtle ways.[34] And at the heart of that paradigm lies a single point of consensus: the term "the poor" circulated among Jesus-followers in the mid-first cen-

---

32. H. Chadwick, *The Early Church* (Harmondsworth: Penguin, 1967), p. 23.

33. M. Hengel, *Acts and the History of Earliest Christianity* (trans. John Bowden; London: SCM, 1979), 118.

34. Bruce Chilton's interpretation is a case in point, for instance. Chilton imagines the poor to be indeed based in Jerusalem (as in the standard paradigm) but not necessarily followers of Jesus (unlike the standard paradigm); instead, they are simply those whose piety and devotion to Israel's deity is expressed according to Nazirite principles of worship in the Jerusalem temple. James himself may well have observed Nazirite vows, at least on occasion, and since the costs involved in observing Nazirite vows were not inconsequential, Gal 2:10 is read by Chilton as instituting a means of alleviating Nazirite costs for Jesus-followers and non-Jesus-followers alike. See Chilton's *Rabbi Paul: An Intellectual Biography* (New York: Doubleday, 2004), pp. 167-68, 218, 224.

tury CE as a "title" designating certain people who resided in Judea/Jerusalem.

This view seems almost to be passed down through the scholarly generations with barely a query as to its legitimacy, precisely on the basis of the presumed relevance of the Ebionite name. So, for instance, Ian J. Elmer can sew the matter up with ease as recently as 2009, when he discusses "the poor" in Gal 2:10 in this way:

> For M. Hengel this is not just the materially poor within the Jerusalem church, but a designation of the whole church. As evidence we note that later the Palestinian Jewish Christians were called Ebionites. . . . [I]t is entirely possible that a similar title emerged at Jerusalem to describe this first community of messianic Jesus people who pooled their resources and established a community in anticipation of the coming eschaton.[35]

The curious thing about such claims, as we have seen, is that there is no evidence throughout most of the first four centuries that "the poor" was ever remembered as being a title for Jerusalem followers of Jesus. Up until the second half of the fourth century CE, the early Jerusalem Jesus-followers were remembered by a variety of titles, but not by the term "the poor." The data, as argued especially by Keck and reinforced by Bauckham, has gone unappreciated in relation to the interpretative paradigm for Gal 2:10.[36]

---

35. Ian J. Elmer, *Paul, Jerusalem and the Judaisers: The Galatian Crisis in Its Broadest Historical Context* (Tübingen: Mohr Siebeck, 2009), p. 202. Notably, Elmer shows no cognizance of Keck's important articles.

36. Even Keck failed to pursue the implications of his work for the interpretation of Gal 2:10. In essence, Keck's work is driven by the question of whether the genitive τῶν ἁγίων in the phrase τοὺς πτωχοὺς τῶν ἁγίων τῶν ἐν Ἰερουσαλήμ at Rom 15:26 is an epexegetical genitive (i.e., "the poor, *that is*, the saints in Jerusalem") or whether it is a partitive genitive (i.e., "the poor *among* the saints in Jerusalem"), rightly supporting the latter (see his "The Poor among the Saints in the New Testament," p. 119). His articles do not press the reading of the Galatian letter, however, with Keck imagining on the basis of 1 Cor 16:1 that the first readers of Gal 2:10 had already been informed by Paul that "the poor" of that verse were based in Jerusalem (p. 122). While this is possible, it is not likely. As M. P. Miller notes ("Antioch, Paul and Jerusalem: Diaspora Myths of Origins," in R. Cameron and M. P. Miller, eds., *Redescribing Christian Origins* [Atlanta: Society of Biblical Literature, 2004], 177-236, p. 224), "despite lengthy passages in the Corinthian correspondence that concern the collection, Paul never indicates that he is making good on a commitment he made in Jerusalem. Thus there is at least no indication that Paul has explained the reason for this project in his churches by a reference to a prior agreement." The same is likely to be true for the Galatian communities as well.

Nonetheless, there are signs that some scholars are uneasy about being too reliant on the traditional Ebionite argument, as will now be noted.

7.4: Argumentational Adjustment within the Contemporary Consensus

Keck's case unsettles what might be thought of as the otherwise secure foundations upon which the established paradigm for interpreting Gal 2:10 has rested. For the most part, Pauline scholarship has failed to take on board the full implications of Keck's work. But there are instances in which scholars side-step the Ebionite foundations of the established paradigm while keeping that paradigm intact. In this section, the work of four prominent interpreters will be used to demonstrate the point: John Dominic Crossan, Dieter Georgi, Jerome Murphy-O'Connor and John Knox. No attempt is made here to outline the "state of the question," or the history of interpretation on Gal 2:10. Instead, our purpose is simply to observe how four influential scholars attempt to maintain a Jerusalem-centric view of "the poor" without having to rely on the traditional argument about the name of the Ebionites in relation to early followers of Jesus in Jerusalem, and to assess the strength of their argumentation accordingly.

When considering the referent of the term "the poor" in Gal 2:10, John Dominic Crossan writes:

> [Regarding "remember the poor" in Gal 2:10,] it is *clear* from other texts that money from Christian pagan communities was to be collected for the benefit of the Christian Jewish community of Jerusalem. That's the easy part. The *difficult* part is whether this was simple poor-relief . . . or whether it was intended to support the Jerusalem community itself under the theologically charged name of the Poor Ones. If we are speaking only of poor-relief, why should the poor of Jerusalem take precedence over the poor of Antioch, Ephesus, Philippi, Corinth, or another Christian pagan community? Why would the Christian poor of Jerusalem be in any worse straits than the Christian poor of any other city? I am inclined, therefore, to consider that the collection was primarily for the Jerusalem community itself and that they called themselves the Poor Ones.[37]

37. John Dominic Crossan, *The Birth of Christianity* (Edinburgh: T&T Clark, 1998), p. 474, emphasis added.

The reasoning is suspect.[38] As will be discussed below (§8.1), equating Gal 2:10 with Paul's later collection without remainder has its deficits. But that issue aside, for our purposes it is enough to notice that Crossan's case is sufficiently weak, in that the argumentation seems devised to support an already-adopted conclusion that the early followers of Jesus in Jerusalem "called themselves the Poor Ones."

The heart of the problem lies in Crossan's question "why should the poor of Jerusalem take precedence over the poor elsewhere?" This formulation of the issue operates on the simple assumption that Paul's collection for "the poor among the saints in Jerusalem" was motivated solely on the basis of alleviating poverty. There can be no doubt that alleviating poverty was, in fact, a notable feature of Paul's collection efforts.[39] But that collection also had *symbolic* value for Paul in a way that Crossan's reductionist formulation fails to allow. Without denying that there was real need within Jerusalem communities of Jesus-followers, and without denying that the collection was partly driven by Paul's concern to alleviate poverty, the collection would nonetheless have also served a highly symbolic role, highlighting the fundamental unity among communities of Jesus-followers, whether they be primarily of gentile constituency and far-flung throughout the Mediterranean basin on the one hand,[40] or primarily of Jewish constituency and based in Jerusalem on the other hand (including, no doubt, all other options intervening between these two descriptors).[41] Moreover, the collection would also have included a strong symbolic gesture with regard to Paul's own success as an apostle among the gentiles, something that seems to have been under review at key moments among some Jesus-followers in Jerusalem. Fur-

---

38. It is even more suspect in John Dominic Crossan and Jonathan L. Reed, *In Search of Paul: How Jesus's Apostle Opposed Rome's Empire with God's Kingdom* (San Francisco: HarperSanFrancisco, 2004), p. 397, where the claim is made that since the Jerusalem Jesus-followers "practiced community life with regard to their possessions, . . . [t]hey were known, therefore, as the Poor Ones."

39. This point will be highlighted in §13.3 below.

40. I take it that most of the distinctively Jesus-groups founded by Paul were primarily of this order, although there would have been some Jewish presence in some of those Jesus-groups.

41. J. Louis Martyn (*Theological Issues in the Letters of Paul* [Edinburgh: T&T Clark, 1997], p. 41) writes: "the collection was Paul's crucial witness to the grand unity of the church of God in the whole of the world." Although Crossan neglects this feature of Paul's collection efforts in his *Birth of Christianity*, he highlights it in John Dominic Crossan and Jonathan L. Reed, *In Search of Paul: How Jesus's Apostle Opposed Rome's Empire with God's Kingdom* (San Francisco: HarperSanFrancisco, 2004), pp. 397-400.

ther, the rationale for his ministry that Paul expressed in Romans might well have helped motivate Paul's collection efforts — i.e., to provoke unbelieving Israel to belief through envy of the grace that Israel's deity is bestowing on the gentiles (Rom 10:19; 11:11, 14). Perhaps Paul hoped that a collection from gentiles to assist Jerusalemites would send strong signals to Jews at the heart of mainstream Judaism (and not merely to Jewish Jesus-followers) that the glorious eschaton had already begun to dawn — signals that would have been significantly muted if the collection had been delivered to a location other than Jerusalem itself.

These pragmatic and symbolic ingredients of Paul's collection pertain exclusively to the community of Jewish Jesus-followers based in Jerusalem, so that Crossan's "either-or" formulation of the issue is wrong-headed from the start. Both parts of Crossan's "either-or" turn out to be misguided: Paul's collection efforts were not motivated solely by a concern to relieve poverty,[42] but neither were the Jerusalem Jesus-followers known as "the poor." Whatever merit Crossan's formulation might have derives from the fact that his conclusion supports the consensus paradigm; apart from that paradigm, the reasoning about what is "clear" and what is "difficult" is recognizable as begging the very question that it seeks to answer.

Dieter Georgi provides a second example of a modern scholar supporting a paradigmatic interpretation of "the poor" without relying explicitly on the Ebionite argument. He writes: "The absolute use of this appellation ['the poor'] in Galatians 2:10 and the fact that it does not need any explanation show that it must have been a title commonly bestowed upon that congregation" of Jerusalem Jesus-followers.[43]

But Georgi's conclusion simply begs the question. He sets up the problem in such a fashion that it seems to contain within itself the seeds of its own solution. Georgi fails to question whether Paul's use of "the poor" is, in fact, an "absolute use of this appellation." His point that the phrase "does not need any explanation" and therefore "must have been a title" is simply tautologous reasoning; Georgi's assumption that an explanation of the term "the poor" would have been unnecessary already presumes that the term cannot refer to the indigenous poor in a general sense. In this rhetorical house of cards, the only way out is to conclude that "the poor" had titular

---

42. So Hurtado ("The Jerusalem Collection," p. 48): "the offering meant more than relief for the poor."

43. Dieter Georgi, *Remembering the Poor: The History of Paul's Collection for Jerusalem* (Nashville: Abingdon, 1992), p. 34.

currency among the earliest Jesus-followers. The flaw in the reasoning is presumably invisible to Georgi, perhaps because his argument was wholly in line with the paradigmatic consensus; if the argumentation provides a conclusion that coheres with the consensus view, then the argumentation must be right. But this puts the cart before the horse. If the argumentation is wrong, then the consensus may well be suspect. Clearly Georgi's straightforward argumentation sits well within an established paradigm of interpretation, but it needs to be recognized for what it is: a form of reasoning whose inadequacies are invisible to its author due to the power of the interpretative paradigm that it pretends to support but which, in fact, supports it.

When Jerome Murphy-O'Connor first considers Gal 2:10 in depth in his *Paul: A Critical Life,* he gets off to a promising start. He notes his dissatisfaction with those who give technical meaning to the phrase οἱ πτωχοί and who translate it with capital letters, as "The Poor." Moreover, he cites with disapproval Georgi's claim that the Jerusalem agreement "stipulated that the Gentile Jesus believers were to give recognition to the exemplary performance on the part of their fellow believers in Jerusalem."[44] Further, he goes on to note the following:

> With the exception of the Christological statement in 2 Corinthians 8:9, Paul always uses "poor" (2 Cor. 6:10; Gal. 4:9) and "poverty" (2 Cor. 8:2) in their natural material sense. The socio-economic meaning is confirmed by his reference to "the poor among the saints in Jerusalem" (Rom. 15:26), where it is most improbable that the genitive is anything but partitive.[45]

So far, so good. We are on track here to read Gal 2:10 with fresh eyes, without restricting "the poor" to the Jerusalem community. But things start to go wrong in Murphy-O'Connor's next sentence: "The natural reading is that some believers were in need." His reference to "believers" is coupled in the next sentence with discussion about "the community," and then to a discussion of the "social conditions in Jerusalem in the first century." Whatever potential there was to read Gal 2:10 in fresh light has been abandoned, by way of compliance with the established but untested paradigm. Argumentation is absent, and assertion fills its place. Assertion can look scholarly when it conforms to paradigmatic givens, but it is assertion nonetheless.

Something similar is evident in the work of John Knox. He adopts the

---

44. Jerome Murphy-O'Connor, *Paul: A Critical Life* (Oxford: Oxford University Press, 1996), p. 144, citing Georgi, *Remembering the Poor,* p. 38.

45. Murphy-O'Connor, *Paul: A Critical Life,* p. 144.

consensus paradigm when he interprets Gal 2:10 as being the occasion when the Jerusalem leaders stipulated "that Paul and his churches should 'remember the poor' *(obviously the poor of the Jerusalem church)."*[46] Why this inference should be so "obvious" to Knox is unclear, precisely since Knox offers no explicit justification for it. If Knox ever provides a defense of his claim, it is in the following sentences:[47]

> There are three, and only three, ways in which this stipulation [to remember the poor] can be understood. (a) The first is as a reference to a regular, more or less constant, effort on Paul's part to raise and send money to Jerusalem, which he is now asked to continue and which he expresses himself as eager to do. (b) The second is as a reference to some special collection for Jerusalem that antedates the offering being raised in the period of the Corinthians letters. (c) The third is as a reference to this offering [i.e., the collection referred to in the Corinthian and Roman letters on behalf of the Jerusalem community]. There are no other alternatives.

The claim that "there are no other alternatives" might well strike a skeptical reader as odd, since in the very next paragraph Knox writes the following: "There is, of course, plenty of evidence in Paul's letters that the churches were expected to care for their poor" — i.e., the indigenous poor.[48] If Knox is of this view, then why is this practice of caring for the localized poor not even raised as a possible category for interpreting the identity of "the poor" mentioned in Gal 2:10? Knox's assumption that the stipulation of Gal 2:10 was "obviously [for] the poor of the Jerusalem church" seems to have resulted in a blind-spot in Knox's analysis. The assumption that "the poor" in Gal 2:10 refers to followers of Jesus *in Jerusalem* has ruled out a whole category of interpretation, even though that assumption has never been given an evidential basis other than that it is "obvious." Basing an interpretation on its being self-evident is not good practice unless, of course, one's discipline permits it within the givens of its "paradigmatic" discourse. In Knox's case, the word "obviously" seems to stand guard in defense of an assumption that has simply gone unchallenged in the discipline of New Testament studies.

46. J. Knox, *Chapters in a Life of Paul*, rev. ed. (London: SCM Press, 1987), p. 37, emphasis added.

47. Knox, *Chapters in a Life of Paul*, pp. 37-38.

48. Knox, *Chapters in a Life of Paul*, p. 38.

7.5: Conclusions

Six texts from Tertullian, Origen, Athanasius and Aphrahat suggest that, at least until the middle of the fourth century, "the poor" of Gal 2:10 was not thought to refer to members of the early Jesus-movement in Jerusalem. By the middle of the fourth century, this had begun to changed, as testified to by Ephrem, Jerome and John Chrysostom. But we have seen reason to believe that this later interpretation of the verse may have resulted from the unfounded view that the Ebionite "poor ones" had retained the name of the earliest Jerusalem Jesus-followers — a view that initially emerged about the same period.

Of course, it might be that the earliest extant consensus on the identity of "the poor" in Gal 2:10 (as testified to by Tertullian, Origen, Athanasius, and Aphrahat) was ill-founded and should defer to the consensus that replaced it (as early as the second half of the fourth century). Clearly, when judged in strict historical-critical terms, early interpreters often got things wrong in their understanding of texts, and the same might be true of the interpretation of "the poor" represented by Tertullian.[49] But for this to be the case, we must imagine that the term "the poor" had initially designated (a part of) the community of Jewish Jesus-followers in Jerusalem, that the designation had quickly lost its geographical specificity, and that it continued to bear a non-specific application until its original specificity was reintroduced in the late fourth century through a spurious connection made in the final half of that century.

It is far simpler, however, to imagine that "the poor" of Gal 2:10 was ubiquitously interpreted throughout the earliest centuries without geographical specificity for good reason, and that the specious linkage of the Ebionite name with the earliest communities of Jesus-followers in Jerusalem has thereby had a disproportionate and misleading effect on the interpretation of that verse ever since. The modern guild of New Testament scholarship seems also to have been under the heavy influence of Epiphanius' specious linkage. Estimates about "the poor" of Gal 2:10 being "undisputedly" and "obviously" and "certainly" based in Jerusalem are usually founded on the conviction that "the poor" was "a religious title which the earliest com-

---

49. For instance, Tertullian's tendency to remove Barnabas from the socio-religious dynamics of Gal 2:9-10 is obviously not a live exegetical option for historical reconstruction. But neither is that feature of Tertullian's interpretation foundational for his view that "the poor" has a general rather than specific referent.

munity adopted and which is preserved in the later designation of the Palestinian Jewish Christians as 'Ebionites.'"[50] Unfortunately there is no trace of this view within the literary record of the first centuries.

It is arguable, then, that, in contrast to the current "undisputed," "obvious" and "certain" consensus of New Testament scholarship, the earliest consensus is founded on a better interpretative premise, precisely because it is unaffected (and uninfected) by the historically illegitimate view that the Ebionites perpetuated the self-designation of early Jewish Jesus-followers based in Jerusalem. If some New Testament interpreters sit lightly to the view that the Ebionites inherited and promulgated the name of the first followers of Jesus in Jerusalem, they continue to show their commitment to the view that those first Jewish Jesus-followers (or sectors within their communities) were known as "the poor." Commitment to that view is evidenced by the manner in which, when interpreting Gal 2:10, interpreters continue to construct system-dependent argumentation or fail to consider all the interpretative options with regard to the term "the poor." Such examples represent attempts to retain the paradigmatic consensus by taking paths around its data anomalies. As if cognizant that the paradigm's foundations are weak, interpreters devise forms of argumentation that skirt around those insecure foundations in efforts to bolster the dubious consensus, but only to advance other forms of highly questionable argumentation in the process.

Instead of continuing to bolster the current scholarly consensus, the way forward is precisely to abandon that consensus and, instead, to work towards a fresh interpretation of the text. To this end, I propose that the earliest paradigm for interpreting Gal 2:10 commends itself notably — that "remember the poor" demarcates caring for the poor without geographical restriction or specificity.[51] It is time to reconsider the structure, the rhetorical force and the theological implications of Gal 2:6-10 in an interpretative paradigm that shows closer affinity to the paradigm of the early church fathers. That will be the goal of the next chapter.

---

50. Hengel, *Acts and the History of Earliest Christianity,* p. 118.

51. So Nicholas Perrin ("Introduction," in Mark Goodacre and Nicholas Perrin, eds., *Questioning Q* [London: SPCK, 2004], 1-12, p. 12): "Sometimes the best step on the path of truth is not a step forward, but a step back" — in this case, a significant step back.

CHAPTER 8

"They added nothing"

The Poor in the Mission of the Early Jesus-movement

It has been argued above that New Testament scholarship is overly reliant on a questionable interpretative framework in its understanding of "the poor" in Gal 2:10, and that an alternative framework of understanding is operative in the earliest stages in the reception history of that verse (from the early third through mid-fourth centuries). To that end, the paragraphs that follow will seek to construct a positive case for interpreting the text of Gal 2:1-10 in a manner that is not indebted to the paradigm that is currently thought to be indisputable.

Four exegetical considerations are entertained in this chapter which interlock to suggest that "the poor" of Gal 2:10 is a reference to the needy who were indigenous to the geographical areas that Paul's gentile mission was to infiltrate. Initially, however, it is important to address an issue that is often deeply entangled with discussion of the identity of the poor of Gal 2:10: that is, the relation of that verse to Paul's collection for "the poor among the saints in Jerusalem."

8.1: Paul's Collection and Galatians 2:10

As with Jerome and Chrysostom, so also in contemporary scholarship an identification is often made between Paul's collection in 53-57 CE and the stipulation (of 48 CE?) to "remember the poor" in Gal 2:10. The argument is straightforward: if 2:10 stipulates a remembrance of "the Jerusalem poor," and if Paul's collection was for "the poor among the saints in Jerusalem" (Rom 15:26),[1] it must simply be the case that Paul's collection efforts are, without remainder, in direct response to the stipulation cited in Gal 2:10.[2] So, for instance, Nils Dahl claims the following:

> The economic need of the Jerusalem church was a fundamental presup-position underlying the project [i.e., Paul's collection for the Jerusalem saints]. But this is not the element which weighed most heavily on Paul. More important for Paul was that the collection was an obligation which he had assumed [i.e., which he had taken onto himself]. . . . Paul and Bar-nabas had promised to "remember the poor" (Gal. 2:10). The fulfillment of this promise symbolized for Paul a ratification of the unity between Jewish and Gentile Christians.[3]

Similarly Lloyd Gaston writes: "According to Paul, the idea of the collection from his Gentile churches for the Jerusalem church came about by mutual agreement," referring the reader to Paul's text in Gal 2:10.[4] David Catchpole asserts that Gal 2:10 "makes perfect sense in its context as a reference solely to the collection."[5] Larry Hurtado thinks it "well known that the Jerusalem collection is mentioned in Gal 2:10."[6] Ian Elmer makes the point confidently:

---

1. In Rom 15:26, the genitive τῶν ἁγίων most likely has a partitive sense, not an epexegetical sense, in the phrase τοὺς πτωχοὺς τῶν ἁγίων τῶν ἐν Ἰερουσαλήμ (contra H. Schlier, *Der Römerbrief* [Freiburg: Herder, 1977], p. 436).

2. See, for instance, Stephan Joubert, *Paul as Benefactor: Reciprocity, Strategy and Theological Reflection in Paul's Collection* (Tübingen: Mohr Siebeck, 2000), pp. 73-115; Michael Goulder, "A Poor Man's Christology," *NTS* 45 (1999): 332-48, p. 333; Timothy J. M. Ling, *The Judaean Poor and the Fourth Gospel* (Cambridge: Cambridge University Press, 2006), p. 138.

3. Nils Dahl, *Studies in Paul* (Minneapolis: Fortress Press, 1977), p. 31.

4. Lloyd Gaston, "Paul and Jerusalem," in P. Richardson and J. C. Hurd, eds., *From Jesus to Paul* (Waterloo: Wilfrid Laurier University Press, 1984), 61-72, p. 65.

5. David R. Catchpole, "Paul, James and the Apostolic Decree," *NTS* 23 (1977): 428-44, p. 433. See also Douglas A. Campbell, *The Deliverance of God: An Apocalyptic Rereading of Justification in Paul* (Grand Rapids: Eerdmans, 2009), p. 142 n. 8.

6. Larry W. Hurtado, "The Jerusalem Collection and the Book of Galatians," *JSNT* 5 (1979): 46-62, p. 50.

"[T]he instigation of [Paul's] collection was at the request of the Pillars [*sic*] Apostles of Jerusalem 'to remember the poor.' . . . Galatians 2:10 explicitly attributes the institution of the collection to the Pillar apostles."[7] Richard Horsley maintains that Paul's collection "evidently originated in the 'apostolic council' (Gal. 2:1-10; cf. Acts 15:6-41)."[8] And Barry Gordon claims that "[a]s a result of this pledge [to remember the poor], Paul was to divert a deal of his time and energy to raising money for 'the saints' in Jerusalem" — an undertaking that, according to Gordon, was intended "to help sustain the faltering [economic] experiment" that the Jerusalem communities had set in motion (and an undertaking that for Paul constituted an "irksome diversion" from what he should have been doing).[9]

Similar estimates could be extensively reproduced. In fact, whole theses have been built on this identification of the stipulation of Gal 2:10 and Paul's subsequent collection, an identification that is usually not defended in much depth, evidently because interpreters imagine that it can be assumed, that it is "well known," or it "makes perfect sense."[10]

---

7. Ian J. Elmer, *Paul, Jerusalem and the Judaisers: The Galatian Crisis in Its Broadest Historical Context* (Tübingen: Mohr Siebeck, 2009), pp. 202-203.

8. Richard A. Horsley, *Covenant Economics: A Biblical Vision of Justice for All* (Louisville: Westminster John Knox Press, 2009), p. 143.

9. Barry Gordon, *The Economic Problem in Biblical and Patristic Thought* (Leiden: Brill, 1989), p. 78.

10. For instance, David Trobisch (*Paul's Letter Collection: Tracing the Origins* [Minneapolis: Fortress Press, 1994], p. 70) mounts an interesting (but ultimately unconvincing) thesis about "Paul's Letter Collection," which lashes together Romans, 1 and 2 Corinthians, and Galatians as a single and early letter collection assembled by Paul himself, their unifying feature being the issue of the collection for the saints in Jerusalem (see also his earlier and more extensive book, *Die Entstehung der Paulusbriefsammlung: Studien zu den Anfängen christlicher Publizistik* [Göttingen: Vandenhoeck & Ruprecht, 1989]). The whole of the thesis relies on Gal 2:10 pertaining to the collection. Trobisch articulates things in this way: "The collection for the poor in Jerusalem is mentioned in Galatians at a crucial point. In the conflict between Paul and the Jerusalem apostles, Paul presents the collection as the only requirement he was asked to follow: 'All they asked was that we should continue to remember the poor . . .' (Gal 2:10). And he readily agrees." I discuss some deficits of Trobisch's position at the start of chapter 9 below.

If the identification of "remember the poor" with Paul's collection is problematized, so too are chronologies of Paul's life that depend on linking the collection project with sabbatical years, with the collection's initial request and the later delivery both falling in sabbatical years. Chronological attempts of this sort can be found in J. Jeremias, "Sabbathjahr und neutestamentliche Chronologie," in his *Abba: Studien zur neutestamentlichen Chronologie und Zeitgeschichte* (Göttingen: Vandenhoeck & Ruprecht, 1966), 233-38, p. 236; A. Suhl, "Der Beginn der selbständigen Mission des Paulus," *NTS* 38 (1992): 430-47.

Not all are convinced that the commonplace of identifying Paul's collection efforts with Gal 2:10 is justified, however. In Paul's discussion of his collection (1 Cor 16:1-4; 2 Cor 8–9; Rom 15:25-33), donations by Jesus-followers are consistently depicted as voluntary expressions of divine grace for other needy Jesus-followers, rather than gestures required of gentile Jesus-followers as a result of a stipulation from the late 40s. As Leander Keck pointed out, in none of the relevant passages is there the appearance of a "fixed, technical terminology for the money itself, as would be the case if the fund were a contractual *sine qua non* for Paul's standing in the 'ecumenical' church."[11] The paucity of that "fixed, technical terminology" within Paul's letters inspires reservation as to the frequently-postulated connection between Gal 2:10 and Paul's later collection. As A. J. M. Wedderburn argues:

> nowhere in all his explicit mentions of the collection (if one does not count Gal 2.10 as such) does Paul connect the project with the carrying out of an agreement reached between himself and the Jerusalem church; nothing suggests that in the raising of the collection he saw himself as carrying out his side of that particular bargain.[12]

Furthermore, as David Downs points out, "it is very difficult to explain Paul's trepidation about the possibility of Jerusalem's rejection of his efforts in Rom 15:30-31 if, in fact, he is doing nothing more than fulfilling an accord previously established with the Jerusalem leadership."[13]

11. Leander E. Keck, "The Poor among the Saints in the New Testament," *ZNW* 56 (1965): 100-129, p. 129.

12. A. J. M. Wedderburn, "Paul's Collection: Chronology and History," *NTS* 48 (2002): 95-110, p. 99. Similarly, James D. G. Dunn assesses the relationship between Gal 2:10 and Paul's collection of the mid-50s in this way (*The Theology of Paul the Apostle* [Grand Rapids: Eerdmans, 1998], p. 706 n. 170): "Gal. 2:10 is unlikely to refer to the collection as such; the references to the collection elsewhere have a similarity in language and tone which is not shared by Gal. 2.10. The collection is more likely to have been conceived by Paul as an attempt to bridge the gulf which evidently opened up between his mission and the Jerusalem or Judean churches following his failure at Antioch (Gal. 2.11-14). That the agreement mentioned in Gal. 2.10 was part of the stimulus to the collection, however, is more than likely; that he should "remember the poor" was the original request of the Jerusalem apostles; that the collection was specifically "for the poor of the saints who are in Jerusalem" was Paul's own intention [sic; perhaps also "invention"] (Rom. 15.26)." The position is reiterated in his *Beginning from Jerusalem: Christianity in the Making,* vol. 2 (Grand Rapids: Eerdmans, 2009), pp. 933-35.

13. David J. Downs, *The Offering of the Gentiles* (Tübingen: Mohr Siebeck, 2008), pp. 35-36. The point is not conclusive in itself, but strongly favors the position advocated by Wedderburn and others.

Consequently, some have postulated that a series of stages marked out Paul's relationship to the stipulation of Gal 2:10. Initially that stipulation bound the Antiochene communities to "remember the Jerusalem poor," but then, once Paul broke from the Antiochene fold (so Gal 2:11-14), he was released from the duty recounted in Gal 2:10. This shift in Paul's responsibility might well account for the terminological differences between Gal 2:10 and Paul's own references to his collection. According to Wedderburn, for instance, we should separate "the agreement of Gal 2.10 with the Antioch church from Paul's eventual collection project . . . [because] what Paul eventually organized was not a direct response to the agreement, but was initiated on a different basis and for rather different reasons."[14] This is laudable reasoning, but it is also reasoning based on the paradigmatic assumption that the poor of Gal 2:10 were based in Jerusalem. Once that assumption is problematized, more needs to be done to conceptualize the relationship between Gal 2:10 and Paul's collection.

To that end, it is enough here to suggest how Gal 2:10 and Paul's collection relate in a frame of reference that includes no geographical specificity within the term "the poor." Notable in that regard is the way that Paul differentiates the collection for the Jerusalem "saints" from caring for all in general, as in 2 Cor 9:13, where he speaks of "your contribution for them (i.e., Jerusalem Jesus-followers) and for all (others)." This suggests that the collection was probably seen by Paul to be a single application of the more general principle of caring for the poor, and perhaps even as one of the most important manifestations of that principle.[15] But while the mid 50s saw Paul engaged in a collection for the Jerusalem poor, there is no compelling reason to imagine that the same group must have been in view in the late 40s when Paul was in discussion with Jerusalem leaders. Interpreting "the poor" of Gal 2:10 without reference to Jerusalem would align that stipulation and Paul's later collection efforts in the same fashion as a species (i.e., the indigenous poor in any location; Gal 2:10) is related to a sub-species (i.e., the Jerusalem poor; Rom 15:26).

This is not to suggest that Paul imagined the "sub-species" to be necessarily distinct from its overarching "species." This is clear from the way that

14. Wedderburn, "Paul's Collection," p. 100.

15. Consequently, I am reluctant to agree with M. P. Miller when he suggests that "[i]t is difficult to see any close relationship between the request in Gal 2:10a and the collection initiated by Paul in his churches" ("Antioch, Paul and Jerusalem: Diaspora Myths of Origins," in R. Cameron and M. P. Miller, eds., *Redescribing Christian Origins* [Atlanta: Society of Biblical Literature, 2004], 177-36, p. 224).

he can apply favored theological terms to the collection that pertain just as much to the gospel itself. If remembering the poor has a rightful place within the all-encompassing "truth of the gospel,"[16] it is not surprising that Paul can portray the Jerusalem collection in similar terms. Again 2 Cor 9:13 is notable, since Paul speaks there of Corinthian involvement in his collection effort as demonstrating their glorification of Israel's deity "by your obedience to the confession of the gospel of Christ" (ἐπὶ τῇ ὑποταγῇ τῆς ὁμολογίας ὑμῶν εἰς τὸ εὐαγγέλιον τοῦ Χριστοῦ). Alongside "obedience," "confession," and "gospel," other favored terms appear in Paul's discussion of the collection in 2 Corinthians 8-9, including: "grace" (χάρις; 8:1, 6-7, 9, 19; 9:8, 14); "service" (διακονία, 8:4; 9:1, 12, 13); "fellowship" (κοινωνία; 8:4; 9:13); and "righteousness" (δικαιοσύνη, 9:9-10) — both the righteousness of Israel's deity and of those who would be obedient to him. For Paul, the collection itself was intricately associated with the very gospel that he proclaimed, a gospel about the righteousness of Israel's deity that sets the world to order through the righteous lives of his devotees.[17]

For reasons of both exegetical and conceptual clarity, however, it is important to differentiate between remembrance of the poor and the collection effort, with remembrance of the poor being the general marker of identity within communities of Jesus-followers (as proposed below; see also chapter 6 above) and the collection for the Jerusalem poor being a specific application of that principle.

Without recognizing the distinction between the two phenomena, errors can all too easily creep into our understanding of Paul and his texts. For instance, as was shown in chapter 1 above, Peter Davids contrasts Paul's view of "charity" with that of the author of James: for the Jacobite author, charity is essential to a life of faithfulness before Israel's deity; for Paul, on the other hand, charity is optional.[18] But as was shown, Davids builds his case on the assumption that Paul's view of "charity" is reducible to, and exhausted by, Paul's view of the collection. But if the simple equating of Gal 2:10 with

---

16. Paul depicts the flip side of the coin in 1 Cor 11:17-34, where getting the economic dimension of the Lord's Supper wrong results in the actual dissolution of the Lord's Supper (11:20), and in bringing judgment down upon oneself (11:29-30), not least because it runs contrary to the community's corporate proclamation of the full meaning of "the Lord's death." See §6.2 above.

17. See further, Dunn, *Beginning from Jerusalem*, pp. 940-44.

18. Peter H. Davids, "The Test of Wealth," in B. Chilton and C. Evans, eds., *The Missions of James, Peter and Paul: Tensions in Early Christianity* (Leiden: Brill, 2005), 355-84, pp. 369-70.

Paul's collection is problematized, then estimates about Paul's view of economic generosity will be skewed when informed primarily or exclusively by Paul's collection texts.

8.2: Galatians 2:10 in Its Close Rhetorical Context

As we have seen, within the flow of Gal 2:1-10, Gal 2:10 is often thought to be "supplementary, unrelated to the main points of the debate" at Jerusalem.[19] To make this claim, however, commentators often have to sit lightly to the function of the word μόνον at the start of 2:10 — usually translated "only" or "except." Hans Dieter Betz claims that the word μόνον "separates the following [verse — i.e., 2:10] from the preceding matter under discussion."[20] It is arguable, however, that the word μόνον does precisely the opposite. Rather than separating 2:10 from 2:6-9, the word "except" connects 2:10 with Paul's claim of 2:6 that the pillar apostles "added nothing" (οὐδὲν προσανέθεντο).[21] That claim in 2:6 modifies two previous references: the closest being in 2:5, where Paul speaks of "the truth of the gospel" (ἡ ἀλήθεια τοῦ εὐαγγελίου), and the furthest being in 2:2 where he speaks of "the gospel that I preach among the Gentiles" (τὸ εὐαγγέλιον ὃ κηρύσσω ἐν τοῖς ἔθνεσιν).[22]

From 2:2 through to 2:10, then, Paul has constructed a discursive web in which the phrase "remember the poor" in 2:10 is expected to be heard within

19. Hans Dieter Betz, *Galatians* (Philadelphia: Fortress Press, 1979), p. 101.

20. Betz, *Galatians*, p. 101.

21. The ἵνα of Gal 2:10 serves to mark an explanatory clause (cf. Johannes P. Louw and Eugene A. Nida, *Greek-English Lexicon of the New Testament Based on Semantic Domains* [New York: United Bible Society, 1988, 1989], §91.15); cf. Matt 5:29; John 15:13. Accordingly, it differs from the purpose clause introduced by ἵνα in Gal 2:9.

22. F. Vouda (*An die Galater* [Tübingen: Mohr Siebeck, 1998], pp. 49-50) asserts that 2:10 does not, in fact, extend the sentence begun in 2:6, but amplifies the main verb of 2:9 (ἔδωκαν), just as the ἵνα-clause of 2:9 does. This interpretation founders on the single word μόνον of 2:10, which Vouda does not seem able to explain in his structuring of the verses. The same claim and weakness are found in B.-M. Kim, *Die paulinische Kollekte* (Tübingen: A. Francke Verlag, 2002), p. 148. I imagine that they are taking the μόνον . . . ἵνα construction in the phrase μόνον τῶν πτωχῶν ἵνα μνημονεύωμεν of Gal 2:10 as comparable to the μόνον ἵνα construction (i.e., "solely in order that") in the phrase μόνον ἵνα τῷ σταυρῷ τοῦ Χριστοῦ μὴ διώκωνται of Gal 6:12. If these constructions are thought to be comparable, then Gal 2:10 could be interpreted as suggesting that the Jerusalem leaders extended the right hand of fellowship to Paul and Barnabas "solely in order that we might remember the poor." In my view, this reconstruction is extremely unlikely, regardless of whether "the poor" are Jerusalem Jesus-followers or not.

the overarching parameters of apostolic efforts to tease out the full implications of the gospel. In Paul's reconstruction of the late-40s meeting, the Jerusalem leadership is depicted as uncompromising in its view that "remembering the poor" is not to be discarded in Paul's mission to the gentiles.[23] On the contrary, remembering the poor is to be an essential feature of that mission to spread the gospel, not least among the gentiles.

8.3: Present Tense Remembrance

It might be argued that, even if the Jerusalem leaders considered remembrance of the indigenous poor to be essential to "the truth of the gospel," they nonetheless considered Paul himself to be deficient in this regard — explaining why the Jerusalem leaders urged Paul and Barnabas to "remember the poor."

But it is not necessarily the case that the Jerusalem leaders thought Paul's regard for the poor was defective. The present form of the verb "remember" (μνημονεύω) in 2:10 might carry a constative sense, rendering the translation: "they added . . . only that we should *continue* to remember the poor."[24] But does this mean "they added only that we should *start and then continue* to remember the poor"? Or might it mean "they added only that we should *continue* to remember the poor *as we had already been doing*"? Although either nuance is syntactically possible, the latter is more likely historically. We have already noted in chapter 6 above that Paul expected care for the economically insecure to be built within the very character of Jesus-groups that he founded. There is no reason to imagine that this only took

23. Here again it is easy to see the deficiencies of the standard interpretation of "remember the poor" in reference to Jerusalem Jesus-groups of one sort or another. Paul's discourse relates that phrase ultimately back to "the truth of the good news." If Paul's reconstruction has merit, it is hard to believe that the Jerusalem leaders included the phrase "send us money" in their definition of the good news. That is the stuff of today's television evangelists, not the stuff of the Jerusalem leaders of the early Jesus-movement, unless we give credence to theories about the Jerusalem leaders wanting a commission in return for their support of the gentile mission, or about the Jerusalem church taxing gentile churches — theories to which I do not subscribe.

24. J. Louis Martyn takes it to mean "remember the poor *regularly*" (*Galatians* [New York: Doubleday, 1997], p. 206). Whereas Martyn works this reiterative interpretation in relation to the poor followers of Jesus in Jerusalem, it is preferable to interpret the verb with reiterative force in relation to the poor of the Greco-Roman world that Paul's gentile communities would encounter.

root in the late 40s, as a consequence of the Jerusalem meeting. The stipulation to "continue to remember the poor" is likely to include a recognition that Paul and Barnabas[25] had already been involved in initiatives for the indigenous poor within communities of gentile followers of Jesus.[26]

8.4: Paul's Devotion and Its Referent

Related to how we should interpret the verb "remember" at the beginning of Gal 2:10 is the issue of how we should interpret the verb at the end of the same verse. In the final clause of Gal 2:10 Paul writes: ὃ καὶ ἐσπούδασα αὐτὸ τοῦτο ποιῆσαι. This is usually translated "and I was eager to do precisely this," with the verb ἐσπούδασα being thought to have "inceptive" meaning — that is, Paul's eagerness to remember the poor *began* at this point in time. Some argue, however, that the verb does not have an inceptive spin; according to F. F. Bruce, for instance, the verb signals "not only that he [Paul] henceforth adopted this policy [i.e., remember the poor], but that he had already done so . . . , that this was a matter in which he had taken the initiative."[27]

25. Within the Lukan corpus, Barnabas is remembered as one who personally offered some of his own resources in order to benefit others (Acts 4:36-37).

26. Several interpreters have suggested that the verb "remember" may have a non-economic dimension. Dieter Georgi has argued that the verb should be glossed "acknowledge the merits." In his view, the agreement mentioned in Gal 2:10 "stipulated that the Gentile Jesus believers were to give *recognition* to the exemplary performance on the part of their fellow believers in Jerusalem" (*Remembering the Poor: The History of Paul's Collection for Jerusalem* [Nashville: Abingdon, 1992], p. 38, emphasis added). Richard N. Longenecker also puts a non-economic spin on the phrase "remember the poor," taking it to mean "continue to keep the welfare of the Jerusalem believers in Jesus also in mind"; for him, the Jerusalem leaders asked that Paul "do nothing in the exercise of his freedom that would impede their outreach to Jews and that he take into consideration the special circumstances of their Jewish mission, supporting them whenever possible" (*Galatians* [Dallas: Word Books, 1990], p. 60). Similarly, see Nicholas H. Taylor, *Paul, Antioch and Jerusalem* (Sheffield: Sheffield Academic Press, 1992), pp. 120-22. The same problem plagues all non-economic interpretations of the verb — that is, the term "the poor" has to be a titular term referring to the Jerusalem community. Once that view is problematized, a non-economic reading of μνημονεύω is problematized as well.

27. F. F. Bruce, *The Epistle to the Galatians* (Grand Rapids: Eerdmans, 1982), p. 126. See also Richard N. Longenecker, *Galatians*, p. 61; David R. Hall, "St Paul and Famine Relief: A Study of Galatians 2:10," *ExpT* 82 (1971): 309-11; Joseph Pathrapankal, *Foundational Perspectives in the New Testament* (Bangalore: Dharmaram Publications, 2004), p. 206. Keith F. Nickle (*The Collection: A Study in Paul's Strategy* [Naperville: Alec R. Allenson, 1966], p. 59) imagines that Paul is thinking both back to the famine relief of Acts 11:27-30 and ahead to his

The main issue in this debate should not be the syntactical significance of the aorist tense, however, for in this case syntactical decisions follow on from prior semantic assumptions. This is because the verb σπουδάζω has a broad semantic field, including within itself two related but different poles of meaning. As Catchpole rightly notes, "σπουδάζω can refer not simply to keenness but to action which expresses that keenness."[28]

In some places, these two meanings can go their separate ways. The issue is well known to commentators of Acts 20:16, where the aorist of σπεύδω (a cognate of σπουδάζω) illustrates the point: ἔσπευδεν γὰρ εἰ δυνατὸν εἴη αὐτῷ τὴν ἡμέραν τῆς πεντηκοστῆς γενέσθαι εἰς Ἱεροσόλυμα (translated in the NRSV as: "he was eager to be in Jerusalem, if possible, on the day of Pentecost"). Does ἔσπευδεν signal that Paul "was earnestly longing" or "was making every effort" to arrive in Jerusalem by the day of Pentecost? Despite their interrelationship, there is a semantic difference between (1) an earnest and diligent *desire* already felt in relation to an intended goal, and (2) an earnest and diligent *action* already being undertaken in order to achieve a goal. At stake is whether or not the earnest desire has resulted in action already. This same breadth of semantic field applies to the verb σπουδάζω, which can signal either a volition (i.e., "to be eager") or an action (i.e., "to make every effort").[29] So, when Paul writes in 1 Thess. 2:17 ἐσπουδάσαμεν τὸ πρόσωπον ὑμῶν ἰδεῖν, does he mean "we have been eager to see you" or "we have made every effort to see you"?[30] If the two senses *can* overlap, they are not necessarily synonymous; their relationship depends on non-semantic factors — i.e., whether Paul's eagerness ever translated into effort.

The same issue pertains to the verb σπουδάζω in Gal 2:10. Is Paul claiming that it was only at the time of the Jerusalem meeting that he began to have an eager *desire* to "remember the poor," or is he claiming that he had already made a keen *effort* to remember the poor even prior to that Jerusalem meeting?

---

subsequent collection. Stephan Joubert proposes (*Paul as Benefactor: Reciprocity, Strategy, and Theological Reflection in Paul's Collection* [Tübingen: Mohr Siebeck, 2000], p. 89) that the aorist signals that Paul's collection is in full swing at the time of writing Galatians. While this is possible, it cannot be demonstrated (contra Joubert) by means of the aorist tense of σπουδάζω in Gal 2:10.

28. Catchpole, "Paul, James and the Apostolic Decree," p. 433.

29. See Eph 4:3; 2 Tim 2:15; 4:9, 21; Tit 3:12.

30. The same breadth of meaning can be recognized in the noun σπουδή, the adjective σπουδαῖος, and the adverb σπουδαίως. See Rom 12:8, 11; 2 Cor 7:11; 8:7-8, 16-17, 22; Phil 2:28; 2 Tim 1:17.

If it is assumed that "the poor" in Gal 2:10 is "the Jerusalem poor," and if it is assumed that the phrase "remember the poor" refers to a future collection for the benefit of Jerusalem communities of Jesus-followers, then the verb σπουδάζω most naturally configures itself on the volitional side of its broad semantic field, emphasizing Paul's eagerness to start a new initiative. This is how the verb is interpreted most commonly, on the basis of this double assumption and in full accord with the standard interpretative paradigm of Gal 2:10. But if this double assumption is problematized, then the verb σπουδάζω can be understood along different lines altogether, putting emphasis on action-already-undertaken rather than on eagerness-to-undertake-a-future-initiative.

This is what we see in Bruce's interpretation, for instance. He argues (along with others) that the initiative for the poor that Paul had already undertaken is the one outlined in Acts 11:27-30, where Paul and Barnabas are said to have brought famine relief to Jerusalem as representatives of the Antiochene communities of Jesus-followers.[31]

This connection between Gal 2:10 and Acts 11:27-30 is possible, although many think (as do I) that Paul's participation in the delivery of the Antiochene collection of Acts 11:27-30 is historically suspect.[32] Even if we *were* to grant the historical reliability of Paul's participation in the famine relief visit of Acts 11, it is not necessary to conclude that Paul's mention of his

31. See, most recently, Downs, *The Offering of the Gentiles*, pp. 33-39; Downs, "Paul's Collection and the Book of Acts Revisited," *NTS* 52 (2006): 50-70, especially pp. 59-62.

32. Most think it likely that the events of Gal 2:1-10 correspond loosely with those of Acts 15, and that Paul is writing Galatians after the Jerusalem council of Acts 15. On the basis that the meeting of Gal 2 equates to the meeting of Acts 15, if Paul had participated in an Antioch relief visit to Jerusalem (i.e., Acts 11:27-30), the fact that he makes no mention of it in his biographical reconstruction of Gal 1–2 would have undermined his credibility among Paul's Galatian audience. Since Paul would not have risked that, his participation in the delivery of the Antiochene relief effort is historically suspect.

I have argued elsewhere, however, that although Paul's delivering of the Antioch initiative in Acts 11:27-30 is historically suspect, it is also rhetorically required in view of the placement of that passage within the structure of Acts. For an outline of the historical problems and for a rhetorical solution, see Bruce W. Longenecker, *Rhetoric at the Boundaries: The Art and Theology of New Testament Chain-Link Interlock* (Waco: Baylor University Press, 2005), pp. 241-52 (see also Mikeal Parsons's *Acts* [Grand Rapids: Baker Academic, 2008] for a commentary based on chain-link structuring). And even if Paul's participation in the delivery of the Antioch initiative is historically suspect, it is still possible that Paul was involved in its *organization* at Antioch, although not its delivery. (In this way, it is possible to speak of Paul having been involved in "collections" for Jerusalem, although the notion needs to be qualified significantly.)

devotion to remembering the poor should therefore be understood in relation to a single event of the past, let alone an event solely for the benefit of Jerusalem communities.[33]

Instead, there is reason to believe that Paul had already been involved in initiatives for the *indigenous* poor as part of his gentile mission in the Mediterranean basin prior to the late 40s. Accordingly, σπουδάζω in Gal 2:10 would connote not a volitional state pertaining to something in the future but, instead, a diligent action, with the aorist form (ἐσπούδασα) articulating a significant claim: "I had already been actively devoted to this cause."[34] This active devotion to the cause of the poor was not first aroused at the Jerusalem meeting of the late 40s, and it had nothing to do with concern for the Jerusalem communities of Jesus-followers. If it could be said that the Jerusalem leaders "added" remembrance of the poor to the deliberations,[35] Paul's

---

33. Even if the famine relief visit of Acts 11:27-30/12:25 might be thought of as contributing to the meaning of Gal 2:10 (as Bruce and others contend), it need not be the case that a Jerusalem reference exhausts the meaning of Gal 2:10; instead, the Antioch relief could easily be viewed as a particular expression of a larger principle, a tangible application of something that had already been implemented by and within Antiochene Jesus-groups.

34. James D. G. Dunn (*The Epistle to the Galatians* [London: A&C Black, 1993], p. 113) translates the final phrase of Gal 2:10 well: "the very thing which I have eagerly done."

35. Here Acts 15 and Gal 2 go their separate ways, since Paul's claim that "they added nothing . . . except that we remember the poor" in Gal 2:10 contrasts with the "addition" in Acts 15 of the apostolic "decree," by which all gentile Jesus-followers were to abide. I find myself in general sympathy (despite exegetical differences) with the view of Catchpole ("Paul, James and the Apostolic Decree," pp. 431-32): "[T]he Decree must be traced to a situation not involving Paul . . . the Decree was not only formulated later than the Gal. ii.1-10 meeting but also represented a sharp move away from that meeting's decision and, moreover, in a conservative and traditional direction." (The phrase "a sharp move away from" might require some adjustment, however.) See also Ernst Haenchen, *Die Apostelgeschichte* (Göttingen: Vandenhoeck & Ruprecht, 1977), pp. 452-55; C. K. Barrett, *Paul: An Introduction to His Thought* (London: Geoffrey Chapman, 1994), p. 163; James D. G. Dunn, *Beginning from Jerusalem; Christianity in the Making,* vol. 2 (Grand Rapids: Eerdmans, 2009), pp. 461-64.

What I cannot explore in this project is whether the devising of this decree within Jerusalem-based Jesus-groups, perhaps in the early 50s, might itself have contributed to Paul's original conceptualization of the collection in 53 CE. In short, there is scope for considering whether the collection might have been Paul's way of proving the theological legitimacy of gentile Jesus-groups in ways that bypass the stipulations of the decree, with which he may not have been in full sympathy. This might also help to explain why the Lukan author chose to overlook Paul's collection efforts in the narrative of Acts, since he may have known that the collection's origins were not wholly free from a polemical edge in relation to Jerusalem-based Jesus-groups. (On the complete absence of Paul's collection from the narrative of Acts, see Downs, "Paul's Collection and the Book of Acts Revisited.")

last clause in Gal 2:10 indicates that they really added nothing at all, since remembrance of the poor within the pagan world was already part of Paul's mission endeavors.

There is, then, no reason to be suspicious about Paul's claim in Gal 2:10 to have already been "devoted to this very thing," or to doubt that remembering the poor had been an established feature of Paul's ministry to the gentiles even prior to the Jerusalem meeting of Gal 2:1-10. Paul's claim to have already been devoted "to this very thing" is itself a counter to the idea that "remembering the poor" was "added" to his ministry due to the influence of the Jerusalem leaders. They may have raised the matter directly in their discussions about the spread of the gospel among the gentiles, but Paul, in typical fashion, is eager to demonstrate in the final phrase of 2:10 that he was already well ahead of the Jerusalem leaders.[36]

But this interpretation of Gal 2:10 simply raises the question, If Paul had so firm a devotion to the poor, why would the Jerusalem leaders see the need to put the issue firmly on the agenda of their deliberations about the identity of Jesus-followers and the mission to the gentiles? The answer to that is evident from the way that Paul has structured the single, complicated sentence of Gal 2:6-10, considered in §8.5 below.

8.5: The Structure of Galatians 2:6-10

Some interpreters suggest that we can read Paul's own psychological discomforts and anxieties right out of the structural oddities of Paul's discourse in Gal 2:1-10. Lou Martyn, for instance, argues that Paul has been thrown so far off-balance by those influencing his Galatian communities that it affects even his syntax, and tortuously so at this point in his letter. So Martyn writes:

> when Paul thinks of the False Brothers [in Gal 2:4], his command of grammatical niceties partly disappears in a cloud of emotional heat.

---

36. Paul's shift from first-person plural in 2:10a (μνημονεύωμεν) to the first-person singular in 2:10b (ἐσπούδασα) simply reflects the way that he tends to peripheralize Barnabas in 2:1-10. Barnabas appears by name in 2:1 and 2:9, and as part of first-person plural verbs or pronouns in 2:5, 2:9 and 2:10 (the plurals of 2:4 pertain to Jesus-followers in general). But otherwise Paul puts himself front and center to the action, without mention of Barnabas. So first-person singular narrative marks out Paul's account in 2:1-3 [five times in historical narrative] and 2:6-10 [six times in historical narrative].

Something similar happens when he turns his attention to the acknowledged leaders of the Jerusalem church. His ambivalent feelings about these persons produce a long sentence (vv 6-10) that is syntactically somewhat disjointed.[37]

Martyn claims that 2:4 is "the first of two glaring syntactical slips in Paul's account of the Jerusalem meeting, the other emerging in vv. 6-9," with both passages involving "grammatical nonsequiturs." This is because, according to Martyn, the "false brothers" and the leaders of the Jerusalem church cause "an increase in his [Paul's] pulse rate." So, says Martyn: "When Paul pictures these groups in his mind, he experiences a degree of mental suffering, and his syntax suffers as well."[38]

Interpretations based on speculation about the author's psychological state are often suspect. Whatever merits they might have in the case of Gal 2:6-10 are superseded by considerations that Martyn has failed to consider and that have gone unrecognized in general. Three things need to be noted in this regard.

1. The "long sentence (vv 6-10) that is syntactically somewhat disjointed" appears to be disjointed precisely because the beginning and the end of the sentence (in 2:6 and 2:10 respectively) are qualified and explained throughout 2:7-9.
2. Precisely because the main sentence is contained in 2:6 and 2:10, it is most likely that the sentence's main weight falls in those two verses. The material contained in 2:7-9 is to be seen as explanatory material that supports the main sentence in some fashion.
3. The material in 2:7-9 has as much to do with 2:10 as with 2:6.

When Gal 2:10 is understood in relation to these three features of Paul's discursive flow, it becomes evident that the concerns of the Jerusalem apostles were not about Paul but about the targets of his mission.

Whereas interpreters frequently put more emphasis on 2:7-9 than on 2:10, the structure of Paul's lengthy sentence in 2:6-10 indicates that, if there is parenthetical material in 2:6-10, it appears in 2:7-9. The structural foundations of Paul's main sentence are found in 2:6 and 2:10: "the ones that seem [to be significant] added nothing to me . . . except that we remember the

---

37. Martyn, *Galatians*, p. 199. Along similar lines, Georgi, *Remembering the Poor*, p. 22; Gaston, "Paul and Jerusalem," p. 65.

38. Martyn, *Galatians*, p. 195.

poor, and I had already been actively devoted to doing this very thing" (ἐμοὶ γὰρ οἱ δοκοῦντες οὐδὲν προσανέθεντο . . . μόνον τῶν πτωχῶν ἵνα μνημονεύωμεν, ὃ καὶ ἐσπούδασα αὐτὸ τοῦτο ποιῆσαι). The material in 2:7-9 does not make 2:10 peripheral to 2:6; instead, 2:7-9 offers explanatory reasoning in relation to the material that surrounds it in both 2:6 and in 2:10, with 2:6 being "amplified by" 2:10.[39]

Paul intends 2:7-9 to assist his claim in 2:6 that the leaders added nothing to his gospel, asserting repeatedly that the leaders saw that he had been given "the grace" to go to the gentiles. But 2:7-9 is not fully explained by its relationship to 2:6. It also offers anticipatory explanation for Paul's claim in 2:10 ("except that we remember the poor"). On four occasions in 2:7-9 Paul points out that he (along with Barnabas) is commissioned to go to the gentiles, in contrast to three occasions in which Peter is said to be commissioned to go to the Jews. Inserted just before the main sentence of 2:6 picks up again in 2:10, this material helps to explain the content of 2:10. That is, it is precisely because Paul and Barnabas are approved in a mission to the *gentile* world that they, and not Peter, are specifically charged to "[continue to] remember the poor."

It is not difficult to see why the charge follows from the material of Gal 2:7-9. Quite simply, in complete contrast to the longstanding traditions of Judaism, the pagan world was not known for its traditions of care for the poor (even if, as was shown in chapter 4 above, care for the poor was not altogether absent from the ancient world). In this light, it is not hard to spot the relationship of the parenthetical material in 2:7-9 to what follows in 2:10. Highlighting the differentiation of proclamation to Jews by Peter and to gentiles by Paul and Barnabas, Gal 2:7-9 sets up the rhetorical context in which 2:10 is to be understood. The Jerusalem leaders might well have assumed that Jews who accepted the "good news" would be unfailing in their attempts to remember the poor, having been immersed in longstanding Jewish traditions regarding the necessity of caring for the vulnerable (see §5.1 above).[40] At the Jerusalem meeting of Gal 2:1-10, the Petrine mission was not

---

39. Catchpole, "Paul, James and the Apostolic Decree," p. 432.

40. Perhaps a powerful witness to such care had recently been modeled in the Jerusalem Jesus-groups in the late 40s, when famines struck Judea. Those famines had no doubt highlighted for the Jerusalem leadership the essential need for communities to care for the/ their needy. And if Paul's meeting with them took place in 48 CE, it coincided with the period in which the famines were having their most pronounced effect on the populace. It is little wonder, then, that the apostolic discussions about the essentials of identity for Jesus-followers were especially keen to the essentiality of remembering the poor: living embodi-

targeted with a stipulation to remember the poor since the targeted audience of that mission was expected to be immersed in such concerns anyway (albeit, most likely the poor within the Jewish community in general). But the Jerusalem leadership appears to have been apprehensive about gentiles who accepted the good news, since there was no guarantee that the previous practices of those gentiles would have been regulated by Jewish traditions about the essential nature of remembering the poor.[41]

In this light, the charge "to remember the poor" was not simply about ecclesial polity between Jerusalem followers of Jesus and those further afield. The Jerusalem leaders were not interested in having money sent to their community from gentile followers of Jesus. Without standing on constant guard to control how such an expectation was being interpreted in far-flung Jesus-groups, a request to "send money to the poor among us here in Jerusalem" may well have sent out extremely confusing signals about patron-client relations between the Jesus-groups. But the charge to "remember the poor" carried no such specificity; instead, it replicated an essential feature of Judeo-Christian identity — that of caring for the needy, without geographical restriction. As such, instead of referring to Jerusalem Jesus-followers, the phrase was probably seen by all parties as an intrinsic part of the good news to the Greco-Roman world which, comparatively speaking, had little such good news.

Gal 2:1-10 is best read as indicating that remembrance of the poor is something that would (continue to) characterize the emergent Jesus-movement in both its mission to the circumcised and to the uncircumcised. Assuming that such remembrance would inevitably characterize the Jewish mission, the Jerusalem apostles were nonetheless concerned that Jewish traditions about caring for the poor might be abandoned in a mission to the

_____

ments of need were all around them. The Jerusalem leaders might have expected that precisely the same care for the poor that the Jerusalem Jesus-groups modeled in the 40s (presumably) should be replicated by the Jesus-groups founded by Paul throughout the Mediterranean basin.

41. The point can be articulated in a more precise fashion for those who envision the agreement in Gal 2:1-10 as one between Jesus-groups of two prominent cities, Antioch and Jerusalem. In that scenario, the Jerusalem leaders were concerned to ensure that what Jerusalem Jesus-groups would be engaged in (i.e., a ministry [for the benefit of Jews] that included caring for the poor) is precisely what Antiochene Jesus-groups would be engaged in (i.e., a ministry [for the benefit of gentiles] that included caring for the poor). The only additional twist to this interpretation would be that, when Paul separated himself from the Antiochene umbrella of mission, he nonetheless carried on the same interest that he had been committed to already (as indicated by the data assembled above).

pagan world. Paul is quick to offer assurances that such would not be the case on his watch.[42] Paul is reminding his readers that the apostles who met in Jerusalem to discuss issues of common identity across all branches of Jesus-followers agreed that circumcision would not be one of those ubiquitous markers, but that care for the poor would be. This, they agreed, was in full conformity to what Paul calls "the truth of the gospel."

8.6: "Remember the Poor" as Mission Strategy

In chapters 4 and 5 above we saw that care for the poor must have existed in the Greco-Roman world, at least in some low-level forms, but that the pagan world was not strongly characterized by this concern, in general contrast to the traditions of Judaism. Perhaps many ancient Jews would have agreed with Gillian Clark's assessment: "No Roman cult groups, not even those that were primarily mutual groups, . . . looked after strangers and people in need. . . . Provision for the poor was not an ethical priority in Roman culture."[43]

A contrast between Jewish and gentile initiatives for the poor seems to lie behind the Jerusalem meeting's stipulation that gentile Jesus-followers should "remember the poor." That contrast may have been a "contrast of kind," sharply distinguishing the gentile and Jewish constituencies.[44] Or it may have been a "contrast of degree," in which differences between the two constituencies were noted but without a sharp edge between them. But in either scenario, the early Jesus-movement seems to have had suspicions that the non-Jewish communities of Jesus-followers might be virtually indistinguishable from pagan counterparts with regard to care for the poor. The stipulation to "remember the poor" was made in an effort to ensure that

---

42. Cf. Dunn, *Beginning from Jerusalem,* p. 935: "in Gal. 2.10 Paul was simply affirming his long-standing and sustained eagerness as a Jesus-believer to maintain the traditional Jewish concerns for the 'poor,' a concern he continued to enact during his days as a church founder without reference to and prior to the idea of the collection as such."

43. G. Clark, *Christianity and Roman Society* (Cambridge: Cambridge University Press, 2004), pp. 23-24.

44. Paul himself utilizes "contrasts of kind" at times in his own letters. For instance, in 1 Cor 5:1 he likens the immorality of some Corinthians to behavior spurned even by the (immoral) gentiles. On two occasions, he adopts a similar worldview, only to abandon it subsequently. So, in Rom 1:18-32 Paul characterizes the immorality that engulfed the pagan world prior to engulfing his Jewish reader in the same world of immorality (2:1ff); in Gal 2:15, he contrasts Jews with "gentile sinners," only to qualify the worldview in the verses that follow (2:16-17).

gentile Jesus-followers were recognizably more "Jewish" than their pagan environment — or better, to ensure that gentile Jesus-followers were recognized more readily as having aligned themselves with and been transformed by the deity of Israel.

This arcs to the narrative of Acts at various points. In Acts 10-11 we are told of Cornelius who, although uncircumcised, feared the deity of Israel and gave alms "to the people" as an expression of his piety (10:2). An angel appears to him to say, "Your prayers and your alms have ascended as a memorial before God" (10:4; see also 10:31). As a consequence of his practical piety, he wins the respect of "the whole Jewish nation" (10:22) and becomes the test case for the full inclusion of gentiles into the early Jesus-movement.[45]

Something of the same is likely to be inherent in the Acts account of Paul arriving in Jerusalem for the final time. The day after his arrival there, Paul is said to have given an account to James and all the elders about "the things that God had done among the gentiles through his ministry," an account that inspires the praise of Israel's deity among the Jesus-followers in Jerusalem (Acts 21:19-20). Although there is no explicit reference to charitable initiatives among gentile Jesus-followers, it is likely to be implied, not least in resonance with the Cornelius incident of Acts 10–11.[46] That incident served as the first occasion in which a Jerusalem-based apostle (i.e., Peter) recognizes the legitimacy of law-free gentile mission, a mission that is fea-

45. That "almsgiving" was expected to ingratiate one to Jews may well be part of the storyline of Paul's demonstration of Jewish piety in the Jerusalem temple; see Acts 24:17 in relation to Acts 21:20-26. See also Downs, "Paul's Collection," pp. 62-70. So too Tabitha, or Dorcas, is said to have been "devoted to good works and acts of charity" (Acts 9:36), and her death prompts Peter to revive her, in view of her high standing within the (predominately Jewish) constituency of the Jesus-movement.

46. Although we know from Rom 15 that Paul's arrival in Jerusalem was the occasion when he delivered his "collection for the poor among the saints in Jerusalem," that knowledge must be held in check when reading the Lukan account of Paul meeting the Jerusalem leaders, since the Lukan audience is not expected to know anything about that initiative. Moreover, if the Lukan author does not make an economic dimension explicit at this point in the narrative, this is in general agreement with his normal tendency with regard to the Pauline mission. Downs ("Paul's Collection," pp. 60-61) makes the point this way: "Paul's epistles are rich with information about the economic life of the earliest Christian communities. . . . For the most part, however, very little is actually recorded in Acts about the economic life of Paul's churches, about issues of wealth and poverty in the Pauline mission, or about the sources of funding for Paul's extensive travels. This stands in contrast not only to the situation represented in the letters of Paul, but also to the portrayal of the Jerusalem church earlier in the narrative of Acts, which provides a number of details about the common life of the first believers."

tured through the efforts of Paul in Acts 13-19. At the completion of Paul's public ministry, he reports back to Jerusalem leaders of the Jesus-movement regarding the success of that ministry. Perhaps readers are to imagine the praise of the Jerusalem leaders to have been prompted not merely by hearing about "signs and wonders" performed through Paul (and Barnabas) among the gentile communities (see Acts 15:12; similarly Acts 10:45), but by the recognition that those communities were demonstrating the same kind of practical and charitable expressions of piety that Cornelius had demonstrated prior to the official undertaking of the gentile mission.[47]

Moreover, if Cornelius is said to have had the respect of "the whole Jewish nation" (10:22), the Lukan narrative may imply that the "praise" that transpired within the Jerusalem community (21:19-20) arose out of that community's concern for the well-being of the mission of the Jesus-movement as a whole, which their leaders oversaw. If their mission could be shown to include turning pagans (i.e., "gentile sinners," Gal 2:15) into people worthy of Jewish respect, then both the mission to the gentile world and the mission to the Jewish world might well progress with reduced levels of antagonism.[48]

These narratological hints within the Lukan account might inform our understanding of the motivation of the Jerusalem apostles in stipulating that the gentile communities should be diligent in their concern for the poor. Precisely because charitable initiatives were highly regarded within the Jewish world, the fact that gentiles were engaging in such practices within communities of Jesus-followers would have increased the chances of success for the mission of the early Jesus-movement. Jews who were not Jesus-followers would have found it hard to dispute that gentiles were fulfilling the Isaianic vision of a people approved by Israel's deity because they "share [their] bread with the hungry, and bring the homeless poor into

---

47. A double emphasis on care for the poor and powerful acts was established by Peter in his speech within the Cornelius episode (10:38). There Jesus is remembered as one who went around "doing deeds of benevolence" (εὐεργετῶν) and "healing all" (ἰώμενος πάντας). In this context, "deeds of benevolence" probably refers to his concern for the poor. And on Cornelius as the paradigmatic gentile convert to the Jesus-movement, see R. D. Witherup, "Cornelius Over and Over and Over Again," *JSNT* 49 (1993): 43-66, especially p. 60.

48. The speech of James and the elders in Acts 21:20-25 connects the success of the gentile mission with the hope that the suspicions of the Jews might be assuaged. In the end, these hopes were dashed, not because of success of the gentile mission, but because of Paul's controversial reputation with regard to Jewish observance of the law, or lack thereof (see also 21:20-22 and 27-29).

[their] house" (Isa 58:7). As a result of these dramatic instances of care for the needy, the deity of Israel makes the following promises to his people (Isa 58:8):

> your light shall break forth like the dawn,
> and your healing shall spring up quickly;
> your vindicator shall go before you,
> the glory of the LORD shall be your rear guard.

Lest the point be lost, it is reiterated a second time in subsequent verses (Isa 58:10-11):

> If you offer your food to the hungry
> and satisfy the needs of the afflicted,
> then your light shall rise in the darkness
> and your gloom be like the noonday.
> The LORD will guide you continually.

It is along these lines that the Jerusalem leadership most likely understood gentile remembrance of the poor.

8.7: Conclusions

Attempts to place the admonition to "remember the poor" in a category of "church politics,"[49] separated off from "gospel," are problematic. Since there is little to suggest that Jerusalem followers of Jesus were known as "the poor," and much to suggest the opposite, the Galatian Jesus-followers were unlikely to have recognized Paul's bald reference to "the poor" as in any way referring exclusively to the Jesus-followers in Jerusalem. Instead, they were far more likely to have heard it as a straightforward reference to a fundamentally socio-economic condition or situation, without any geographical qualifiers or connotations whatsoever. (That is, they would have heard it as referring to some even within their *own* communities.) Since Paul's Anatolian audience were unlikely to have shared the current consensus view about the identity of "the poor" in Gal 2:10, their understanding of the passage would have been much different to those normally postulated in academic treatises on Paul and the early history of the Jesus-movement.

49. Betz, *Galatians*, p. 99.

This interpretation of Gal 2:6-10, unencumbered by views about "the poor" being Jerusalem Jesus-followers (or a subset within them), reveals that the Jerusalem apostles urged Paul to (continue to) remember the poor (as he was already actively doing) not because they were worried about *his* credentials on this matter, but because they were worried about the credentials of *his target audience* — pagans of the Roman world who perhaps had never been influenced by the traditions of Judaism with regard to the poor. The Jerusalem leaders were anxious that the good news preached by Paul and Barnabas, a good news free from the requirement of circumcision, should nonetheless continue to look like a Jewish good news in relation to one of Judaism's most socially distinctive features: that is, its care for the poor. The Jerusalem leaders wanted to be sure that, in the far-flung cities of the Greco-Roman world, non-circumcised followers of Jesus in the "Pauline orbs" of ministry would be aligned with circumcised followers of Jesus in the "Petrine orbs" of ministry, being characterized not by a uniformity of ethnic practice and identity, but instead by a proclamation about faith in/of Christ[50] and a practical concern for the poor. The handshake of Gal 2:9 represents the defining moment in which representatives from major strands within the early Jesus-movement agreed on the basic character of identity and praxis within the diverse communities of Jesus-followers. The Jerusalem leadership of the Jesus-movement agreed not only that circumcision is nonessential across the spectrum of Jesus-groups but also that care for the poor is essential in all incarnations of Jesus-groups, not simply among Jewish followers of Jesus. In these ways, along with the essentiality of faith in/of Christ, the gospel to the circumcised and the gospel to the uncircumcised would be united in both the proclamational content of the good news and its practical embodiment, ensuring that even "the poor" would benefit by the good news.

Consequently, it is not adequate to describe "the character of the economics of the Pauline epistles" in the manner of Barry Gordon, who imagines that, for Paul, Jesus-followers "are not to make their incorporation in Christ an occasion for a plunge into experimentation with economic relationships."[51] This estimate not only devalues Paul's understanding of the gospel, but also runs contrary to a defining moment in the history of the early Jesus-movement.

---

50. In Gal 2:16, Paul depicts πίστις Χριστοῦ as something that "we know" (εἰδότες) to be part of the message about righteousness. He is probably referring to a tradition commonly and "centrally" held within the Jesus-movement.

51. Barry Gordon, *The Economic Problem in Biblical and Patristic Thought* (Leiden: Brill, 1989), p. 78.

As a result of this study, it is imperative that we never again hear from Christian interpreters that Gal 2:1-10 demonstrates Paul's resolve to preach a gospel that was "free from all mixture of Judaism."[52] Such a defective formulation is ignorant of the main theological issues that the Jerusalem agreement of Gal 2:10 was intended to preserve — i.e., the very Jewish character of the gospel in contradistinction to the general ethos of the Greco-Roman world. That same ignorance is evident in Constantine's remembered words:

> Let us, then, have nothing in common with the Jews, who are our adversaries. For we have received from our Savior another way. A better and more lawful line of conduct is inculcated by our holy religion. Let us with one accord walk therein, my much-honored brethren, studiously avoiding all contact with that evil way.[53]

If Constantine did utter words of this sort, he was simply showing his own historical and theological ignorance. For unless we are entrenched Marcionites, Gal 2:10 indicates that leaders of the early Jesus-movement envisaged Jesus-groups to be not "free from all mixture of Judaism" (Henry) nor groups that avoided "all contact with that evil way" (Constantine). Instead, what the early leaders envisaged was a movement of Jesus-groups that, as part of their good news, propelled Judaism's rich traditions of concern for the needy into the harsh Greco-Roman world that could all too easily be characterized as intransigent towards the needy. Historically speaking, in the Jerusalem meeting we see a Judaism legitimating the spawning of other forms of Judaism to offset deep-rooted need in the name of the deity of Israel and a single Galilean Jew, whose own ministry was marked by concern for the poor as one of its primary features.

One additional advantage for reading Gal 2:10 in this way is that it relieves us from having to imagine that James, for instance, would consider it justified to redirect the minimal resources of gentile groups of Jesus-followers away from the indigenous populations of the Mediterranean basin in order to support the poor of the Jerusalem communities. It is far more likely that the James depicted in the Jacobite letter would have preferred to be seen as the sponsor of a movement (spearheaded by his brother Jesus, who himself struck a strong pose in defense of the poor) in which the poor

---

52. *Matthew Henry's Commentary* (condensed), public domain electronic text, downloaded from the Bible Foundation e-Text Library: http://www.bf.org/bfetexts.htm; hypertexted and formatted by OakTree Software, Inc., Version 2.5.

53. From Theodoret, *Hist. eccl.: Dial.* 1.9.

throughout the diaspora were aided by indigenously-entrenched groups of Jesus-followers. In this light, it is little wonder that James and other Christian leaders in Jerusalem stipulated that the Jesus-groups founded by Paul should be encouraged to remember the poor in their own localized contexts (Gal 2:10), not least in order to assist in the spreading of the good news in both Jewish and pagan sectors of the Greco-Roman world.

For Paul, the meeting of Gal 2:1-10 resulted in the affirmation that the Jesus-movement in all of its indigenous forms was to be marked out by concern for the poor. We have no reason to think that he gave his assent to this begrudgingly, as if it verged on "salvation by human works" or a "social gospel" or "Marxist revolution."[54] Instead, he gave his assent wholeheartedly, having already been wholly committed to this task precisely because it lay at the very heart of his gospel of transformation-through-grace. Paul knew from Israel's scriptures that the deity of Israel had staked his own reputation as the cosmic sovereign to the overthrowing of unjust systems and the refreshment of the disadvantaged; and Paul probably knew from early remembrances of the Jesus-movement that Jesus himself had invoked the Isaianic narrative to encapsulate his own kingdom-message of "good news to the poor." Moreover, as will be shown in chapter 12 below, care for the poor within groups of Jesus-followers has a solid place within Paul's own theology of corporate enlivenment by the Spirit of the sovereign deity of Israel. If "remember the poor" is not simply "church politics," neither does it represent a dubious, second-rate theology. It lies at the very core of Judaeo-Christian tradition, having been showcased in Israel's scriptures, in Jesus' proclamation and ministry, and in the best practices of the early Jesus-movement — including those Jesus-followers whose corporate life had been established and nurtured by Paul.[55]

Care for the poor as an outworking of divine grace did not, in itself, dis-

54. Compare the comments by E. Earle Ellis cited in chapter 1 above.

55. On the relation of "grace" and "works" in Paul's theology, see, for instance, John M. G. Barclay, "Grace and the Transformation of Agency in Christ," in F. E. Udoh et al., eds., *Redefining First-Century Jewish and Christian Identities* (Notre Dame: University of Notre Dame Press, 2008), pp. 372-89. An earlier essay that still repays study is John Howard Yoder's "Justification by Grace through Faith," in his *The Politics of Jesus* (2nd ed.; Grand Rapids: Eerdmans, 1994 [1972]), pp. 212-26. The artificiality of the distinction between "social gospel" and "spiritual gospel" is articulated well by Aaron Kuecker, "The Spirit and the 'Other,' Satan and the 'Self': Economic Ethics as a Consequence of Identity Transformation in Luke-Acts," in Bruce W. Longenecker and Kelly Liebengood, eds., *Engaging Economics: New Testament Scenarios and Early Christian Interpretations* (Grand Rapids: Eerdmans, 2009), 81-103, pp. 102-103.

tinguish the Jesus-movement from other forms of Judaism. On the matter of the poor, the Jesus-movement distinguished itself from other Judaisms only in its specified enlistment of *gentiles* in the project of caring for the poor, to which Israel's deity had long ago called his people. This calling was something that gentile followers of Jesus found themselves expected to act on, as a consequence of their new identity as those who were invaded by the generous love of the deity of Israel. This resulted from their hearing of the good news for all, which included the charge to remember the poor. If interpreters in the early centuries put Paul at the heart of that enterprise of remembering the poor, later interpreters have often found other ways of reading Paul's good news. As a consequence, theological components that Paul held together in a holistic package have all too often become broken up into atomistic parts. In such cases, Paul might have said to his later interpreters words similar to those that he said to the Galatians: "Even if we or an angel from heaven should proclaim to you a gospel contrary to what we proclaimed to you, let that one be accursed!" (Gal 1:8). With regard to the "gospel imperative" of remembering the indigenous poor, the Jerusalem leaders themselves would seem to have heartily affirmed the same.

CHAPTER 9

"Fulfill the law of Christ"

The Poor in the Rhetoric of Galatians

9.1: The Galatian Biography and the Needy
9.2: The Galatians, the Needy and the Mosaic Law

It has been argued that "remember the poor" in Gal 2:10 was stipulated in order to obligate gentile Jesus-groups to care for the needy within their local orb of responsibility, thereby ensuring that Jewish and gentile Jesus-groups would be identical in certain key respects, even if they went their separate ways with regard to circumcision. The point needs to be pressed here, then, as to how this understanding of Gal 2:10 plays into Paul's letter to the Galatians. Why did Paul feel it necessary to recount this stipulation for Galatian Christians at precisely the time when they were finding the prospect of circumcision to have some appeal? Why were they to hear that the Jerusalem meeting included a stipulation that gentile communities of Jesus-followers (like their Jewish counterparts) would be sure to "remember the poor"?

The rhetorical function of Gal 2:10 within the broader confines of Paul's Galatian letter is an issue that is rarely given due consideration. Perhaps the neglect arises from the (unlikely) view that what is being referred to in that verse is a collection for the Jerusalem poor, in which case the phrase pertains to things other than "the truth of the gospel" that was primarily under discussion in the Jerusalem meeting and that had little relevance to the Galatian auditors. In other words, precisely because "remember the poor" is usually considered to be peripheral to the main issues of both the Jerusalem and the

Galatian situations, it consequently is assumed to have little or no resonance within the rest of the Galatian letter. But the question still remains, why did Paul make reference to the stipulation in his Galatian letter?

The difficulties that this question poses for those who imagine that "remember the poor" pertains to Jerusalem Jesus-followers is most evident, perhaps, in David Trobisch's work. Trobisch argues that Romans, 1 and 2 Corinthians, and Galatians were all assembled as a mini-canon of sorts by Paul himself, in an effort to lash together his own texts that dealt with the collection for "the poor among the saints in Jerusalem." In this view of things, Gal 2:10 carries significant rhetorical weight, since it must simply pertain to Paul's collection efforts in order for Trobisch's thesis to survive. But Trobisch's is an awkward thesis, in that he has simultaneously to augment and diminish the significance of Gal 2:10. So at the start of one paragraph Trobisch claims that the "saints in Jerusalem" and "the collection for the poor" are "a major topic of Galatians," while at the end of that same paragraph he notes that the "central topic [of Galatians] . . . is different."[1] This distinction between the "major" and "central" topics of the letter seems to be the discursive loophole that allows Trobisch not to pursue the obvious question: If the collection is a "major topic" of Galatians (which might surprise the majority of Pauline interpreters), how does the (alleged) reference to that collection in 2:10 resonate with and/or support the theological contours of the letter in general? Trobisch fails to offer an answer, even on his own terms of reference.

The issue gains further significance when we note what else Paul fails to mention when recalling the highpoints of the Jerusalem meeting — i.e., other important emphases that might well have been mentioned in that meeting. For instance, New Testament texts attributed to James, Peter and John suggest that they regularly admonished others to exceed in practices such as the following:

> the appropriation of scripture within Christian communities; having a good reputation among the populace; avoiding malice and anger; taming the tongue; being humble and merciful; watching out for gluttony and covetousness; honoring the marriage bed; standing fast against adversity and compromise; praying without ceasing; loving one's neighbor, correcting others in love; being submissive to the governing authorities, honor-

---

1. David Trobisch, *Paul's Letter Collection: Tracing the Origins* (Minneapolis: Fortress Press, 1994), p. 89. Contrast James D. G. Dunn (*Beginning from Jerusalem: Christianity in the Making*, vol. 2 [Grand Rapids: Eerdmans, 2009], p. 933), who speaks of Paul's collection being mentioned "across three letters" (i.e., 1 and 2 Corinthians, and Romans).

ing all people; being patient for and prepared for the Lord's return; commending the faith to anyone.

If Paul is simply recalling something tangential to the main topic of the Jerusalem meeting when recounting the "remember the poor" stipulation, why this tangential nugget and not some other one? If Paul had written, for instance, "They added nothing to me, except to appropriate scripture wisely within the life of Christian communities," interpreters would see it as their duty to link that reminder to other places within the Galatian letter. The same would apply if Paul had said "They added nothing to me, except to be humble and merciful," or "except to stand fast against adversity and compromise," or "except to love one's neighbor," or "except to correct others in love." Any of these helpful apostolic admonitions would arc to other passages within Galatians, and interpreters would be quick to note the arc and explain its significance for the Galatian situation. But because the phrase "except remember the poor" is thought to indicate the collection for Jerusalem, and since that issue is not on the surface of the text, interpreters fail to pursue the issue of whether the phrase has a strong rhetorical function within the Galatian letter.

As will be seen in this chapter, however, once the stranglehold of the Jerusalem collection is removed from the phrase "remember the poor," and once that phrase is seen in relation to care for the indigenous needy among the pagan world, Gal 2:10 bears notable rhetorical weight within the theological frame of the Galatian letter. This is true especially with regard to the general situation of which the Galatian communities were a part. So if those "agitating" the Galatians were proposing that circumcision should mark out all the followers of Jesus, Paul highlights how the Jerusalem meeting ended in the affirmation that what would unite Jewish and gentile communities of Jesus-followers would not be circumcision but care for the poor. But we need also to trace the argument out in more detail, showing how the stipulation to "remember the poor" relates to two key issues within Galatians: (1) the biography of the Galatian followers of Jesus, and (2) the Galatian interest in observing the law. These points are developed in §9.1 and §9.2 below.

9.1: The Galatian Biography and the Needy

In his Galatian letter, Paul reconstructs the biography of the Galatians in starkly simplistic terms, at least chronologically speaking. The Galatian followers of Jesus had previously been "enslaved" to the elemental forces of the universe (4:3, 9) that control vast swathes of "the present evil age" (1:4). This enslavement was disrupted when the Galatians received Paul into their midst (4:12-15), accepted the gospel by faith, and experienced the workings of the Spirit in their communities (3:1-5). This state of divine blessedness (4:15) was disrupted, in Paul's view, when others sought to influence the Galatians in ways that undermined their alignment with the ways of Israel's deity (e.g., 3:1; 4:16-17; 6:12-13). Paul is now writing this letter with the hopes that proper alignment with Israel's deity can be re-established and that Christ might (again) be "formed" among them (4:19) in the expectant "hope of righteousness" that is to come (5:5).

If the sequence of "what you were in the past prior" and "what you have become 'in Christ'" is a simple one, so too is the moral fabric that Paul interweaves within that chronological sequence. The "present evil age" is depicted as being comprised of savage competitiveness and fiercely-engrained self-interestedness (e.g., 5:19-21). But the way of life enlivened by "the Spirit of [God's] Son" is altogether different, being enlivened after the pattern of the son "who gave himself" (τοῦ δόντος ἑαυτόν, 1:4; παραδόντος ἑαυτόν, 2:20). For Paul, quite simply, the characteristic of cruciform self-giving is requisite to divine favor (or divine "blessedness," as he calls it in 4:15).

It is this pattern of self-giving for others' benefit that Paul calls upon to adjudicate whether or not the Galatians are living favorably before the deity of Israel. If they previously belonged to "the present evil age" (i.e., the age of life under "the elemental spirits of the world"), they are at risk of moving back into the world once again. This risk has been introduced to them by "agitators" (as we will call them) who have recently been influencing the Galatian Jesus-followers. According to Paul, their own way of life testifies to the competitive self-interestedness that marks out the present evil age. Although the Galatians had welcomed Paul into their midst previously, under the influence of self-interested agitators Paul now feels himself in danger of being perceived as an "enemy" (4:16) against whom the Galatians must protect themselves. The contagion of self-interestedness has left the Galatians as pawns in a power-struggle between suprahuman forces, a struggle carried out in the character of individuals and the communities to which they belong. Blessedness from the one true deity (i.e., that blessedness associated with the dawning of the new age) emerges in communities marked out by patterns of life that conform to the cruciform pattern of the self-giving Christ.[2]

---

2. More could be said along these lines. See especially Bruce W. Longenecker, "'Until Christ is formed in you': Suprahuman Forces and Moral Character in Galatians," *CBQ* 61

The phrase "remember the poor" of Gal 2:10 needs to be fed into this matrix of character inventory. And the point is virtually self-evident. In the "moral universe" that Paul constructs in Galatians, the stipulation to "remember the poor" is not simply good moral exhortation. Instead, it lies right at the heart of the "truth of the gospel" that Paul was defending in Jerusalem precisely because it is wholly in line with the cruciform configuration of gospel morality. In Paul's view, what the apostles were rubber-stamping in Jerusalem was not merely a decision about circumcision. Instead, it was a decision about the moral matrix that was to mark out all communities of Jesus-followers, and at the heart of that matrix lies care for the vulnerable.[3]

As noted in chapter 8 above, the Jerusalem apostles seem to have imagined that Jewish communities of Jesus-followers would be marked out by a self-giving character because care for the economically vulnerable was deeply infused within Jewish scripture and tradition; but they seem less convinced that the same kind of character would characterize gentile communities of Jesus-followers, due to suspicions about the (relative) lack of care for the poor in the gentile world. Paul's assurance that he had already been devoted to inspiring care for the poor within his gentile communities is meant to carry rhetorical force with his Galatian audience in relation to other aspects of the Galatian letter as it unfolds. For instance, if they had not already known it, Paul's audiences will discover in the course of hearing Paul's letter that, in nurturing cruciform care within their midst, they testify to their corporate enlivenment by the Spirit and to their habitation within the framework of the gospel.

Moreover, with Gal 2:6-10 already establishing the express desires of the Jerusalem apostles for the gentile mission, later chapters of Paul's letter will provoke thematic linking with those verses. That is, if they had not already known it, Paul's Galatian audience will note that practices of cruciform care, which Paul is so intent to enliven, would align the Galatians wholly with the expectations of the Jerusalem apostles. In Galatians, Paul is upholding the moral character of cruciformity as the test against which the Galatians are to measure their current situation — with respect both to the agitators (whose character is depicted as falling far short of the standard; 6:12-13) and to

---

(1999): 92-108; Longenecker, *The Triumph of Abraham's God: The Transformation of Identity in Galatians* (Edinburgh: T&T Clark, 1998), pp. 69-88, 147-71.

3. It is little wonder, then, that in 1 Cor 11 Paul charges the Corinthians with having lost the essence of the good news when, in their corporate gatherings, economic relationships are skewed in disservice to the economically insecure.

themselves. The agitators may have argued that observing circumcision (and other stipulations within the law) would align the Galatians with the wishes of the Jerusalem apostles. To the contrary, Paul suggests that, as he and the Jerusalem apostles understand it, the "truth of the gospel" excludes the necessity of circumcision but includes a definite moral configuration. In this way, Paul's Galatian letter demonstrates that his gospel promotes the very "responsibility" that the Jerusalem apostles aired years earlier, in conjunction with Paul's own view on the matter. He has never wavered from the framework that was established at that meeting: circumcision is not an essential component of identity for Jesus-followers, but caring for the indigenous poor is, as an expression of the cruciform gospel that the early Jesus-movement unanimously preached.

The irony of Paul's presentation emerges from the fact that, in Paul's biography of the Galatians, they had already been living in conformity with the wishes of the Jerusalem apostles (and more importantly, in conformity with the moral world of the gospel) prior to the coming of the agitators. This is the subtext behind the account of Paul's arrival among the Galatians in 4:12-15 — verses that have been largely neglected in the history of interpretation, but which play a key role in Paul's theological biography of the Galatians.[4]

Paul recounts how he initially came to the Galatians "because of a weakness of the flesh" (δι' ἀσθένειαν τῆς σαρκός) — i.e., a physical ailment of some notable kind. Paul makes three lexical choices in this passage that indicate how he wants this initial encounter to be viewed. He notes that, although his condition put the Galatians to the test (τὸν πειρασμὸν ὑμῶν, 4:14), they did no "wrong" to him (οὐδέν με ἠδικήσατε, 4:12), and did not "spit" at him (οὐδὲ ἐξεπτύσατε, 4:14). These descriptions of Paul's initial encounter with the Galatians operate wholly within the context of popular

4. A more recent form of "neglect" has appeared in the work of Thomas Witulski, who imagines 4:8-20 to be an interpolation into the text from a time when the imperial cult was making inroads into the Galatian context (*Die Adressaten des Galaterbriefes: Untersuchungen zur Gemeinde von Antiochia ad Pisidiam* [Göttingen: Vandenhoeck & Ruprecht, 2000]). Rather than noting the essential structural and theological position of this passage, this kind of approach merely adds error on top of neglect. On the essential role of this passage within the Galatian letter, see Longenecker, "Until Christ is formed in you." See also Justin K. Hardin, *Galatians and the Imperial Cult: A Critical Analysis of the First-Century Social Context of Paul's Letter* (Tübingen: Mohr Siebeck, 2008), who follows Witulski's view that 4:8-20 pertains to the imperial cult (as well as the issue of circumcision), but who drops Witulski's spurious view that the passage is a later addition (pp. 101-102).

(but not ubiquitous) notions of illness in the ancient world. When someone entered territory where he was not known to the local population, it was prudent for the locals to be cautious, in case that person was coming with malicious intent. This was all the more the case when that person exhibited an illness, as was the case with Paul, since such a person would be a prime candidate to wield the much-feared evil eye — that is, the belief that individuals of certain types possess the power to bring misfortune to things animate and inanimate simply through their glance. Through manipulation of supra-human forces, the wielder of the evil eye was thought to be able to snatch away the health of others in order to offset his own ailments. The wisest measures, then, were to shun such a person, to exclude him from their midst, and to take precautions against the effects of the evil eye, one of which was to spit at the suspicious person.[5]

Paul notes, however, that the Galatians did none of this. Although they were "tested" upon his arrival, they chose not to "do him wrong" by shunning him and "spitting." Instead, they "welcomed" Paul (4:14), despite his illness. Moreover, they welcomed him in a most gracious manner, even to the extent that they "would have plucked out [their] eyes and given them" to him (ἐδώκατέ μοι; compare Jesus' self-giving, highlighted in 1:4 and 2:20), if that could have been possible (4:15).

What we see in this theological biography of the Galatians is the way that Paul depicts their own encounter with him as itself an occasion of Spirit-inspired cruciform morality. Rather than observing practices of prudent self-preservation that were dictated by their culture, the Galatians had already exhibited practices of culturally imprudent self-giving to one in need (and dangerously so) — practices that could only have been enlivened by the Spirit of the Son, in Paul's view. In short, when despite his physical in-

---

5. Paul's health deficit would normally have excluded him from being a worthy recipient of hospitality. In theory, a stranger might be targeted for, or might successfully request, hospitality. But when the stranger is also one who is infirmed, Greco-Roman hospitality dissipated, being replaced by suspicion that the stranger might be a wielder of the evil eye. That evil-eye codes rather than hospitality codes are the "register" of Paul's arrival among the Galatians is indicated by Paul's use of the verb "spit," which has nothing to do with hospitality codes and everything to do with evil-eye prevention. Andrew Arterbury (*Entertaining Angels: Early Christian Hospitality in Its Mediterranean Setting* [Sheffield: Sheffield Phoenix Press, 2005], pp. 95, 102) does not take note of this important difference. There may be grounds for exploring Gal 4:12-15 in light of hospitality conventions, however, since Paul's point is that instead of acting out the script of evil-eye protection, as expected, they acted out the script of hospitality — astonishingly so, and only through the influence of the Spirit (the latter is only implied, but strongly so).

firmity the Galatians welcomed Paul, they were showing themselves to be already living within the moral matrix of the all-transforming gospel — i.e., bearing the burdens of another, even at great risk to themselves.[6]

In this way, the stipulation of the Jerusalem apostles in Gal 2:10 is not unrelated to the actions whereby the Galatians welcomed Paul at great risk to themselves. Paul's Galatian audiences are to see themselves having already been living in accordance with the cruciform moral universe that the Jerusalem apostles had defined in the presence of Paul years before the Galatian crisis had emerged.

Paul did not intend his initial reception by the Galatians to be the sole demonstration of Galatian cruciformity. To this end, an arc is notable between the stipulation of Gal 2:10 and the biography of Galatians, by means of Gal 6:9-10. These two verses, which have been considered already in §6.2 above, fall right at the end of what has often been seen as the "ethical" section of Paul's Galatian letter — i.e., Gal 5:13–6:10. Gone are the days, however, when interpreters divided Galatians up into sections "theological" and "ethical" with a rather strained relationship between them. Paul's theologizing in the early chapters of Galatians must bear fruit in relation to lifestyle and practice, if it is to be seen as offering a viable alternative to the "gospel" being advocated by the agitators. And much of what Paul writes in Gal 5:13–6:10 clearly pertains to the Galatian situation, at least from 5:13 through to, say, 6:2. But the few verses that precede the postscript of Gal 6:11-18 continue to give the impression of being rather general ethical maxims that are not really grounded in the theological resources of the letter or the contours of the situation. Perhaps Paul was simply in a flow of thought that continued to run on until it petered out in 6:10. Perhaps prior to picking up the writing instrument himself and inscribing Gal 6:11-18 in his own hand, Paul had simply been on ethical autopilot in the verses immediately preceding 6:11.

Regardless of how we might imagine the rhetorical utility of Gal 6:3-8, however, Paul's comments in 6:9-10 are not nearly so arbitrary and negligible as all that. As noted above, the emphatic construction ἄρα οὖν ("therefore, then") in Gal 6:10 seems devised to hammer home a point that is vitally important to Paul's argument. Paul wants his readers to sit up and take note of where his argument has taken him, and he does not pick up the writing instrument until his case reaches that point. And what he emphasizes, of

---

6. For more on this, see Longenecker, "Until Christ is formed in you"; and Longenecker, *The Triumph of Abraham's God*, pp. 150-62.

course, is that followers of Jesus should willingly initiate financial expenditures in order to offer assistance to those in need — the same point made a verse earlier, ensuring therefore that the reader gets a double dose of the point: "Let us not grow weary in doing good. . . . Therefore, then, as often as God gives the opportunity, let us work the good for all people, especially for those of the household of faith." The exhortations to "do good" in 6:9-10 are not an indication that Paul's moral vision here has reached "the utmost point of generality," as commentators occasionally suggest.[7] Instead, those exhortations have moved more in the direction of specificity. That is, the apostolic stipulation that gentile Christians should remember the poor is reinforced by Paul in the final verses of 5:13–6:10. Paul's exhortations of 6:9-10 form a practical application and reinforcement of the apostolic exhortation of 2:10. That apostolic exhortation arcs outwards to its final grounding point in the very culmination of Paul's theologizing prior to his epistolary postscript. Just as 2:10 takes pride of place in the account of the Jerusalem meeting of Gal 2:1-10, so too 6:9-10 takes pride of place in the structure of Paul's Galatian letter, not least because of its theological relationship to the apostolic stipulation of 2:10.[8]

As noted at the beginning of this chapter, only rarely do interpreters ask the question, "How does the stipulation of Gal 2:10 function within the rhetorical context of the Galatian letter?" One of the few to ask this question is Larry Hurtado.[9] Notably, just as we have done here, Hurtado links 2:10 to Gal 6:6-10. But according to him, all of those verses comprise an implicit "exhortation to participate in the Jerusalem collection."[10] Hurtado is on pre-

---

7. Ernest de Witt Burton, *A Critical and Exegetical Commentary on the Epistle to the Galatians* (Edinburgh: T&T Clark, 1921), p. 345.

8. According to Larry W. Hurtado ("The Jerusalem Collection and the Book of Galatians," *JSNT* 5 [1979]: 46-62, p. 53), "[t]he whole of Gal 6:6-10 . . . is a single, cohesive appeal urging the Galatians to share their material goods with others." Although this fits well with my thesis, I am not convinced, however, of Hurtado's claim that the same economic dimension is in full force in 6:7-8. Of those verses, Hurtado writes: "To 'mock' God, in this context then, would mean to profess brotherhood but not to demonstrate it by sharing. To 'sow to one's own flesh' would mean to keep all one's goods selfishly for one's own enjoyment. 'Sowing to the Spirit' would mean giving one's goods in response to the clear impulse of God's Spirit to the needs of others."

9. Hurtado, "The Jerusalem Collection."

10. Hurtado, "The Jerusalem Collection," p. 53. Walter Schmithals has the same view ("Die Kollekten des Paulus für Jerusalem," in C. Breytenbach, ed., *Paulus, Die Evangelien und Das Urchristentum* [Leiden: Brill, 2004], 78-106, p. 90): "Aber nicht nur Gal 2,10 enthält einen indirekten Hinweis auf die bereits angelaufene Kollektierung. Deutlich und für die

cisely the right track in linking Gal 2:10 and 6:9-10, but he is wrong to think that all of these verses are about Paul's collection for the saints in Jerusalem.[11] Once the Jerusalem-centric interpretation of Gal 2:10 is jettisoned, the link between 2:10 and 6:9-10 has nothing to do with Paul's collection and everything to do with what Paul calls "the truth of the gospel" (2:5, 14) that he and the Jerusalem apostles had already confirmed. Deep within that gospel is to be found a cruciform morality — a character demonstrated in the provision of support for those in economic hardship. Rather than Gal 6:9-10 tailing off into generalities, or comprising an exhortation to participate in Paul's collection, in those verses Paul is emphatic in his efforts to demonstrate that the kind of lifestyle (to be) generated within Jesus-groups is a lifestyle that coheres perfectly with the apostolic stipulation of Gal 2:10.[12]

Accordingly, Gal 2:10 established one point of an arc that is grounded in at least two other points within the Galatian letter: 4:12-15 and 6:9-10. Gal 4:12-15 assess one point in the theological biography of the Galatians in relation to the apostolic stipulation, and Gal 6:9-10 attest that Paul's theology becomes grounded in practices which cohere with that stipulation. For Paul, the point is simple: if the Galatians abide by Paul's theology and exhortations, they would find themselves to be living in complete alignment with the moral world that was endorsed and sanctioned by the Jerusalem apostles in agreement with Paul.

9.2: The Galatians, the Needy and the Mosaic Law

Proving that his gospel falls in line with the apostolic stipulation of Gal 2:10 is not the only thing that Paul wants to establish in Galatians. He is also intent on demonstrating that, as the Galatians live in accord with the gospel

---

Galater unmißverständlich nimmt Paulus auch in Gal 6,9f, gegen Ende des eigentlichen Briefkorpus, darauf Bezug."

11. On weaknesses within Hurtado's approach, see especially John M. G. Barclay, *Obeying the Truth: Paul's Ethics in Galatians* (Edinburgh: T&T Clark, 1988), p. 163 n. 59, and p. 166 n. 69.

12. The same might be said in more traditionally familiar terms in the words of Hans Dieter Betz (*Galatians* [Philadelphia: Fortress Press, 1979], p. 310): "As the conclusion to the parenetical section, the statement sums up . . . what the Apostle regards as the ethical task of the Christian community. Hence, it serves also as a definition of Christian ethics." Betz's comments might simply be glossed by saying that this is not simply Paul's view, but is the agreed apostolic view, as Paul has already demonstrated in Gal 2:10.

that he preaches and give generously to the needy, they will also be aligning themselves with the moral world that was endorsed and sanctioned in the scriptures of Israel (at least when read through the prism of the gospel).

The thesis is not at all difficult to demonstrate, as even a cursory reading of the letter reveals. One cannot get past Gal 5:13-15 without noting the point:

> For you were called to freedom, brothers and sisters; only do not use your freedom as an opportunity for self-indulgence, but through love become slaves to one another. For the whole law is summed up in a single commandment, "You shall love your neighbor as yourself." If, however, you bite and devour one another, take care that you are not consumed by one another.

Paul's sketch of agonistic competition and self-interest at the start and finish of this section is the backdrop against which he contrasts the loving of others through service and self-giving. For our purposes, the point to notice is simply that Paul lists cruciform morality (here amplifying the "love your neighbor" of Lev 19:18) as itself the means of fulfilling "the whole law" (ὁ πᾶς νόμος). If the Galatians were enthralled not simply with the prospect of undergoing circumcision but, more broadly, with the issue of observing the law, Paul undercuts the need for a literal observance of the particulars of the Mosaic law by postulating that the law finds its fulfillment in patterns of cruciform morality within communities of Jesus-followers.

Paul registers much the same in Gal 6:2: "Bear one another's burdens, and in this way you will fulfill the law of Christ" (ἀλλήλων τὰ βάρη βαστάζετε καὶ οὕτως ἀναπληρώσετε τὸν νόμον τοῦ Χριστοῦ). Once again, cruciform morality is the means of fulfilling what Paul calls here the "law of Christ" — by which he seems to mean the law as interpreted through the cruciform pattern exhibited in the life of Jesus who "loved and gave himself" (2:20; see also 1:4).[13]

For Paul, the notion of "love" is grounded in the gritty realities of self-

---

13. It is not uncommon to find this phrase interpreted without reference to the Mosaic law, since the "law of Christ" can so easily be understood as the social teaching of Jesus or in a more general way as a "norm" or "principle" (νόμος) of living patterned on Christ's own model. There is some cause to think that Paul is redefining things here somewhat, but it seems unwise to erode all reference to the Mosaic law in this phrase; the links between 5:13-14 and 6:2 are too strong to suggest otherwise. Both passages (1) speak of relationships of mutuality and service among Jesus-followers in connection with (2) the verb "fulfill" (πληρόω/ ἀναπληρόω) and (3) the noun "law" (νόμος).

giving for the benefit of others. It is little wonder, then, that when Paul lays out his list of the fruit of the Spirit (5:22-23), he includes the action of generous giving to those in need (ἀγαθωσύνη, 5:22) as one example of the kind of cruciform love he has in mind.[14] For Paul, this kind of generous goodness to the needy exemplifies and characterizes precisely the "faith working practically through love" (πίστις δι' ἀγάπης ἐνεργουμένη, 5:6) by which the Mosaic law is fulfilled.

The apostolic agreement about remembering the poor resonates throughout the theological echo-chamber that Paul establishes in these later parts of his letter.[15] As Paul pointed out to his Galatian communities in 2:1-10, the apostles had all agreed that the Mosaic requirement of circumcision was not applicable to gentile Jesus-followers, but also that generous care for the needy was a pattern of life to be enlivened among all followers of Jesus universally. In Paul's letter to the Galatians, precisely the cruciform pattern that underlies the stipulation to "remember the poor" is said to be the means of fulfilling "the whole law." If the Galatians are intent on aligning themselves with the law, Paul holds out cruciform morality as the means of doing precisely that — i.e., bearing one another's burdens, being servants of one another, being generous towards others, remembering the poor. In this way, the apostolic stipulation to "remember the poor" establishes a foothold for the notion of generous living that Paul later goes on to develop in relation to the Mosaic law, with which the Galatians were so anxious to align themselves.

It is little wonder, then, that Paul includes mention of that stipulation in his reconstruction of the apostolic agreement. In fact, Gal 2:6-10 may qualify as a record of the first attempt within the Jesus-movement to devise something of a universal "rule of faith" through which the scriptures are to be read wisely in the various (and diverse) Jesus-communities. This embryonic rule of faith was agreed to by key figures across the spectrum of the Jesus-movement, and represents their initial deliberations regarding the extent to which certain aspects of Israel's scriptures pertained to their common life. Whereas the biblical commands regarding circumcision were recognized as being non-essential to the diverse membership of the Jesus-movement, the

14. Johannes P. Louw and Eugene A. Nida center the semantic range of ἀγαθωσύνη on this notion of generous giving (*Greek-English Lexicon of the New Testament Based on Semantic Domains* [New York: United Bible Societies, 1988/89], §57.109): "the act of generous giving, with the implication of its relationship to goodness."

15. Gal 5:13-15, 22-23; 6:2; also, as shown in §9.1 above, 4:12-15; 6:9-10. For more on these and other important passages in Galatians, especially with regard to Paul's presentation of "the law" in that text, see my *The Triumph of Abraham's God*.

biblical values regarding the remembrance of the poor were recognized as being a necessary (albeit not sufficient) component of any and all Jesus-groups. For Paul, remembrance of the poor seems to have been a prime attribute of the cruciform pattern of life — a pattern of life whereby the whole law is fulfilled (in accordance with the embryonic "rule of faith" established by a cross-section of apostolic figures) through the enlivenment of the eschatological Spirit.[16]

At this point, the interest in Paul that has predominated in chapters 6 through 9 gives way to an interest in the constitution of communities founded by Paul — in particular, the socio-economic profiling of those communities and the extent to which they would have been attractive to urbanites within the Greco-Roman world. But although the next two chapters shift their focus, they do not leave Paul behind. He continues to pop back into the frame at key points, not least when considering his theology of the body of Christ in chapter 12 below, and then again in chapter 13, when the conclusions of this book are laid out in relation to key features of Paul's own life. But we can proceed no further in our investigation of the poor in Pauline perspective without focusing more concretely on life within urban Jesus-groups, including the socio-economic profiles of those who gathered in Jesus-groups that Paul established.

16. See Appendix 2 below, "Non-Pauline Configurations of Generosity and the Mosaic Law," where this feature of Paul's theology is compared to views held by others.

CHAPTER 10

"Not many of you were of noble birth"

Economic Profiles within Paul's Communities

Interest in the socio-economic profile of the first urban Jesus-followers has a long history, having a strong foothold even in patristic literature of the early centuries CE.[1] But only recently has discussion about the issue taken on a controversial edge in an unprecedented way. The debate derives its importance not from some speculative interest in the size of the "wallets" of the first urban Jesus-followers. Nor is it that the socio-economic level of the earliest urban Jesus-followers derives its primary utility in relation to the inter-

---

1. See, for instance, Origen, *Cels.* 3; Augustine, *Div.* 10.14; Chrysostom, *Laud. Paul.* 4.11. On similar interest in 1 Cor 1:26 by Theodore of Mopsuestia and Theodoret, see John Anthony Cramer, ed., *Catenae in Sancti Pauli Epistolas ad Corinthios,* vol. 5 of *Catenae Graecorum Patrum in Novum Testamentum,* ed. John Anthony Cramer (1841; repr. Hildesheim: Georg Olms, 1967), pp. 30-31; Karl Staab, ed., *Pauluskommentare aus der griechischen Kirche,* 2nd ed. (Münster: Aschendorff, 1984), p. 174.

pretative nuances of a few texts of the early Jesus-movement. Instead, the issue is central for understanding things like: (1) how early urban Jesus-groups may have attracted or deterred first-century urban dwellers, and (2) how those groups were internally constituted. In order to address issues of that kind, socio-economic factors need to be taken into full account, even if they may fall short of providing all-encompassing explanations.

10.1: What Are They Saying about the Socio-Economic Status of the First Urban Jesus-Followers?

Wayne Meeks's landmark study *The First Urban Christians* stands tall in explorations of matters such as these. Although published in 1983, it continues to command high respect with regard to the issues that it dealt with, as it reconstructed what it might have been like for ordinary people to join urban communities of Jesus-followers.[2]

One of the most important contributions of that book is its consideration of the extent to which the rise of the Jesus-movement in first-century urban contexts was affected by socio-economic factors. Since innumerable (other) clubs and associations existed within Greco-Roman urbanism, Meeks was interested in understanding what particular attractions early Jesus-groups might have offered urban dwellers, without resorting to sociological reductionism. In this, Meeks sought to take full account of the fact that, in the ancient world (and today as well), a full register of a person's status involved a blend of diverse factors, with the economic dimension being only one.[3] Meeks alerted his readers to a variety of features that would have contributed to a person's social profile: ethnic origins, *ordo*, citizenship, personal liberty, wealth, occupation, age, sex, public offices or honors, and family heritage.[4]

2. Wayne A. Meeks, *First Urban Christians: The Social World of the Apostle Paul* (New Haven: Yale University Press, 1983). See now the volume edited by Todd Still and David Horrell, *After the First Urban Christians* (London: Continuum, 2009), in which more often than not Meeks's book is shown to stand most of the tests of time in the intervening twenty-five years.

3. On contemporary forms of "honor capture" and its negative effects on society, see Robert H. Frank, *Luxury Fever: Money and Happiness in an Era of Excess* (Princeton: Princeton University Press, 1999). So he writes (p. 172): "The evidence we have seen suggests that concerns about relative position are a powerful element of human nature. Given the intensity of these concerns, we are confronted at almost every turn with opportunities to pursue actions that are smart for one, dumb for all."

4. Meeks, *First Urban Christians*, pp. 54-55. That status was multivalent in the ancient

To what extent might status issues shed light on the rise of the early Jesus-movement? At the forefront of Meeks's proposals are people who were "status-inconsistent" in the Greco-Roman world.[5] For Meeks, such people occupied "an ambiguous position in society," and Jesus-groups offered those people a means to resolve their socially-perceived status inconsistency. For any in this bracket, some indicators would have registered higher up the status scale while others would have registered lower down.[6] In Meeks's view, two intertwined factors would have served to attract status-dissonant middling urbanites to Jesus-groups, as opposed to other Greco-Roman associations. Meeks outlines this double-attraction in the final paragraphs of *First Urban Christians:* (1) the "good news" of divinely empowered "change" would have been attractive to "status inconsistents," since the structures of society were generally stacked against beneficial change, and (2) the intimacy that transpired within Jesus-groups would have been attractive to status inconsistents, since corporate intimacy would have offset the inevitable "anxiety" and "loneliness" of status-dissonant urbanites through the

---

Mediterranean basin is clear from a text like Paul's letter to Philemon. In that letter Paul tries to pull off a difficult balancing act with regard to social profile and authority. In a manner not unlike the swing of a pendulum, Paul finds it necessary at times to recognize Philemon's authority, based on certain aspects of his profile (e.g., Philem 2, 7, 14a, 19a, 20), and at other times to insist on his own (i.e., Paul's) authority, based on certain aspects of his profile (e.g., Philem 8-9, 14b, 19b, 21). The letter indicates that, in certain situations, status negotiation was tricky business involving a delicate register of factors that fed into the mix of social profiling. Or as David J. Downs says ("Is God Paul's Patron? The Economy of Patronage in Pauline Theology," in Bruce W. Longenecker and Kelly Liebengood, eds., *Engaging Economics: New Testament Scenarios and Early Christian Reception* [Grand Rapids: Eerdmans, 2009], 129-56, p. 135), "when read in light of a sociological definition of patronage, much of the letter turns on the question, 'Who is the patron of whom?'"

Compare also the fact that Prisca (Priscilla), a woman, is frequently mentioned before her husband Aquila in New Testament texts; Acts 18:18, 26; Rom 16:3; cf. 2 Tim 4:19 (contrast Acts 18:2; 1 Cor 16:19). Or the case of the young Jesus who taught with authority in the Temple precincts (Luke 2:43-51). Or the case of Peter, as a guest of Simon, inviting the representatives of Cornelius to enjoy hospitality in the house of Simon (Acts 10:23).

5. When the broad canvas of status complexity is lost from view, focusing on a "middle class" can too easily lead to the view that the early Jesus-movement was part of a "class struggle" of a kind favored by Marxist analysis. By keeping the breadth of status in view, Meeks is able to avoid anachronistic analysis of this kind.

6. So Keith Hopkins, "Elite Mobility in the Roman Empire," *Past and Present* 32 (1965): 12-26, p. 26: "Romans expected a high degree of status congruence" as opposed to "status dissonance," which involved a person rating "highly on some status dimensions but not on others."

"emotion-charged language of family and affections and the image of a caring, personal God."[7]

Meeks's thesis is derived primarily from evidence within Paul's corpus of texts, since that corpus, more than any other within the early stratum of the Jesus-movement, testifies to the urban context of the first generation of the Jesus-movement. Accordingly, Meeks entitles the second chapter of his book "The Social Level of Pauline Christians." And it is a pivotal chapter, making a strong arc directly into the closing paragraphs of his book. Meeks's concluding explanation for the rise of the early Jesus-movement takes full account of the issues of socio-economic status that were explored in his second chapter. In fact, the end of the "social level" chapter concludes much as the book does, with the claim that "the most active and prominent members of Paul's circle . . . are people of high status inconsistency" (p. 73). Meeks then asked the pressing question:

> Is that more than accidental? Are there some specific characteristics of early Christianity that would be attractive to status-inconsistents? Or is it only that people with the sorts of drive, abilities, and opportunities that produced such mixed status would tend to stand out in any group they joined, and thus to be noticed for the record?

The chapters that follow the second in Meeks's *First Urban Christians* are very much directed at giving a "non-accidental" explanation for the presence of people of high "status inconsistency" in communities founded by

---

7. Meeks, *First Urban Christians*, p. 191. Note, however, Meeks's point (p. 79) that the "primary goals" of associations "were fellowship and conviviality," so it is not clear whether the demarcation between Jesus-groups and other associations is one of kind or degree. Moreover, it is not wholly clear whether Meeks intends to ascribe "anxiety" and "loneliness" to the "middle-status" members or to others at lower economic levels. H. W. Pleket (Review of *First Urban Christians* by Wayne Meeks, *VC* 39 [1985]: 192-96, p. 195) understands Meeks to ascribe these psychological states to the status inconsistents, whereas Bruce Malina (Review of *First Urban Christians* by Wayne Meeks, *JBL* 104 [1985]: 346-49, p. 349) understands Meeks to ascribe them to others. On this, Pleket has the better reading. On p. 191 Meeks postulates that status-inconsistents would have endured anxiety and loneliness. Meeks may imagine that anxiety and loneliness characterized people beyond the status-inconsistents, of course. On p. 104, for instance, Meeks speaks of societal "complexity — its untidiness to the mind" as likely having been "felt with special acuteness by people who were marginal or transient, either physically or socially or both, as so many of the identifiable members of the Pauline churches seem to have been." There may be some (intentional) ambiguity in that sentence, although the word "identifiable" in the final phrase makes a gesture to status-inconsistent members.

Paul, noting how those communities offered resources to offset the deficits that accompanied status inconsistency. Those who found their middling form of "status inconsistency" to be offset in urban Jesus-groups provided the resources for corporate life among Jesus-followers, and consequently are the key for understanding the expansion of the early Jesus-movement within the Mediterranean basin.

Criticism has been leveled at Meeks's attempt to explain the socio-economic attractions of the early urban Jesus-movement in relation to the resolution of "status inconsistency." Since status inconsistency was arguably a phenomenon that pertained to a wide spectrum of people, it consequently fails to have the explanatory power that Meeks affords it in relation to a narrower band within that spectrum.[8]

For instance, psychological factors such as "anxiety," which carry significant weight in Meeks's analysis of motivational bases, are not themselves restricted to middling status inconsistents.[9] Clearly, anxiety would have marked out the existence of low-status holders who lived near or at poverty levels; moreover, we should not fail to recognize the extent to which the elite themselves were subject to anxiety.[10] Few, if any, were ever removed from the precarious prospect of loss: "The fear of loss, of the downward mobility that was so common, was nearly universal," involving "deep-seated and often undifferentiated fears about powerlessness and lack of control in life."[11] Philo

8. See R. Lane Fox, *Pagans and Christians* (London: Viking, 1986), pp. 319-22. There he notes that "[p]eople's views of their own status are enchantingly complex and unexpected, and perhaps 'consistency' is a rarer condition than its theorists imply." John Milbank (*Theology and Social Theory: Beyond Secular Reason* [Oxford: Basil Blackwell, 1990], p. 118) makes the point in relation to a caution about sociological reductionism: "Christianity was not uniquely well-adapted to those suffering from status inconsistency, and the problem which sociology cannot answer is why *this* solution [i.e., Christianity] . . . with its unprecedented effectiveness?" Nonetheless, the status inconsistency explanation is given full articulation by Jerome Murphy-O'Connor, *Paul: A Critical Life* (Oxford: Oxford University Press, 1996), pp. 268-71.

9. Neville Morley ("The Poor in the City of Rome," in M. Atkins and R. Osborne, eds., *Poverty in the Roman World* [Cambridge: Cambridge University Press, 2006], 21-39, p. 34) postulates that "urban society, especially in the great metropolis . . . , was characterised by alienation, anonymity and purely instrumental relationships."

10. Seneca (*Marc.* 9.1) reflects on how easily the elite can be reduced to beggary. This is ironically depicted in Ovid *Tr.* 5.8.13-14, in which a woman who had stubbornly failed to give food to the poor suddenly found herself having to beg for it herself.

11. Richard L. Rohrbauch, "Methodological Considerations in the Debate over the Social Class Status of Early Christians," *JAAR* 52 (1984): 519-46, p. 543. He continues: "the theological message [of the early Jesus-movement] is to be understood as speaking to persons

(*Ios.* 144) makes the point with polemical acuteness when speaking to the elite with this rhetorical question and subsequent instruction: "Does everything succeed with you according to your wish? Fear a change [μεταβολὴν εὐλαβοῦ]."[12] The fact that the elite generally seem not to have sought shelter against anxiety in the earliest Jesus-groups suggests that scenarios placing anxiety about status front and center are not fully nuanced.

Meeks's discussion of "the social level of Pauline Christians" contributes to a dispute that was long-standing in 1983 and still continues today. Much of the scholarship dedicated to the issue in the twentieth century showed a marked indebtedness to Adolf Deissmann's analysis. Deissmann's postulate of a "close inward connection between the gospel and the lower classes" was understood (rightly or wrongly) to mean that the early Jesus-movement was a movement of and for the destitute.[13] So in 1975 John Gager could speak of

---

who are not so much thwarted in their social aspirations as they are frightened by the precarious nature of their position in the world. Whatever influence the desire for social prestige may have had on both early Christianity and the New Testament, it was probably of modest proportions alongside the hope for an alternative future, for a new and different kind of kingdom."

12. He says much the same in *Spec.* 2.17: "For the accidents of human life are numerous, and life is not always anchored on the same bottom, but is apt to change like the fickle wind which blows in different directions at different times." Cf. Jerome Murphy-O'Connor, *Paul: His Story* (Oxford: Oxford University Press, 2004), p. 83: "It was an age of anxiety. The arbitrariness of chance generated an interior world inhabited by dread and uncertainty."

13. G. A. Deissmann, *Light from the Ancient East: The New Testament Illustrated by Recently Discovered Texts of the Graeco-Roman World* (London: Hodder & Stoughton, 1910), p. 403. Meeks himself attributes scholarly thinking about the social level of early Jesus-followers to Deissman in this way (*First Urban Christians*, pp. 51-52]): "Of particular importance in shaping this century's common view of Paul and his congregations was the opinion of Adolf Deissmann. . . . The prevailing viewpoint has been that the constituency of early Christianity . . . came from the poor and dispossessed of the Roman provinces." Arguably, however, Deissmann did not mean to suggest that only the desperately poor were attracted to the early Jesus-movement. For a helpful discussion of how Deissmann's view has been (mis)interpreted, see Steven J. Friesen, "Poverty in Pauline Studies: Beyond the So-called New Consensus," *JSNT* 26 (2004): 323-61, pp. 324-26. Note, for instance, Deissmann's comments in *Paul: A Study in Social and Religious History* (New York: Harper & Brothers, 1957 [1925]), pp. 241-43: "The people whose souls were moved by the mission of Paul and his faithful companions were — the overwhelming majority at least — men and women from the middle and lower classes. . . . Paul mentions by name certain fairly well-to-do Christians. Those who possessed rooms so large that 'house churches' could assemble there for edification . . . cannot have been poor. . . . It is noteworthy that several women whose names are honourably mentioned in connection with Paul's missionary labours, appear to have been possessed of means." Meeks rightly notes the nuances within Deissmann's position in *First Urban Christians*, p. 52.

"something approaching a consensus" within scholarship, with the early Jesus-movement being depicted as "essentially a movement among disprivileged [*sic*] groups in the Empire."[14] The point has been championed most starkly in relation to an economic profiling of early urban Jesus-followers by Justin Meggitt, whose influential work has already been noted in chapter 3 above. As we have seen, he characterizes communities founded by Paul in this way:

> The Pauline Christians *en masse* shared fully the bleak material existence which was the lot of more than 99% of the inhabitants of the Empire. . . . To believe otherwise . . . , given the near universal prevalence of poverty in the first-century world, is to believe the improbable.[15]

But alternative emphases have also been strongly registered along the way. In 1960, for instance, Edwin Judge claimed that "the Christians were dominated by a socially pretentious section of the population of the big cities," with those "socially pretentious" members of the community supporting "a broad constituency" that included predominately "the household dependants of the leading members."[16] In the early 1970s Wilhelm Wuellner argued that the earliest urban Jesus-followers were largely "from fairly well-to-do bourgeois circles, with a fair percentage also from upper class people as well as the very poor,"[17] while Jurgen Becker found the early urban Jesus-

---

14. John G. Gager, *Kingdom and Community: The Social World of Early Christianity* (Englewood Cliffs: Prentice-Hall, 1975), p. 96. Bengt Holmberg (*Sociology and the New Testament* [Minneapolis: Fortress Press, 1990], p. 28) characterizes this view as maintaining that the early Jesus-movement was "a religion of the slaves and the oppressed, made up of poor peasants and workers."

15. Justin J. Meggitt, *Paul, Poverty and Survival* (Edinburgh: T&T Clark, 1998), p. 99.

16. Edwin A. Judge, "The Social Pattern of the Christian Groups in the First Century: Some Prolegomena to the Study of New Testament Ideas of Social Obligation," originally published as a book (London: Tyndale, 1960), now reprinted in David M. Scholer, ed., *Social Perspectives on Christians in the First Century: Pivotal Essays by E. A. Judge* (Peabody: Hendrickson, 2008), 1-56, p. 43. The description is reiterated on p. 119.

17. Wilhelm H. Wuellner, "The Sociological Implications of I Corinthians 1:26-28 Reconsidered," in *Studia Evangelica* VI, ed. Elizabeth A. Livingstone, TU 112 (Berlin: Akademie Verlag, 1973), 666-72, p. 672. Gail O'Day confirmed his interpretation in her 1990 article "Jeremiah 9:22-23 and 1 Corinthians 1:26-31: A Study in Intertextuality," *JBL* 109 (1990): 259-67, p. 263. Wuellner and O'Day translate 1 Cor 1:26 as "Look to your call, brothers and sisters, were not many of you wise according to the flesh, were not many strong, were not many of noble birth?" Patristic interpretations of this verse, however, show no signs of cognizance of this reading, and it remains extremely unlikely.

movement to have been driven by "a self-confident, urban bourgeoisie with entrepreneurial spirit and sizeable wealth."[18] By the late 1970s and early 1980s, other strong voices were being heard along similar lines, including those of Gerd Theissen,[19] Abraham Malherbe,[20] Robin Scroggs,[21] and of course Meeks himself. Instead of the primary appeal of the Jesus-movement being seen in terms of its attractions for the poor, it was common to characterize the early Jesus-movement as having been comprised of socially diverse members who were supported in communities by its most prominent members. Those members were predominately "the urban middle-status holders,"[22] who enjoyed "an elevated status" (at least by comparison with the numerous poor).[23] This view took such a prominent hold that in 1977 Malherbe noted the emergence of "a new consensus" in Pauline scholarship.[24] R. Russell reconstructs the "new consensus" with accuracy: "The 'new consensus' claims that the early Jesus-movement represented by Paul's communities reflects an urban social mixture with a minority of higher social ranking members that are dominant within a community which includes dependent clients, freedmen, and slaves."[25]

Both sides of the debate have advocates among scholars twenty-five years after the appearance of Meeks's *First Urban Christians*.[26] It is common

18. Jürgen Becker, "Paul and His Churches," in J. Becker, ed., *Christian Beginnings* (Louisville: Westminster John Knox Press, 1993), 132-210, p. 168.

19. Although numerous publications could be cited, fundamental is Gerd Theissen, *The Social Setting of Pauline Christianity* (Philadelphia: Fortress Press, 1982), especially ch. 2, "Social Stratification in the Corinthian Community."

20. Abraham J. Malherbe, *Social Aspects of Early Christianity* (Philadelphia: Fortress Press, 1977/1983).

21. Robin Scroggs, "The Sociological Interpretation of the New Testament: The Present State of Research," *NTS* 26 (1980): 164-79.

22. T. Schleich, "Missionsgeschichte und Sozialstruktur des vorkonstantinischen Christentums," *Geschichte in Wissenschaft und Unterricht* 33 (1982): 269-96, especially p. 288, translation mine ("der städtischen Mittelschichten"); see too p. 279.

23. This is how F. Bovon describes the urban community and readership of the Lukan writings (*Das Evangelium nach Lukas 1* [Zürich: Benziger Verlag; Neukirchen-Vluyn: Neukirchener Verlag, 1989], p. 300): "Soziologisch sind Lukas, seine Gemeinde und seine potentielle Leserschaft in einer oberen Schicht angesiedelt."

24. Malherbe, *Social Aspects*, p. 31.

25. R. Russell, "The Idle in 2 Thess 3:6-12: An Eschatological or Social Problem?" *NTS* 34 (1988): 105-119, p. 110.

26. Compare, on the one hand, Meggitt's *Paul, Poverty and Survival* and Friesen, "Poverty in Pauline Studies"; and on the other hand, David G. Horrell, *The Social Ethos of the Corinthian Correspondence: Interests and Ideology from 1 Corinthians to 1 Clement* (Edinburgh:

to depict the two positions in terms of those who advocate the "new consensus" (i.e., Theissen, Meeks, etc.) over against the "old consensus" (i.e., Deissmann, Meggitt, etc.). But in fact, the differences between these two positions has at times been unnecessarily overdrawn. I suggest this for two reasons. First, most recognize a spread of some sort within the socio-economic profile of urban Jesus-groups, so that the debate often has most to do with particular nuances and refinements to the overall picture. For instance, when Theissen writes that the "majority of the members . . . come from the lower classes" but that "a few influential members . . . come from the upper classes,"[27] it is only the second clause about "a few influential members" that is in any way contentious for some.[28] As Russell rightly notes, the "shift" from the old to the new consensus "is one primarily of focus — the 'old consensus' emphasized the lower social level but realized the middle class was represented in the churches as well, whereas the 'new consensus' underscores the reverse."[29]

Second, the debate may have been overdrawn due to terminological variation within academic parlance. Arguably, for instance, some who speak of the attractions of the early Jesus-movement for the "lower classes" mean to include by that designation the vast swathes of people, all of whom fell below the elite but at varying points. If the terms "elite" and "upper classes" can refer to those endowed with enormous amounts of status resources, the terms "the poor" and "the lower class" have at times been used to demarcate all the rest. This is where a lack of clarity can potentially arise, because a term

---

T&T Clark, 1996), especially pp. 91-101. Note also Horrell's slight qualification to his earlier position in his "Aliens and Strangers? The Socio-Economic Location of the Addressees of 1 Peter," in Bruce W. Longenecker and Kelly D. Liebengood, eds., *Engaging Economics: New Testament Scenarios and Early Christian Reception* (Grand Rapids: Eerdmans, 2009), 176-202, p. 177 n. 7.

27. Theissen, *Social Setting*, 69. The word "class" is an unfortunate English translation of Theissen's original "Schicht," which, as Horrell rightly notes (*Social Ethos*, p. 95 n. 189), should be translated "stratum."

28. Compare V. H. T. Nguyen's unnuanced (and consequently highly suspect) depiction of "a minority group" within Corinthian communities that was comprised of "elite individuals" (*Christian Identity in Corinth* [Tübingen: Mohr Siebeck, 2008], p. 133). Nguyen claims to be outlining the positions of Judge, Theissen and others, but it is also a position that he himself advocates on pp. 132-35. See also the claim of Robert S. Dutch that some members of the Corinthian communities were among "the educated elite" (*The Educated Elite in 1 Corinth: Education and Community Conflict in Graeco-Roman Context* [London: T&T Clark, 2005]).

29. Russell, "The Idle in 2 Thess 3:6-12," p. 110.

like "lower class" can be used to demarcate either *status* deficiencies (more broadly) or *economic* deficiencies (more narrowly). Not unlike the ancient rhetorical practice of distinguishing between the few *honestiores* and the many *humiliores*,[30] some have adopted the discourse of "the lower class" to refer not simply to those at or near the poverty line but to a broad category of people, including those that others would describe as among the economically middling groups.[31] Terminological ambiguity within scholarly discourse cannot account for all points of scholarly disagreement, of course. But it may go some way towards blunting what might at times look to be a debate unnecessarily entrenched in polar opposites.[32]

The point might be made, in the first instance, by comparing Meeks's position with Gager's. Although they usually fall on either side of the divide with regard to the economic level of the early Jesus-movement, Meeks and Gager reconstruct the social function of that movement in much the same way:

> Those who were attracted to the Christian movement as a religion with unmistakably revolutionary implications were not those who stood at the very bottom of the social ladder, that is, the deprived in an absolute sense, but rather those with social aspirations who found their path blocked by the rigidity of the Roman social structure.

The words are Gager's in 1982,[33] but the position resonates well with that of Meeks in 1983.[34]

The debate between proponents of the so-called "old consensus" and "new consensus" can at times take on virtually comical dimensions. Take, for instance, the debate between Gager and Malherbe. In his 1979 review of the first edition of Malherbe's *Social Aspects of Early Christianity* (1977), Gager notes that "the proponents of this new view [i.e., the 'new consensus'] see themselves as correcting earlier presentations of early Christianity as exclu-

---

30. Morley, "The Poor," p. 29: "elite sources often treat the rest of the population as an undifferentiated mass, and apply the vocabulary of poverty indiscriminately."

31. See Friesen, "Poverty in Pauline Studies," pp. 324-26, as in n. 13 above.

32. The issue may involve more than simply terminological imprecision. It may also involve issues pertaining to the "sociology of knowledge." On this, see Rohrbaugh, "Methodological Considerations," pp. 530-31; Friesen, "Poverty in Pauline Studies," pp. 323-37.

33. J. G. Gager, "Shall We Marry Our Enemies?" *Int* 36 (1982): 256-65, p. 262. Also Gager, *Kingdom and Community*, p. 95.

34. Meeks (*First Urban Christians*, p. 215 n. 20) identifies Gager's "relative deprivation" thesis as being "closely related" to his own "status inconsistency" thesis.

sively proletarian, a movement of slaves, laborers, and outcasts of various sorts." So far, so good. But Gager goes on to claim that "it may be seriously doubted that such a view [i.e., a brash version of the 'old consensus'] ever existed apart from a few romantics and early Marxists."[35] Malherbe sees this as a blatant contradiction on Gager's part. So in the second edition of his *Social Aspects* book (1983), Malherbe offers a quotation from Gager's book of 1975, *Kingdom and Community,* in which Gager claimed that "a consensus has emerged . . . that for more than two hundred years Christianity was essentially a movement among dispossessed groups."[36] Malherbe then makes this simple observation:

> It would appear to me that the effect of this statement on the consensus, which Gager has evidently accepted, is to widen the consensus beyond the few romantics and early Marxists. . . . Gager has now either shifted ground somewhat . . . or his qualifications in the two statements (. . . "exclusively," "essentially") obscure what he really means.[37]

The oddity, however, is that within the covers of his own book, Malherbe himself can be seen to "shift ground somewhat" or to "obscure what he really means." At one point, Malherbe notes that "the majority of his [Paul's] converts came from among the poor," while not many pages later he makes the following claim: "I do not think that the majority of Christians were from the lower strata."[38] What we are witnessing is two very capable scholars dancing around an issue without the conceptual tools and terminological precision to do adequate justice to the full complexity of that issue. The apparent contradictions of both scholars arise from these deficits.

With the assistance of an economy scale, we might refine the claims of these two scholars. When Gager said in 1975 that the early Jesus-movement emerged from "dispossessed groups," we might imagine him to be referring to the sub-elite of ES4 through ES7, especially perhaps ES5 and downwards; and in 1979 he might have been intimating that his own view, like that of others, cannot be caricatured as depicting the rise of the early Jesus-movement as restricted to those at, say, ES6 and ES7. Once refined by the economy scale, Gager's position need not be seen as blatantly self-

---

35. John Gager, Review of *Social Aspects of Early Christianity* by Abraham Malherbe, *RelSRev* 5 (1979): 174-80, p. 179.

36. Gager, *Kingdom and Community,* p. 96.

37. Malherbe, *Social Aspects,* p. 120.

38. Malherbe, *Social Aspects,* pp. 77 and 121 respectively.

contradictory. And similar refinements might be used to iron out Malherbe's position. When he said that the early Jesus-movement emerged from "among the poor," we might likewise imagine him to be referring to the sub-elite of ES4 through ES7 (perhaps with more of an emphasis on ES4 than Gager's position); and when he said that the early Jesus-movement did not emerge "from the lower strata," we should probably imagine him to be envisioning levels ES6 and ES7. While the two interpreters have their own emphases and interests, their apparent contradictions are, like the dispute itself, overblown. The economy scale will not erase the dispute, but it will help us to introduce precision where in the past there has been a deficit of clarity.

Meeks's position with regard to the social profile of communities founded by Paul has itself, it seems, been subject to occasional misinterpretation. Steve Friesen, for instance, understands Meeks to say that, despite having a broad membership from several social levels, urban Jesus-groups "did not include the . . . lowest strata of society."[39] But it is not clear that this description adequately represents Meeks's position. The relevant paragraph from Meeks is as follows:

> We have found a number of converging clues . . . that permit an impressionistic sketch of these groups. It is a picture in which people of several social levels are brought together. The extreme top and bottom of the Greco-Roman social scale are missing from the picture. It is hardly surprising that we meet no landed aristocrats, no senators, *equites*, nor . . . decurions. But there is also no specific evidence of people who are destitute — such as the hired menials and dependent handworkers. . . . There may well have been members of the Pauline communities who lived at the subsistence level, but we hear nothing of them.[40]

Meeks does not say that urban Jesus-groups "did not include" the lowest strata of society (contra Friesen), only that there is "no specific evidence" of such people, allowing for the fact that "[t]here may well have been members of the Pauline communities who lived at the subsistence level." Hearing nothing about the destitute does not mean that the destitute were absent from communities that Paul addressed; it means only that their imprint has not been left on the surviving material record.

There is reason to be more optimistic than Meeks allows about the data pertaining to the destitute among urban Jesus-groups. Regardless of

39. Friesen, "Poverty in Pauline Studies," p. 326 n. 10.
40. Meeks, *First Urban Christians*, pp. 72-73.

whether we have "specific evidence" (by which I take it Meeks means specific names and descriptors — i.e., prosopographic data), the grain of New Testament data runs in the direction of signaling that those communities must have included a significant number of destitute members. This view is based not merely on the occasional reference to such people within Paul's letters (e.g., "those who have nothing," 1 Cor 11:22).[41] It is based primarily on those texts that demonstrate that Paul expected communal funds for the poor (or their equivalent) to be established within communities that he founded, with the urban destitute-beyond-the-confines-of-a-household probably having a strong presence within those communities, many of them having been attracted to such communities for whatever economic support might have been provided.[42] This feature helps to explain, for instance, how Paul can laud communities like those in Thessalonica for their "work of faith and labor of love" that had been reported throughout the region of Macedonia and Achaia (as says Paul hyperbolically in 1 Thess 1:3-10).

41. I interpret τοὺς μὴ ἔχοντας in 1 Cor 11:22 in absolute terms as "those who have nothing." Bruce W. Winter qualifies τοὺς μὴ ἔχοντας in relation to the οἰκία of the same verse (*Seek the Welfare of the City: Christians as Benefactors and Citizens* [Grand Rapids: Eerdmans, 1994], p. 203), so that the phrase differentiates between those with household connections and those without connections to householders. This is possible, and in either reconstruction the economic level of those referred to is likely to be much the same; the difference will simply be in whether τοὺς μὴ ἔχοντας pertains only to those beyond households or might also include some within households. Meggitt's claim (*Paul, Poverty and Survival*, pp. 119-20) that τοὺς μὴ ἔχοντας refers to "those who do not have bread and wine" seems less likely.

42. These textual indicators are strongly reinforced by the study of early Christianity in Rome by Peter Lampe (*Die stadtrömischen Christen in den ersten beiden Jahrhunderten: Untersuchungen zur Sozialgeschichte* [Tübingen: Mohr Siebeck, 1989; now *From Paul to Valentinus: Christians at Rome in the First Two Centuries*, trans. M. Steinhauser [Minneapolis: Fortress Press, 2003]). Lampe demonstrates that one of the locations in which the early Jesus-movement was likely to have taken root in Rome was the Trastevere, "a harbor quarter, a workers quarter." According to Lampe, this section accommodated people such as: harbor workers, warehouse porters, sailors, brickyard workers, shopkeepers, craftsmen of small shops, millers, and tanners. He calls this quarter the "city quarter of the lowest strata of the population" (p. 50). Two other sectors in which early Jesus-groups are likely to have become established were not so depressed, including the area near the Appian Way and, especially, the Aventine. But Lampe's work has been subjected to important criticisms; see for instance Peter Oakes, "Methodological Issues in Using Economic Evidence in Interpretation of Early Christian Texts," in Bruce W. Longenecker and Kelly D. Liebengood, eds., *Engaging Economics: New Testament Scenarios and Early Christian Reception* (Grand Rapids: Eerdmans, 2009), 9-34, pp. 25-26; also David L. Balch, "Paul, Families and Households," in J. Paul Sampley, ed., *Paul in the Greco-Roman World* (Harrisburg: Trinity Press International, 2003), 258-92, p. 259.

It is also important to note that Meeks's analysis works well if we imagine early Jesus-followers to have been embedded within household structures. A typical household would have been comprised of a householder, the householder's family and a group of servile functionaries. Many of those slaves would have been poor in and of themselves, although being embedded within a household would often have provided some relative security. Similarly, as a householder joined a group of Jesus-followers, so too would those within the household (or those whom the householder designated).[43] Furthermore, the Roman *domus* was not simply a housing for a "single-family unit"; instead, the *domus* resembled more an urban neighborhood than a single house. Andrew Wallace-Hadrill describes it as "a 'big house' inhabited by a 'houseful' rather than a household; [it was] not only a parent-children-slaves unit, but a cluster" linked by any number of familial, patronal, servile and/or commercial relationships.[44]

More recently, however, interpreters have been toying with other organizational models as the context for the meetings of the earliest followers of Jesus.[45] In these cases, the influence of a householder is greatly reduced or is altogether absent. For instance, David Horrell has noted "the considerable variety of possible types of domestic space — from country villas to peasant homes, smart town apartments to rooms behind or over a shop, not to mention the more ramshackle and temporary dwellings of the destitute." So he warns against imagining any of them as necessarily "typical" settings in the rise of the early Jesus-movement: "NT studies should pay more attention to the varieties of domestic space in the urban setting of Corinth and other cities of the Roman empire, and consider these as possible settings for early Christian meetings."[46] Robert Jewett and Justin Meggitt imagine groups of Jesus-followers to have been organized within *insulae* — tenement buildings with numerous small apartments stacked tall above the ground floor shops

43. So Edwin A. Judge, *Social Perspectives on Christians in the First Century: Pivotal Essays,* ed. D. M. Scholer (Peabody: Hendrickson, 2008), for whom the rise of the early Jesus-movement was primarily an urban phenomenon of household conversions (pp. 44, 119).

44. Andrew Wallace-Hadrill, "*Domus* and *Insulae* in Rome: Families and Housefuls," in David L. Balch and Carolyn Osiek, eds., *Early Christian Families in Context: An Interdisciplinary Dialogue* (Grand Rapids: Eerdmans, 2003), 3-18, p. 4.

45. Exceptions to the household conversion model are evident in 1 Cor 7:12-16, 1 Tim 6:1-2 and 1 Pet 3:1-2.

46. David Horrell, "Domestic Space and Christian Meetings at Corinth: Imagining New Contexts and the Buildings East of the Theatre," *NTS* 50 (2004): 349-69, pp. 366 and 369. The point was made well also by Meggitt, *Paul, Poverty and Survival,* pp. 120-21, especially n. 227.

and workshops, and found in most urban centers of the ancient world. Such groups, or "tenement churches," would have gathered within the tenement building, in one of the ground-floor workshops or upper-level apartments. As Jewett points out, in such cases "the church would not be meeting in space provided by the patron but rather in rented or shared space provided by the members themselves."[47] While Meeks's reconstruction works especially well in relation to the household model, where (middling group) householders hold predominant forms of power, it will have less explanatory force when other models are adopted as heuristic tools for considering the social context from which earliest groups of Jesus-followers emerged. Nonetheless, as will be shown in §12.2 below, Paul's theology of economic generosity operates best not in tenement scenarios, with groups of ES6 and ES7 members supporting themselves in some form of creative economic mutuality, but in situations whereby certain members have some accumulated resources that can be put to the service of the community (presuming a minimum of an ES5 profile). A household situation is ideal in that regard, with some members seeming to belong to ES4.[48]

As noted already, Meeks alerts his readers to the commonplace that status was multidimensional in the ancient world. Quite simply, economic profiling is only one dimension of status profiling.[49] With that said, however, Meeks's analysis includes a strong economic focus.[50] This is not necessarily surprising, nor is it illegitimate. It is arguable that, generally speaking, status was intricately connected to economic resources. Access to economic resources augmented one's chances of status improvement, and improved sta-

47. Robert Jewett, *Romans* (Minneapolis: Fortress, 2007), p. 65.

48. Further, there are evolutionary possibilities to consider. Some groups might have morphed from tenement settings to household settings by attracting low-grade forms of "patronage" from those with some minimal resources (i.e., ES5). Such a group, originally comprised predominately of ES6 members, might have found their structures and identity to have been reshaped in relation to their ES5 patron. In some cases, Jesus-groups may have had attraction to someone in ES4 (although there would also have been notable disincentives, as considered in §11.1 below). There does not seem to have been much evolution past ES4 in this regard in the early generations of the first century.

49. The prominence of economic resources in the status-registers of affluent cultures of the 21st century is captured in the words of Ted Turner: "In America, money is how we keep score."

50. All examples of status inconsistency in the final paragraphs of Meeks's book include an economic component (*First Urban Christians*, p. 191): "independent women with moderate wealth, Jews with wealth in a pagan society, freedmen with skill and money but stigmatized by origin."

tus usually enhanced one's access to economic resources.[51] So classicist Greg Woolf rightly notes that in the ancient world one's access to wealth was "one of the most explicit and formal measures of an individual's social standing and a key component of his public identity."[52]

10.2: Towards a Prosopographic Survey of Individuals Named in Paul's Letters

A full socio-economic profiling of communities addressed by Paul requires a prosopographic analysis of the few status indicators revealed to us when Paul speaks about individual members of the Jesus-groups he founded. But prosopographic surveys are plagued by difficulties in knowing how to assess certain indicators. For instance, what factors would indicate that someone has "comfortable" economic resources? Perhaps travel? Or being an artisan engaged in a trade? Or being a householder? Or providing hospitality? Or having a slave? Or allowing a Jesus-group to meet in one's home? Or opening one's home to a collective of Jesus-groups? Such indicators are interspersed within Paul's texts, but none of them is a wholly reliable or transparent indicator for composing prosopographic profiles.[53] The best course of action, then, regarding the socio-economic level of figures within urban Jesus-groups is not necessarily to remain agnostic but, instead, to recognize the tentative nature of any particular reconstruction, including the ones that appear in 10.3 below.

In shifting our focus to consider the "social standing" and "public iden-

---

51. So Paul Veyne, *Bread and Circuses: Historical Sociology and Political Pluralism* (London: Penguin, 1990), p. 44: "[T]he notables are in power by virtue of their prestige, which results from their wealth, and that same wealth which gives them the political authority . . . confers on them power in all other spheres." This is a better way of putting it than the oft-said platitude that "in the ancient world, power was the means to wealth" (Rohrbauch, "Methodological Considerations," p. 542). The opposite was also the case. This is most clearly evident in relation to the *Augustales,* as noted in Appendix 1 below.

52. G. Woolf, "Writing Poverty in Rome," in *Poverty in the Roman World,* 83-99, p. 92. He continues: "One consequence was that impoverishment carried with it the threat of a form of social death." See also Meggitt, *Paul, Poverty and Survival,* p. 6; John R. Patterson, *Landscape and Cities: Rural Settlement and Civic Transformation in Early Imperial Italy* (Oxford: Oxford University Press, 2006), p. 188. Of course, other features of one's status could at times register more forcefully than economic profile.

53. The fact that there is more data pertaining to Paul himself might suggest that a prosopographic profile of Paul would be relatively easy. But such has not necessarily been the case. On this, see §13.2 below.

tity" of members of urban Jesus-groups, it will serve our purposes to link our discussion to the economy scale outlined in chapter 3 above — precisely the sort of thing that was absent in the oft-times tortuous debates of scholars in the past. That economy scale will serve as the basis for the following sections of this chapter. A prosopographic survey of selected individuals named in Paul's texts appears in §10.3 through §10.6;[54] and §10.7 considers Paul's rhetorical construct of the general economic level of Jesus-groups he had founded.

10.3: Those Belonging to ES4: Erastus, Gaius and Phoebe

Erastus

Of all the people mentioned in the letters of Paul, the person whose socio-economic status is potentially the most significant is also one whose socio-economic status is the most highly disputed: Erastus, a member of one of the Corinthian communities, mentioned by Paul in Rom 16:23. The name Erastus also appears (or so it seems; see below) on an ancient inscription discovered at Corinth from the first or second century CE. The Erastus honored by that inscription had donated a pavement to benefit the city in return for having been appointed as a Corinthian aedile (a one-year administrative appointment of civic duty and honor).[55] Clearly this Erastus was a man of notable civic esteem, probably one of the civic elite (i.e., ES3 and above). Is this the same man who sends greetings to the Roman Jesus-followers in Rom 16:23? If the identification of the two figures is sound, then the phrase Ἔραστος ὁ οἰκονόμος τῆς πόλεως in Rom 16:23 should be translated "Erastus the city treasurer." In the view of Theissen and others, the correlation of this data makes it evident that Corinthian Jesus-groups included within their membership a man well entrenched within the upper echelons of society, a wealthy elite who was, in fact, born into a "powerful" and "well-bred" family (1 Cor 1:26: δυνατοί, εὐγενεῖς).[56] According to

54. No attempt is made here to be exhaustive in the analysis of each and every named person in Pauline texts. Instead, the individuals selected are those for whom prosopographic analysis is the most promising.

55. See John Harvey Kent, *The Inscriptions, 1926-1950* (Corinth VIII.3; Princeton: ASCSA, 1966), 99-100.

56. E.g. Theissen, *Social Setting*, pp. 75-83. So also Nils Dahl (*Studies in Paul* [Philadelphia: Fortress Press, 1977], p. 27): "It is quite likely that the congregation at Corinth did have some rich members, even if they did not belong to the intellectual or social elites."

Helmut Koester, the Erastus of Romans 16 "was certainly a member of the ruling class."[57]

This view has rarely gone undisputed.[58] It may even be wrong-headed from the start. Since the Corinthian inscription has been broken off just at the point where the "e" of "Erastus" begins, it is possible that the visible "e" may have been preceded by other letters, in which case the name might have been not Erastus but Eperastus.[59] But even assuming that the full name has been retained in the broken inscription, the following points make problematic any attempt to identify the "epistolary Erastus" with the "inscriptional Erastus":[60]

- The dating of the Corinthian inscription is uncertain, but more likely is to be dated to the late first century or early second century than to the middle of the first century CE;
- As recent studies have shown, the name "Erastus" is much more common than was first thought after the discovery of the Erastus inscription, so the identification of one Erastus with another is statistically unlikely;[61]
- The phrase ὁ οἰκονόμος τῆς πόλεως that Paul uses to characterize a member of Corinthian Jesus-followers is not itself a technical term designating a single civic office (i.e., city treasurer), since the phrase was used to denote a variety of civic functionaries, from high ranking elites to low ranking servants of the civic administration.[62]

---

57. Helmut Koester, "The Silence of the Apostle," in Daniel N. Schowalter and Steven J. Friesen, eds., *Urban Religion in Roman Corinth* (Cambridge, MA: Harvard University Press, 2005), 339-49, p. 339. See also Murphy-O'Connor, *Paul: A Critical Life*, pp. 268-71.

58. For one detractor from the early twentieth century, see Henry Cadbury, "Erastus of Corinth," *JBL* 50 (1931): 42-58.

59. The surviving pieces of the inscription are best reconstructed in this way: "[. . .] *erastus pro aedilit[at]e s(ua) p(ecunia) stravit.*"

60. These points have been voiced most effectively by Justin J. Meggitt, "The Social Status of Erastus (Rom. 16:23)," *NovT* 38 (1996): 218-23; now reprinted in Edward Adams and David G. Horrell, eds., *Christianity at Corinth: The Quest for the Pauline Church* (Louisville: Westminster John Knox Press, 2004), pp. 219-26; and Steven J. Friesen, "The Wrong Erastus: Ideology, Archaeology, and Exegesis," in Steven J. Friesen, Daniel N. Schowalter, and James Walters, eds., *Corinth in Context: Comparative Studies on Religion and Society* (Leiden: Brill, forthcoming).

61. So Pleket, Review of *First Urban Christians*, p. 194: "Erastus is too common a name for such identifications."

62. So Pleket, Review of *First Urban Christians*, p. 194: "[T]he true parallel for the status

Accordingly, the notion that the Erastus of Rom 16:23 equates to the Erastus of the Corinthian inscription (or was it Eperastus?) is far from likely.

Consequently, the socio-economic profile of Erastus of Rom 16:23 needs to be considered without regard to the Corinthian inscription. The title that Paul uses of him, ὁ οἰκονόμος τῆς πόλεως, suggests service within the civic arena in some fashion, but its breadth of usage probably spreads across at least two economic categories, including the lower levels of the elite (i.e., ES3) and the upper end of the middling groups (i.e., ES4a).[63] Without further information on the identity of this Erastus, statistical probability speaks against putting the Erastus that Paul refers to into ES3, and favors ES4. Meggitt is likely to be correct, then, when he concludes that the Erastus of Rom 16:23 "cannot be used as evidence of the spread of the new faith amongst the socially powerful of the Principate"[64] — if "socially powerful" refers to the elite of ES1 through ES3. Paul draws the attention of Roman Jesus-followers to an Erastus who seems to fall somewhere in the elongated mix of ES4 — although it needs to be reiterated that those toward the top of ES4 had significant forms of socio-economic power of their own.

But if the Erastus of Rom 16:23 falls within ES4, this makes the second of Meggitt's two conclusions problematical: "Erastus' socio-economic situation

---

of such an *oikonomos* [i.e., the Erastus of the Corinthian inscription] is an inscription from Stobi (*SEG* XXIV 496), where a certain Diadoumenos *as slave* fulfills that function, rather than Hellenistic civic decrees which mention free-born and respectable *oikonomoi*." See especially, Friesen, "The Wrong Erastus."

It follows from this that Paul might have included the term οἰκονόμος τῆς πόλεως not to give due respect to a civic elite but to differentiate this Erastus from another Erastus known to Jesus-followers (compare the Erastuses of Acts 19:22 and 2 Tim. 4:20, who are often thought to be different to the Erastus of Rom 16:23). On this point, see Colin Hemer, *The Book of Acts in the Setting of Hellenistic History* (Tübingen: Mohr, 1989), p. 235. Relatedly, James D. G. Dunn writes (*Romans 9–16* [Dallas: Word Books, 1988], p. 911): "The definite article [ὁ, in the phrase ὁ οἰκονόμος τῆς πόλεως] does not necessarily indicate that there was only one oikonomos" in the city of Corinth. This may be true. But Dunn goes on to reason that the term "could just mean the oikonomos who was a Christian." While it is true that the article might play a "restrictive" or "identifying" role in this verse, the article ὁ may not delineate a "Christian" *oikonomos* from a "non-Christian" *oikonomos,* but might delineate one Erastus from another Erastus within a Jesus-group or Jesus-groups — i.e., the Erastus who is a civic *oikonomos,* as opposed to another Erastus within the Corinthian communities. On the other hand, Friesen ("The Wrong Erastus") postulates that the Erastus of Rom 16 is not even a Jesus-follower.

63. Friesen ("Poverty in Pauline Studies," pp. 354-55) puts Erastus in ES4 or ES5. In my view, ES5 is too low for a bearer of this title.

64. Meggitt, "The Social Status of Erastus," p. 225.

was most likely indistinguishable from that of his fellow believers." If Erastus is not to be placed among the elite, and if one adopts a rigidly binary model (as Meggitt does), then a conclusion of this sort will suffice. But in a more nuanced model of economic stratification, it is not at all obvious that Erastus is economically "indistinguishable" from his fellow believers. At ES4 (and probably ES4a), he would be significantly better off than many of his fellow believers. He might well have had patron-client connections with some in ES3.

Gaius

The name "Gaius" appears in two of Paul's letters, and both occasions refer to someone based in Corinth. Although it is conceivable that both texts refer to the same person, this cannot be proved, since the name was exceedingly common in the ancient world. The earlier of the two references appears in 1 Cor 1:14, where Paul mentions having baptized Gaius (along with Crispus and, as in 1:16, the household of Stephanas). The later reference is in Rom 16:23, where Paul intimates that a man named Gaius functioned as the "host" to him and to "the whole church" in Corinth (ὁ ξένος μου καὶ ὅλης τῆς ἐκκλησίας). The nuance here is of one who "welcomed and took care of us in his home."[65] When Paul mentions gatherings of "the whole church" meeting in Gaius's house, he seems to envisage the (occasional) coming together of various Corinthian Jesus-groups within one single *domus*, or household complex. If, on a very conservative estimate, we imagine three communities comprised of only fifteen members each, then Gaius' *domus* would have needed to be suitable and welcoming to a gathering of at least 45 people. Even on such a conservative estimate, this would probably put Gaius' domus within ES4 levels. To have acted as the corporate host on a number of occasions (which is presumably what Paul infers) would likely put him well above the bottom of ES4.[66] I err on the side of placing him towards the middle of ES4. He might have been higher up the economy scale (i.e., ES4a), but we have no data to permit pegging him higher than the middle of ES4.

---

65. Johannes P. Louw and Eugene A. Nida, *Greek-English Lexicon of the New Testament Based on Semantic Domains* (New York: United Bible Society, 1988, 1989), §34.60.

66. The view that Gaius might be Titius Justus (= Gaius Titius Justus) in Acts 18:7, in whose house Paul took refuge, is possible but cannot be confirmed.

Phoebe

Paul describes Phoebe in Rom 16:1-2. Although the translation is disputed at various points, the NRSV reads as follows:

> I commend to you our sister Phoebe, a deacon (διάκονον) of the church at Cenchreae, so that you may welcome her in the Lord as is fitting for the saints, and help her in whatever she may require from you, for she has been a benefactor (προστάτις) of many and of myself as well.

From this depiction of Phoebe, Meeks estimates that she was a "patroness [προστάτις] of many Christians" and, moreover, she was likely to have been

> an independent woman (she is probably traveling to Rome on business of her own, not solely to carry Paul's letter) who has some wealth and is also one of the leaders of the Christian group in the harbor town of Cenchreae.[67]

But this portrait of Phoebe as a "benefactor" (NRSV) or "patroness" (Meeks) is disputed. The issue is whether the word προστάτις should be translated by terms that include a socio-economic timbre, such as "benefactor" or "patroness," or by terms that are potentially devoid of such nuances, such as "helper" or "leader."

The case against seeing Pheobe as a "patroness" of Cenchreaen Jesus-groups has recently been articulated by Friesen. According to him, Paul does not mean to describe Phoebe as a "patroness" since προστάτις is not the normal term for a benefactor. This is further confirmed by the fact that Paul "asks the Romans to help her when she arrives," since this act of requesting assistance "would be inappropriate for a client (Paul) to do on behalf of his benefactor." For Friesen, the fact that Paul "requested help for her from the saints in Rome . . . indicates that her financial standing was not high."[68] This

---

67. Meeks, *First Urban Christians*, p. 60. Anxieties about travel must have been heightened for women such as Phoebe and, perhaps, Lydia, a merchant woman probably some way up in the ES4 category. So Meeks (*First Urban Christians*, p. 17): "For merchants such as Lydia the dealer in purple goods, who was from Thyatira (Asia Minor) but met Paul in Philippi (Macedonia) (Acts 16:14), travel was an occupational necessity — and hazard. Anxieties about travel and its dangers — brigandage and piracy, shipwreck, and hardships on the road — were among the fears that often sent such people to astrologers or dream interpreters."

68. Friesen, "Poverty in Pauline Studies," p. 355. So also Meggitt, *Paul, Poverty and Survival*, p. 148.

view dovetails nicely with the case that merchants who traveled were not merchants of great wealth.[69]

Conversely, the case for interpreting προστάτις as "patroness" continues to be advocated by a number of exegetes. David Downs, for instance, notes that the relationships between patrons and clients did not always operate in ways that Friesen supposes, since clients were permitted to ask for favors from others on behalf of their patrons or benefactors, and were even expected to take on financial responsibilities on behalf of their patrons:

> [A]ccording to Dionysius of Halicarnassus's account of the origins of patronage, clients were regularly expected to perform services on behalf of their patrons, including paying for dowries for the marriages of the daughters of patrons, paying ransom if someone in the patron's family was kidnapped, and paying public fines incurred by their patrons.[70]

For Downs, then, the possibility that Phoebe was a "patroness" of the Cenchreaen communities cannot be ruled out, as Friesen does, on the basis of Paul's commendation of her. Moreover, Downs notes that the masculine form προστάτης designates benefactors in a variety of ancient inscriptions.[71] Plutarch even notes that the term is used synonymously with πάτρων, "patron," by Romans of his day (*Rom.* 13.3-4). The terminological dispute, then, seems to favor a technical sense to the term προστάτις, rendering it "patroness."[72]

Consequently, it is quite likely that Phoebe should be placed within the economic level ES4.[73] Although ES5 cannot be ruled out, Paul's description

69. Pleket, Review of *First Urban Christians*, p. 194: "Travelling is frequently interpreted [by Meeks] as a sign of wealth and independence. But surely the itinerant artisan does not belong to the top of the artisans; on the contrary, being itinerant as a craftsman is a sign of economic hardship rather than of prosperity." Pleket's point is a helpful control in our attempt to locate economic levels of named individuals in Paul's letters, ensuring that the likes of a Phoebe do not end up in ES3, which in Friesen's model includes some wealthy merchants, or even ES4a. But travelling would not necessarily exclude us from including artisans or merchants within ES4b or ES5.

70. Downs, "Is God Paul's Patron?" p. 147. Downs also notes the following: "One wonders also if Paul endorses Phoebe in such strong terms because her gender would have diminished her status from the perspective of some members of the Roman churches."

71. For example, *LSJ* 1526; *IG* II² 1369, 4747; *IGR* 1.5.1172.

72. For a further defence of this view, see Carolyn Osiek and David L. Balch, *Families in the New Testament World: Households and House Churches* (Louisville: Westminster John Knox Press, 1997), pp. 98-99; Joan Cecelia Campbell, *Phoebe: Patron and Emissary* (Collegeville, MN: The Liturgical Press, 2009), pp. 78-82.

73. Much of what Richard S. Ascough says about the "ways in which Lydia may have ac-

of her in Rom 16:1-2 suggests a higher economic level than that, not least when Paul refers to her as "patroness *of many*" (προστάτις πολλῶν).[74]

Although Friesen's assessment of the status registers of Paul and Phoebe in Rom 16:1-2 is not compelling, it is nonetheless true that status issues are involved in Paul's recommendation of Phoebe. Here it has to be remembered that ancient status was a multi-faceted phenomenon, with some status indicators being higher than others in a person's socio-economic profile. In this regard, status indicators register differently with regard to Paul and Phoebe. Paul's own high status in respects other than socio-economic profile is highlighted right at the start of his Roman letter. There he depicts himself as "a servant of Jesus Christ, called to be an apostle, set apart for the gospel of God . . . to bring about the obedience of faith among all the Gentiles for the sake of his name" (Rom 1:1, 5; see also 16:26). Since Paul is entrusted with the task of enlivening faith among the gentiles, it is also Paul who in Rom 16:1-2 commends Phoebe to the Jesus-followers in Rome, since she is the one who has enhanced the (predominately) gentile communities of Jesus-followers in Cenchreae. Because of Paul's (high-status) responsibilities to gentile communities of Jesus-followers, Paul is perfectly entitled to commend Phoebe, who has served the communities that Paul has established in the Corinthian region.

In this light, Paul's commendation of Phoebe may take on a dimension of meaning beyond what is actually stated in the letter. Given the mixed status signals between Paul and Phoebe, Paul in Rom 16:1-2 is virtually playing the role of patron to Phoebe, a role he can adopt legitimately in view of his own status as one divinely commissioned as the apostle to the gentiles. In this role, Paul may have written Rom 16:1-2 in order to bring Phoebe's financial dealings to the attention of Jesus-followers of a similar socio-economic profile, with the hopes that they, in turn, might be able to open doors of economic opportunity for her while she was in Rome.[75] This implication is

---

quired her economic fluidity" might also be said of Phoebe; see Ascough, *Lydia: Paul's Cosmopolitan Hostess* (Collegeville, MN: Liturgical Press, 2009), p. 51. On the increasing opportunities for women to make their presence felt within the civic arena, see especially Bruce W. Winter, *Roman Wives, Roman Widows: The Appearance of New Women and the Pauline Communities* (Grand Rapids: Eerdmans, 2003); and Carolyn Osiek and Margaret Y. MacDonald, *A Woman's Place: House Churches in Earliest Christianity* (Minneapolis: Fortress Press, 2006), pp. 199-209.

74. See Jewett, *Romans,* especially pp. 89-91, 941-48. Jewett depicts Phoebe as "upper-class" (*Romans,* p. 90); so also Campbell, *Phoebe,* p. 82: "Phoebe was a woman of means who belonged to the local elite of Kenchreai . . . hailing from the elite sector of society."

75. So too Theissen, *Social Setting,* p. 88. Compare Peter Oakes on Lydia's connections

probably present in his comment "help her in whatever she may require from you" (Rom 16:2). By doing this, they would not simply be boosting Phoebe's own business prospects; instead (or so it is implied), they would be enhancing the corporate life of Jesus-followers beyond their own vicinity.[76]

It is interesting to note, in this regard, that just prior to Rom 16:1-2, Paul has already drawn attention to how financial assistance is flowing from Jesus-followers of one area for the benefit of Jesus-followers of another area. In Rom 15:25-28a and 15:30-33, Paul has showcased his own collection efforts, involving the sharing of resources between those bound together in faith despite their geographical locality (especially 15:26-27). Perhaps it is not too far afield, then, to imagine the unstated assumption of Rom 16:1-2 to be that Phoebe's improved financial success in Rome will result in the furtherance of communities of Jesus-followers beyond Rome. And if Cenchreae is one place where this might be so, the same might be the case for prospective communities of Jesus-followers in Spain — a region that Paul has set his sights on, as he highlights in the verses prior to Romans 16 (15:23-24, 28b-29). Perhaps Jesus-followers of ES4 (and/or ES5) who are based in Rome are to imagine that, by enhancing Phoebe's business prospects, they themselves might be playing their own part in assisting prospective Jesus-groups in Spain, since Phoebe's resources might conceivably be used to assist Jesus-followers even beyond the Corinthian region.[77] Paul already has first-hand

---

within Philippi (*Philippians: From People to Letter* [Cambridge: Cambridge University Press, 2001], p. 59): "Lydia and her household would . . . have represented a range of other social points of entry into the Philippian population: in her own case, among Asian migrant traders of reasonable wealth." Jesus-followers of ES4 and ES5 within the Roman Jesus-groups would have had similar social points of entry into the urban context of Rome.

76. Something similar took place among the *Augustales* of ES4, who at times assisted each other in enhancing business prospects. Cf. John H. d'Arms, *Commerce: Social Standing in Ancient Rome* (Cambridge, MA: Harvard University Press, 1981), p. 148: The *Augustales* met "to exchange shipping information derived from various ports, to share news of market rates and property values, to learn of current developments in the building trade, in the ferry services, in naval construction and the other specialized collegia where, as individuals, Augustales discharged professional functions, and to sift and synthesize these reports through common discussion in a common meeting place."

77. This suggestion is much like the one championed by Robert Jewett (see his *Romans*; also his "Ecumenical Theology for the Sake of Mission: Romans 1:1-17 + 15:14–16:24," in David M. Hay and E. Elizabeth Johnson, eds., *Pauline Theology*, Vol. 3: *Romans* [Minneapolis: Fortress Press, 1995], 89-108, p. 90). Jewett's case is far more developed than the simple one that I am proposing here. And at places we go our separate ways. Whereas Jewett imagines Phoebe to be in Rome primarily to lay the foundations for the Spanish ministry that she has agreed to sponsor, I see no reason to imagine that Phoebe is in Rome for any reason other

experience of Jesus-followers from one location helping Jesus-followers in other locations.[78] Perhaps something similar is being implicitly envisioned in Rom 16:1-2. In a densely packaged sentence, Paul negotiates the complexities of status in relation to the economic enhancement of one whose steadfast "patronage" of Jesus-groups might itself be expanded to facilitate new orbits of ministry.[79]

10.4: Those Belonging to ES4 or ES5: Stephanas, Philemon, Crispus

Stephanas

The economic profile of Stephanas remains contested. Theissen puts him among "the upper classes" (probably ES3, if his case were filtered through the economy scale).[80] Friesen put him at ES5, perhaps ES6.[81] Meeks imagined him to be "a person of wealth" and "fairly high on the scale of wealth, though probably not so high as Gaius and Crispus."[82]

Friesen is right to register dissent from Theissen's estimate. That Stephanas was the head of a household, that he "served" the Corinthian Jesus-followers, and that he traveled to meet Paul in Ephesus as a representative of Corinthian communities, these things do not necessarily add up to an elite profile. But neither is it likely that Stephanas should be placed within

---

than (a) her own financial dealings, and possibly (b) to interpret Paul's letter to the Roman Jesus-groups while she is in Rome. More significantly, I imagine Jewett's reconstruction of the economic level of Roman Jesus-groups in general to be too restricted to ES5 and below; there must have been a greater presence of ES4 Jesus-followers than he allows for, not least if his view about the purpose of Romans is to carry weight; on this, see n. 11 in chapter 12. Nonetheless, while the view that Paul wrote Romans in order to garner support for his Spanish ministry "falls short of being a complete explanation" for why Paul wrote Romans (so Douglas A. Campbell, *The Deliverance of God: An Apocalyptic Rereading of Justification in Paul* [Grand Rapids: Eerdmans, 2009], p. 477), it may be the overarching explanation under which a fuller taxonomy of factors assemble themselves.

78. This is evident from 2 Cor 11:9 and Phil 4:15-16, demonstrating how Philippian funds have been used to establish communities of Jesus-followers in both Thessalonica and then Corinth.

79. Did Paul already have this in mind when writing 2 Cor 10:15-16? There he writes: "our hope is that, as your faith increases, our sphere of action among you may be greatly enlarged, so that we may proclaim the good news in lands beyond you."

80. Theissen, *Social Setting of Pauline Christianity,* p. 95.

81. Friesen, "Poverty in Pauline Studies," p. 352.

82. Meeks, *First Urban Christians,* p. 58.

ES6. Either ES5 or the lower end of ES4 would seem to be the best estimate. Stephanas and his household are depicted as "devoting themselves to the service of the saints" in work and wearisome toil (1 Cor 16:15-16). While depictions such as this do not necessarily translate into economic descriptors, it is people in ES4 and ES5 that were generally expected to provide the economic resources of communities of Jesus-followers, and the phrase "service of the saints" is probably indicative of that role.

Philemon

The clear data pertaining to Philemon is that he provided a house for Jesus-group meetings (Phlm 2), and Paul could presume upon him to provide housing and hospitality for guests such as himself (Phlm 22). The fact that Philemon owns a slave, Onesimus, is not indicative of much, since poor households could include the odd slave. But it might be that Philemon's household included a number of slaves, since Paul's discussion of sending Onesimus back to Philemon says nothing of the hardship that Onesimus' departure has caused on the running of Philemon's household. This is speculative, of course, but we should probably imagine Philemon to fall within either ES4 or ES5. It is not possible to be more precise.[83]

Crispus

In 1 Cor 1:14-16, while noting that he had baptized Gaius and the household of Stephanas, Paul also mentions having baptized Crispus. Since Gaius is probably to be placed in ES4 and Stephanas within ES4 or ES5, perhaps by

---

83. It is possible, however, that instead of speaking of Philemon we should actually be speaking of Archippus, mentioned in the second verse of Paul's letter to Philemon, Apphia and Archippus. On the basis of Philem 2 (καὶ Ἀρχίππῳ τῷ συστρατιώτῃ ἡμῶν καὶ τῇ κατ' οἶκόν σου ἐκκλησίᾳ), John Knox has argued that Archippus rather than Philemon is the householder that Paul is addressing. See his *Philemon among the Letters of Paul* (Nashville: Abingdon Press, 1935). But whether Philemon or Archippus is the main addressee, that addressee is depicted by Joseph A. Fitzmyer as "a successful businessman, who traveled much and met Paul in the course of his travels" (*The Letter to Philemon* [New York: Doubleday, 2000], p. 12). James D. G. Dunn (*The Epistles to the Colossians and to Philemon* [Grand Rapids: Eerdmans, 1996], p. 301) imagines on the basis of Philem 17-18 that Paul might have been Philemon's business partner.

association Crispus should fall somewhere within ES4 or ES5. This impression might be strengthened by the fact that the author of Acts notes that a Crispus was leader of the Corinthian synagogue (ὁ ἀρχισυνάγωγος) and became a follower of Jesus due to Paul's ministry (Acts 18:8).[84] If this is the same Crispus as the one mentioned in 1 Cor 1:14 (which seems probable), his position as the synagogue leader would seem to locate him at ES5 at least, since it is not likely that someone at subsistence level (ES6) would have had the opportunity to lead a synagogue. This is not wholly conclusive, of course, since others might have financially supported Crispus in this role.[85] But synagogue leaders could be sustained in their positions more easily if they had economic resources of their own, with those resources themselves having contributed to the development of interpretative, rhetorical and organizational skills that were important to the role.[86] Consequently, it seems more likely that Crispus lived somewhat above subsistence level, at the level of either ES5 or ES4.

10.5: Those Belonging to ES5 or ES6: Prisca and Aquila

Dwelling places of Prisca (or Priscilla) and Aquila were used as bases for communities of Jesus-groups in both Ephesus (1 Cor 16:19) and Rome (Rom 16:3-5) and probably in Corinth as well. We know nothing, however, about the number of Jesus-followers who may have converged on those dwellings, nor do we know whether those dwellings were owned or rented by Prisca and Aquila, so this data yields little prosopographic insight. According to Peter Lampe, the names Prisca and Aquila had "no affinity to circles of slave origin" and probably designated two freeborn individuals, but there is little economic pay-off in that observation. Consequently, from the Pauline data

---

84. Compare also the Sosthenes of Acts 18:17, a leader of the synagogue (Σωσθένην τὸν ἀρχισυνάγωγον), whom the Corinthian "Jews" beat when their efforts against Paul came to nothing. Is he the same person who is listed as the co-author of 1 Corinthians (1 Cor 1:1)?

85. This would be an instance of economic status diverging from other status indicators — in this case, stature in religious wisdom or rhetoric. Compare the story of the young Jesus in the Temple precincts (Luke 2:41-51).

86. The surviving evidence suggests that a synagogue leader was prominent in his community, often being "a wealthy member of the community" (Lee I. Levine, *The Ancient Synagogue: The First Thousand Years* [New Haven: Yale University Press, 2000], p. 116; cf. p. 396). See, for instance, the Theodotos inscription (Levine, *Ancient Synagogue*, p. 55) and the Acmonia inscription (Levine, *Ancient Synagogue*, p. 115). Of course, inscriptional data of this sort cannot be used to reconstruct an economic profile of synagogue leaders in general.

alone, there is little on which to build a prosopographic profile of this wife (Prisca) and husband (Aquila).

Despite this, most scholars tend to imagine Prisca and Aquila as belonging "to a prosperous merchant-class, having homes used by the church in one way or another in Corinth, Ephesus, and Rome."[87] Carolyn Osiek and Margaret MacDonald propose, for instance, the following:

> Whether rented or owned, the typical house of Prisc(ill)a and Aquila is most likely to have been a *domus* (even if fairly modest) and similar to the houses owned by such prominent male householders as Stephanas (1 Cor. 1:16; 16:16-18) or Gaius of Corinth (Rom. 16:23; 1 Cor. 1:14), whose house was apparently large enough to hold the whole of the Corinthian community.[88]

Peter Oakes has suggested that we could liken Prisca and Aquila to the artisan (a cabinet-maker) who resided in House 7 of the Insula of the Menander in the archaeological remains of Pompeii. That craftsman lived in a house "larger . . . than 70 percent of householders — a fair way up the scale of householder wealth, and even further up the scale than we could get if we included non-householders."[89] Accordingly, on the assumption that Prisca and Aquila may be artisans of a similar economic profile to this Pompeian artisan, Oakes notes that in a house such as this they

> would have a garden, a small colonnade, and a couple of rear-facing dining rooms that, altogether, could probably host a meeting of a few dozen. They could, if they wanted, afford a couple of nice Greek mythological paintings on the wall, but they could not run to expensive decoration in every room. Overall, they would have about six times as much housing space as the average person among the bottom 34 percent of householders.[90]

Such a reconstruction would place Prisca and Aquila in something like the lower tiers of ES4.

---

87. E. Earle Ellis, *Pauline Theology: Ministry and Society* (Grand Rapids: Eerdmans, 1989), p. 142.

88. Osiek and MacDonald, *A Woman's Place*, p. 32.

89. Peter Oakes, "Methodological Issues in Using Economic Evidence in Interpretation of Early Christian Texts," in Bruce W. Longenecker and Kelly D. Liebengood, eds., *Engaging Economics: New Testament Scenarios and Early Christian Reception* (Grand Rapids: Eerdmans, 2009), 9-34, p. 33.

90. Oakes, "Methodological Issues," p. 34.

Nonetheless, when data from 2 Corinthians 11 are read in relation to Acts 18, a somewhat different picture tends to emerge, as Lampe has suggested. According to Acts 18:3, Paul resided with Aquila and "Priscilla" while their paths crossed in Corinth; but in 2 Cor 11:9 Paul speaks of being "in need" while he was in Corinth and of how that need had been met "by 'the brothers' (οἱ ἀδελφοί) who came from Macedonia." If the time period for these two references coincide, as seems likely, it is not unreasonable to conclude, as does Lampe, that "the employment in Aquila's Corinthian workshop . . . appears to have yielded little profit."[91]

It is possible, of course, that Aquila and Prisca lived at different economic levels when moving between different locations; in that case, an ES6 or possibly ES5 existence in Corinth might not have corresponded with the economic level of their existence at either Ephesus or Rome. But if Aquila and Prisca lived at ES6 or ES5 levels in Corinth, it is hard to imagine them having had the security of an ES4 existence in Ephesus. In 51 CE, they went to Ephesus to prepare the way for (what was to become) Paul's Ephesian-based ministry (cf. Acts 18:19), uprooting themselves from whatever networks and connections they may have established during the two years of their residence at Corinth (49-51). Changing their location was likely to have introduced economic vulnerability into their prosopographic profile during their time in Ephesus, at least initially.[92] In all likelihood, then, their lifestyle in

91. Lampe, *From Paul to Valentinus*, p. 191. When comparing Prisca and Aquila to the Pompeian artisan of House 7, Oakes fails to take full account of Lampe's observations with regard to how this husband and wife team are to be considered when both Acts 18:3 and 2 Cor 11:9 are held in view simultaneously.

On Paul residing within residences of others without drawing on the resources of patrons, see S. Fowl, "Know Your Context: Giving and Receiving Money in Philippians," *Int* 56 (2002): 45-58, p. 55 n. 33. Paul's decision not to accept funds from certain members of the Corinthian community seems to have caused much of the initial problems for him at Corinth. Compare the governor of Chiapas in Mexico who refused to accept gifts from those whom he was seeking to assist: "it was felt that such a man could not be trusted in personal relations" (J. Pitt-Rivers, "Postscript: The Place of Grace in Anthropology," in J. G. Peristiany and J. Pitt-Rivers, eds., *Honour and Grace in Anthropology* [Cambridge: Cambridge University Press, 1992], 215-46, p. 220).

If Paul lived (for a time) with Aquila and Prisca in a difficult economic situation during his initial stay at Corinth (50-51), when he returned to the city in the mid-50s he seems to have resided in a more affluent setting, staying in the house of ES4 Gaius (Rom 16:23).

92. Cf. Jerome Murphy-O'Connor, *Paul, His Story* (Oxford: Oxford University Press, 2004), p. 98: Prisca and Aquila "were the advance team whose job it was to prepare a comfortable base against the day when Paul would finally join them [in Ephesus]. . . . [Paul] was asking a lot of Prisca and Aquila. They would lose the business which they had laboriously

Corinth and in Ephesus (and perhaps in Rome before and after their residency in these two cities) was likely to have been at the ES5 level at best.

10.6: Things Said and Unsaid

If some things are better left unsaid, there are snippets of potentially useful data which, because they cannot be correlated with other data, lead nowhere with regard to the economic profile of individuals within Jesus-groups founded by Paul. This is the case, for instance, for the one who is talked about extensively in Paul's letter to Philemon. We know almost nothing about Onesimus, the slave who had run away from Philemon's household and who seems to have become a Jesus-follower through Paul's efforts one way or another — either within Philemon's household prior to his "escape" or as a consequence of meeting Paul after it. Although Onesimus was a slave, that in itself gives no indication of his economic profile, since slaves could fall anywhere between ES7 and ES4. We simply cannot be more precise than that.

Similarly, from the (deutero-Pauline?) letter to the Colossians we hear of a community that meets in the house of Nympha (Col 4:15). Because hosting a meeting is a very general descriptor, it would operate as a very tenuous base for prosopographic reconstruction. The same pertains to the sparse data we have about Chloe (1 Cor 1:11, who may not be a Corinthian, and may not even be a Jesus-follower),[93] and about a variety of other named individuals from Paul's texts. The reference to "those of Caesar's household" (οἱ ἐκ τῆς Καίσαρος οἰκίας) in Phil 4:22 is too cryptic to feed into a prosopographic analysis.

Moreover, the prosopographic data from the Acts of the Apostles have not been factored into consideration here. For many, those Lukan data have the potential to distort the portrait of Jesus-groups founded by Paul, since it seems to move those communities in an economically more secure direction than is recoverable from Paul's own texts.[94] The Lukan depiction of Jesus-

---

built up in Corinth, and with it the support of their lifestyle. They would have to begin anew in a strange city, scraping a living as they struggled to attract clients."

93. In my view, the most likely scenario is that Chloe is based in Ephesus, and her "people" (i.e., οἱ Χλόης, 1 Cor 1:11) who report to Paul are her servants who have returned to Ephesus from Corinth. The servants are presumably Corinthian Jesus-followers, and so too, perhaps, is Chloe. Probably she falls within ES4, but ES5 remains a possibility.

94. On the socio-economic levels of Paul's associates in Acts, see Steven J. Friesen, "Injustice or God's Will: Early Christian Explanations of Poverty," in Susan R. Holman, ed.,

groups frequently includes economic descriptors that are elevated above what seems to be the case from Paul's own letters, demonstrating "Luke's proclivity for presenting men and women of substance as founding members of Jesus groups."[95] From start to finish (i.e., from Acts 13 through 19),[96] Paul's public ministry is enclosed by encounters with and connections to members of the civic elite, including: Sergius Paulus at ES1 (Acts 13:6-12), the "leading men" of various cities at ES2-ES3 (Acts 13:50; 17:12); the "leading women" of various cities at ES2-ES3 (Acts 13:50; 17:4, 12), and Asiarchs at perhaps ES3 (Acts 19:31), who held positions of public office and served as benefactors of their cities (although these could well be likened to the *Augustales*,

---

Wealth and Poverty in Early Church and Society (Grand Rapids: Baker Academic, 2008), 17-36, pp. 26-32. He writes: "In Acts . . . Paul is portrayed as interacting easily with people in the top 1 percent of the poverty scale; Sergius Paulus, Asiarchs in Ephesus, the unnamed chiliarch who arrests Paul in Jerusalem, King Agrippa II, the procurator Felix, his wife, Drusilla (who was also a sister of Agrippa II), Festus (procurator after Felix), the chiliarch Lysias, and Bernice (sister of Drusilla, sister and consort of Agrippa II, later consort of Titus until he became emperor). . . . [T]he author of Acts portrays Paul . . . as a man of the highest social skills who commands respect from some of the wealthiest and most powerful Roman imperialists" (pp. 30-31).

In principle, however, there is some scope for imagining that, at times, the Lukan scenario of supra-ES4 interest in the Jesus-movement has some historical veracity, with the early Jesus-movement having had some connections with the civic elite through patron-client links with Jesus-followers at ES4. (For example, is the Aristarchus of Acts 19:29 and 20:4 one of the politarchs of Thessalonica? On this, see Colin J. Hemer, *The Book of Acts in the Setting of Hellenistic History* [Tübingen: Mohr Siebeck, 1989], p. 236.) And the mention of Manaen in Acts 13:1, where he is described as the σύντροφος ("close friend from childhood," or "foster brother"?) of Herod the tetrarch, is especially notable, not least since it seems to be embedded within Antiochene traditional material. But the Lukan scenario is likely to be hyperbolic, nonetheless. For instance, when we compare the Lukan portrait of members from a single community with Paul's portrait of that same community, a lack of alignment is notable. Acts 17:4 shows Paul as having the support of Thessalonian "leading women" — i.e., women from among the ranks of the elite of ES3 and above; Paul, however, places his Thessalonian communities in ES5 and below in both 1 Thess 4:11 and 2 Cor 8:2-4. And on Sergius Paulus of Acts 13:6-12, even the relatively conservative Rainer Riesner concludes (*Paul's Early Period: Chronology, Mission Strategy, Theology* [Grand Rapids: Eerdmans, 1998], p. 146): "the connection between the account of Acts and this particular Roman official is very unlikely."

95. Richard S. Ascough, *Lydia: Paul's Cosmopolitan Hostess* (Collegeville, MN: Liturgical Press, 2009), p. 5.

96. Elsewhere, I delineate Acts 13-19 as a self-contained section of Acts that encloses Paul's public ministry; see Bruce W. Longenecker, *Rhetoric at the Boundaries: The Art and Theology of New Testament Chain-Link Transitions* (Waco: Baylor University Press, 2005), pp. 226-35.

most of whom fell within the top end of ES4).[97] The portrait of elite participation in Jesus-groups founded by Paul is so uniform, and diverges so significantly from what we see in the prosopographic data of Paul's own letters,
that for the most part it is best to err on the side of seeing in these data a
Lukan tendency to nudge upwards the economic profile of those who
aligned themselves with Paul's ministry, in the interest of fortifying the public profile of the Jesus-movement within its early Greco-Roman context.[98]
Nonetheless, the Lukan portrait of Lydia as a Roman woman sponsoring the
development of the Jesus-group within Philippi (Acts 16:11-15) falls in line
with what we see in other urban centers, especially if Lydia is to be placed
within the spectrum of ES4.[99]

With regard to prosopographic reconstruction, it needs to be restated
that the useable data are partial and, therefore, inherently unstable, since
they can often span a variety of economic levels. Accordingly, prosopographic profiles are never to be held tenaciously. But with that said, even
though prosopographic data is handled differently by different interpreters,
attempts at prosopographic analysis do not usually result in dramatically
different reconstructions. Differences in prosopographic reconstruction are

97. Some (e.g., Steven J. Friesen, *Twice Neokoros: Ephesus, Asia and the Cult of the
Flavian Imperial Family* [Leiden: Brill, 1993]) consider the Asiarchs to have been promoters
of the imperial cult, thereby making them strange bed-fellows of Paul. The claim has not
gone unchallenged; see, for instance, R. A. Kearsley, "The Asiarchs," in D. W. J. Gill and
Conrad Gempf, eds., *The Book of Acts in Its Graeco-Roman Setting*, vol. 2 of *The Book of Acts
in Its First Century Setting* (Grand Rapids: Eerdmans, 1994), pp. 363-76.

98. There is a possibility that the Aristobulus mentioned in Rom 16:10 was the
Aristobulus mentioned by Josephus (*Ant.* 20.1.2) — i.e., the Aristobulus who was the grand-
son of Herod the Great and the brother of Agrippa I, and who died in the late 40s. If a link
could be made, it would connect one group of Jesus-followers in Rome with a member of
the elite. But since the name was not uncommon and since Paul is writing Romans almost a
decade after Aristobulus' death, attempting to link "those of the house of Aristobulus" (τοὺς
ἐκ τῶν Ἀριστοβούλου) with the Herodian dynasty is somewhat tenuous. There may be
Herodian links with the early Jesus-movement in the textual record (i.e., Manaen in Acts
13:1, and one of Jesus' followers, Joanna, is described in Luke 8:3 as "the wife of Herod's stew-
ard Chuza"), but the reference to Aristobulus probably does not provide such a link.

99. Ascough's study of Lydia puts her into ES4, as someone "well-off, but not elite"
(*Lydia*, p. 99). Questions of the historicity of the Lukan account aside, note Margaret Y.
MacDonald's estimate ("The Role of Women in the Expansion of Early Christianity," in David L. Balch and Carolyn Osiek, eds., *Early Christian Families in Context: An Interdisciplinary
Dialogue* [Grand Rapids: Eerdmans, 2003], 157-84, p. 177): "Lydia herself may never have existed, but women like her almost certainly contributed to the rise of Christianity from Paul's
day onward."

inevitable, of course, but in general they seem more like differences in degree than differences in kind.

This claim might seem surprising in light of the amount of literature dedicated to prosopographic profiling, but a simple trawl through three prosopographic analyses from the last three decades (i.e., those of Meeks in 1983, Horrell in 1996, and Friesen in 2004) illustrates how relatively stable prosopographic analyses have been during that time, even across the "consensus" divide.[100] Similarities between Meeks and Horrell may not be particularly notable, since Horrell does not do much to differentiate himself from the "new consensus" that Meeks represents. Friesen, on the other hand, mounts a significant challenge to that consensus. Despite this, however, Friesen's prosopographic itemization does not differ in any significant measure from the sort of conclusions that Meeks himself drew. Of course, there are differences here and there. In general, Friesen errs on the side of depressing the prosopographic features, whereas Meeks errs on the side of inflating them. But despite these differences, Friesen's prosopographic conclusions with regard to specific individuals are not a world away from similar analyses by some that are firmly within the "new consensus."

In Friesen's estimate, for instance, up to seven individuals mentioned by Paul "can be classified as having moderate surplus resources,"[101] including: Chloe (if a member of a Jesus-group) and Gaius at ES4; and Erastus, Philemon, Phoebe, Aquila and Prisca at either ES4 or perhaps ES5. Once again, there are, of course, differences between Meeks and Friesen, as is generally the case when two scholars assess the same data.[102] But the differences are generally not all that significant. With the exception of Erastus (Rom 16:23) and perhaps one or two others,[103] neither includes the elite of ES1-ES3 in the prosopographic mix of early Jesus-groups, for instance, and each has a spread of adherents from the middling groups downward. Perhaps there is more in common than is sometimes thought between those who challenge the "new consensus" and the more "responsible" advocates of the "new con-

---

100. Meeks, *First Urban Christians*, pp. 55-63; Horrell, *Social Ethos*, pp. 91-101; Friesen, "Poverty in Pauline Studies," pp. 348-58. See too Dale B. Martin, *The Corinthian Body* (New Haven: Yale University Press, 1995), pp. xv-xvii.

101. Friesen, "Poverty in Pauline Studies," p. 348.

102. For example, Meeks (*First Urban Christians*, pp. 57-58) includes Stephanas within this upper-band of the "wealthiest" Jesus-followers (relatively speaking, although lower than Erastus, Gaius and Crispus), whereas Friesen ("Poverty in Pauline Studies," p. 352) puts Stephanas in ES5 or ES6.

103. Meeks (*First Urban Christians*, p. 59) puts Erastus in the position of a civic elite.

sensus."[104] Here again is some evidence of how the debate can too easily be stereotyped and overdrawn.

If scholarly differences of opinion are generally not all that significant with regard to individuals mentioned by Paul, the differences become more interesting with regard to how scholars map out the proportion of those individuals in relation to the larger make-up of early urban Jesus-groups. To what extent are ES4 members indicative of the economic profile of urban Jesus-groups in general? If a rough guide is to be found in this regard, it involves a double approach: (1) taking into account Paul's rhetorical construct of the economic location of the communities he addresses, and (2) making educated guesses about the potential attractions of those communities for different economic levels. The first of these issues is explored in the following section, and the second in the next chapter.

10.7: Paul's Rhetorical Construct of His Communities' Economic Level

Most of the individuals whom Paul mentions by name, and whose economic profile can be tentatively reconstructed, seem to fall within ES4 or ES5. It is notable, then, that when he envisions the general economic profile of the Jesus-groups he addresses, Paul's descriptions seem to drop a level, gravitating towards the ES5 level primarily, with some resonance with ES6.[105] His descriptions usually exclude the categories on either side of these economic levels (i.e., ES4 and ES7).

Paul gives advice in 1 Cor 16:1-2 about how Corinthian Jesus-followers should put a little aside every week in preparation for the collection. This advice makes the most sense if it is directed to those of ES5, and possibly ES6. Those among ES7 would have had nothing to put aside, while those in ES4 would probably have had resources that are out of alignment with the kind

---

104. John M. G. Barclay ("Poverty in Pauline Studies: A Response to Steven Friesen," *JSNT* 26 [2004]: 363-66, p. 365) makes the point this way: "To place a few, as Friesen tentatively does, among the 7% in PS 4 is to make a claim for substantial wealth stratification in the Pauline churches — much as claimed by Theissen and Meeks, though with different vocabulary."

105. This view refines that of Friesen: "The group references that have economic significance assume that most of the saints lived at subsistence level" ("Poverty in Pauline Studies," 350). Instead of ES6, as Friesen implies, a higher economic register is often noted in Paul's group references.

of advice that Paul offers.[106] So Paul's description of the Corinthian situation (along with that of his Galatian communities, also mentioned in 1 Cor 16:1-2) rhetorically excludes ES7 and gravitates primarily towards ES6 and, especially, ES5. This does not mean that the Corinthian (and Galatian) communities had no representatives from ES4 and ES7, but simply that Paul is not addressing ES4 and ES7 members when giving the advice outlined in 1 Cor 16:1-2.

This instance resonates with the preponderance of other data. On those occasions when Paul's discourse includes an indicator of his audience's economic level, that level gravitates to ES5 especially. Of particular interest is the use of the phrase "work with your own hands." Of relevance are the following passages where this phrase appears: 1 Cor 4:11-13, 1 Thess 4:11-12, Eph. 4:28, and Acts 20:34-35 (the latter two with slight changes to the form). While the phrase might conceivably be appropriate to a variety of levels, it would exclude most in the ES4 descriptor (except upper level artisans). In 1 Cor 4:12 Paul makes use of the phrase in a list of entries meant to illustrate the extremely low end of status levels. In 1 Cor 4:11-13, Paul offers a catalogue of hardships demonstrating that he embodies all that is held in disrepute according to cultural standards and expectations. He is nothing other than "the world's scum" (περικαθάρματα τοῦ κόσμου) and "the scrapings from everyone's shoes" (πάντων περίψημα ἕως ἄρτι).[107] He counters these lowly status indicators with another that he expects to trump them all — that of Paul being the Corinthians' progenitor in faith (πατήρ, 4:15). The Corinthians are in the odd situation of being status-inconsistent with their own "spiritual father." For they imagine themselves to be enjoying overabundance (κεκορεσμένοι ἐστέ), to have been made rich (ἐπλουτήσατε), and to have been established as kings (ἐβασιλεύσατε), as ones who are strong (ἰσχυροί) and honored (ἔνδοξοι). But Paul glories in his weakness and disrepute, marshalling evidence to prove his cultural dishonor. He has experienced hunger, thirst, homelessness; he has had a lack of proper clothing and has suffered abuse, persecution and slander. Among these dishonorable entries Paul includes "working with our own hands" in 4:12 (ἐργαζόμενοι ταῖς ἰδίαις χερσίν).

While most of the entries in Paul's catalogue of vices in 1 Cor 4:11-13

---

106. Paul must have expected those at ES4 to be involved in his collection, but his advice in this passage does not apply to them primarily.

107. The translation is that of A. C. Thiselton, *The First Epistle to the Corinthians* (Grand Rapids: Eerdmans, 2000), p. 344.

could well apply to ES7 situations, it would be wrong to assign, by association, the phrase "working with hands" to that same economic level. That phrase resonates with sub-elite levels ES6 and ES5, with slight resonances at the low end of ES4b. The "working with hands" phrase may be at home in Paul's "low-status hardship list," but it does not drop to the bottom of that list as some other entries do. Paul incorporates his manual labor into the frame because it is a live issue among his audience (see 1 Cor 9:1-18; 2 Cor 11:7-11; 12:14-15; also 1 Thess 2:7-12; 3:8-9) and, relatedly, because manual labor was generally despised by the elite and used as a mark of inferiority by the rich who enjoyed overabundance and high-levels of social honor.[108] Accordingly, even if the phrase "working with hands" is rhetorically aligned here with ES7 descriptors, it is best taken as a descriptor of economic levels higher than ES7. Conversely, if the phrase resonates well at ES6 and ES5 levels, it nonetheless starts to become a bit thinly stretched as a descriptor of ES4, precisely in view of its rhetorical utility in Paul's hardship list.

A similar picture emerges in 1 Thess 4:11-12, where Paul advises the Thessalonian Jesus-followers "to work with your own hands, as we directed you, so that you may command the respect of outsiders and be dependent on no one [μηδενὸς χρείαν ἔχητε]." Here Paul's advice seems targeted at those in ES5 primarily, with some resonance with ES6, but excluding ES7, who were in real need and were wholly dependent on others.[109]

The passage is important beyond initial appearances, since Paul makes it clear that this advice replicates advice that he and his associates had given earlier ("as we directed you"). Meeks writes:

> [T]his is a paraenetic reminder of instruction given the Thessalonian converts when the church was first organized there. It is not a unique admonition fitted to special needs of the Thessalonians . . . but represents the kind of instruction that Paul and his associates generally gave to new converts.[110]

It is not surprising, then, that a similar economic characterization of communities founded by Paul is maintained in two other disputed Pauline

---

108. See Moses I. Finley, *The Ancient Economy* (London: Chatto & Windus, 1975), pp. 40-43.

109. So Dale Martin, *The Corinthian Body*, p. 79: "most if not all of these [Thessalonian] converts were themselves manual laborers."

110. Meeks, *First Urban Christians*, p. 64. Paul's words in 2 Thess 3:10 have the same importance; on this, see Jewett, *Romans*, p. 69.

texts. The author of 2 Thessalonians advises that Jesus-followers should "do their work quietly and earn their own living" (2 Thess 3:12). The author of Ephesians proposes that, as a consequence of joining communities of Jesus-followers, "thieves must give up stealing" and must instead "labor and work honestly with their own hands, so as to have something to share with the needy" (Eph 4:28). The double-tasked prospect of working with one's hands and sharing with others puts the rhetorical target above the level of ES7, being rhetorically centered primarily in ES5, and possibly ES6. Of course, both of these admonitions occur in disputed Pauline letters, but implications regarding the economic characterization of urban Jesus-groups is not undermined by that. Instead, if either one or both texts is/are thought to have been authored by someone other than Paul, we would simply have a consistent depiction of the economic characterization of urban Jesus-groups by one or two authors alongside of Paul himself.

It is also notable that, when imagining Paul to gather together with members of Jesus-groups he had founded, the Lukan author also placed those members generally at the level of ES5. In Acts 20:34-35, when meeting with members of the Ephesian Jesus-groups among whom he had lived for several years, Paul says: "You know for yourselves that I worked with my own hands to support myself and my companions. In all this I have given you an example that by such work we must support the weak (δεῖ ἀντιλαμβάνεσθαι τῶν ἀσθενούντων)." The "weak" of Acts 20:35 must overlap considerably with the economically "poor," to the extent that the two are likely to be virtually identical. The Paul of Acts 20 is not speaking to people of ES7, and perhaps not to those of ES6. His scenario of working with one's hands to support oneself and in order to support the needy corresponds most closely to the ES5 economic level.[111]

In two instances Paul's economic register focuses on those who fell within ES7 — a category included in the reference to "the weak" of Acts 20:35. In 1 Cor 11:22, Paul discusses the situation of "those who have nothing" (τοὺς μὴ ἔχοντας) in relation to the Corinthian observance of the Lord's Supper.[112] Here Paul's discourse focuses on, and seeks to negotiate, the disparity between those who fall within ES7 (and perhaps ES6) and those higher up the economic registry. This instance does not provide us with a rhetorical construct of the Corinthians' general economic profile, but shows

---

111. Paul's self-description in Acts 20 accords well with the same in 1 Cor 9:12-18; 2 Thess 3:7-12.

112. On interpreting this phrase, see n. 41 above.

Paul addressing a situation that involved particular individuals who fell predominately within ES7.

2 Corinthians 8:1-6 provides us with another instance of Paul constructing an economic location of ES7 for some among urban Jesus-groups. There he describes the economic situation of Macedonian Jesus-groups (i.e., Thessalonica; Philippi). According to Paul, those communities had already given generously to the collection despite their "severe ordeal of affliction" and "extremely onerous poverty" (ἡ κατὰ βάθους πτωχεία αὐτῶν). Since Paul's advice of 1 Thess 4:11-12 envisions a higher economic register for Thessalonian Jesus-groups (i.e., ES5) than in 2 Cor 8:1-6 (i.e., ES7), it may be that in 2 Corinthians Paul is intentionally depressing the economic situation of the Macedonian congregations. This would have had the rhetorical effect, first, of accentuating Macedonian generosity in order, second, to motivate Corinthian generosity through emulation of the Macedonian communities. It is noteworthy, then, that Paul can shift his construct of Macedonian economic identity between ES5 (or so) in 1 Thess 4:11-12 and ES7 in 2 Cor 8:1-6, according to the requirements of rhetorical utility.[113]

A similar shift out of ES5 for purposes of rhetorical effect is likely to be evident in 2 Cor 8:14, although in this case moving up the scale rather than down it (as in 2 Cor 8:1-6). Paul's depiction of the Corinthian "abundance" (περίσσευμα) in 2 Cor 8:14 might be said to describe a community that falls predominantly within ES4 rather than ES5 and below. But this rhetorical construct must be interpreted with some caution. Paul is likely speaking of Corinthian "abundance" in terms relative to the Jerusalem communities. Or the reference to "abundance" might be a subtle way of arm-twisting those in ES4 from within the Corinthian communities, seeking a generous donation from them for Paul's collection efforts (having already instructed those in ES5, and perhaps ES6, in 1 Cor 16:1-2).[114] Either way, the term is probably being used with an extra dose of rhetorical spin in this case, and should not be

---

113. When Paul speaks of "churches of Macedonia" offering him financial assistance (2 Cor 8:1; cf. 2 Cor 11:9), he is probably basing his point on support given by Philippian instead of Thessalonian Jesus-followers. But Paul's blanket description of support coming from "churches of Macedonia" in 2 Cor 8:1 would have given (some) Corinthian Jesus-followers a less specific impression. On the socio-economic locations of Philippian and Thessalonian Jesus-groups, see Richard S. Ascough, *Paul's Macedonian Associations: The Social Context of Philippians and 1 Thessalonians* (Tübingen: Mohr Siebeck, 2003), pp. 115-29, pp. 165-76.

114. There were likely to be more Corinthians in ES4 than those defined as such in the prosopographic survey above; see Dale Martin, *The Corinthian Body*, pp. 70-79, 88-92.

used to raise the general profile of the Corinthian communities beyond a general average of ES5, with some falling into higher and some into lower categories.[115]

In general, then, Paul seems to address urban Jesus-groups as if they were comprised primarily of people belonging to ES5. At times the rhetorical target is broad enough to incorporate both ES5 and ES6, but when advice about working with one's hands is combined with exhortations to support others in need, ES5 seems to be most in Paul's sights — or at least, his hortatory pressure comes to bear most notably on them. At times Paul moved the level of economic characterization up or down from that point, for rhetorical effect, or when addressing particular people or people groups. But in general, ES5 seems to be where his own mental averaging of urban Jesus-groups gravitates most naturally.

In this chapter, the economic profiles of selected urban Jesus-followers have been canvassed, and Paul's "mental averaging" of the economic status of urban Jesus-groups has been noted. We are now in a position to consider more specifically the extent to which Jesus-groups would have been found to offer attraction to urbanites along the economic spectrum — the primary focus of the next chapter.

---

115. Other indicators are also neutral economic indicators, such as the fact that some Corinthian Jesus-followers were engaged in lawsuits against others. Lawsuits in themselves are not indicative of economic location; see Meggitt, *Paul, Poverty and Survival,* pp. 122-25, 152. Nonetheless, it was the norm for the legal system to be stacked against those who fell lower on the social strata; see especially L. de Ligt, "Restraining the Rich, Protecting the Poor: Symbolic Aspects of Roman Legislation," in W. Jongman and M. Kleijwegt, eds., *After the Past* (Leiden: Brill, 2002), 1-46, pp. 1-2.

CHAPTER 11

"You would have plucked out your eyes"

The Economic Attractions of Paul's Communities

11.1: Economic Levels and Affiliation Attractions

11.2: Further Possible Attractions for Those at ES4 and ES5

11.3: Reference Groups and Status Realignment

11.1: Economic Levels and Affiliation Attractions

As Wayne Meeks rightly noted, "motivational bases for becoming part of the *ekklēsia* would likely vary from one member to another."[1] And identifying possible "motivational bases" requires an attentiveness to socio-economic location. While socio-economic factors alone will not provide a sufficient explanation for the spread of the early Jesus-movement and the promulgation of its good news, we need nonetheless to consider the extent to which such factors may have played some part in that spread.[2]

---

1. Wayne A. Meeks, *The First Urban Christians* (New Haven: Yale University Press, 1983), p. 77.

2. For a classic statement of the socio-economic attractions of the Jesus-movement in an age philosophically influenced by Hellenistic democratic and egalitarian ideals, see S. Dickey, "Some Economic and Social Conditions of Asia Minor Affecting the Expansion of Christianity," in S. J. Case, ed., *Studies in Early Christianity* (New York: Century, 1928), pp. 393-416. Immersed in the ideals of prosperity and justice induced by Hellenistic philosophy, the majority of the population continued to experience little other than economically-adverse situations, so that "when Christianity entered with its promise of a 'new age' of righteousness inaugurated by divine power, which included 'feeding the hungry with good

We should guard against the assumption that the only "motivational bases" worthy of note are those of the middling-status artisans and house-holders, and that servile functionaries had no "motivational bases" to be considered since they simply followed the initiatives of the householder. Having already noted Paul's commitment to the poor in chapters 6 through 9 above, we must also consider the motivational bases not simply of middle-class artisans and members of households but also those beyond the security of households and in economically vulnerable positions. While some at the lower end of the socio-economic scale were embedded within a Jesus-group by reason of their attachment to a householder who had joined a Jesus-group, others were members of Jesus-groups on their own initiative without belonging to a household. For this reason, consideration of "motivational bases" needs to be extended beyond the middle-status holders to include also the poor and destitute beyond household structures.

Arguably, the early Jesus-movement offered a great deal to impoverished urbanites, especially those beyond the relative security of a household.

---

things' and 'exalting those of low degree,' it could not help but get a hearing" (p. 411). Compare R. Lane Fox's view (*Pagans and Christians* [London: Viking, 1986], p. 321): The early Jesus-movement offered "an alternative community and range of values to those who were disenchanted by the display of riches, by the harshness of the exercise of power and the progressive hardening of the gradations of rank and degree. Only a simple view of human nature will expect such people to be none but the poor and the oppressed themselves." Along these lines, see also Lawrence L. Welborn, "'Extraction from the Mortal Site': Badiou on the Resurrection in Paul," *NTS* 55 (2009): 295-314, p. 304: Paul's converts, like many others, were likely to have been "increasingly isolated individuals, wracked by obsessive emotions and a sense of supine powerlessness."

Note also Dale Martin's suggestion that the Jesus-movement might have been seen as a vehicle for protection against malevolent forces (*Inventing Superstition* [Cambridge, MA: Harvard University Press, 2004], p. 243): "Christianity may indeed have been as successful as it was because, among other factors, it offered answers to a problem that most people considered a real one: the threat of harm from possibly malicious daimons. Christianity, unlike classical philosophy, did not answer the problem by insisting that evil daimons did not exist. Instead, it offered an antidote more powerful than the poison, a drug stronger than the disease; healing and exorcism in the name of Jesus. . . . In its demonology, Christianity tapped into an assumed reality and met a need in a way classical philosophy had failed to do. So it was more successful eventually in winning over the masses than philosophy had ever been." See also P. Gray, *Godly Fear: The Epistle to the Hebrews and Greco-Roman Critiques of Superstition* (Atlanta: Society of Biblical Literature, 2003). There would be a socio-economic dimension even in this, of course. The same would be true for the view that the attraction of early Christianity lay in its promise that its adherents would overcome death and receive a restored and comfortable physicality in the afterlife; on this, see Dag Oistein Endsjo, *Greek Resurrection Beliefs and the Success of Christianity* (New York: Palgrave Macmillan, 2009).

If Jesus-groups set up communal funds for the poor and gathered to share food and drink in corporate dinners and other occasions, it is relatively easy to see what economic attraction such communities would have held for people in ES6 and ES7 who fell beyond the structures of a household. Moreover, this dimension might have distinguished early Jesus-groups from other urban associations, since Greco-Roman associations generally did not accumulate their membership from among ES6 and ES7 levels (see below).[3] While economic benefit is probably not a sufficient explanation for the attractions of Jesus-groups among those in ES6 and ES7, it would nonetheless have served as a powerful means of attraction, alongside any other "noneconomic" factors that might be considered.[4]

At the other end of the economy scale, the early Jesus-movement seems to have had little attraction among the elite of ES1 through ES3. As Edwin Judge noted half a century ago, early Jesus-groups "did not draw upon the upper order of the Roman ranking system. . . . Their social needs were very amply gratified by the exclusive circles to which they were admitted."[5] By the end of the first century CE at the latest, this situation began to change, with

---

3. Paul Veyne (*Bread and Circuses: Historical Sociology and Political Pluralism* [London: Penguin, 1990], p. 34) claims that "none of these [Greco-Roman] associations ever allotted anything for assistance to members who had become poor." This is not true; see §4.2 above. But it is true that if members of associations dropped to ES6 or ES7 levels, they would have been in an exceptional position within the membership, since most associations had memberships drawn predominantly from ES4 and ES5.

4. This is the dimension of attraction that Meggitt taps into when he depicts urban Jesus-groups as based on principles of economic "mutuality." Meggitt arrives at this characterization on the basis that almost all people of the Roman world lived in desperate poverty, resulting consequently in a monochrome depiction of Pauline Jesus followers as similarly grouped at subsistence level. The only economic strategy for such a group would be mutualism — a sharing of resources. Apart from the weakness of binary constructions of this kind, it is not clear that such a strategy would amount to much of an increase in levels of security and survival; very little plus very little still leaves very little, especially when increasing the numbers of those sharing very little. So instead of being characterized by mutuality among the desperately poor, the early Jesus-movement must have had injections of resources from those who were more economically secure.

5. Edwin A. Judge, *Social Perspectives on Christians in the First Century: Pivotal Essays* (ed. D. M. Scholer; Peabody: Hendrickson, 2008), p. 37. So also Lane Fox, *Pagans and Christians*, p. 321: "Christianity was least likely to attract the people who were most embedded in social tradition, the great families of Rome, the upper families who filled the civic priesthoods and competed in public generosity." Contrast the rather undisciplined view of Rodney Stark, *The Rise of Christianity* (Princeton: Princeton University Press, 1996), p. 89: "Christians were not a mass of degraded outsiders but from the early days had members, friends, and relatives in high places — often within the Imperial family."

elite adherents beginning to appear within Jesus-groups.[6] Before that time, it is unlikely that they had much of a presence within urban groups of Jesus-followers.[7] It would be unwise to completely rule out the prospect of elite membership in the early urban groups of Jesus-followers, of course, and the Lukan account of the spread of the early Jesus-movement builds much on precisely this feature of its historiography, as noted above (see §10.6). But it is a Lukan feature that continues to be suspect. In the mid-second century, Celsus characterized Christian groups as being attractive only to the poor, the uneducated and the stupid.[8] Even allowing for rhetorical hyperbole,[9] his depiction must have been generally reliable in order to score its rhetorical points. But neither does it exclude a low-level presence of elite members in some gatherings of Jesus-followers, especially as the Christian groups began to become increasingly visible in the second and third centuries CE, for reasons beyond our purview.[10]

6. Peter Lampe, *From Paul to Valentinus: Christians at Rome in the First Two Centuries,* trans. M. Steinhauser (Minneapolis: Fortress Press, 2003), p. 139: In the Jesus-movement "[r]eally 'rich people' . . . become discernible for the first time [only] in the 90s of the first century." Cf. Jerome Murphy-O'Connor, *Paul: His Story* (Oxford: Oxford University Press, 2004), pp. 41-42.

According to Eusebius, many Roman converts of his day (i.e., the fourth century) were "most distinguished by their riches and their birth" (*Hist. eccl.* 5.21.1). See also Tertullian, *Apol.* 37; *Scap.* 4–5.

7. It would be hasty to exclude their presence altogether from early groups of Jesus-followers, at least from the middle of the first century onwards. On the other hand, it is uncertain whether 1 Cor 1:26 can be used to prove the point, when Paul implies that some Corinthian Jesus-followers were δυνατοί and εὐγενεῖς. The adjective δυνατός is a relative term without a clear economic correlative, while εὐγενεῖς might mean little more than having a freedman as a father or grandfather (perhaps like Paul himself; see §13.2 below).

8. Origen, *Cels.* 1.27; 3.18, 44, 50, 52, 55, 59, etc.

9. That Celsus's statement is hyperbolic is evident from Pliny's letter to Trajan, as in n. 10 below.

10. Lampe, *From Paul to Valentinus,* p. 139: "In the second century the group of socially elevated increases constantly. By the time of Hermas this group is already polymorphic and, in the last fifth of the second century, it stretches into the upper classes, even into senatorial circles." See also Pliny's description of Jesus-followers/Christians living in Pontus in the early second century (*Ep. Tra.* 10.96.9): they are comprised of "a great many individuals, of every age, of every class [*omnis ordinis*], both men and women."

The fact that Christianity attracted elite in the late first century onwards has been seen to explain why the Letter of James had no impact on the extant Christian literature prior to Irenaeus (cf. 180 CE) — i.e., its radical critique of wealth would have been a hindrance to the spread of Christianity among the elite at precisely the time when the movement was seeking to ingratiate itself with the elite. The position is advocated by Görge K. Hasselhoff ("James

If there is some clarity with regard to the relative attractiveness of Jesus-groups for those at either end of the economic spectrum, more convoluted is any attempt to theorize as to the possible attractions of early Jesus-groups for those in the middle of the economy scale. In relation to both ES4 and ES5, it is best to proceed by analogy with Greco-Roman *collegia* or associations,[11] for which we have enough data to extrapolate somewhat in relation to early Jesus-groups. Such associations were numerous in the first century, and urban Jesus-groups shared some notable similarities with them.[12]

In a world where identity was calculated in relation to social honor, establishing oneself as a benefactor of an association would have had some obvious attractions. This was true especially for those at the upper end of the middling groups (i.e., ES4a). They would have had both the resources and the motivation to act as an association's benefactor. Being a benefactor of a *collegium* had its own rewards in a number of ways. First, it allowed one to be the equivalent of "a big fish in a (relatively) small pond."[13] Second, it

2:2-7 in Early Christian Thought," in Susan R. Holman, ed., *Wealth and Poverty in Early Church and Society* [Grand Rapids: Baker Academic Press, 2008], 48-55, p. 55), but is unlikely to offer a full explanation. John Painter ("James as the First Catholic Epistle," in Karl-Wilhelm Niebuhr and Robert W. Wall, eds., *The Catholic Epistles and Apostolic Tradition* [Waco: Baylor University Press, 2009], 161-82, p. 166) is on better ground, perhaps, when he suggests that because the letter was composed after James's death "at a time [post-70 CE] when the Jerusalem church was no longer preeminent and Gentile Christianity had become dominant, an epistle directed to the Jewish Diaspora had little appeal to the church at large."

11. Richard S. Ascough (*Lydia: Paul's Cosmopolitan Hostess* [Collegeville, MN: Liturgical Press, 2009], p. 79) suggests that we call these "elective social formations," although I am not sure that the description will stick.

12. The relationship between Jesus-groups and Greco-Roman associations has received notable attention since the mid 1990s, not least with the publication of John S. Kloppenborg and Stephen G. Wilson, eds., *Voluntary Associations in the Graeco-Roman World* (London: Routledge, 1996), and followed up by Richard S. Ascough's case for seeing Jesus-groups as associations; see, for instance, Ascough, *What Are They Saying about the Formation of Pauline Churches?* (Mahwah, NJ: Paulist Press, 1998); Ascough, "The Thessalonian Christian Community as a Professional Voluntary Association," *JBL* 119 (2000): 311-28; and Ascough, "Voluntary Associations and the Formation of Pauline Christian Communities: Overcoming Objections," in A. Gutsfeld and D.-A. Koch, eds., *Vereine, Synagogen und Gemeinden im kaiserzeitlichen Kleinasien* (Tübingen: Mohr Siebeck, 2006), pp. 149-83.

13. So John S. Kloppenborg ("Collegia and Thiasoi: Issues in Function, Taxonomy and Membership," in Kloppenborg and Wilson, *Voluntary Associations*, pp. 16-30, here p. 18): "The association afforded each member a say in who joined the group and how the group was run, fellowship and conviviality, and perhaps the opportunity to become an officer or magistrate — in short, to participate in a *census honorum* to which he or she could never aspire outside of the association."

would have enabled the benefactor to increase in social visibility, since *collegia* benefactors were frequently honored by the members of associations in ways that increased their public honor. Consequently, and third, sponsoring an association would have increased the benefactor's chances of entering into an advantageous patronage relationship with someone more prominently situated, on the grounds that the benefactor would have had influence within sectors of the populace.

By analogy, we might well imagine similar attractions having motivated some to establish themselves as benefactors of urban groups of Jesus-followers. Early communities of Jesus-followers might well have served as vehicles for social honor for some ES4 figures engaged in the never-ending hunt for honor-capture that marked out Greco-Roman urbanism. This might cohere well with Meeks's proposal that some urban "status-inconsistents" found that adhering to a Jesus-group gave some resolution to their status inconsistency within Greco-Roman culture.

It needs to be noted, however, that at least three factors would have made the prospect of becoming a benefactor of an urban Jesus-group less than wholly appealing. First, there is a difference between the economic profile of *collegia* in general and urban Jesus-groups. While there were *collegia* whose membership included "poorer" sectors of society (i.e., funerary associations of the second century CE and beyond),[14] *collegia* members generally were "drawn from the upper echelons of the urban *plebs* and can best be characterized as 'employers' rather than 'employees.'"[15] The depiction of

---

14. Kloppenborg makes the case ("Collegia") that funerary associations were not prominent in the first century CE. Note also that funerary associations themselves had a membership that was unlikely to include the destitute. As O. M. van Nijf notes ("*Collegia* and Civic Guards: Two Chapters in the History of Sociability," in W. Jongman and M. Kleijwegt, eds., *After the Past* [Leiden: Brill, 2002], 305-340, p. 308), "these funerary activities were not a last resort for urban paupers, but rather symptomatic of the social ambitions of individuals of a certain standing in society." If someone already had some stature-traction in society, he might well seek to preserve it after death as well as possible; funerary associations helped to serve that purpose.

15. John R. Patterson, *Landscapes and Cities: Rural Settlement and Civic Transformation in Early Imperial Italy* (Oxford: Oxford University Press, 2006), p. 255. This generalization pertains to what Kloppenborg calls "private associations . . . [whose] membership was for the most part drawn from the non-elite" rather than the "Roman sacerdotal colleges and sacred sodalities . . . [that] drew upon the elite for their members" ("Collegia," p. 16). The "private associations" are generally thought to have been characterized by a relatively "homogenous social membership, often influenced by common trades and crafts" (W. O. McCready, "*Ekklēsia* and Voluntary Associations," in Kloppenborg and Wilson, eds., *Voluntary Associations*, 59-73, p. 63).

collegia as the virtual equivalent of self-help organizations for the very poor, offering a refuge for orphans and paupers, is now recognized to be "no longer tenable."[16] Instead, as Onno van Nijf notes, the associations

> recruited their members mainly from among the upper levels of the urban plebs: craftsmen and traders of at least moderate wealth, . . . a relatively well-off segment of the population. . . . The *collegia* . . . seem to have covered a broad band of society. At the highest level we find individuals who were merging with the ruling order of decurions, but most *collegiati* appear to have been men of more moderate means. They occupied the social position for which the Romans used the term *plebs media*.[17]

This characterization would place the primary membership of *collegia* within ES5 and ES4 (perhaps ES4b especially), with the *collegia's* benefactor standing higher up on the economic spectrum (ES4a and higher). As John Patterson has demonstrated, the fact that *collegia* members were not normally drawn from among the needy is both "implied by the costs involved in belonging to a *collegium*" and "reflected in the level of generosity shown to *collegia* members as part of formal distributions or banquets."[18] This is evident in various inscriptions listing the distribution rates to various sectors of society. So Patterson writes:

> [A]n inscription dated to the reign of Commodus records that during a distribution at Urvinum Mataurense organized by C. Vesnius Vindex, patron of the town, the *decuriones* [i.e., ES3] received 20 HS, the members of the *collegia* 16 HS, and the *plebs* 12 HS; at Verulae in 197, *decuriones* and *seriri* received 16 HS each, *dendrophorio* [i.e., members of a *collegium*] 12 HS, and the *populus* 4 HS. At a distribution in Pisaurum, *decurions* again received 20 HS, but *collegia* members 8 HS and the *plebs* in general only 4 HS.

---

16. Van Nijf, "*Collegia* and Civic Guards," p. 307. For an extended discussion animated by this older view, see F. M. Ausbüttel, *Untersuchungen zu den Vereinen im Westen des römischen Reiches* (Kallmünz: Lassleben, 1982), pp. 71-84.

17. Van Nijf, "*Collegia* and Civic Guards," pp. 308-309.

18. Patterson, *Landscapes and Cities*, p. 255. See also van Nijf, "*Collegia* and Civic Guards," p. 308; David J. Downs, *The Offering of the Gentiles* (Tübingen: Mohr Siebeck, 2008), p. 110. Both of the latter point to the association fees depicted in *CIL* XIV, 2112: "whoever wishes to become a member of this society shall give as a personal entrance fee 100 sesterces and an *amphora* of good wine, also he shall pay a monthly subscription of 5 asses." As Downs notes (p. 110), "[m]ost pagan voluntary associations were composed of those of middling status and wealth."

According to Patterson, *collegia* members were comprised of "the wealthier elements within the *plebs*." He makes the point in relation to mounting levels of urban growth:

> [U]rban growth led to increasing profits for artisans and traders of the city, leading to an increasing influence on their part and a growing differentiation between them and the destitute. . . . Part of this additional wealth financed the development of *collegia*.[19]

Describing *collegia* members as primarily artisans and traders who were differentiated from the destitute and who enjoyed the increasing profits of urban growth, Patterson places them squarely within the ES5 and ES4 economic levels.[20]

If honor was ascribed to benefactors of *collegia* whose membership usually fell predominately within ES5 and ES4 economic levels, it is not clear that similar forms of honor could be expected for benefactors of Jesus-group *ekklēsiai* whose profile included significant levels of ES5 members as well as high percentages of members from ES6 and ES7. Accordingly, the prospect of a member of the elite establishing a patronage relationship with a benefactor of a Jesus-group comprised primarily of people in ES5 through ES7 may not have been as attractive as patronage connections with sponsors of (other kinds of) associations.

Second, those who sought to establish a relationship of benefaction with a Jesus-group "association" might soon have been repulsed by a general vacuity of ascribed honor that would have been expected to be shown by those within that association. In this regard it is, of course, impossible to at-

---

19. Patterson, *Landscapes and Cities*, p. 261.

20. Patterson's data problematizes the view that members of *collegia* were normally entrenched in poverty. Kloppenborg gives voice to this view ("Collegia," p. 23): "It would seem that the majority of associations, with the exception of the priestly sodalities, were composed of the urban poor, slaves and freedmen." More nuanced is Stephen G. Wilson, who in his editorial introduction to a co-edited volume with Kloppenborg, takes on Kloppenborg's view directly ("Voluntary Associations: An Overview," in Kloppenborg and Wilson, eds., *Voluntary Associations*, 1-15, p. 10): "It is often noted that membership in associations was confined largely to the lower classes — typically the urban poor, slaves, and freedmen. This is generally true, though it can also give a misleading impression. For one thing it tells us only that they [i.e., voluntary associations] catered to all but an elite minority. For another, the categories slave and freedman cover a wide range of people, from the abjectly poor and beholden to the relatively wealthy and influential." Wilson's view coincides with Kloppenborg's point that "many of the members of these guilds became *Augustales*" ("Collegia," 24), since the *Augustales* were "secure" economically speaking (usually ES4a).

General Economic Levels of *Collegia* and Jesus-Groups

Level	*Collegia* in General	Jesus-Groups
ES4	Predominant Membership Levels	
ES5	Predominant Membership Levels	Predominant Membership Levels
ES6		Predominant Membership Levels
ES7		Predominant Membership Levels

tribute to early communities of Jesus-followers anything more than a general proclivity towards "culturally transgressive" norms. Certain texts from the early Jesus-movement reflect how, in some occasions, honor was ascribed within Jesus-groups in ways that adhered relatively well with normal social codes. But in each case, the texts' authors are quick to point out that the good news they preach frequently runs contrary to the cultural canons of honor.[21] In the early days of the Jesus-movement's spread into Mediterranean urban contexts, there is little to suggest that members of Jesus-group *ekklēsiai* were expected to follow their sponsor through the streets among an entourage that publicly proclaimed their sponsor's merits. No lists of honor pertaining to benefactors of Jesus-groups are evident in the literary or archaeological data of the earliest Jesus-movement. Instead, Jesus-groups told stories about their Lord who was remembered as speaking words like these:

> The kings of the Gentiles exercise lordship over them; and those in authority over them are called benefactors. But not so with you; rather the greatest among you must become as the youngest, and the leader like one who serves. (Luke 22:25-26)

> When you give a luncheon or a dinner, do not invite your friends or your brothers or your relatives or rich neighbors, in case they may invite you in

21. With regard to Paul, for instance, David G. Horrell writes (*The Social Ethos of the Corinthian Correspondence: Interests and Ideology from 1 Corinthians to 1 Clement* [Edinburgh: T&T Clark, 1996], p. 155): "It would certainly be inaccurate to suggest that Paul's teaching reflected these people's social interests [i.e., the interests of the socially strong]; he does not affirm or legitimate their social position." So also Meeks, *First Urban Christians*, p. 78.

return, and you would be repaid. But when you give a banquet, invite the poor, the crippled, the lame, and the blind. And you will be blessed, because they cannot repay you, for you will be repaid at the resurrection of the righteous. (Luke 14:12-14)

In words of this kind, communities of Jesus-followers remembered their Lord as having defamed those engaged in honor-bound benefaction and patronage practices, all the way up the socio-economic scale, and remembered him as promoting relationships that escalate honor among those at the bottom of the scale. As Halvor Moxnes says about texts such as these, "Compared to Hellenistic and later Christian texts, it is remarkable that there is no expectation of reciprocity, not even in the form of gratitude from the poor. . . . This is the end of a patron-client relationship in a traditional sense."[22] It is little wonder, then, that Paul called the good news "foolishness to the gentiles" (1 Cor 1:23), precisely because that news was frequently interpreted to run contrary to normal codes of social honor.

Third, prospective benefactors of early Jesus-groups might have been hesitant to establish themselves as sponsors because of the potentially dubious reputation of the Jesus-movement with regard to the Roman imperial order. Historians of the early Jesus-movement have begun to revisit this issue with vigor in recent years, exploring the extent to which the good news of the Jesus-movement included a politically subversive or anti-imperial dimension. Romanism was primarily an urban phenomenon, and the Roman imperial cult was at the heart of Roman urbanism in the provinces across which the Jesus-movement was spreading.[23] Within urban contexts, social advancement was generally inconsistent with anything anti-Roman.

In this light, the relationship between social advancement (on the one hand) and adherence to the good news (on the other) might well have been seen as inversely proportional in certain contexts. The more subversive the early Jesus-movement would have appeared, the less attraction it would have

22. Halvor Moxnes, *The Economy of the Kingdom: Social Conflict and Economic Relations in Luke's Gospel* (Philadelphia: Fortress Press, 1988), p. 133. For Lane Fox (*Pagans and Christians*, p. 321), this problematizes any attempt to link the attraction of the Jesus-movement to patronal interests.

23. On urban centers as the prime location for exploring identity in relation to Roman imperialism, see especially Louise Revell, *Roman Imperialism and Local Identities* (Cambridge: Cambridge University Press, 2009). On Roman influence within urban centers, see William L. MacDonald, *The Architecture of the Roman Empire*, Vol. 1: *An Introductory Study*, rev. ed. (New Haven: Yale University Press, 1982); William L. MacDonald, *The Architecture of the Roman Empire*, Vol. 2: *An Urban Appraisal* (New Haven: Yale University Press, 1986).

held for those enthralled by honor and advancement within Roman urbanism. And at the heart of the good news that Paul proclaimed lay the drama
of one crucified on a Roman cross. Throughout the Mediterranean basin,
crucifixion was the recognized punishment for those convicted of anti-
social and, ultimately, anti-Roman sentiment. It was "horrendous, ignomin-
ious, and reserved for the scum of society."[24] Consequently, crucifixion not
only removed anti-Roman criminals but promoted fear among the populace
and symbolically reenacted Roman victory over the nations and the forces of
chaos. A century before Paul, Cicero had said (*Rab. Post.* 5.16): "The very
word 'cross' should be far removed not only from the person of a Roman citizen but from his thoughts, his eyes, and his ears."[25] In urban contexts of
highly-charged pro-Romanism, it is not difficult to imagine that "some aspects of early Christian communal life . . . could be seen as politically or socially destablilizing."[26] Whatever else we might say, at times in its early history the Jesus-movement was seen as part of the civic problem, holding back
urban progress and the Roman program.[27] The deities were thought to over-

24. J. C. Beker, *Paul the Apostle* (Minneapolis: Fortress Press, 1980), p. 206. Cf. Martin
Hengel, *Crucifixion in the Ancient World and the Folly of the Message of the Cross* (Minneapolis: Fortress Press, 1977), p. 51.

25. As Welborn points out ("Extraction from the Mortal Site," pp. 307-308), while elite
literature complies with Cicero's advice, "[t]he omnipresence of the cross in popular literature portraying the lives of slaves stands in striking contrast to the social constraint upon
discourse about the cross in the literature of the elite . . . the rarity of references to crucifixion in canonical literature is not an historical accident, but a reflection of the social and aes-
thetic values of upper-class writers." Moreover he notes that "the cross was not only the omi-
nous specter around which the consciousness of the slave cringed, but because the cross was
the evil instrument by which the legal institution of slavery was maintained, that extracted
the surplus upon which the power of the ruling class depended, the cross may be identified
as the dark, gravitational center which, whether recognized or repressed, allotted places to
all those who lived within the socio-symbolic edifice of the Roman Empire, and compelled
thought to consent to those places."

26. Wilson, "Voluntary Associations," p. 3. He continues: "[N]either Jews nor Christians were entirely quietist. . . . [T]hey were not unwilling to pillory the religious practices
and social mores of pagan society and [to engage in] sharp criticism of the ruling classes." So
too John Barclay notes how the early Jesus-movement could be seen as dangerous to the fabric of social cohesion in the Greco-Roman world because Jesus-followers were "self-
consciously socially innovative"; see his "Money and Meetings: Group Formation among
Diaspora Jews and Early Christians," in A. Gutsfeld and D.-A. Koch, eds., *Vereine, Synagogen
und Gemeinden im kaiserzeitlichen Kleinasien* (Tübingen: Mohr Siebeck, 2006), 113-27, pp.
125-26. For a helpful study on conflict between Jesus-followers and others, see Barclay's
"Conflict in Thessalonica," *CBQ* 55 (1993): 512-30.

27. Traces of this view are evident in a passage like Acts 17:1-10 (where the Jesus-

see the well-being of the Greco-Roman cities, and consequently the more pronounced the claim that "for us there is one God, the Father . . . and one Lord, Jesus Christ" (1 Cor 8:6), the more Jesus-followers might have been suspected of being those who held back the welfare of the cities.

The degree to which the good news of the Jesus-movement was socially and politically subversive is an issue currently entangled in debate, and cannot be entertained in any detail here. For our purposes, however, the point is simple: The extent to which potential benefactors considered the good news of the Jesus-movement to have a subversive religio-political dimension (rightly or wrongly) might well have approximated the extent to which the same prospective benefactors would have been hesitant to act as sponsors of Jesus-groups in urban contexts engulfed in pro-Romanism.[28]

In light of these three factors, sponsoring a Jesus-group might have been a less attractive prospect for would-be benefactors than sponsoring some other association or group (of which there were numerous varieties). When faced with the prospect of sponsoring an urban Jesus-group, one would have

---

movement proved itself an easy target for anti-imperial slander), Acts 19:23-41 (where the proclamation of the Jesus-movement's message is recognized as having dire implications for artisan business in the service of the deities), and of course the correspondence between Pliny and Trajan in the early second century CE. Paul's letters themselves suggest a low-grade form of "persecution" against the early Jesus-movement in Macedonia: cf. 1 Thess 1:6; 2:14 (if original); 3:3; 2 Thess 1:4; 2 Cor 8:1-2; Phil 1:28-30. The canonical Gospels register warnings about persecution coming against Jesus-followers by local authorities: Mark 13:9-11; Matt 10:17-20; Luke 12:11; John 15:18-27. And Nero's scapegoating of Jesus-followers (in the aftermath of the burning of Rome in 64 CE) is suggestive of a general suspicion (at least) about Jesus-followers in relation to the goals of the Roman imperial order.

28. My own view is that the theology and practice of the early Jesus-movement nurtured a malleable hybridity with regard to the Roman imperial order. Anti-Roman ingredients within the good news may have risen to prominence in some contexts, remained obscure in others, and been relatively denuded in still others. This is evident, for instance, in the Lukan Gospel and Acts. The Lukan author frequently tries to establish that the good news of the Jesus-movement is not a threat to those in positions of civic responsibility, while at the same time registering ingredients of that news that run against the grain of Roman society and honor. With regard to Paul's letters, a subversive dimension is noticeable in 1 Thessalonians, but is obscured in Romans 13. On hybridity in Paul's approach to the Roman imperial order, see John W. Marshall, "Hybridity and Reading Romans 13," *JSNT* 31 (2008): 157-78. See also W. Jordaan and J. Jordaan, *People in Context*, 3rd ed. (Johannesburg: Heinemann, 1998), pp. 635-36. Along slightly different but helpful lines, see Dale B. Martin, *Inventing Superstition: From the Hippocratics to the Christians* (Cambridge, MA: Harvard University Press, 2004), pp. 135-39. What has been neglected in studies of Paul and the Roman imperial order is the fact that one could be critical of aspects of Roman rule without necessarily being anti-Roman; this happened frequently in the Roman world.

had to weigh up both the potential advantages and the potential disadvantages in relation to the register of his/her social honor. Various factors were thrown into the socio-economic mix and would have been synthesized in different ways by different people in different situations. While sponsoring a Jesus-group might have had some aspects of potential attraction, it might also have introduced considerable vulnerability to any in the ES4 economic level who were also immersed in the quest for civic honor and status advancement (especially those in E4a). Often, many in ES4 must have imagined that involving themselves in the Jesus-movement would have added to their status inconsistency within the civic arena rather than reducing it.

To someone in ES5, an urban Jesus-group might have had some of the same benefits as other associations — i.e., enjoyment of resources (food, drink, conviviality) provided by more economically-secure benefactors.[29] And it might have had additional attractions. There is little to suggest that urban Jesus-groups, unlike other associations, had a membership fee that was paid to the association's treasurer to enhance the goals of the association.[30] Perhaps, then, we are to imagine a scenario in which those in ES5 could enjoy the benefits of a benefactor's generosity without being expected either to make membership payments or to be involved in public acclaim of the benefactor. Such a group could well have been attractive to people at this economic level.

On the other hand, from around 53-57 CE Paul targets ES5 members (along with ES4 members, no doubt, although they are not targeted in his letters) with the financial responsibility of raising funds for the collection for the Jerusalem poor (1 Cor 16:1-4).[31] This might have been a variation on (or an addition to) the expectation that, instead of paying membership fees, ES5 members would voluntarily contribute to the communal funds for the poor within urban Jesus-groups whenever possible. In general, then, while

29. So Meeks, *First Urban Christians*, p. 104: "For many members, especially those of the humbler social strata, the Christian assemblies and meals provided a more than adequate substitute for benefits, both physical and social, that they might otherwise have obtained from membership in collegia of various sorts or from the various municipal festivals." This "motivational base" for joining *collegia* by "those of the humbler social strata" pertains especially to those at ES5, for whom membership of *collegia* was something of an option; it is less evident as a motivational descriptor of those below ES5, where such an option was rarely a live one.

30. Are association fees what Paul has in mind in 2 Cor 9:7 when contrasting generosity in communities of Jesus-followers with payments made "reluctantly or under compulsion" (ἐκ λύπης ἢ ἐξ ἀνάγκης)? See also Justin, *1 Apol.* 67.6; Tertullian, *Apol.* 39.5.

31. On the dating of Paul's collection efforts, see Appendix 3 below.

there might have been additional economic attraction to join a Jesus-group (i.e., lack of a membership fee) instead of some other urban association, someone in ES5 might have found joining an urban Jesus-group to have similar economic dynamics to the (other) associations in the urban market-place, at least with regard to financial outlay.

Accordingly, to ascribe the primary motivational bases of ES4 and ES5 Jesus-followers to the quest for a heightened or resolved socio-economic status would be, it seems, to err on the side of doing a disservice to many of them.[32] The economic expectations and implications built into the socio-theological dynamics of the urban Jesus-groups meant that the ES4 and ES5 members bore the brunt of oiling the corporate machinery of the urban Jesus-groups, at least economically speaking.

11.2: Further Possible Attractions for Those at ES4 and ES5

A further possibility needs to be considered with regard to the attraction of the Jesus-movement for some urban dwellers, an attraction that involves economic considerations of a different sort. As was shown in chapter 4 above, it is not the case that, prior to the rise of the Jesus-movement, the Greco-Roman world was wholly devoid of charitable initiatives towards the poor. Charitable initiatives had a foothold within Greco-Roman urbanism, albeit in a low-level fashion.

Consequently, it needs to be considered whether some Greco-Roman urbanites found the "Judeo-Christian" message to be attractive in relation to their own charitable initiatives.[33] Quite simply, those who were in the habit of undertaking charitable initiatives of one form or another might well have found the good news of the Jesus-movement to be attractive in crediting and rewarding those initiatives. Here was a deity who did not just promote hospitality towards those worthy of it, as in the case of Zeus Xenios. Here was a deity whose reputation was marked out most prominently by concern for the poor of ES6 and ES7, and who took initiatives to reward those who cared for the

---

32. In this regard, what Wilson says about associations in general needs also to be heard in relation to the early Jesus-movement ("Voluntary Associations," p. 14): "It would . . . be a mistake to suppose that the motive for joining these groups was always compensatory, making up for something otherwise lacking in family or political life."

33. Reference to "Judeo-Christian" is necessary at this point, since concern for the poor among Jesus-groups is ultimately rooted in Jewish scripture and tradition, with the Jesus-movement being one of various species within the overarching genus of "Judaism."

needy. If some ancients suspected that piety should include gestures that bene-fitted the needy (see §4.4 above), Israel's deity had, in a sense, staked much of his reputation on ensuring that the poor were provided for, and on rewarding those who extended care to the needy. As was noted in §8.6, the text of Isaiah, so favored among the early Jesus-followers, speaks in blatant terms along pre-cisely these lines, when the deity of Israel makes the following promises to those who share bread with the hungry, who bring the homeless poor into their houses, and who satisfy the needs of the afflicted (Isa 58:8, 10-11):

> Your light shall break forth like the dawn,
> and your healing shall spring up quickly;
> your vindicator shall go before you,
> the glory of the LORD shall be your rear guard . . .
> your light shall rise in the darkness
> and your gloom be like the noonday.
> The LORD will guide you continually.

These were mainstays not only of the Jewish scriptures and traditions, but of the "good news" spread by the early Jesus-movement — a movement that included within the "truth of the gospel" the mandate to "remember the poor." It was a "good news" that included the rewarding of those who do precisely that (i.e., remember the poor) and the penalizing of those who fail to do precisely that.[34] Perhaps some Greco-Roman urban dwellers found the good news of the Jesus-movement to offer the chance of turning their "char-itable assets" into "salvific capital" to a previously unequaled extent.[35]

I raise this as a possibility not least since it resonates with Paul's own de-

---

34. This emerges both from the Isaianic substructure of Jesus' own proclamation of "good news to the poor" (cf. Isa 61:8: "For I the Lord love justice, I hate robbery and wrong-doing"), and from early remembrances of Jesus as one who pronounced blessing on those who extended care for the needy (cf. Luke 19:8-9) and woes on the well-off who did not (cf. Luke 6:24-26; 12:13-21; 16:19-31).

35. The point cannot be pressed too far, since at times the deities were themselves thought of as avenging moral deficits and rewarding virtues. So *SIG* vol. 3, 985 outlines the regulations of a private association of Zeus, including certain practices to avoid and others to perform. The deities are said to "watch over these things, and will not tolerate those who transgress the ordinances." So, "evil curses" will come "from the gods for disregarding these ordinances. For the god does not desire these things [i.e., transgressions] to happen at all, nor does he wish it, but he wants obedience. The gods will be gracious to those who obey, and always give them all good things, whatever gods give to men they love" (cited by Ascough, "Voluntary Associations and the Formation of Pauline Christian Communities," p. 179).

scription of the former pagans who joined Jesus-groups in Galatia. The point was made in §9.1 above in relation to Gal 4:12-15, where Paul outlines his initial encounter with them:

> You did me no wrong [i.e., when I came to you]. You know that it was because of a physical infirmity that I first announced the good news to you; though my condition put you to the test, you did not scorn me or spit at me (ἐξεπτύσατε); instead, you readily received me (ἐδέξασθέ με) as if I were an angel of God, as Christ Jesus. What has become of your blessedness before God (ὁ μακαρισμὸς ὑμῶν)? For I testify that, had it been possible, you would have torn out your eyes and given them to me.[36]

As was shown earlier, at the heart of this simple description lies a stark contrast between practices of self-preservation that were deeply embedded within the Mediterranean basin on the one hand and, on the other, the generous behavior demonstrated by the Galatians when Paul first came to them. Instead of shunning Paul as they would have been expected to do, the Galatians "readily received" him, even as one in need of assistance, and even to the extent of tearing out their own eyes in order to help him, if they could have.

Perhaps what we have in this account is a rare sub-elite testimony of the existence of low-grade forms of care for the needy within Greco-Roman society.[37] If so, it is also important to note that Paul links the Galatians' caring treatment of him to a state of "blessedness" by the deity of Israel.[38] The Galatians did not shun the ailing Paul, as cultural codes would normally have dictated. And precisely because they had extended assistance to him despite his needy condition, the Galatians received favor from the all-powerful deity of the Jews. For those pagans who "seek to imitate" Jewish care for the

36. The translation is mine.

37. Note the similarities between Galatians and Romans on this score. In Galatians, Paul imagined that the counter-intuitive behavior of the Galatians (i.e., putting themselves at risk, according to the cultural codes of self-preservation) was a mark of the Spirit of Israel's deity acting in their lives and resulted in attitudes and practices at odds with the patterns of life that characterize the "present evil age" (1:4). So too, in Rom 12:13 Paul identifies hospitality (φιλοξενία) as one of the features that characterize communities of Jesus-followers who are not "conformed to this world" but have been "transformed" (Rom 12:2). Presumably, then, Paul would have consistently accredited low-level forms of charity and hospitality within the Greco-Roman world to the working of the Spirit, or to the image of the sovereign deity within humanity, or both.

38. On a full-bodied theological sense of ὁ μακαρισμὸς ὑμῶν in Gal 4:15, see Bruce Longenecker, "Until Christ is formed in you," *CBQ* 61 (1999): 92-108.

needy (Josephus, *C. Ap.* 2.283), a gentile-friendly form of Judaism such as the Jesus-movement would have had its obvious attractions, not least with regard to an all-powerful deity who bestowed blessings on those who cared for the poor and needy.

If Paul imagined that the deity of Israel had blessed the Galatians who had extended care to the needy, he works the other side of the street when addressing the Corinthians. As noted in §6.2, in 1 Corinthians 11 Paul speaks harsh words of criticism against Corinthian communities, having heard that those who are economically insecure were being disadvantaged when the "Lord's Supper" was being observed. With extreme vehemence, he seeks to overturn this injustice by reminding the Corinthians of the narrative of the self-giving Jesus and expecting the Corinthians to follow in the narrative's wake. In being a community where resources are shared with the needy, the Corinthian Jesus-followers will be "proclaiming the Lord's death until he comes" (τὸν θάνατον τοῦ κυρίου καταγγέλλετε ἄχρι οὗ ἔλθῃ, 1 Cor 11:26). Paul understands the Lord's Supper to include the recognition of the needs of the poor and to set in motion practices offsetting those needs, under divine auspices. Accordingly Paul links Corinthian abuse of the Lord's Supper to divine judgment (11:30). If caring for the poor results in being blessed by Israel's deity, so failing to care for the poor results in the wrath of Israel's deity.

To these same Corinthian Jesus-followers, however, Paul can also take the line that he adopted in Gal 4:13-15. So in 2 Corinthians 9, Paul encourages the Corinthians to contribute to his collection for "the poor among the saints in Jerusalem" through the analogy of sowing and reaping: "the one who sows sparingly will also reap sparingly, and the one who sows bountifully will also reap bountifully" (9:6), and "He who supplies seed to the sower and bread for food will supply and multiply your seed for sowing and increase the harvest of your righteousness" (9:10). Since "God loves a cheerful giver" (9:7), Paul assures the Corinthians that by giving of their economic resources "you will be enriched in every way for your great generosity" (9:11). Regarding Paul's strategy in this passage, Christopher Stanley notes the following:

> The idea that God would bless the Corinthians for their generosity is the linchpin of Paul's final argument regarding the collection. . . . By appealing simultaneously to the Corinthians' religious sentiments and their self-interest, Paul framed his appeal in a manner that few could resist.[39]

---

39. Christopher D. Stanley, *Arguing with Scripture: The Rhetoric of Quotations in the Letters of Paul* (New York: T&T Clark, 2004), 109.

If Paul can make use of self-interest as a means of motivating Corinthian Jesus-followers to participate in his collection efforts, he might just as easily have made use of it as a means of motivating Greco-Roman urbanites with a proclivity for economic generosity to join a Jesus-group — along the lines of his reflections in Gal 4:13-15. Paul seems not to have been averse to depicting Israel's deity as one who rewards economic generosity and is angered by its absence.

This might be a neglected socio-economic factor in explaining how the early Jesus-movement got some traction among gentiles of the Greco-Roman world. Those of the Greco-Roman world who were in the habit of offering support to the needy might well have been attracted to the early Jesus-movement's "good news" about Israel's deity. They would have heard about a powerful deity who blesses those who, regardless of their socio-economic status, act beneficently towards the poor. Perhaps, in brief, the early Jesus-movement was able to balance both other-interestedness (i.e., care for the poor) with self-interest (i.e., blessing by Israel's sovereign deity) in what was perceived by many to be a win-win situation.

11.3: Reference Groups and Status Realignment

If it is the case that joining a group of early Jesus-followers might have *increased* the problem of "status inconsistency" for some middling-level urbanites (as outlined in §11.1 above), does this make any thesis about status inconsistents finding status resolution within groups of Jesus-followers wholly untenable? Not necessarily. Instead, it might simply heighten the significance of what early Jesus-groups offered to middling-group urbanites. The early Jesus-groups must simply have offered something quite attractive to such status-inconsistents if they were willing to brave the prospect of further status inconsistency within the civic order in order to enjoy the benefits of the Jesus-groups. The more it was the case that status inconsistency would have been compounded by participation in a group of Jesus-followers, the more things like fictive kinship within those groups become significant in our understanding of the rise of the Jesus-movement in urban contexts.

This highlights the importance of reference groups for understanding the growth of the early Jesus-movement. Reference groups are those groups or arenas that a person prioritizes in terms of defining her identity and status.[40]

---

40. Meeks explains a reference group anecdotally (*First Urban Christians,* p. 215 n. 20):

The rise of household groups of Jesus-followers might best be attributed to the fact that some people in the Greco-Roman middling groups must, to some extent, have shifted their primary reference group away from the burgeoning, highly stratified and agonistic civic arena and towards the fledgling, intimate and expectant fellowships of Jesus-followers.[41] This shift in primary reference groups helps to explain how joining a group of Jesus-followers might at one and the same time have had two different consequences for middling-group members of the Greco-Roman world: (1) the potential for status reduction within the civic arena, and (2) the potential for status realignment within the corporate context of early Jesus-groups. The more the first is emphasized, the more the second is required.

A quick glance at Wayne Meeks's publications in the wake of his *First Urban Christians* helps to make the point. Precisely because the benefits of belonging to a Jesus-group must have had significant attraction, Meeks's exploration of the early Jesus-movement did not stop where *First Urban Christians* ends. Instead, Meeks's project extends into those books that Meeks went on to write subsequently: *The Moral World of the First Christians* in 1986 and *The Origins of Christian Morality* in 1993.[42] In one sense, these three books belong together as a triumvirate, in that they showcase the "moral world" of the early Jesus-movement as holding the key to the historical suc-

---

"I am not likely to feel oppressed nor are the people who matter to me likely to snub me because I shall not ever receive a peerage in the British realm." In this example, Meeks's reference group is shown not to place a particular value on the peerage status within Britain, even if other reference groups might; Meeks's reference group values other markers of identity instead. For a fuller discussion of reference groups in Paul's moral admonitions, see Wayne A. Meeks, "The Circle of Reference in Pauline Morality," in *Greeks, Romans, and Christians: Essays in Honor of Abraham J. Malherbe* (Minneapolis: Fortress Press, 1990), pp. 305-317, where he summarizes his case as such (pp. 316-17): "Not only are multiple reference groups and individuals implicit in the exhortations of Paul's letters, but in any given instance, several different bases of reference may be operative, sometimes in tension with one another. . . . [Paul does not] simplify the process of moral formation by stating a hierarchy [of reference groups]. It is in the give and take of dialogue that the community itself must work out what is σύμφορον (advantageous) . . . [and what] οἰκοδομεῖ (builds up)."

41. Elsewhere Meeks notes two types of shifts in reference-group loyalties (*The Moral World of the First Christians* [New Haven: Yale University Press, 1986], p. 14): "I may . . . convert [from one group to another] because the world of the other community has come to seem truer to me than that of my former society. Or I may be forced into the new setting and only gradually come to understand and adopt its world view."

42. Wayne A. Meeks, *The Origins of Christian Morality: The First Two Centuries* (New Haven: Yale University Press, 1993).

cess of that movement. As Meeks writes toward the end of *The Origins of Christian Morality:*

> Perhaps . . . it was in certain of their social practices that the Christian groups most effectively distinguished themselves from other cult associations, clubs, or philosophical schools — [1] their special rituals of initiation and communion, [2] their practice of communal admonition and discipline, [and 3] the organization of aid for widows, orphans, prisoners, and other weaker members of the movement.[43]

Here Meeks puts his finger on the explanation of why some Greco-Roman urbanites might have found attraction in a Jesus-group, even if joining such a group would have included disincentives in one form or another. For some middling-level urbanites, and for many others at lower socio-economic levels, benefits such as those suggested by Meeks may well have (1) offset the relentless quest for honor-capture in the civic arena, and (2) provided the basis for status realignment in spirited groups of the first urban Jesus-followers. For Paul, such things were the product of the moving of the Spirit within fledgling Jesus-groups, where Jesus-followers found resources for moral regeneration and corporate refreshment in ways that could only be explained as prefigurements of the eschatological reign of Israel's deity.

43. Meeks, *The Origins of Christian Morality,* p. 213.

CHAPTER 12

"There were none in need"

Care for the Poor in Paul's Theology

12.1: The Resourcing and "Ownership" of Jesus-communities

Of the various results considered thus far in this project, three need to be recalled here: (1) if there were members of the economic elite within Jesus-groups that Paul established, they were very few and far between; (2) some members within those communities belonged to the economic middling groups of the Greco-Roman world (ES4), with a few of them possibly registering quite high on that economic level; and (3) when Paul characterizes the economic level of urban Jesus-groups to whom he writes, he tends to do so at a level of ES5, perhaps with some overlap into ES6.

From these three data, we may be tempted to conclude that groups of Jesus-followers gravitated between ES5 and ES4, with members from ES6 and ES7 being absent from or poorly represented within those communities. But the temptation should be avoided. The lower economic categories were presumably a large part of the constituency of groups of Jesus-followers that Paul founded. The fact that ES6 and ES7 levels are not strongly represented in texts where Paul performs a "mental averaging" of the economic profile of urban Jesus-groups should not cause us to succumb to the "referential fallacy," in which the world of the text corresponds without remainder to the realities of the situation that it addresses. Instead, we should consider the rhetorical advantages of Paul's mental averaging.

In this regard, it is important to note that Paul addresses urban Jesus-groups as if they were comprised of ES5 primarily in contexts where he encourages Jesus-followers to use their economic resources either (1) to help others in need (1 Cor 16:1-2; see also Eph 4:28) or (2) to avoid dependence on others (1 Thess 4:11-12; see also 2 Thess 3:12); the author of Acts combines both aspects in Paul's final speech to the Ephesians (Acts 20:34-35). The convergence of these two goals within texts written by Paul and by others remembering Paul (regardless of how many of these texts fall into each category) is notable. We would do well, then, to consider the strategic advantages of profiling urban Jesus-groups at ES5 levels with regard to each of these two purposes.

It was clearly prudent for Paul to target ES5 members when seeking to shore up corporate resources for those in need. ES4 members were assumed to be resourcing communities to a significant level already, to the benefit of all members, so there is not much in Paul's instructions that pertains primarily to them by way of expecting further economic support for those in need. And evidence of Paul's appreciation for ES4 adherents appears in Paul's commendation of Phoebe in Rom 16:1-2. But Paul seems also to have wanted to tap into the potential economic resources of members a level or so lower than ES4, in order to maximize the economic possibilities of urban Jesus-groups, not least in their efforts to "remember the poor" (whether that be providing assistance for the indigenous poor in general or the specific practice of providing assistance for the poor in Jerusalem communities of Jesus-followers, or both). Communities that put caring for the needy at the heart of their identity require economic resourcing from as many economic levels as possible, and Paul sought to ensure that ES5 members played a part in that effort, rather than allowing communities to be overly reliant on ES4 members.

There may be more to Paul's instructions to ES5 Jesus-followers, however. Something else may be going on than simply bolstering corporate resources by ensuring that as many people as possible within Jesus-groups heightened their economic involvement. From Paul's Corinthians texts, for instance, we know of his hesitation about being overly reliant on some (Corinthian) ES4 Jesus-followers in the promotion of the good news. In Paul's suspicions, the more that communities became reliant on a few "prominent" figures (economically speaking), the more those communities ran the risk of having their corporate life determined by the wishes and interests of that influential minority.[1] Commissioning ES5 (and ES6?) members to enhance their own economic resourcefulness may have been a subtle way for Paul to offset the potential for a few prominent individuals to acquire an authoritative stature based merely on their economic prominence.

Instead of simple "mental averaging," then, when Paul challenges sub-ES4 members to undertake economic initiatives for others in need, he may have been attempting not only to resource Jesus-groups to their maximum potential but also to instill a sense of corporate "ownership" within the sub-ES4 membership of Jesus-groups. This would help to ensure that Jesus-groups continued to be nurtured by the "good news" of the early Jesus-movement instead of becoming engulfed in the honor-quest that marked out the Greco-Roman world. In essence, the tasking of sub-ES4 Jesus-followers with economic responsibilities may have been Paul's way of ensuring that Jesus-groups did not focus inordinately on the economically privileged and thereby lose their concern for the economically un(der)privileged.

12.2: Economic Well-Being and Paul's Theology of the "Body of Christ"

Paul's expectation that people at different economic levels have different economic responsibilities allocated to them within the context of Jesus groups dovetails nicely with Paul's view of Jesus-groups being something like a living "body" — a body comprised of various individual parts, each of which contributes in various ways to the health and vitality of the whole. The metaphor is elaborated in both 1 Corinthians 12 and Romans 12, and might best be summed up in Rom 12:4-5: "For as in one body we have many members, and not all the members have the same function, so we, who are many, are one body in Christ, and individually we are members one of another." It is this context of thought that best animates Paul's view of differences in economic tasking within communities of Jesus-followers.

1. Cf. David J. Downs ("Is God Paul's Patron? The Economy of Patronage in Pauline Theology," in Bruce W. Longenecker and Kelly Liebengood, eds., *Engaging Economics: New Testament Scenarios and Early Christian Reception* [Grand Rapids: Eerdmans, 2009], 129-56, p. 150): "Paul's own decisions regarding the financial support of his ministry by the Corinthians appear to have been shaped, at least in part, in response to his desire to minimize vertical relationships of patronage between apostle and church."

Putting the discussion of economic tasking within the context of Paul's theology of the body of Christ might help to stave off two potential misreadings of Paul. The first misreading would be to interpret Paul as suggesting that economic generosity is a gift of the Spirit that is thereby to be practiced by only a few "designated" members of the community. This potential misreading of Paul takes its cues from two verses that elaborate the body metaphor. In both 1 Corinthians 12 and Romans 12, Paul mentions gifts given by the Spirit to distinct individuals within Jesus-groups, and each list of spiritual gifts includes reference to making resources available to the poor. In 1 Cor 12:28, Paul lists assistance to those in need (ἀντιλήμψεις)[2] as one of the gifts given by the Spirit to Jesus-communities through the empowerment of specific individuals. And in Rom 12:8 Paul speaks of economic generosity as a gift given by the Spirit to particular individuals within and for the benefit of the community as a whole. There the term "the generous giver" (ὁ μεταδιδοὺς ἐν ἁπλότητι) captures this sentiment.[3] Another gift of the Spirit in Rom 12:8 overlaps with this one significantly — that is, "the one who does acts of mercy with cheerfulness" (ὁ ἐλεῶν ἐν ἱλαρότητι).[4] In light of Paul's comments in 1 Cor 12:28 and Rom 12:8, then, it might be argued that Paul expected generosity to be exercised by only some individuals within Jesus-groups, rather than being an integral feature of the identity of each member of those groups.

But the view would be problematic, not in its reading of particular verses but in its failure to read beyond them. For just past Rom 12:8 Paul gives two general admonitions (Rom 12:13, 16) that highlight care for the needy as a definition of the love that is to mark out the life of Jesus-followers

---

2. The word ἀντιλήμψεις clearly has this meaning in Jewish literature prior to the Common Era; see Ps. LXX 21:20; 1 Esdr 8:27; Sir 11:12 (where "the slow one who needs assistance" [νωθρὸς προσδεόμενος ἀντιλήμψεως] is also cited as one who "abounds in poverty" [πτωχείᾳ περισσεύει]); 51:7; 2 Macc. 15:7.

3. So, for instance, Douglas J. Moo (*The Epistle to the Romans* [Grand Rapids: Eerdmans, 1996], p. 768) interprets the phrase to mean "one who shares his or her own resources with those less fortunate." So too James D. G. Dunn (*Romans* [Dallas: Word Publishers, 1988], p. 730): "it is probably the sharing of food or wealth or possessions which is in view." According to Dunn (p. 735), with this theme of generosity in 12:8 "Paul seeks to bring his major theological insights of the earlier part of the letter into practical everyday expression."

4. We need not determine whether this term denotes "almsgiving" specifically (so Dunn, *Romans*, p. 723) or simply "any act of mercy toward others, such as visiting the sick, caring for the elderly or disabled, and providing for the poor" (so Moo, *Romans*, p. 769). In my view, Moo probably underestimates the sense to which the verb ἐλεέω, when used of human interaction, had acquired almost a technical sense for almsgiving. But either way, almost all of Moo's examples involve an economic dimension.

in general. Similarly, Paul's discussion in 1 Corinthians 12 cannot be divorced from his praise of love in 1 Corinthians 13, with love being defined consistently within the Pauline corpus as self-giving and burden-bearing, and without being restricted to particular individuals but being embodied in some form by every individual in the group.[5] Along similar lines, we have seen in Gal 5:22 that Paul lists the act of giving to those in need (ἀγαθωσύνη) as one of "the fruit of the Spirit" that Paul expected to come alive in all Jesus-followers.

It might be difficult to systematize Paul's understanding (1) economic generosity as a general attribute of identity among Jesus-followers and (2) economic generosity as a gift of the Spirit awarded to select individuals. But even if the relationship between these two features is not crystal clear, it is notable that economic generosity can so markedly saturate Paul's hortatory discourse in relation to the internal workings of Jesus-groups. If there is something more systematic to it than that, it might be that Paul imagined that (1) those who have economic resources and who graciously fortify the community by making some of those resources available for use in and by the community are, *de facto,* those specially tasked for this purpose by the Spirit; and (2) such "resourcefully-gifted" people (economically speaking) embody in a concentrated fashion (one form of) the ideal of social ethics among Jesus-followers — that is, the giving of one's self for the benefit of others.

But Paul would probably also say that those *without* material resources are not "gifted" by the Spirit in terms of *economic* generosity, even if they are gifted for generosity in other ways. If material resources are (or become) available to certain members and if economic generosity is aroused among them (as Paul suggests in 2 Cor 8:1-5), this might well be interpreted as a special gifting by the Spirit or as the enlivenment by the Spirit of the ideal of self-giving for the benefit of others.[6] But for those without material re-

---

5. Paul is enough of a realist, however, to know that self-giving does not automatically come under the category of love. In 1 Cor 13:3 he writes: "If I give away all my possessions, and if I hand over (παραδῶ) my body so that I may boast [or 'to be burned'], but do not have love, I gain nothing." Paul is aware that acts of generosity may be motivated by interests other than benefitting others. A generous action may be selfishly motivated if, by performing such an action, one seeks to capture the attention of others or enhance one's own reputation. In this way, even self-giving has the potential to be fully immersed in the game of honor-capture that marked out the Greco-Roman world. The point was noted when discussing charitable initiatives in the Greco-Roman world in §4.3 and §4.4 above.

6. As was shown in chapters 9 and 11, Paul interprets Galatian generosity along precisely such lines as these.

sources, economic generosity is not required of them, even though the group of Jesus-followers to which they belong needs to be characterized by economic generosity.

Essential to the core identity of Jesus-followers is a corporate generosity that ensures that the economically poor are "remembered" within groups of Jesus-followers, even if not all Jesus-followers are in a position to demonstrate economic generosity themselves. Those who are unable to be economically generous will be "gifted" in ways other than economic generosity.

This gets us some way towards addressing the second potential misreading of Paul, in which the destitute are perceived as, at best, second-class followers of Jesus since they are not able to offer economic assistance within the community of Jesus-followers. Christian theology in the patristic era began to assign to the destitute the important role of providing the occasion for wealthy persons to offer alms. In this perspective, a synergistic relationship was envisioned in which the needy and the wealthy supplied each other with what the other lacked — that is, the rich were afforded the *opportunity to offer* resources, and the poor were afforded the *opportunity to receive* resources. In this view, the poor are not second-class, but perform a primary function within the community, in their very role of being poor.[7]

This view cannot be attributed to Paul himself, and it might all too easily run the risk of acquiescing in the assumption that things are pretty much acceptable as they are, without needing to address issues of structural injustice and reform. But with regard to the indispensable place of the poor

---

7. This view is already evident in Hermas, *Sim.* 1–2. So *Similitude* 2 outlines the situation as follows: "The rich man has much wealth, but is poor in matters relating to the Lord, because he is distracted about his riches; and he offers very few confessions and intercessions to the Lord, and those which he does offer are small and weak, and have no power above. But when the rich man refreshes the poor, and assists him in his necessities, believing that what he does to the poor man will be able to find its reward with God — because the poor man is rich in intercession and confession, and his intercession has great power with God — then the rich man helps the poor in all things without hesitation; and the poor man, being helped by the rich, intercedes for him, giving thanks to God for him who bestows gifts upon him. And he still continues to interest himself zealously for the poor man, that his wants may be constantly supplied. For he knows that the intercession of the poor man is acceptable and influential with God. Both, accordingly, accomplish their work. The poor man makes intercession; a work in which he is rich, which he received from the Lord, and with which he recompenses the master who helps him. And the rich man, in like manner, unhesitatingly bestows upon the poor man the riches which he received from the Lord. And this is a great work, and acceptable before God, because he understands the object of his wealth, and has given to the poor of the gifts of the Lord, and rightly discharged his service to Him."

within communities of Jesus-followers, the view represented in patristic literature is not inconsistent with Paul's perception of things.[8] Paul seems content that care for the poor marked out the communities of Jesus-followers that he founded, and that everyone within those communities *who was able to contribute* to those initiatives was, in fact, contributing to those initiatives; if the destitute were excluded from contributing by default, it was not to their shame or detriment. Presumably Paul expected their contribution to the community to lie in some other area of corporate service or enrichment. Paul would certainly have imagined it to run contrary to the identity of Jesus-groups if Jesus-followers with economic resources failed to act generously toward others, but he would not have imagined the same to have been the case for Jesus-followers without economic resources. Paul was pragmatic enough to have known that care for the poor was not something for the destitute to be doing; unless resources became available to them (as in 2 Cor 8:1-5), such acts of generous initiative were not envisioned as falling within their responsibility, their tasking, or their gift. Their contributions lay elsewhere.

One final observation emerges from this. While Paul's expectation that Jesus-groups will support the economically needy might resonate with a broad variety of corporate configurations, his comments about the Spirit gifting certain people with economic generosity seem to presuppose Jesus-groups being economically supported by those in ES4 and ES5 who give from their "disposable" resources. Scenarios of Jesus-followers at ES6 and ES7 levels sharing their scarce or non-existent resources do not resonate well with the kind of dynamics that Paul's discourse of generosity as-spiritual-gift envisages. Instead, even when writing to Jesus-groups that he has not founded and has never visited (i.e., those in Rome), Paul imagines some to be "gifted" with a generous spirit beyond others (albeit in conformity with the ideal to which all members would conform, if opportunity allowed and as resources permitted). In economic terms, ES5 or ES4 levels are best envisioned here. Little wonder, then, that household codes are prominent in Colossians and Ephesians; whether written by Paul or not, those texts highlight Paul's interest in ES4 and ES5 urban households as key components in the spread of the early Jesus-movement.[9] Of course, while a household context is one of the most natural environments for this theology of gifting and

---

8. It coheres well with Paul's theology of the body in 1 Cor 12. Moreover, when speaking of his collection, Paul sees the givers and the recipients as interlocked in a relationship of reciprocity; so Rom 15:27; 2 Cor 8:13-14.

9. So Roger W. Gehring, *House Church and Mission: The Importance of Household Structures in Early Christianity* (Peabody: Hendrickson, 2004), pp. 193, 291-95.

generosity to be played out, it is not the only environment in which such a theology would resonate. Nonetheless, it would seem that Paul's theology of gifting operates best in relation to Jesus-groups that had some members at ES5 and above,[10] allowing for both a lesser and a greater "corporate stretch" — i.e., from ES7 through ES5 (perhaps Thessalonian Jesus-groups) and from ES7 through ES4 (probably Corinthian Jesus-groups).[11]

10. Jerome Murphy-O'Connor (*Paul: His Story* [Oxford: Oxford University Press, 2004], p. 30) says that ES4 members (my term) were the people "from which he [Paul] had to recruit one or two believers in each city if he was to find a house large enough to assemble his converts."

11. As John M. B. Barclay has shown ("Thessalonica and Corinth: Social Contrasts in Pauline Christianity," *JSNT* 47 [1992]: 49-74), the Jesus-groups in Corinth and Thessalonica were different in terms of their relationships with "outsiders," probably because of notable differences in their socio-economic composition. See also James Walters, "Civic Identity in Roman Corinth and Its Impact on Early Christians," in Daniel N. Schowalter and Steven J. Friesen, eds., *Urban Religion in Roman Corinth* (Cambridge, MA: Harvard University Press, 2005), pp. 397-417. Because Friesen seeks to deflate the economic stretch of the Corinthian communities, he ends up arguing a rather different line to that of Barclay; instead of contrasting Corinthian and Thessalonian communities, he argues for their general similarities. So Friesen, "Prospects for a Demography of the Pauline Mission: Corinth among the Churches," in Schowalter and Friesen, eds., *Urban Religion in Roman Corinth,* 351-70, p. 369): "While most of the evidence comes from Corinth, it is probably representative for other Pauline assemblies as well."

On the Thessalonian Jesus-groups as groups of "agape communalism," see especially Robert Jewett, *Romans* (Minneapolis: Fortress Press, 2007), pp. 66-69. He reconstructs a Thessalonian situation dominated by "a communally supported system of love feasts . . . provided by community members rather than by patrons" (*Romans*, pp. 66, 68). This assessment represents a notable adjustment to the one he adopted in his earlier work. In his book *The Thessalonian Correspondence* (Philadelphia: Fortress Press, 1986), Jewett wrote (p. 120): "there are no indications, in contrast to the Corinthian congregation, that there were slaves in the Thessalonian church. The paucity of patrons with high status or wealth in the congregation may well have reduced the likelihood of slaves being incorporated into the church as members of the patrons' households. It would be inappropriate to lay too much weight on this argument from silence, however, because at least one patron with wealth, Jason [Acts 17:6-9], is linked with the congregation, and . . . the archaeological evidence in the Greek cities renders it essential to assume the presence of a few patrons whose houses were large enough to serve as centers for house churches."

With regard to Jesus-groups in Rome, I find Jewett's position to be unclear. He believes that the majority of Roman Jesus-groups would have been economically deprived tenement groups rather than the more economically "liquid" household groups of the kind evident in Corinth. This might well be the case. And yet, Jewett's view of the purpose of Paul's letter (i.e., "the unification of the Roman house churches so that they would be able to cooperate in the support of the Spanish mission," p. 90) requires a dimension of economic viability

We should be wary of imagining that all communities founded by Paul matched the blueprint of ES4 household-based groups; to do so allows the Corinthian data to dictate and exhaust our historical reconstruction. In household contexts, Paul shows concern that ES4 members should not be seen as "patrons" of communities who thereby acquire a status beyond what is healthy for Spirit-enlivened communities. Instead, in both Romans and 1 Corinthians he places the generosity of such people in the category of spiritual gifting, alongside other forms of gifting that are just as essential to the health of the community. In doing so, however, he in no way expects to compromise on the vision of Spirit-enlivened people being characterized by generosity whenever resources are available, as a demonstration of the generosity of Israel's deity.

12.3: Not Communism, Not Charity, but Community

How are we to characterize Paul's view of economic generosity within Jesus-groups? Peter Brown depicts Paul as one who advocated the "leveling out" or "equalizing . . . of resources between the brethren."[12] But language of this sort endangers a proper conceptualization of socio-economic relationships and responsibilities within urban Jesus-groups. At no point do we get the sense that the ES4 members were selling all of their resources in an effort to

---

that would appear to be absent from the tenement groups ("he [Paul] needed the full resources of many of the congregations in Rome," p. 89). According to Jewett, Paul hopes that Roman Jesus-groups will milk their contacts there, not least with "Roman bureaucrats charged with responsibilities there" (p. 88), and "providing bases of operation in each of the three provinces for Paul and his missionary colleagues, finding logistical support for their travels and lodging, and recruiting translators capable of moving from Greek to Latin as well as other languages. . . . If inappropriate local patrons were chosen, the entire mission would be jeopardized." Jewett's view of the purpose of Romans appears to be out of alignment with his view of the economic resources within (some) Roman Jesus-groups. The tasks that Jewett imagines the Roman Jesus-groups to be carrying out would seem to require a stronger presence of ES4 Jesus-followers in Rome than Jewett allows.

This also problematizes Jewett's case (*Romans*, p. 89) that "[i]n view of the impoverished status of congregations in Rome, it is inconceivable that a woman of her [i.e., Phoebe's] social class could hope to gain help from them in her business." If there was a higher percentage of ES4 members of Roman Jesus-groups than Jewett allows, the scenario that he rejects is not at all inconceivable.

12. Peter Brown, *Poverty and Leadership in the Later Roman Empire* (Hanover, NH: University Press of New England, 2002), p. 18. He uses Paul's collection as evidence of this, thereby over-egging Paul's discourse in 2 Cor 9.

equalize the economic profile of all Jesus-followers. There is no sense that Paul expected all members of urban Jesus-groups to pool their resources and distribute them equally between all of the members. Economic differences continued to exist within communities of Jesus-followers that Paul established, and Paul imagined nothing to be wrong with that, as long as the needs of the poor were being met.

As noted already, members of Jesus-groups who fell into the higher economic categories of ES4 and ES5 are likely to have borne the brunt of the economic health of Jesus-groups. In communities with ES4 members, those members probably opened their homes to provide venues for corporate gatherings, and probably provided many of the economic and material resources for those meetings at their own expense. ES5 members and, no doubt, ES4 members were expected to contribute to Paul's collection efforts of 53-57 CE. Moreover, if 2 Cor 9:13 is indicative of Paul's expectation, these Jesus-followers were not only to be contributing to his collection efforts but were also expected to continue their efforts to offset the needs of the locally impoverished (at least the impoverished among Jesus-groups; but see also §12.4 below), possibly through some communal fund to which they contributed.

Something similar is evident, for instance, in rabbinic sources, with the synagogue being depicted as an "economic center" for the distribution of goods to the needy among their number.[13] So we hear of efforts performed for the poor by appointed synagogue members called "public supervisors of the poor" and "charity supervisors":

> Public supervisors of the poor who had money left over after making their distribution to the poor should not purchase with it produce on consignment, because of the [possibility of] loss to the poor. But they purchase [produce] with it at the lowest price and [mark up] to the highest price [for sale, in order to give the surplus to the poor].[14]

> Charity supervisors who did not find poor folk among whom to distribute the beans [that they had collected for the poor] may sell them to others. But they may not sell them to themselves.[15]

---

13. Ben-Zion Rosenfeld and Joseph Menirav, "The Ancient Synagogue as an Economic Center," *JNES* 58 (1999): 259-76, pp. 262, 267-68. They claim their evidence to pertain to "the first century CE in Palestine and in the Diaspora" (p. 268), although much of their evidence is from a later period.

14. Tosefta, *Šeqal.* 2.8.

15. Tosefta, *B. Meṣiʿa* 3.9.

Elsewhere, we read of synagogue initiatives to assist the poor, such as soup kitchens and communal funds:

> Whoever has sufficient food for two meals may not take [food] from a soup kitchen. [Whoever has sufficient] food for fourteen meals may not take [money] from the [communal] fund. [Money for] the [communal] fund is collected by two [people] and distributed by three [people].[16]

Similar dynamics are evident in Pauline passages like 2 Thess 3:6-12 and 1 Tim 5:3-16 (noted in §6.2 above), where the Pauline author (whether Paul himself or someone writing in his name) is having to put restrictions on the availability of communal funds within communities founded by Paul, in view of the vulnerability of those funds and the potential for their misuse. The pattern of better-off members contributing to communal funds in order to alleviate the needs of the poor puts urban Jesus-groups in general alignment not only with rabbinic comments on synagogue care for the poor but also with the Jerusalem communities of Jesus-followers, at least as they are depicted in Acts 2:44-47, 4:32-37 and 6:1-6.[17]

We have already seen that, for Paul, economic initiatives to benefit the poor were themselves part of a larger theology of the body of Christ. Here we need to press the point further. For Paul, the poor were not simply to be "remembered" by tossing the odd coin to them on the streets. Such a gesture may be well motivated, but it fails miserably as a testimony to and advertisement of the good news of the early Jesus-movement. Paul would not have

16. *m. Pe'ah* 8:7, translation by Jacob Neusner, *The Mishnah: A New Translation* (New Haven: Yale University Press, 1988). See also *m. Demai* 3:1; *t. Pe'ah* 4:9. This evidence is generally thought to be later than the New Testament period, so I make no claims about influence from synagogual practices to practices within urban Jesus-groups.

17. If those instances in which Jesus-groups met for common meals and/or the Lord's Supper provided the occasions for Jesus-followers to make offerings to the corporate funds, to be used then in assisting the poor, this might help to explain the enormity of Paul's distress concerning the way that the Lord's Supper was being observed in Corinth (1 Cor 11:17-32), as practices were being introduced that had the potential to side-line the economically disadvantaged within the community's eucharistic observances. According to Nils Dahl (*Studies in Paul* [Minneapolis: Fortress, 1977], p. 30), the community's "celebration of the Eucharist was . . . a common meal, the time when the congregation offered its gifts, gifts which were later distributed to the poor." If this is right, it is possible that certain of the more affluent Corinthian Jesus-followers may not have imagined their practice of the Lord's Supper to be problematic. The poor were being supported in those occasions through the collection of donations for their betterment; in that way, their practice was indeed a means of "discerning the body" (and "remembering the poor").

wanted Jesus-groups simply to keep the poor at arm's length through charitable gestures. Instead, to the extent that such was possible, the poor were to
be welcomed into the very heart of those communities of fellowship and
"gifted" as contributing members within it. No different from anyone else,
the economically poor were expected to contribute their own "gifts" and to
participate in the nurturing of a group of fictive kin who supported each
other in various ways, not all of which were economic. Whatever initiatives
for the poor arose within such contexts were not seen simply as "charity,"
which can all too often be ineffectual in alleviating poverty. Paul did not
imagine the corporate meals of urban Jesus-followers to be a means of simply filling stomachs. Instead, he imagined them to be incarnations of the
kingdom or empire of Israel's deity. In that empire (in contrast to the empires of this age, including that of Rome), the rich do not accumulate resources at the expense of the poor and furnish their tables with food that the
poor have no access to (unlike Jesus' parable of the rich man and Lazarus in
Luke 16:19-31). Instead, in the empire of Israel's deity, the poor "are welcomed to the messianic banquet alongside the rich, where they find not only
a place but a voice"[18] — or better, perhaps, a place where their voice is heard
and where their needs are met, as they themselves help to contribute to an
empire in which the various needs of all are (being) met, as the people of a
generous deity give expression to their "faith working practically through
love" (Gal 5:6).

It seems, then, that Paul imagined initiatives for the poor within their
communities to be incarnations of a divine order that was invading the very
structures of the not-yet-restored world.[19] Minute efforts of economic generosity within Jesus-groups were themselves advertisements of a "kingdom"
that rested on foundations contrary to the structures of "this age." It was a
kingdom or empire empowered by the sovereign creator and loving re-
deemer, whose own righteousness was at stake in relation to the care for the
poor through the "grace-full" and grace-enlivened efforts of those devoted

18. Michael S. Northcott, *A Moral Climate: The Ethics of Global Warming* (London:
Darton, Longman and Todd, 2007), p. 251. According to Timothy Patitsas ("St. Basil's Philanthropic Program and Modern Macrolending Strategies for Economic Self-Actualization,"
in Susan R. Holman, ed., *Wealth and Poverty in Early Church and Society* [Grand Rapids:
Baker Academic Press, 2008], 267-86, p. 283), "charity can substitute for formal capital investment . . . as it establishes genuinely mutual interpersonal networks."

19. D. Georgi (*The City in the Valley: Biblical Interpretation and Urban Theology* [At-
lanta: Society of Biblical Literature, 2005], p. 307) makes the point simply: "The poor call up
the not-yet of society."

to him (2 Cor 9:9-10). In this way, and in a fashion that coincided fully with Jesus' own vision (see §5.3 above), Jesus-groups founded by Paul probably were to imagine even their low-level initiatives to publicize and participate in the structural rectification inherent in the reign of Israel's deity that was invading the world in and through their communities. As Paul would have it, they would be right to imagine their miniature acts of generosity to be part of a much grander narrative of the structural reform that would eventually change things forever, through the abundant power and generosity of the sovereign deity.[20]

12.4: Care for Poor Insiders Exclusively?

It is against this backdrop that we need to consider whether Paul imagined care for the poor to be something exercised only within groups of Jesus-followers and only for their members. If so, then some parallels can be drawn between communities founded by Paul, synagogual Judaism and (other?) Greco-Roman associations, since offering generosity to other members of a group was a characterizing feature of many urban associations and of synagogual Judaism alike.

In general, it is most likely that care for the poor was primarily practiced intra-communally within Jesus-groups. In view of the huge number of destitute and poor within the ancient urban context, and the relatively limited resources of Jesus-groups, it would be foolhardy to imagine much other than an intra-communal practice of extending support in limited supply to a few within a community. Anything beyond that was probably unlikely to transpire. Although the alleviation of poverty was one part of a grand narrative of what Israel's deity was doing in and through communities of Jesus-followers, and although that narrative was getting some traction in the cor-

20. Kenneth Arrow argues ("Gifts and Exchanges," *Philosophy and Public Affairs* 1 [1972]: 343-62, p. 355) that "altruistic motivation" is a "scarce resource" that can all too easily be "use[d] up recklessly" whenever ethical consideration is brought to bear on economic issues. That might be, although I imagine that some early Jesus-followers might have theorized that altruistic motivation is not a "limited good" that is depleted with use, but is more like a muscle that develops and grows stronger when exercised, at least in relation to a "spirited" community. On the relationship of divine grace and human good works in Paul, see John M. G. Barclay, "Grace and the Transformation of Agency in Christ," in F. E. Udoh et al., eds., *Redefining First-Century Jewish and Christian Identities* (Notre Dame: University of Notre Dame Press, 2008), pp. 372-89.

porate life of Jesus-groups, those groups simply did not have the resources to do much beyond alleviating some of the needs of their own members. The point was made earlier (§4.6 above) that sub-elite levels of the population did not have the power to address the structural features of the ancient economic system, and precisely the same would have been the case for the earliest Jesus-followers. Their own attempts to offset economic need were relatively small-scale endeavors and, probably by necessity, had to be restricted primarily to members of their own communities. To have done much more would have been to spread their very limited resources more thinly than they already were.

Nonetheless, although Jesus-followers had to restrict their primary efforts to the offsetting of the needs of the poor within their own communities, that focus did not exclude the possibility of extending care to others beyond the community, at least if the Pauline data is anything to go by. His texts fall across a continuum of emphases. In Rom 12:13-16, he identifies care for the needy as an integral feature of intra-corporate love. In Gal 6:10, he speaks of doing good "to all," but adds "especially to those of the household of faith."[21] Yet, in 1 Thess 5:15 he endorses "pursuing the good" (τὸ ἀγαθὸν διώκετε) in relation to both the corporate community (εἰς ἀλλήλους) and broader society in general (εἰς πάντας).[22] And in 1 Thess 5:14 he extols helping the weak in general, without qualifiers of any kind.[23] Paul seems to have imagined that, while alleviating the needs of the poor within communities of Jesus-followers was never to be compromised, neither was that practice to be set in opposition to caring for those beyond Jesus-communities.[24]

21. As an aside, the final phrase of Gal 6:10 cannot be read as Douglas A. Campbell would have us read it: "especially to the households belonging to the faithful one (i.e., Christ)" (*The Deliverance of God: An Apocalyptic Rereading of Justification in Paul* [Grand Rapids: Eerdmans, 2009], p. 894). Even as a paraphrase, this runs contrary to too many rudimentary features of the text.

22. So Greg K. Beale, *1-2 Thessalonians* (Downers Grove: InterVarsity Press, 2003), p. 167.

23. Compare Herm. *Sim.* 10.4.2-4: "Every person [*omnem hominem*] must be helped out of his need. For whoever starves and suffers want of the most necessary things of daily life endures great pain. . . . Whoever knows of the need of such a person and does not help him out commits a great sin." Contrast Clement of Alexandria, *Quis div.* 33, where it is said that, in order for the poor to receive alms, they must be Christians, who look respectable, who are clean, and who are neither needy nor in rags.

24. In this way, "money" could become something that not only solidified the identity of Jesus-groups but also kept their boundaries permeable rather than rigid. John Barclay does well to emphasize the former point ("Money and Meetings: Group Formation among

The contrast with Greco-Roman associations is instructive. There is little reason to think that associations had interest in caring for the needy of ES6 and ES7 who were virtually "locked into" conjunctural poverty. If the economic status of one of their members became precarious, association members did what they could to support him, and that, of course, was generous and laudable. But were there to be instances where all of their members enjoyed economic security, there is little reason to think that associations would have turned their attention to the needy beyond their own membership. This is where associations generally differed from Jesus-groups, at least if Paul's ethical exhortations are anything to go by. In a hypothetical situation in which members of a Jesus-group had no real economic needs among them, Paul would presumably have instructed them to make their extra resources available to the needy, taking the initiative to implement creative measures to assist the poor and, thereby, advertising the "good news" of "the Lord's death until he comes." Seemingly this would not have entailed the simple gesture of tossing coins to beggars on the street while keeping them at arm's length. Instead, it would have entailed getting involved in the lives of the poor, embedding them within their communities in some fashion.

This is not because early Jesus-followers were better people than those belonging to other Greco-Roman associations. Instead, it owes to the fact that they had been immersed in an overarching narrative about Israel's deity, and that narrative spurred them on and held them to account with regard to care for the needy even beyond their struggling membership. It is little wonder, then, that the Galatians' welcoming of Paul into their midst, despite his repellent illness and despite being an outsider to their locale, was interpreted by Paul as the influence of the Spirit upon them even at that early stage in their encounter with the good news. The outsider had been welcomed, cared for, and nurtured to health, as he himself contributed his spiritual gift for their benefit.

It would be unfair, then, to claim that Jesus-followers were "morally su-

---

Diaspora Jews and Early Christians," in A. Gutsfeld and D.-A. Koch, eds., *Vereine, Synagogen und Gemeinden im kaiserzeitlichen Kleinasien* [Tübingen: Mohr Siebeck, 2006], 113-27, pp. 116, 121): "The close tie between giving (or receiving) money and membership of the association meant that all such financial transactions served to solidify the social identity of the group, and clarify the boundaries between insiders and outsiders. . . . [T]hese patterns of giving within the community create a solidarity . . . [so that] every act of charity within the community clarifies and reinforces its social boundary." But since "acts of charity" were not wholly restricted to members of the Jesus-group (at least in theory), they could also serve as symbolic reminders of the permeability of the social boundaries of Jesus-groups.

perior" to their Greco-Roman contemporaries. But it might be fair to say that they shared a powerful narrative that held within it the theological motor that drove them to care for the poor in notable ways. The issues discussed in chapter 4 are again relevant here, in an attempt to get the historical balance right. While it would be wrong to deny charitable initiatives to the Greco-Roman world, similarly it would be wrong to deny that the early Jesus-movement set in motion a wave of "Judeo-Christian" concern for the poor that, once underway, became a powerful force for good within the Greco-Roman world. Such was virtually the inevitable result of the narrative of their "good news" about how Israel's deity was restoring the world through communities committed to following the narrative pattern of Jesus' life, whom they called "Lord" of the very structures of reality.

12.5: An Economic Profile of a Typical Urban Group of Jesus-followers

At this point, I hazard to construct a socio-economic profile of what a household-based Jesus-group might have looked like. In this, I imagine a community comprised of slaves, freedmen, artisans and families, evidencing an economic spread from ES7 through to ES4 and being structured primarily around a householder in the ES4 economic level. This, it must be emphasized, is a highly speculative exercise, and it might be wiser to omit the enterprise altogether. Nonetheless, the task is worth undertaking, if only to assemble some pieces of the puzzle in a suggestive exercise that heuristically fuels our imagination about how things might have worked in a certain configuration. Other configurations were possible, and certainly the profiling offered here is not meant to exhaust our historical imagination. The profile is based on nothing other than estimates (i.e., "guesses," but hopefully educated ones nonetheless), with the hope that the very attempt of constructing an economic profile of an ES4 household-based Jesus-group can bring certain features of its corporate life to light.

It must be pointed out, however, that no part of the argumentation of this book rests on this speculative exercise. It is a stand-alone and self-contained exercise, drawing especially on the results of chapters 10 and 11 above, but in no sense are the results of those chapters dependent on this imaginative exercise.

I include this speculative exercise intentionally within this chapter, subsumed in a sense within the context of discussing Paul's theology of the corporate body and the internal taskings of Jesus-communities. The exercise could easily have been appended to the end of chapter 11, for instance, but I prefer to put it here, precisely to immerse the economic profile of this hypothetical community in a theological setting — i.e., precisely how Paul would have imagined it. But it also sits here in the wake of the observation of §12.3 above that Paul's theology of gifting operates with full vitality in corporate contexts configured around ES4 households.

With these provisos in place, I offer the following thumbnail sketch of what a conventional urban group of fifty Jesus-followers in an ES4 household context might have looked like in its economic profiling:

1. Roughly 10% of this community is among the middling groups of Roman urbanism (ES4), not without economic risk, but also with a relatively significant level of economic security. In this community of fifty Jesus-followers, this equates to five members at this economic level.
2. Roughly 25% of this community has some minimal economic resources (ES5). In this community of fifty Jesus-followers, this equates to about twelve members at this economic level.
3. Roughly 65% of this community is marked out by subsistence-level existence (ES6 to ES7). In this community of fifty Jesus-followers, this equates to about thirty-three members at these economic levels.

	Economy Scale Percentages	Percentages for this Urban Jesus-Group	Numbers in this Urban Jesus-Group
ES1–ES3	3	0	0
ES4	15	10	5
ES5	27	25	12
ES6–ES7	55 (30; 25)	65 (35; 30)	33

One ES4 family of four comprises the heart of this household group (= four ES4 members), with perhaps its three servants (= three ES6 or ES7 members). One artisan enjoys ES4 status as well. Dependent on the resources of the ES4 family and the ES4 artisan, but injecting their own limited resources as well, are two ES5 families (= nine ES5 members), each with their single servant (= two ES6 or ES7 members), two ES5 artisans and one ES5 merchant. Four family-groups border on subsistence level, usually managing to survive but occasionally dropping precariously below survival standards (= eighteen ES6-ES7 members); some occasionally contribute to the resources of the community, when times place them well enough into the upper strand of ES6. Ten members also are characterized by subsistence-level existence or below (ES6 and ES7), being unprotected by household structures; some of these might be among the continually destitute.[25]

In this imaginative reconstruction, the highest point on the economy scale from which the community's economic resources come is the one ES4 family and the one independent ES4 artisan. Enhancing the corporate resources would be the limited but not insignificant funds of the two ES5 families, the two ES5 artisans, and the ES5 merchant. The economically needy requiring support would not have included the five servants of the ES4 and ES5 families (10% of the community), since they were embedded within relatively secure households. Many of the other twenty-eight members at the ES6-ES7 borderline will not have required economic assistance, if their position within ES6 was stable. Others within that number will have required constant support, and still others will have required occasional support. Of these, we might imagine the number of ES7 members requiring constant assistance to be ten (or 20% of the community) and the number of ES6 members requiring assistance at any given point to be four (8% of the community). In this scenario, at any given point in the life of this imagined group of fifty Jesus-followers, 28% of the community would be engulfed in dire economic situations, being economically supported by the community's resources.

Again, I need to reiterate that this is not in any way a template of any particular community that we might know of from Paul's texts. The intent is, in the first instance, to propose what an urban community of Jesus-followers might have looked like, in a household configuration, in order to earth our imagination in a historically-informed (albeit conjectural) delineation.[26]

25. That the family sizes of this group average between four and five people is not a reflection of modern demographics but corresponds closely with ancient realities. So Tim G. Parkin and Arthur John Pomeroy, *Roman Social History: A Sourcebook* (London: Routledge, 2007), p. 45: "Poorer families, and even richer families who did not want to spread their wealth too widely, limited their family size. . . . [Despite] relatively high fertility rates, mortality rates ensured that family size was small." With regard to those "richer families," Averil Cameron (*The Mediterranean World in Late Antiquity, AD 395-600* [London: Routledge, 1993], p. 147) notes that "[a]mong the better-off classes, family size comparable to the modern nuclear family seems to have been the norm."

26. In the scenario offered here, there are at least two vulnerable points pertaining to household slaves. First, the ten members that are the most economically exposed are envisioned as falling beyond the structures of the household (i.e., they are not slaves). It is possible that the number of ES6/ES7 members should be enlarged further to include slaves whose masters did not belong to the imagined Jesus-group, on the assumption that slave owners

Other scenarios could be entertained, of course. We might do well to chart a group with a complete absence of ES4 members, for instance. Notably, if we were to extract all the ES4 members (and their servants) from the hypothetical community envisioned above, not only would the resource potential be substantially reduced, but also the percentage of those within the community who were in economic need would significantly increase — i.e., from 28% to 33.5%. For these simple reasons, despite his hesitations about "patronizing" the gospel, and without imagining that he ever did the calculations, perhaps Paul would have sensed the overall advantages of building communities around ES4 households wherever possible.[27]

If these proposals are anywhere close to hitting the mark of what an urban Jesus-group might have looked like, we might think it remarkable that Paul places such a heavy theological overlay onto the economic relationships within fledgling and unimpressive communities of this sort. But heavy theological overlays are what Paul was best at. And because it is counterproductive to characterize Paul as having "an outright retreatist attitude to economic engagements,"[28] we should not be surprised that Paul interprets the economic engagements of such insignificant communities through a rich theological matrix.

---

did not (always) dictate the religious affiliation of their slaves. (On this see Carolyn Osiek and Margaret Y. MacDonald, *A Woman's Place: House Churches in Earliest Christianity* [Minneapolis: Fortress Press, 2006], pp. 157-58, 235-36.) This would add further slaves to the profile of this Jesus-group, although they are not economically vulnerable (relatively speaking), since they are embedded within a household.

Second, the scenario imagines that slaves would normally have been expected by their owners to join Jesus groups when those owners themselves joined Jesus-groups. In contrast to the first point (in which non-Jesus-followers allowed their slaves to participate in a Jesus-group), this second point assumes that Jesus-followers would often have expected their slaves to participate in a Jesus-group. If the hypothetical Jesus-group is restricted to 50 members (solely for ease of percentile calculations), a different scenario could be imagined without affecting the proposed percentage of people requiring economic support in this Jesus-group; that is, if (in view of the second vulnerability) the five ES6/ES7 household slaves were removed from the hypothetical Jesus-group, five others (acting independently of their owners) could easily be added (in view of the first vulnerability).

27. Compare the estimate of Osiek and MacDonald, *A Woman's Place*, p. 212: "Why did [Paul] baptize Crispus, Gaius, and the household of Stephanas if he did not see baptizing as part of his mission (1 Cor. 1:14-17)? The best answer is that these were the ones Paul perceived as most prominent, those who would sponsor his gospel to their dependents, and the ones under whose patronage he could carry out his mission and the church could thrive."

28. Barry Gordon, *Economic Analysis before Adam Smith* (New York: Harper & Row, 1975), p. 88.

CHAPTER 13

"Content with whatever I have"

The Poor in the Life of Paul

13.1: Summary of the Main Argument
13.2: Paul's Socio-Economic Locations
13.3: Paul, Peril, and the Poor

13.1: Summary of the Main Argument

Previous chapters of this project have contained their own set of conclusions, and no attempt will be made here to reiterate them exhaustively. Nonetheless, the argumentation of this book with respect to Paul can be summarized in relatively straightforward terms, encapsulated by the following nine points:

1. Paul, the follower of Jesus and apostle to gentiles of the Greco-Roman world, was concerned about the plight of the poor in the urban contexts in which he operated.
2. Although this was not his sole interest, and although he was not forced to deal with it extensively in his extant letters, care for the economically needy was a matter that he deemed to be characteristic of the identity of Jesus-followers.
3. Communities of Jesus-followers that Paul established were expected to offer care for the poor — albeit in their own groups in the first instance, although theoretically beyond those confines as well, if/as resources permitted.

4. Paul shared this conviction with other sectors of the early Jesus-movement that were committed to caring for the poor, and with leading figures of the early Jesus-movement — including its influential "founder" (i.e., Jesus) and that founder's influential brother (i.e., James).

5. With Paul properly situated in this respect, care for the poor is recognized to have been practiced fairly ubiquitously across the spectrum of first-century proto-orthodox circles of the Jesus-movement.

6. The early Jesus-movement, including Paul's own mission to Greco-Roman urbanites, embodied and exemplified values long embedded within mainstream forms of Early Judaism.

7. Rightly or wrongly, Paul and other leading figures of the early Jesus-movement imagined (along with some other Jews of their day) that care for the poor was not a notable feature of Greco-Roman paganism.

8. Paul imagined care for the poor among gentile communities of Jesus-followers to be an expression and embodiment of the invading triumph of the deity of Israel who had made himself known in the scriptures of Israel, in the life, death and resurrection of Jesus, and now through the Spirit/spirit that enlivened small groups of Jesus-followers.

9. Proto-orthodox forms of Christianity from the second through fourth centuries are known to have enormously augmented the strategies and institutions for caring for the poor to an unprecedented extent in the Greco-Roman world. Those efforts are organically related to more low-level forms of similar efforts evident throughout the early Jesus-movement, with Paul taking a prominent lead in spearheading such efforts among the gentile urbanites of the Greco-Roman world.

One of the keys in this recharacterization of Paul has been a reinterpretation of the phrase "remember the poor" of Gal 2:10 in its literary, historical and theological contexts. For long, the notion that Paul lacked any real concern for the poor has contributed to the interpretation of that verse, along the lines that, if "the poor" in Gal 2:10 does not refer to the *Jerusalem* poor, then the verse makes no sense, since Paul had no interest in "dealing with socio-economic problems" within urban Jesus-groups (so Hoppe). But as we have seen, this approach is shot through with misplaced assumptions (i.e., that Paul had no concern for alleviating the needs of the poor) and untested conjectures (i.e., that relatively simple lines can be drawn from Gal 2:10 to Paul's collection) in relation to defective historical foundations (i.e., that the "poor" was a technical term for the Jerusalem community) and an inadequate expla-

nation for the place of Gal 2:10 in the rhetorical strategy of Paul's Galatian letter. By contrast, this project has sought to articulate a literary, historical and
theological basis for a fresh interpretation of that key verse in particular.

In tandem with that exegetical contribution, this project has sought to
overhaul Paul's reputation with regard to the poverty of the Greco-Roman
world and the tasking of Jesus-groups in offsetting the needs of the urban
poor. It was through the vehicle of the gentile-friendly wing of the Jesus-
movement (in which Paul was a key and instrumental player) that Judaism's
concern for the poor spread throughout the cultures of the ancient world,
giving visibility to the poor in an unprecedented fashion. In that sense, the
preceding chapters recount one crucial episode in the story of how Judaism
bequeathed to the world a concern for the economically poor by way of the
early Jesus-movement — an episode that features the controversial figure
Paul. He imagined urban Jesus-groups to be miniature oases of eschatological refreshment amid the harsh economic conditions of the Greco-Roman
world.

Two areas that relate to the central thesis of this project nonetheless remain unexplored in this book. First, if I have succeeded in demonstrating
that concern for the poor was a stable feature in the rise of the early Jesus-
movement (since "even Paul" shared that concern), I have not sought to engage with the issue of whether the economic dimension of its message
shifted and changed as the movement developed to include a diversity of adherents across the economic spectrum. In this regard, there may be some
truth in the view that as the Jesus-movement took root across the Mediterranean basin, it "softened Jesus' critique [of wealth] and focused on the moral
dangers of 'love of money'" — a danger "more apparent to those who had
money than to those who did not."[1]

Second, many New Testament interpreters are currently of the view that
the earliest Jesus-movement was a counter-cultural movement that provided
protection against the bleak realities of the Roman imperial order while at
the same time denouncing that order's pattern of socio-economic injustice.[2]

---

1. Douglas Oakman, "Money in the Moral Universe of the New Testament," in
W. Stegemann, B. J. Malina and G. Theissen, eds., *The Social Setting of Jesus and the Gospels*
(Minneapolis: Fortress Press, 2002), p. 346, emphasis removed.

2. For instance, see the volumes edited by Richard A. Horsley, *Paul and the Roman Im-
perial Order* (New York: Trinity Press International, 2004); *Hidden Transcripts and the Arts of
Resistance: Applying the Work of James C. Scott to Jesus and Paul* (Atlanta: Society of Biblical
Literature, 2004); *Paul and Politics* (Harrisburg: Trinity Press International, 2000); *Paul and
Empire: Religion and Power in Roman Imperial Society* (Harrisburg: Trinity Press Interna-

Although the characterization of Paul advocated here need not be placed into an anti-imperial context, neither would it be out of place within it.[3] But the argument of this book is not dependent on how the matter is adjudicated one way or another. In fact, whether Paul was politically conservative or subversive has no impact on the thesis of this book.

One further issue cannot be addressed within the covers of this book: that is, how its findings pertain to contemporary Christian theological reflection on issues of poverty and wealth in the globalized context of the twenty-first century. If the findings of this study make the issue a pressing one, it is also far from a simple and straightforward one. One thing is relatively simple and straightforward, however — that is, Paul probably would imagine that contemporary Christian theology is legitimate to the extent that it includes such issues within its central remit, and not peripherally so.

Two related issues will be addressed in the final two sections of this book: (1) the extent to which Paul's concern for the poor had a bearing on his own socio-economic location; and (2) the extent to which Paul was willing to put his life on the line as a result of his concern for the poor. As will be shown, Paul's concern for the poor had considerable impact on the way that he lived his life, so much so that he was willing to compromise himself in terms of both the quality of his life and quantity of his days.

13.2: Paul's Socio-Economic Locations

In the prosopographic analysis of selected Jesus-followers offered in chapter 10 above, the precariousness of prosopographic reconstruction was noted, since such exercises are often required to be based on minimal data that themselves are not wholly transparent. The same is true with regard to a prosopographic analysis of Paul, since the useable data are neither sizeable nor self-interpreting. But the exercise needs to be done, and has some relevance to our overall impression of Paul and poverty.

---

tional, 1997). Similarly, see John Dominic Crossan and Jonathan L. Reed, *In Search of Paul: How Jesus's Apostle Opposed Rome's Empire with God's Kingdom* (San Francisco: HarperSanFrancisco, 2004).

3. The most profitable area of comparison in this regard might be in the area of economic dimensions of the Jesus-movement on the one hand and the imperial "good news" about the dawning of the Golden Age of plenty. On imperial Golden Age ideology, see L. de Ligt, "Restraining the Rich, Protecting the Poor: Symbolic Aspects of Roman Legislation," in W. Jongman and M. Kleijwegt, eds., *After the Past* (Leiden: Brill, 2002), 1-46, pp. 23-25.

According to the author of Acts, Paul was a Roman citizen (Acts 16:37-39) and had been born with Roman citizenship to his merit (22:25-29). If Paul had been born a citizen of Rome, he would have inherited that citizenship, since Roman citizenship was passed from one generation to the next. But the possibility that Paul was a Roman citizen is made problematic by the fact that there is no reference to Paul's Roman citizenship in his own letters. How are we to interpret this lacuna? The question is best enunciated in this way: Are there any points in Paul's argumentation that would have been enhanced by the mention of his alleged Roman citizenship? If not, then the absence of reference to Roman citizenship in Paul's letters is not necessarily a determinative factor. In fact, it is hard to imagine instances within the extant Pauline corpus where Paul's discourse could have been aided by mentioning his alleged citizenship. The possible exception is in Phil 3:4-6 when Paul registers a list of honorable things that had marked out his life that he now "considers to be as worthy as excrement" (Phil 3:8), and there he makes no mention of Roman citizenship. But the objection is not a strong one, since in that passage Paul is listing precisely *Jewish* features of his status (cf. 2 Cor 11:21-22).[4] In fact, Paul's discourse in Romans 13 is arguably the discourse of a citizen (even if it be the discourse of a citizen who might have occasion to be critical of the Roman imperial order, although not in this context).[5]

Harder to explain is the fact that, by his own admission, Paul had undergone civic floggings on three occasions (2 Cor 11:25), a scenario generally out of alignment with Roman citizenship.[6] It is possible, however, that on those occasions Paul had "kept quiet about his Roman citizenship deliberately in order to follow Christ in his sufferings."[7] This might coincide with the situation depicted in Acts 16:35-40 when, having already been beaten by the Philippian magistrates, Paul protests by introducing only then that he (along with Silas) was a Roman citizen. It might also cohere with the sense of Gal 6:17, where

---

4. Moreover, to include Roman citizenship in a list of what Paul now considers to be "excrement" would not have been a prudent rhetorical strategy in a fiercely pro-Roman context.

5. Neil Elliott's valiant attempt to interpret Rom 13:1-7 through the lens of "fear," and thereby to demonstrate that this is actually a subversive passage, seems to me to clutch at straws; see his "Romans 13:1-7 in the Context of Imperial Propaganda," in Richard A. Horsley, ed., *Paul and Empire: Religion and Power in Roman Imperial Society* (Harrisburg: Trinity Press International, 1997), pp. 184-204. A more productive position is that of John W. Marshall, "Hybridity and Reading Romans 13," JSNT 31 (2008): 157-78. See n. 28 in chapter 11.

6. It is precisely, and solely, on this basis that Crossan and Reed (*In Search of Paul,* p. 5) argue against Paul having had Roman citizenship.

7. Martin Hengel, *The Pre-Christian Paul* (London: SCM, 1991), p. 6.

Paul's satisfaction at his own imitation of Jesus shows through the page with full clarity: "From now on, let no one make trouble for me; for I carry the marks of Jesus branded on my body."[8] Moreover, it is not at all clear that Roman citizenship would have prevented Paul from being flogged. In situations of civic tumult (such as those depicted frequently in Acts in relation to the early Jesus-movement), city magistrates would not have been able to do thorough citizenship checks in order to mete out different kinds of punishments.[9] And citizenship did not protect some Roman citizens from being put to death by the distinctively Roman means of capital punishment — crucifixion.[10]

Most telling, however, is the fact that Paul's journey from Jerusalem to Rome, as outlined in Acts 22–28, cannot be feasibly understood apart from his alleged Roman citizenship. As Martin Hengel notes, if Paul was not a Roman citizen, "he would very probably have been condemned in Judaea without much fuss."[11] If the Lukan reconstruction of events in Acts 22–28 has historical merit even in its most basic outline, then the consequent corollary is that Paul was, in fact, a Roman citizen, since appeals to the emperor to hear one's case in unsatisfactory disputes was a privilege afforded only to Roman citizens. If some features of the Lukan narrative are historically vulnerable, this one is probably not.[12]

Most likely, then, Paul was a Roman citizen who, on at least one occasion, used that citizenship to afford leverage for himself and his mission — that is, his appeal to Caesar (i.e., Acts 22–28).[13] At other times, Paul's citizenship was not used to his advantage, resulting in him being flogged; in those situations we must imagine that his citizenship could not be legitimated, that the situation did not permit citizenship checks, or that Paul chose not to

8. A similar sentiment is found in 2 Cor 4:10, where Paul speaks of "carrying in the body the death of Jesus."

9. See Jerome Murphy-O'Connor, *Paul: A Critical Life* (Oxford: Oxford University Press, 1997), pp. 40-41. Justin J. Meggitt (*Paul, Poverty and Survival* [Edinburgh: T&T Clark, 1998], p. 78 n. 14) notes that "the rights of citizens were often ignored." See further Peter D. A. Garnsey, "Legal Privilege in the Roman Empire," *Past and Present* 41 (1968): 3-24.

10. See Hengel, *Pre-Christian Paul*, p. 7.

11. Hengel, *Pre-Christian Paul*, p. 7.

12. On Paul's citizenship, there is no better starting point than Hengel, *Pre-Christian Paul*, pp. 1-17. See also Ben Witherington, *The Paul Quest* (Downers Grove: InterVarsity Press, 1998), pp. 69-73; Murphy-O'Connor, *Paul: A Critical Life*, pp. 39-41; Paul Barnett, *Paul: Missionary of Jesus* (Grand Rapids: Eerdmans, 2008), pp. 28-29.

13. Hengel, *Pre-Christian Paul*, p. 8: Paul "was a Roman citizen who made use of the fact in particular circumstances. . . . As he urgently wanted to get to Rome, he will have thrown his Roman citizenship on the scales at the decisive moment to achieve his purpose."

make use of it in self-defense. Nor did he make rhetorical use of his Roman citizenship within his extant letters.

Of course Paul's Roman citizenship does not necessarily plug straight into a particular ES-level. But certain factors lead us to imagine that, in Paul's case, his citizenship went hand in hand with something of a middling economic profile, at least in his family's recent past. The most likely reason why a non-elite would have inherited Roman citizenship is manumission from servitude. Presumably Paul's father or grandfather had been granted citizenship on the occasion of gaining his freedom from a Roman master.[14] Servitude itself spanned the middling through lower economic categories, but manumission is likely to have characterized the middling economic levels, since gaining freedom usually involved awarding the Roman master with significant forms of financial compensation. So the likelihood that Paul's citizenship resulted from a forebear's manumission may suggest a middling economic profile for that forebear.

But the likelihood that one of Paul's forebears was manumitted and acquired Roman citizenship in the process does little to testify as to the economic profile of Paul's family. The significant costs involved in funding manumission might suggest not only that, at the time of manumission, Paul's forebear enjoyed a middling economic profile but also that Paul's family continued to draw on middling-level economic resources.[15] Or perhaps the full expense of manumission had left his family in relative poverty.[16]

---

14. So too, patristic interpreters of Paul imagined him to have gained his citizenship through familial manumission; see Hengel, *Pre-Christian Paul*, p. 14. Manumission from servitude is also the likely situation behind the construction of the "synagogue of freedmen" in Jerusalem (Acts 6:9).

15. Martin Hengel (*Pre-Christian Paul*, primarily pp. 4-6, 14-15, 37-39) envisions the following: Paul's grandfather had been based in Judea, but was then taken to Italy as a prisoner of war in the hostilities after the sacking of the Jerusalem Temple by Pompey in 63 BCE; Tarsus was either the home city or the adopted city of the Roman master of Paul's family; that Roman would have received a sizeable amount in compensation for the freeing of Paul's father or grandfather, who might well have remained in the employ of the Roman in some regard, perhaps even acting as manager of the Roman's estate in Tarsus; and at a later date, Paul's father or grandfather also purchased citizenship of the city of Tarsus. A simpler scenario is outlined by Murphy-O'Connor, *Paul: His Story* (Oxford: Oxford University Press, 2004), p. 4: Paul's parents were taken as slaves from Galilee in the aftermath of Sepphoris's destruction in 4 BCE, and brought to Tarsus; there "Paul's parents would have been bought by a Roman citizen . . . , and would have automatically acquired Roman citizenship when he set them free." Here Murphy-O'Connor (knowingly) sits light to the evidence of Acts 22:28 that Paul had been born a Roman citizen.

16. Compare G. E. M. de Ste. Croix (*The Class Struggle in the Ancient Greek World: From*

At least two indicators suggest that, during his upbringing, Paul enjoyed a certain level of economic security. The first of these indicators is Paul's attitude towards manual labor. As an apostle, Paul seems to have preferred to engage in manual labor (i.e., leather work) in order to support himself, rather than to rely on the patronage or (on occasion) the assistance of others. His reasoning for this preferred *modus operandi,* which he probably adopted only during the apostolic years of his life, was probably multifaceted.[17] But it is also notable that Paul's attitude towards manual labor betrays a man who imagines manual labor to be beneath his normal station in life. This emerges in a passage like 2 Cor 11:7: "Did I commit a sin by humbling myself (ἐποίησα ἐμαυτὸν ταπεινῶν) so that you might be exalted, because I proclaimed God's good news to you free of charge?" Here Paul depicts his manual labor as a form of self-humiliation. This is not the language of one who imagined that manual labor was a normal part of his everyday life — i.e., an attitude that would have predominated in ES6 and ES5. Something similar emerges from 1 Cor 9:22 (see also 9:19), where he speaks of making himself "weak" (probably economically vulnerable) "in order that I might win the weak."

Such passages reveal something about Paul's own sense of his "natural" economic profile, with manual labor being out of sync with his ingrained sense of status — except, of course, for his status as an apostle of Jesus Christ. Abraham Malherbe puts it this way:

> Paul's attitude towards his labor is reflected by the fact that he lists it in a series of hardships (1 Cor. 4:12) and that he regards it as servile (1 Cor. 9:19) and an act of abasement (2 Cor. 11:7).[18]

We can presume, then, that Paul's upbringing and life prior to his christophanic experience had been marked out by a middling economic profile.

---

the Archaic Age to the Arab Conquests [London: Duckworth, 1981], p. 178): Many freedmen "must have been poverty stricken wretches" who had been "allowed to buy their freedom with every penny they had managed to accumulate as their peculium during slavery."

17. Dale Martin outlines the various reasons; see his *Slavery as Salvation: Metaphor of Slavery in Pauline Christianity* (New Haven: Yale University Press, 1990), pp. 118-26. Even if commencing a trade in later life was rare, it was not unknown; see for instance, the case of Corbyle (Lucian, *Dial. Meretr.* 293), as noted by Meggitt, *Paul, Poverty, and Survival,* p. 88 n. 58.

18. Abraham J. Malherbe, *Paul and the Thessalonians: The Philosophic Tradition of Pastoral Care* (Philadelphia: Fortress Press, 1987), p. 56 n. 83. See too his *Social Aspects of Early Christianity* (Philadelphia: Fortress Press, 1977/1983), pp. 29-59.

This might receive additional support in light of Paul's rhetorical ability. When fed through rhetorical matrices, Paul's letters often display an array of rhetorical techniques that augment their communicative effectiveness. While his letters are not paradigmatic of ancient high literature, they nonetheless fare rather well in their use of rhetorical strategies and structures. This is suggestive of an author whose education was of a higher level than many of his day, and who had some acquaintance with some rhetorical training beyond the norm for the sub-elites.[19] Paul's own denials of rhetorical prowess themselves display the hallmarks of rhetorical skill (e.g., 1 Cor 1:17-20; 2:1-5).[20] Accordingly, Dale Martin sums up the situation in this way:

> To more and more scholars, who have become more and more cognizant of Greco-Roman rhetoric, it is inconceivable that Paul's letters could have

19. On this, see Dale Martin, *The Corinthian Body* (New Haven: Yale University Press, 1995), pp. 47-68; S. K. Stowers, "Romans 7:7-25 as a Speech-in-Character (προσωποποιία)," in Troels Engberg-Pedersen, ed., *Paul in His Hellenistic Context* (Minneapolis: Fortress Press, 1995), pp. 180-202; Glenn Holland, "Paul's Use of Irony as a Rhetorical Technique," in Stanley E. Porter and Thomas H. Olbricht, eds. *The Rhetorical Analysis of Scripture* (Sheffield: Sheffield Academic Press, 1997), pp. 234-48; Frederick Danker, "Paul's Debt to the *De Corona* of Demosthenes: A Study of Rhetorical Techniques in Second Corinthians," in D. F. Watson, ed., *Persuasive Artistry: Studies in New Testament Rhetoric in Honor of George A. Kennedy* (Sheffield: Sheffield Academic Press, 1991), pp. 262-80; G. A. Rowe, "Style," in Stanley E. Porter, ed., *Handbook of Classical Rhetoric in the Hellenistic Period, 330 BC–AD 400* (Leiden: Brill, 1997), pp. 121-57; Raymond Collins, *1 Corinthians* (Collegeville, MN: Liturgical Press, 1999), pp. 8-10; John R. Levison, "Did the Spirit Inspire Rhetoric? An Evaluation of George Kennedy's Definition of Early Christian Rhetoric," in Duane Watson, ed., *Persuasive Artistry: Essays in Honor of George Kennedy* (Sheffield: JSOT Press, 1991), pp. 25-40.

My own demonstration of Paul's rhetorical use of chain-link construction cannot be used to make the point, however (see my *Rhetoric at the Boundaries: The Art and Theology of New Testament Chain-Link Transitions* [Waco: Baylor University Press, 2005]). The ancient technique of structuring neighboring sections of a text through chain-link interlock was not restricted to Greco-Roman schools of rhetoric, but was a technique widespread in oral cultures of the ancient world. If it was taught in rhetorical schools (e.g., Quintilian, Lucian of Samosata), it also is evident in texts that antedate and/or have no dependence on such schools.

20. See, for instance, Duane Litfin, *St. Paul's Theology of Proclamation: 1 Corinthians 1–4 and Greco-Roman Rhetoric* (Cambridge: Cambridge University Press, 1994). According to Dale Martin (*Corinthian Body,* p. 49), "[w]hen Paul calls himself a 'layman with regard to speech,' . . . he is saying that he is not a professional orator or a teacher of rhetoric; but he is not denying that he had a rhetorical education. In fact, in both his disparagement of rhetoric and his claim to be only a layman, Paul stands in a great tradition of rhetorical disavowals of rhetorical activity." On the Corinthian charges behind 2 Cor 10:1-11, see Dale Martin, *Corinthian Body,* pp. 52-55.

been written by someone uneducated in the rhetorical systems of his day. Paul's rhetorical education is evident on every page.[21]

Putting an economic level to match such observations about Paul's use of rhetoric is, again, difficult to do with any certainty, but it is not a wholly speculative exercise. Many of the elite would have been extensively trained in schools of rhetoric, and most of the poor at ES6 to ES7 would have not. It is unlikely that many in ES5 would have had the resources to afford much rhetorical training, nor would it necessarily have been a skill they would have much needed or cherished. But those at ES4 would have had the resources to afford some form of rhetorical training and many within that economic level would have found benefit in undergoing some rhetorical education. If Paul's letters do, in fact, testify to a certain level of rhetorical education, it is most likely that he had enjoyed an ES4 kind of existence during his upbringing.[22] On the basis of Paul's rhetorical ability, Jerome Murphy-O'Connor concludes that "[t]here can be little doubt that he was brought up in a socially privileged class."[23] Although his phrase "privileged class" lacks proper nuancing, the claim is probably on target nonetheless.

Other features of Paul's life have occasionally been suggested as indicative of a middling economic level; many of them are weak indicators.[24] But the likelihood that Paul was a Roman citizen carries with it an implication about the economic profile of his forebear/forebears, an implication that triangulates well with Paul's own attitude to work and with the rhetorical level of his own literary products. Accordingly, it is best to postulate that Paul's pre-apostolic life had been marked out by an ES4 economic existence.

Against this backdrop, Paul's economic profile as an apostle for Jesus Christ drops a level or two — that is, from ES4 to the manual labor of ES5, perhaps even ES6 at times (see §10.5 above).[25] Even allowing for rhetorical

21. Dale Martin, *Corinthian Body*, p. 52. I cannot consider here whether Paul was educated in Jerusalem, as in Acts 22:3. This complicated issue adds relatively little to the matter at hand. Once again, however, Martin Hengel provides the best analysis of the matter; see his *The Pre-Christian Paul*, pp. 18-39.

22. See also Dale Martin, *Corinthian Body*, p. 52.

23. Jerome Murphy-O'Connor, *Paul: His Story* (Oxford: Oxford University Press, 2004), p. 190.

24. Meggitt (*Paul, Poverty and Survival*, pp. 75-97) takes full advantage of exposing their weaknesses. However, in my view he fails to undermine the three points used here to reconstruct the prosopographic profile of Paul's pre-christophanic life.

25. On Paul's downward economic profile following his christophany, see Edwin A. Judge, "Paul's Boasting in Relation to Contemporary Professional Practice," *ABR* 16 (1968):

hyperbole, Paul's comments in 1 Cor 4:11-12 are nonetheless illustrative of how he envisioned his own apostolic experiences: "To the present hour we are hungry and thirsty, we are poorly clothed and beaten and homeless, and we grow weary from the work of our own hands." And this is matched by the much longer catalogue of hardships that Paul lists throughout 2 Cor 11:23-27. There, along with the mention of experiences of imprisonment, floggings, stonings, shipwrecks, and other dangers, Paul mentions having been "in toil and hardship, through many a sleepless night, hungry and thirsty, often without food, cold and naked." Friesen (using terminology of "poverty scale" and "PS" levels) locates the Paul of the letters along ES5 through ES7 in this way:

> Paul's hard life as an itinerant artisan is indicated briefly in his letters (1 Thess. 2.9; 2 Cor. 11.29). . . . Paul's days would have been dominated by long hours of difficult physical labor for meager wages. . . . While Paul's economic situation certainly vacillated throughout his adult life (Phil. 4.12), his experiences would have been primarily in categories 5-7 of the poverty scale. There were probably times when he stayed in households with moderate surplus resources (PS4), and he occasionally received gifts from assemblies he had visited in the past (2 Cor. 11.7-9), but his normal practice was apparently to do manual labor to support himself (1 Thess. 2.9; 1 Cor. 9.3-12).[26]

According to Ronald F. Hock, Paul's manual labor would not have supplied him "with enough to make him anything but a poor man and sometimes not even with that much, so that hunger and thirst and cold were at times his lot."[27] Such experiences were likely to have been in relative contrast with those of Paul's pre-apostolic days.

37-50; Judge, "The Social Identity of the First Christians," *JRH* 11 (1980): 201-217; Dale Martin, *Corinthian Body*, pp. 51-52, 118-35; Martin, *Slavery as Salvation*, pp. 79-86; E. P. Sanders, *Paul* (Oxford: Oxford University Press, 1991), p. 11.

26. Friesen, "Poverty in Pauline Studies," *JSNT* 26 (2004): 350. Meggitt (*Paul, Poverty and Survival*, pp. 77-79) challenges the view that Paul drew on more sources of personal income than just his own manual labor.

27. Ronald F. Hock, *The Social Context of Paul's Ministry: Tentmaking and Apostleship* (Philadelphia: Fortress Press, 1980), p. 68. Todd D. Still ("Did Paul Loathe Manual Labor? Revisiting the Work of Ronald F. Hock," *JBL* 125 [2006]: 781-95) offers an important corrective to Hock and others who err on the side of inflating Paul's pre-christophanic socio-economic profile, not least in speaking of Paul's "snobbish and scornful attitude" to work (Hock, "Paul's Tentmaking and the Problem of His Social Class," *JBL* 97 [1978]: 555-64,

As far as we can reconstruct, this plunge in Paul's economic profile was his preferred *modus operandi*, the result of his own choice, his intentional taking of the road less traveled. He claims that his choice of downward mobility was driven by a strategy to become economically "weak" (ἀσθενής) in order to win precisely those who are similarly "weak" (1 Cor 9:22). This "kenotic" move on Paul's part was motivated (or so he presents it) by a concern "to gain those who are themselves of lower status."[28] In 1 Thess 2:8-9 Paul identifies his working night and day in labor and hardship as the means whereby he and his coworkers were able to impart to the Thessalonians "not only the gospel of God but also our own lives."

For the purpose of this project, the point can hardly be overemphasized. The economic profile that Paul adopted in his mission to proclaim the gospel to the nations was seemingly lower than the economic profile that he had enjoyed in his earlier and formative period. As Dahl notes, "Paul's financial sacrifice is likely to have been greater than we can determine from his letters, but he chooses not to talk about it."[29] Perhaps his own economic autobiography shows through the page of Phil 4:11-13:

> I have learned to be content with whatever I have. I know what it is to have little, and I know what it is to have plenty. In any and all circumstances I have learned the secret of being well-fed and of going hungry, of having plenty and of being in need. I can do all things through him who strengthens me.

It should not be overlooked that, since Paul saw care for the needy as an integral component of the gospel he proclaimed, his self-imposed economic demotion was motivated, partially but nonetheless surely, by a concern to help alleviate the needs of the poor in the Greco-Roman world through the establishment of communities of Jesus-followers across the Mediterranean basin. Those communities that Paul "lowered himself" to serve were expected to "proclaim the Lord's death until he comes," a proclamation that included caring for the economically vulnerable as a central feature. In order to work

---

p. 564) or of Paul having been born into "a wealthy family" with a silver spoon in his mouth (Ernest Best, *Paul and His Converts* [Edinburgh: T&T Clark, 1988], p. 74).

28. Dale Martin, *Slavery as Salvation*, p. 124.

29. Nils Dahl, *Studies in Paul* (Philadelphia: Fortress Press, 1977), p. 36. He speculates as to what Paul, after his christophanic experience, might have done with any economic resources he may have acquired during his middling-economic days: Paul, like Barnabas, probably "gave his property to the congregation's common fund, or perhaps he used the money to support himself during his early years of service as a missionary for Christ."

toward the realization of that vision, Paul willingly compromised his own economic well-being. Making himself economically more vulnerable seems to have resulted from a conviction that Israel's sovereign deity was at work in Jesus-groups, where the needs of economically vulnerable people were expected to be met as divine grace flowed through the lives of Jesus-followers.

13.3: Paul, Peril, and the Poor

If Paul gave up some economic status in his commitment to the gospel (with care for the poor embedded within it), it seems he was also willing to put his life on the line for the same commitment. In this regard, the pattern of his life is not a world away from that of the one whose death and resurrection he proclaimed. The gospel story of Jesus' own self-giving for the benefit of others provided a theological basis for Paul's own efforts to build up communities in which the poor were not overlooked but were explicitly targeted as deserving of corporate support. This is the case in 1 Corinthians 11, for instance, where the abuse of poorer Jesus-followers within the Corinthian community is offset in relation to the story of Jesus' last night with his disciples, in which he demonstrated his own self-giving for the benefit of others. The same is true of other texts too, with the story of Jesus serving as the foundation for Paul's practical exhortation to support others in need. So, Paul's admonition "to do good to all" in Gal 6:10 may be said to derive ultimately from the narrative of "the Son of God, who loved me and gave himself for me" (Gal 2:20; cf. 1:4), a narrative now refracted through other paraenetic passages in Galatians, such as Gal 5:13 ("through love be servants of one another") and 6:2 ("bear one another's burdens, and so fulfill the law of Christ").

Paul's strategy of using the narrative of the self-giving Christ to foster concern for the needy was applied throughout the mid-50s to the project that, as we have seen, was of such importance to him: his sponsorship of the collection from gentile Jesus-followers to help alleviate the poverty of some needy Jewish Jesus-followers in Jerusalem. The christological underpinning for this effort comes to the fore in 2 Cor 8:9: "Although he [our Lord Jesus Christ] was rich, yet for your sake he became poor, so that by his poverty you might become rich." For Paul, this "rich" christological narrative should inform the narrative of the Jesus-groups in Corinth, so that they too should give of themselves and their "riches" (relatively speaking) to assist "the poor among the saints in Jerusalem."

Paul drove this collection effort for a number of years from 53 CE, experiencing a number of setbacks along the way, not least in Corinth (and perhaps in Galatia as well). In about 57 or 58 CE Paul himself took the monetary yield to Jerusalem, where he experienced a setback of an altogether different order than any he had experienced in Corinth. In Jerusalem, life-threatening dynamics were in play for Paul. Even before Paul undertook his journey to deliver the collection to its destination, Paul was keenly aware of the personal dangers that would face him not only on the journey itself but also when he arrived in Jerusalem — dangers having to do with his controversial reputation regarding observance of the law. That Paul was aware of this danger is clear from his letter to the Romans, written in 57 CE. Towards the end of that letter, Paul encourages his addressees "to join me in earnest prayer to God on my behalf, that I may be rescued from the unbelievers in Judea, and that my ministry to Jerusalem may be acceptable to the saints" (Rom 15:30-31). It seems that Paul was right to suspect that trouble awaited him in Jerusalem, since "it is hard to shake off the suspicion that the collection was not welcomed and possibly not even received by the Jerusalem church."[30] If the narrative of Acts is reliable in its depiction of Paul's return to Judea, an outcry against Paul led to his subsequent arrest in Jerusalem and his journey as

---

30. James D. G. Dunn, *Beginning from Jerusalem: Christianity in the Making*, vol. 2 (Grand Rapids: Eerdmans, 2009), p. 972; see his fuller discussion on pp. 970-72. In his *Unity and Diversity in the New Testament* (London: SCM Press, 1977), Dunn writes: "Paul was widely regarded as a renegade for abandoning the law, and it would seem that little or nothing had been done within or by the Jerusalem church to defend him on this score (21.20-24; despite 16.3 and 18.18). Then when Paul was arrested and put on trial we hear nothing of any Jewish Christians standing by him, speaking in his defence — and this despite James's apparent high standing among orthodox Jews. . . . Where were the Jerusalem Christians? It looks very much as though they had washed their hands of Paul, left him to stew in his own juice."

If, as Dunn imagines, the collection money was not accepted by the Jerusalem Jesus-followers, what would have happened to it? Perhaps it was used to gain Paul his hearing before the emperor. Note J. C. Lentz, *Luke's Portrait of Paul* (Cambridge: Cambridge University Press, 1993), p. 127: "A Roman citizen in the provinces was a privileged person. His citizenship could, at times, save him from non-Roman provincial justice. Yet only those citizens who also possessed wealth and prestige as well as the citizenship were in the position to procure any certain legal advantages." Along with this, note that the collection's funds must have been considerable. As Jerome Murphy-O'Connor says (*Paul: A Critical Life*, p. 345), "The symbolic value of the gesture would have been negated were the sum derisory (1 Cor 16:2); it would have been seen by the Jerusalemites as an expression of contempt." Perhaps this is one reason why Paul's collection effort seems to have extended for a significant amount of time (i.e., from 53 to 57 CE).

a Roman prisoner to the imperial city, where his case was to be heard. After this, evidence is precariously patchy. Paul's life may have ended in Rome sometime between 62 and 64 CE, as a martyr who was unsuccessful in his attempt to clear his name.[31] Alternatively, he may have been released from house arrest in Rome, and gone on to have a ministry in the Spanish west and then again in the east somewhere, before finally returning to Rome in the aftermath of Nero's persecutions and himself becoming a martyr sometime between 65 and 67 CE.[32]

If Paul died in the early to mid-60s, the collection looms large as one of the most significant of his initiatives as a "free agent," prior to his arrest and eventual death. If, however, Paul died in the mid- to late 60s, the collection maintains its central prominence in his career of the mid-50s but does not arc to his death in such a direct fashion. In either case, it is the collection that demonstrates just how far Paul was willing to risk his own life in order to promote the gospel and, consequently, remember the poor of the Greco-Roman world. Interpreters have debated what Paul's full motivation for undertaking his collection might have been, and no clear consensus has emerged.[33] But in the attempt to pinpoint possible motivations for Paul's trip to Jerusalem, one motive can all too easily get lost in the mix: that is, Paul's desire "to be of service to them" (ἐν . . . λειτουργῆσαι αὐτοῖς, Rom 15:27), with the "them" being identified as "the poor among the saints in Jerusalem" (15:26). That is, Paul's motivations included "serving the poor," the very thing that he identifies in Gal 2:10 as something he had long been zealously devoted to. There would need to be other lines of connection as well, of course. His trip to Jerusalem in 58 CE cannot be motivated simply by the desire to help out needy followers of

31. This is the most likely outcome if none of the Pastoral Epistles were written by Paul. This view is advocated by Crossan and Reed, *In Search of Paul,* pp. 400-403.

32. The best advocate of this position is Murphy-O'Connor, *Paul: A Critical Life,* pp. 356-71. He bases this view on the authenticity of 2 Timothy.

33. Some options, beyond an interest in expressing the unity of Jewish and gentile wings of the early Jesus-movement, include: (1) Paul sought to fulfill prophecy about the Gentiles bringing gifts to Zion (although Paul never quite says so much); (2) Paul sought to provoke Jews to jealousy and thereby to place their faith in Jesus Christ (a view developed on the basis of Rom 11:13-14); (3) Paul was attempting to replicate the half-shekel Temple tax paid by Jews (although the comparison does not work in certain respects); (4) Paul wanted to demonstrate, right in the heart of the city/community where opposition to him was (sometimes) most evident, the validity of his gentile mission, and thereby his own apostolic legitimacy, by demonstrating how Israel's deity was working graciously among the gentiles. On these options, see Victor Furnish, *II Corinthians* (Garden City: Doubleday Press, 1984), pp. 409-413; M. E. Thrall, *II Corinthians* (Edinburgh: T&T Clark, 2000), pp. 511-15.

Jesus, for obviously such people were spread throughout the Mediterranean basin. Nonetheless, although this motive of "serving the poor" cannot explain everything about Paul's collection, neither can everything about Paul's collection be explained without this motive.

To elaborate, in all probability two goals stood front and center as motivating Paul to bring a collection right into the heart of Jerusalem. First, he hoped that the collection would unleash unifying forces among different streams of the early Jesus-movement.[34] Second (but not unrelated), he hoped that the collection would demonstrate the legitimacy of his own apostolic efforts.[35] The collection would serve these purposes by removing the offense of the early Jesus-movement's "law-free" mission that targeted the gentiles. Perhaps two further consequences would follow in the wake of these primary goals: it would assist in the proclamation of the good news to Judeans who were not Jesus-followers, and it would undermine the efforts of any who sought to influence the communities Paul had established in ways that ran contrary to his understanding of the good news.

An underlying conviction must be seen to lie behind any and all of these possible motivations, and one that intertwines economics and salvation history at every point. For Paul, the fact that gentile Jesus-followers had given some of their limited resources in an effort to alleviate the needs of the poor is testimony to the working of the Spirit in their midst and of the legitimacy of their acceptance by Israel's all-powerful deity, despite their non-circumcised status.[36] Years earlier, the Jerusalem apostles had stipulated that gentile Jesus-followers (like their Jewish counterparts) were to be unfailing in their efforts for the poor (precisely the thing that Paul himself insisted on,

34. Interpreters often highlight this as the most pressing factor motivating Paul's collection efforts. So Nils Dahl (*Studies in Paul* [Minneapolis: Fortress Press, 1977], p. 32) states: "the gift of money expresses what is for Paul most important: the unity of Jews and Gentiles in the church of Christ. This is the reason that it was so important to Paul to deliver the gift in person, even though he fully understood the risk of a journey to Jerusalem."

35. Compare Annette Clark Wire ("Response: Paul and Those Outside Power," in R. A. Horsley, ed., *Paul and Politics* [Harrisburg: Trinity Press International, 2000], 224-26, p. 224): "The collection seems to me to have [as its primary purpose the vindication of] one Judaism in the eyes of another. Is Paul not working, first and foremost, to vindicate his messianic mission to the Gentiles in the eyes of, as he puts it, 'the saints in Judea' (messianic Jews) and unbelievers (nonmessianic Jews)?"

36. Something along these lines contributes to the significance of the Cornelius story in Acts 10–11, as well as motivating the stipulation of the Jerusalem apostles that communities of former pagans should be unerring in remembering the poor, as in Gal 2:10. Along somewhat similar lines, see K. Berger, "Almosen für Israel," *NTS* 23 (1977): 180-204.

he says); by 53 CE, however, Paul became enamored with the idea that Jerusalem communities would themselves become the beneficiaries of the generosity of gentile Jesus-followers. There could be no better way to prove the legitimacy of a "law-free" gentile mission to those in Jerusalem who were skeptical of it, and to those who advocated the need for circumcision and law observance even among gentile followers of Jesus. Taking the proceeds of gentile generosity right into the heart of Jerusalem itself would speak volumes about the transformation of gentile followers of Jesus — precisely since generosity was the very thing that gentiles were generally not known for (or at least were not credited with). When Jewish Jesus-followers in Jerusalem were brought face-to-face with tangible evidence of the generosity of gentile Jesus-followers (not only for the indigenous poor but also for the poor among Jesus-followers in Jerusalem), the legitimacy of "law-free" Jesus-groups among the gentiles would be virtually self-evident. As a consequence, the collection would serve to undermine all further efforts to force gentile followers of Jesus to conform to the law in any way other than to fulfill it through their efforts of bearing the burdens of others.

One can compare here Josephus's story of Izates and his mother Queen Helena of Adiabene who, as noted in §5.1 above, demonstrated their piety and obeisance to Israel's deity by donating funds for those who were in desperate need; for Josephus, this characteristic was the indisputable mark that their fidelity to Israel's deity was deep-rooted and genuine. And long before the first century CE (and long after as well), Jewish traditions had come to include generosity to the poor as a key component of "righteousness" before Israel's deity.[37]

It is not at all surprising, then, that the collection's symbolism about unity among different wings within the early Jesus-movement was itself founded on what the collection indicated about the legitimacy of Paul's controversial mission to the gentiles, which itself was founded on what the collection indicated about the transformation of gentile Jesus-followers, as demonstrated by their generosity towards those in need. The latter is nothing other than one expression of the injunction to "remember the poor" — the injunction stipulated by the Jerusalem apostles, who, upon receiving the collection of the gentiles' generosity, would have tangible and incontrovert-

---

37. In Greek translations of the Hebrew Scriptures (i.e., the LXX), the term צדקה ("righteousness") is normally translated with the term ἐλεημοσύνη ("almsgiving"). On this, see especially Roman Garrison, *Redemptive Almsgiving in Early Christianity* (Sheffield: Sheffield Academic Press, 1993), pp. 46-59; James D. G. Dunn, *The Epistle to the Galatians* (London: A&C Black, 1993), pp. 112-13.

ible proof of the transformative power of Israel's deity among the pagan nations of the world. Herein lies the basis for all the other theological and symbolic layers of meaning that Paul had packaged into his collection efforts. If that foundation is removed or neglected, all other levels of meaning have the potential to lose their interconnected coherence, or to collapse altogether.

Throughout the early to mid 50s, then, Paul unfailingly put his own energies into a new financial initiative, made possible by the resources of urban Jesus-groups that remained loyal to him. It came on-stream alongside efforts to care for the indigenous poor in the pagan world and was designed to offset the material destitution of a specific group of needy people — those based in communities of Jesus-followers in Jerusalem. This new initiative had the additional merit of being a highly symbolic initiative, crystallizing a gamut of Paul's interests in one powerful emblem of the identity of all Jesus-groups and the solidarity among them.

Paul continued to drive this new initiative with vigor despite opposition from within some Jesus-groups and despite the risk to his own reputation and his own life. Arguably it was precisely because of its larger symbolic significance (rather than just alleviating the needs of the poor in Jerusalem communities of Jesus-followers) that Paul was willing to put his life on the line.[38] But even so, the larger significance of the collection included the legitimacy of gentile communities of Jesus-followers, precisely because they were communities that cared for the economically needy, which itself was to be a marker of Jesus-groups across the spectrum of the Jesus-movement.

No matter how we slice it, then, it looks as if care for the poor was something for which Paul was willing to put his life on the line. Just as Paul's gospel is not reducible to caring for the poor, so his motivation for undertaking the Jerusalem collection cannot be reduced to that. But just as caring for the poor is an integral dimension to Paul's larger gospel, so concern for the poor

38. For this reason, it is unproductive to consider whether Paul hoped that his collection would help establish improved long-term economic structures among the Jerusalem Jesus-followers, along the lines that Dieter Georgi follows (*The City in the Valley: Biblical Interpretation and Urban Theology* [Atlanta: Society of Biblical Literature, 2005], p. 306): "In all probability, heavy investment in the creation and maintenance of the economic stability of the Christ community in Jerusalem remains the direct financial objective of the collection. . . . Some real estate and building projects for the meeting purposes of the Christ community in Jerusalem and their guests may be in the picture as well." This overstretches the import of the collection. For Paul, the collection was symbolic of the fact that the gentile Jesus-followers were demonstrating the kind of practices that only the deity of Israel could nurture, and that, therefore, there should be unity between Jewish and gentile Jesus-followers.

was also an integral feature in Paul's larger motivational pool for undertaking his collection. The devotion to the cause of the poor that Paul says had marked out his early ministry (Gal 2:10) seems to have continued to characterize his ministry throughout the 50s, as evidenced by the fact that he was willing to put his life on the line in his delivery of the collection, despite the dangers that he knew were likely to face him in that very undertaking.

*   *   *   **

We have seen that Paul's concern for the poor had considerable impact on the way that he lived his life, to the point of risking his own life in "putting his money where his mouth was." This should surprise us only if, unlike Paul, we imagine the "good news" that transformed Paul from persecutor to apostle to be devoid of an economic dimension. But since Paul envisioned an economic component to lie deeply embedded within the good news of the Jesus-movement, the fact that his concern for the poor influenced his manner of living and his approach to peril falls wholly in line with all that we know of this man who, when committing himself to a cause, did so wholeheartedly, and with spirited enthusiasm.

Perhaps, then, the recovery of Paul's concern for the poor goes some way towards bridging the gap that is often postulated between the so-called "Jesus of history" and the "Christ of faith." John Dominic Crossan articulates the issue in challenging fashion:

> Maybe Christianity is an inevitable and absolutely necessary "betrayal" of Jesus, else it might all have died among the hills of Lower Galilee. But did that "betrayal" have to happen so swiftly, succeed so fully, and be enjoyed so thoroughly?[39]

With regard to Jesus' proclamation of "good news to the poor," however, we have seen reason to think that Paul's gospel of Jesus Christ was not the least bit complicit in any "betrayal" of the message of Jesus of Nazareth. Whereas Jesus is remembered as one who brought good news to the poor who are blessed in the kingdom of God, Paul is (to be) remembered as one whose gospel included "remembrance" of the poor as an integral part of the proclamation about (and embodiment of) what Israel's deity had accomplished through the life, death and resurrection of Jesus.

39. John Dominic Crossan, *The Historical Jesus: The Life of a Mediterranean Jewish Peasant* (San Francisco: HarperSanFrancisco, 1991), p. 424.

An Early Critique of Steven J. Freisen's 2004 Poverty Scale

A1.1: Adjusting Friesen's 2004 Poverty Scale
A1.2: Profiling Some Important Middling Groups

This appendix includes some aspects of my 2009 critique of Steve Freisen's 2004 "poverty scale" (renamed here "economy scale," with PS-values consequently shifting to ES-values).[1] The critique needs to have a foothold within the covers of this book, since (1) it offers the rationale for most of the figures proposed for the economy scale in chapter 3 above, building on Friesen's proposed percentages in 2004, and (2) it outlines the reasoning behind an "optimistic" interpretation of the data presented by Scheidel and Friesen in 2009.[2]

My 2009 critique of Friesen was fuller than the case that appears in this appendix. I have not, for instance, included any mention of Scheidel's 2006 view that the middling groups comprised 20-25% of the Greco-Roman population. In my article of 2009 I showed cautious indebtedness to this view (although I imagined his figure to be at least 5% too high), but I do not replicate Scheidel's earlier argument here since he went on to abandon it three years later.

1. Steven J. Friesen, "Poverty in Pauline Studies: Beyond the So-called New Consensus," *JSNT* 26 (2004): 323-61; Bruce W. Longenecker, "Exposing the Economic Middle: A Revised Economy Scale for the Study of Early Urban Christianity," *JSNT* 31 (2009): 243-78. This appendix lightly edits parts of the latter article.
2. Walter Scheidel and Steven J. Friesen, "The Size of the Economy and the Distribution of Income in the Roman Empire," *JRS* 99 (2009): 61-91.

In what follows, then, Friesen's original figures for his "poverty scale" (ES1-3 at 3%; ES4 at 7%; ES5 at 22%; ES6 at 40%; and ES7 at 28%) will be considered in relation to (1) his manner of calculating those percentages, and (2) my reasons for adjusting some of those percentages.

Also included in this appendix is the discussion of prominent middling groups — i.e., the *apparitores* and the *Augustales*. This discussion was originally included in my 2009 article in order (1) to demonstrate something of the elongated stretch of ES4, and (2) to note something of the political character that may have predominated at the upper end of ES4. While serving those same purposes here, this discussion takes on another dimension in the wake of the Scheidel and Friesen article of 2009 — that is, to position the *Augustales* primarily within the ES4 economic band rather than placing them among the economically elite.

*   *   *

A1.1: Adjusting Friesen's 2004 Poverty Scale

It will be argued here that Friesen's percentages are subject to significant qualification with regard to ES4, ES6 and ES7. Initially, however, it should be noted that there is no real need to call into question the percentages that Friesen awards to the upper end of the scale. Friesen's percentage for the urban elite (ES1 through ES3) is relatively secure (a point that is addressed briefly in §3.3 above). At roughly 3%, this figure is the most reliable on the scale, being standard within studies of economic profiling in the Roman world, which usually place the urban elite somewhere between 1% and 5% of the population.[3]

Less reliable, however, are the percentages applied to the lower end of the spectrum, due to the way in which Friesen arrived at his percentages for ES6 and ES7. When determining percentages for those economic levels,

---

3. Friesen includes an appendix in which he outlines his reasoning in support of these percentages. According to Walter Scheidel ("Stratification, Deprivation and Quality of Life," in M. Atkins and R. Osborne, eds., *Poverty in the Roman World* [Cambridge: Cambridge University Press, 2006], 40-59, p. 51), land registry evidence suggest that a "truly tiny membership [within the elite orders] would hardly have been possible"; consequently, Scheidel imagines the elite landholders to have comprised "the top 3 to 5 per cent of the population" (p. 54). E. W. Stegemann and W. Stegemann (*The Jesus Movement: A Social History of Its First Century* [Minneapolis: Fortress Press, 1999], p. 77) place the figure at "between 1 and 5 percent."

Friesen is heavily reliant on an important study by C. R. Whittaker, who supplied estimates of how much of the population was engulfed in poverty in ancient Rome.[4] Whittaker estimated that those in the equivalent of ES7 comprised 24% through 28% of the urban population.[5] Taking Whittaker's upper percentage estimates, Friesen identifies 28% of the urban population as belonging to ES7. Whittaker also estimated that some 30-40% of the population fell into the equivalent of ES6. Taking Whittaker's upper percentage estimate, Friesen fills ES6 with 40% of the urban population. In this way, when compiling his percentages for ES7 and ES6, Friesen has simply applied Whittaker's *upper* estimates in each case.[6]

But this is precisely what makes Friesen's percentages vulnerable. Whittaker's figures allow for a variable of 14 percentage points for those two levels — a potential slippage that Friesen's model simply erases. When ES6 and ES7 are pegged to percentage points at the upper-most limit suggested by Whittaker, there is a consequent knock-on effect upon percentages for ES4 and ES5. These two levels on Friesen's scale are derived by adding the percentages of the population already allocated to ES1 through ES3 and ES6 through ES7, and then making a rough guess as to how much of the remaining percentage should be allocated to ES4 and ES5. With 71% of the population already assigned to the other five points on the poverty scale (ES1 through ES3: 3%; ES6: 28%; ES7: 40%), Friesen estimates that most of the remaining 29% should be allocated to ES5, making ES4 much smaller than ES5 "because of the endemic character of poverty in the Roman empire, because of structural impediments in the economy, and because of the large amounts of wealth required to move up the poverty scale."[7] So Friesen awards percentages of 7% to ES4 and 22% to ES5. In theory, however, if we choose to work with the percentages suggested by Whittaker, any or all of the indefinite 14% of Whittaker's ES6 and ES7 groups could have been entered within ES4 or ES5,

---

4. C. R. Whittaker, "The Poor in the City of Rome," in *Land, City and Trade in the Roman Empire* (Aldershot: Variorum Ashgate, 1993), article 7 [there is no sequential pagination throughout the book; internally the article's pagination is from 1-25].

5. Whittaker, "The Poor in the City of Rome," p. 4. In Whittaker's analysis, this group is comprised of two sub-groups: those "unable to earn a living," who comprised 4-8% of the population, and those "permanently in crisis" who comprised 20% of the population.

6. Since Whittaker's figures are themselves extrapolations from figures for pre-industrial cities, the figures that Friesen adopts are not tied to Rome's own profile — itself a city with quite a distinctive economic profile in relation to the urban centers of the ancient world.

7. Friesen, "Poverty in Pauline Studies," p. 346.

in any proportion, taking the combined percentage of those two categories up from 29% to a maximum of 43%. As will be shown below, there is good reason for thinking that the percentage for ES4 requires augmentation.

Friesen speaks early in his article of wanting to get beyond binary constructions of poverty: "The problem with binary terminology of rich and poor is that the term 'the poor' has to cover at least 90% of the population with little or no differentiation among them."[8] In a later article he made the same point in this way: "most specialists use only two opposing terms — rich and poor — instead of employing a graduated series of terms to describe more accurately the situations of the vast majority of people in the Roman Empire."[9] Clearly Friesen's seven-point scale is well suited to get beyond a binary form of construction.

But when Friesen applies his percentages to his seven-point model, his scale becomes interpreted in heavily binary terms, with heavy differentiation between the upper end (ES1 through ES3) and the lower end (ES5 through ES7), and with only a small 7% group in the middle. Friesen's seven-point scale is weighted in such a way and with such a glaring gap between the upper end and the bottom that it amounts to little more than a nuanced binary system.[10]

Friesen's somewhat binary instincts (i.e., attributing only 7% to ES4) are explicitly indebted to the influential work of Cambridge classicist Moses Finley. Finley argued that ancient economies, being almost exclusively agrarian in character, were without notable stimulation from either integrated commercial trade or significant technological advance.[11] Within that eco-

---

8. Friesen, "Poverty in Pauline Studies," p. 340.

9. Steven J. Friesen, "Prospects for a Demography of the Pauline Mission: Corinth among the Churches," in Daniel N. Schowalter and Steven J. Friesen, eds., *Urban Religion in Roman Corinth* (Cambridge, MA: Harvard University Press, 2005), 351-70, p. 362.

10. The same is true of the Stegemanns' proposed stratification (Stegemann and Stegemann, *The Jesus Movement,* pp. 53-95). For them, three economic levels differentiate the tiny number of Greco-Roman elite, while three levels also differentiate the massive number of poor. This six-point taxonomy is little other than a nuanced binary schema.

11. Moses I. Finley, "Technical Innovation and Economic Progress in the Ancient World," *Economic History Review* 18 (1965): 29-45; Finley, *The Ancient Economy* (London: Chatto & Windus, 1975), especially chapters 5 and 6. Similarly Justin J. Meggitt (*Paul, Poverty and Survival* [Edinburgh: T&T Clark, 1998], p. 42) advocates an "essentially 'primitivist' position," believing that the Greco-Roman economy "remained weak and rudimentary, with little or no growth." According to Meggitt, "the Empire's economy was . . . incapable of sustaining a mid-range economic group . . . [so that] in real terms there were few economic differences between those that found themselves outside of the rarefied circles of the élite" (p. 7).

nomic environment, there is little opportunity for middling groups to become established. Friesen cites his indebtedness to Finley in this way:

> The crucial scholar in this . . . is Moses Finley [who] succeeded in demonstrating that the ancient economy was qualitatively different from modern economies. The ancient economy was agrarian and relatively static. It allowed for little growth or entrepreneurial initiative because the organization and use of resources was acquisitive rather than productive. Hence, there was no united market for the commercial exploitation of the empire nor any middle class to undertake such activities. So most inhabitants of the empire were born into poverty, and their only chance to escape it was the tomb.[12]

Finley's position has served as a discursive watershed in the study of the Greco-Roman economy for the past four decades or so. One of its most notable influences has been its feeding of binary economic models that virtually obliterate economic levels between the elite and the poor. In an economic situation of the kind imagined by those adopting "Finleyan orthodoxy," there is little scope for an innovative and emergent middling group.[13]

Acknowledging his indebtedness to Finley, Friesen awards a figure of only 7% to the middle group of ES4. What Friesen's account fails to make clear to its readers, however, is the extent to which Finley's position has been repeatedly and significantly challenged. For some, Finley's reconstruction requires only some tweaking, while for others it is largely problematic. But either way, there arises more scope than Finley had allowed for a range of different levels of wealth to emerge between the two binary extremes.

Within ten years of the publication of Finley's monograph, for instance, Keith Hopkins (one of Finley's students) had argued repeatedly that Finley's model required revision in order to take account of economic growth in the first two centuries of the common era — a growth largely facilitated by "the

---

12. Friesen, "Poverty in Pauline Studies," pp. 338-39.

13. For discussion of the extent to which Finley has been misrepresented, see R. Saller, "Framing the Debate over Growth in the Ancient Economy," in W. Scheidel and S. von Reden, eds., *The Ancient Economy* (Edinburgh: Edinburgh University Press, 2002), pp. 251-69. For a critique of Saller's view, see M. Silver, Review of *The Ancient Economy* by Walter Scheidel and Sitta von Reden (eds.), EH.NET Economic History Services, Jan 3 2003; URL: http://eh.net/bookreviews/library/0570; accessed 11 March 2008. For purposes of this article, it is notable that Friesen taps into Finley's (alleged) position when advocating a minimalist view of middling economic groups.

spread of technical and social innovations."[14] Hopkins did not consider the data he presented to completely overturn Finley's model of Roman economy, since "the Finley model of the ancient economy is sufficiently flexible to incorporate this modest dynamic."[15]

More recently, however, scholars have not been quite so generous to Finley. This is especially the case, for instance, in the work of archaeologists Kevin Greene and Andrew Wilson. Taking note of "Finley's minimalist interpretations and dismissive attitude towards archaeological evidence,"[16] both have presented significant archaeological evidence indicating that technological progress within the Roman world was not at all inconsequential.[17]

14. Keith Hopkins, "Introduction," in P. D. A. Garnsey, K. Hopkins, and C. R. Whittaker, eds., *Trade in the Ancient Economy* (London: Chatto & Windus, 1983), ix-xxv, p. xiv. See also Hopkins, "Economic Growth and Towns in Classical Antiquity," in P. Abrams and E. A. Wrigley, eds., *Towns in Societies: Essays in Economic History and Historical Sociology* (Cambridge: Cambridge University Press, 1978), pp. 35-77; Hopkins, "Taxes and Trade in the Roman Empire, 200 BC–AD 400," *JRS* 70 (1980): 101-25.

15. Hopkins, "Introduction," p. xxi.

16. Kevin Greene, "Technological Innovation and Economic Progress in the Ancient World," *Economic History Review* 53 (2000): 29-59, pp. 29-30.

17. Kevin Greene, *The Archeology of the Roman Economy* (London: Batsford; Berkeley: University of California Press, 1986); Greene, "Industry and Technology," in A. K. Bowman, P. D. A. Garnsey and D. Rathbone, eds., *The Cambridge Ancient History;* Vol. 11, *The High Empire, A.D. 70-192* (Cambridge: Cambridge University Press, 2000), pp. 741-68; Greene, "Technological Innovation and Economic Progress in the Ancient World"; Andrew Wilson, "Machines, Power and the Ancient Economy," *JRS* 92 (2002): 1-32; Greene, "Cyrenaica and the Late Antique Economy," *Ancient West and East* 3 (2004): 143-54; Greene, "The Economic Impact of Technological Advances in the Roman Construction Industry," in Elio Lo Cascio, ed., *Innovazione tecnica e progresso economico* (Bari, Italy: Edipuglia, 2006), pp. 225-36.

For others involved in correcting the position of Finley, see M. W. Fredriksen, "Theory, Evidence and the Ancient Economy," *JRS* 65 (1975): 164-71; John H. D'Arms, "M. I. Rostovtzeff and Moses I. Finley: The Status of Traders in the Roman World," in J. H. D'Arms and J. W. Eadie, eds., *Ancient and Modern: Essays in Honor of Gerald F. Else* (Ann Arbor: University of Michigan Press, 1977), pp. 157-79; K. Christ, "Grundfragen der römischen Sozialstruktur," in W. Eck, H. Galsterer and H. Wolff, eds., *Studien zur Sozialgeschichte* (Cologne: Böhlau, 1980), 197-228; F. Vittinghoff, "Soziale Struktur und politisches System in der hohen römischen Kaiserzeit," *Historische Zeitschrift* 230 (1980): 31-55; A. Carandini, "Italian Wine and African Oil: Commerce in a World Empire," in K. Randsborg, ed., *The Birth of Europe: Archeology and Social Development in the First Millennium AD* (Rome: L'Erma di Bretschneider, 1989), pp. 16-24; H. W. Pleket, "Wirtschaft," in F. Vittinghoff, ed., *Europäische Wirtschafts- und Sozialgeschichte in der römischen Kaiserzeit* (Stuttgart: Ernst Klett Verlag, 1990), pp. 25-160; R. Descat, "*L'économie antique* et la cité grecque," *Annales* 50 (1995): 961-89; John J. Paterson, "Production and Consumption," in P. Jones and K. Sidwell, eds., *The World of Rome: An Introduction to Roman Culture* (Cambridge: Cambridge University Press, 1997),

In contrast to Finley, for instance, Wilson paints a picture of an "economic boom of the first and second centuries A.D.," which can be attributable to a variety of factors. One factor is

> the boost to state finances given by the use of advanced mining technologies, on top of a very healthy agrarian base which grew in the provinces under the stimulus of the opening up of new markets as vast swathes of territory came under Roman control.[18]

For Wilson, certain forms of economic growth stimulated even further forms of economic growth. This is testified to, for instance, in the material record of the construction industry, which underwent notable technological improvements during this period.[19] For example, through the modularization of materials and the standardization of material sizes, building materials could be produced for mass distribution, rather than simply for local or regional distribution. This helps to explain why bricks forged in one region have ended up in buildings far from where they were originally forged.[20]

The benefits that followed in the wake of expansive trade opportunities would have been accrued at various points along the economic spectrum. It would not be surprising if the elite would have had their fingers in the eco-

---

pp. 181-207; the preponderance of articles in D. J. Mattingly and J. Salmon, eds., *Economies Beyond Agriculture in the Classical World* (London: Routledge, 2001); Jean Andreau, "Twenty Years after Moses I. Finley's *The Ancient Economy*," in Scheidel and von Reden, eds., *The Ancient Economy*, pp. 33-49.

For discussion of the place of Finley's views in their historical context, see Andrew Wilson, "Machines, Power and the Ancient Economy," *JRS* 92 (2002): 1-32, p. 2. For discussion of the ideological function of Finley's views, see Neville Morley, "Narrative Economy," in P. F. Bang, M. Ikeguchi, and H. G. Ziche, eds., *Ancient Economies, Modern Methodologies* (Bari: Edipuglia, 2006), 27-47, pp. 41-44. Whereas Finley and others question the extent to which archaeological evidence can negotiate between economic models, Greg Woolf rightly contends that "archaeology offers the best means of choosing between these alternatives"; see Woolf, "Imperialism, Empire and the Integration of the Roman Economy," *World Archeology* 23 (1992): 283-93, p. 283. See also Andreau, "Twenty Years after Moses I. Finley's *The Ancient Economy*," pp. 37-40.

18. Wilson, "Machines, Power and the Ancient Economy," p. 30.

19. Wilson, "The Economic Impact of Technological Advances."

20. In contrast to the view that economic growth was restricted to the imperial west, S. E. Alcock ("The Eastern Mediterranean," in W. Scheidel, I. Morris, and R. Saller, eds., *The Cambridge Economic History of the Graeco-Roman World* [Cambridge: Cambridge University Press, 2007], 671-97, p. 696) argues that "[a]ggregate growth in production — to some as yet unquantifiable, but arguably considerable degree — must be accepted for the early imperial east."

nomic pie of any developing "industry" and would have benefited richly from it, but benefits of technological advances would not have been restricted simply to them. According to Wilson, private brick makers and artisans throughout a broad expanse of the empire would have benefited economically — i.e., some of those listed in Friesen's ES4 and others at the top end of ES5 (i.e., traders).[21] Similarly, according to John Patterson, urban growth and prosperity "led to increasing profits for artisans and traders of the city . . . and [for] social groupings just below the traditional elite" — i.e., those within Friesen's ES4.[22] Similarly, Dennis Kehoe notes that during the early imperial period:

> Fortunes could be made in commerce and manufacturing, which certainly occupied a significant place in the Roman economy. . . . [T]he chief beneficiaries of the opportunities that the Roman empire offered for generating wealth in these sectors were generally people of more modest social and economic status [than the elite], from wealthy freedmen to independent artisans.[23]

Such examples of technological and trade improvements are causing many to question the adequacy of radical binary modeling of the Greco-Roman world. According to Wilson, historians have failed to properly consult the archaeological record and, consequently, "have massively underestimated the degree of technological development in antiquity and its impact on the economy." Wilson and others advise that we should abandon "the assump-

---

21. In Wilson's reconstruction, it is not hard to imagine brick makers of ES5 finding ways of capitalizing on the increasing economic expansion that technological advances in the construction industry provided, with some of the more fortunate moving into ES4 as a consequence. See also D. J. Mattingly and J. Salmon, "The Productive Past: Economies Beyond Agriculture," in D. J. Mattingly and J. Salmon, eds., *Economies Beyond Agriculture in the Classical World* (London: Routledge, 2001), 3-14, p. 10: local production "may in some instances have been significant in the accumulation of local prosperity, and probably also of individual fortunes."

22. John R. Patterson, *Landscapes and Cities* (Oxford: Oxford University Press, 2006), p. 261.

23. D. P. Kehoe, "The Early Roman Empire: Consumption," in Scheidel, Morris and Saller, eds., *The Cambridge Economic History of the Graeco-Roman World*, 543-69, p. 550; see also p. 569: "it is likely that there were many . . . people who could take advantage of the business opportunities that Roman rule created." See the case study by J. F. Drinkwater, "The Gallo-Roman Woolen Industry and the Great Debate: The Igel Column Revisited," in Mattingly and Salmon, eds., *Economies Beyond Agriculture in the Classical World*, pp. 279-308.

tion that the ancient economy was either stable or stagnant," favoring instead a model of "intensive *per capita* economic growth in the first two centuries A.D."[24] Or as Mattingly and Salmon contest, "much work since (and, of course, before) Finley, especially that which depends essentially on archaeological evidence, demonstrates that both individuals and groups successfully established and exploited markets in particular cases, often on a large scale."[25]

If Finley erred by underestimating growth within Roman trade and technology, his many detractors at times have a tendency to err by overemphasizing the importance of that growth. Two issues intertwine here, but should not be confused: (1) the effect of technological advance and improved trade on the Roman economy overall, and (2) the implications of technological advance and improved trade on the modeling of Roman (socio-) economic stratification, of the kind that Friesen has pioneered.

With regard to the first issue, if it is right to imagine 75-80% of the Roman economy being agriculturally based, developments in trade and industry may not have much overall effect on economic growth in the Greco-Roman world, at least on a macro scale. The point has been made by Richard Saller,[26] for instance, and by Walter Scheidel and Sitta von Reden.[27] Whereas the debate has primarily been framed as an either-or (i.e., Finley or anti-Finley), a middle-way seems preferable. The material record testifies to the existence of various kinds of economic systems within the Greco-Roman world. The predominant economic system was agrarian and leaned towards elite "acquisitiveness," benefiting the elite landholders primarily; to a notable degree, then, the basic Finleyan model remains intact. But other economic influences were also in evidence, "economies beyond agriculture,"[28] many of

24. Wilson, "Cyrenaica and the Late Antique Economy," p. 144. See also R. B. Hitchner, "Olive Production and the Roman Economy: The Case for Intensive Growth in the Roman Empire," in M.-C. Amouretti and J.-P. Brun, eds., *La production du vin et de l'huile en Méditerranée* (Athens: École française d'Athènes, 1993), 499-508; Wilson, "'The Advantages of Wealth and Luxury': The Case for Economic Growth in the Roman Empire," in J. Manning and I. Morris, eds., *The Ancient Economy: Evidence and Models* (Stanford: Stanford University Press, 2005), pp. 207-22; W. M. Jongman, "The Early Roman Empire: Production," in Scheidel, Morris and Saller, eds., *The Cambridge Economic History of the Graeco-Roman World*, 592-618, pp. 612-15.

25. Mattingly and Salmon, "The Productive Past," p. 9.

26. Richard P. Saller, "Framing the Debate over Growth in the Ancient Economy," in Scheidel and von Reden, eds., *The Ancient Economy*, pp. 251-69.

27. Scheidel and von Reden, *The Ancient Economy*, p. 71.

28. To borrow the title of the Mattingly and Salmon volume, *Economies Beyond Agriculture in the Classical World*.

which were disengaged from agrarianism to one extent or another (e.g., ceramics, textiles, mining and quarrying). The Roman world was comprised of various economic motors, only some of which Finley's model does justice to.

With regard to the issue of modeling economic stratification, correcting Finley's underestimation of trade and technology in the first two centuries CE has the potential to destabilize severely binary schematizations that are indebted to Finley. The Greco-Roman world testifies instead to "a spectrum of statuses between the wealthiest senators at the top and the most oppressed slaves at the bottom."[29] The consequence is that the size of the Greco-Roman middling groups may well have been notably underestimated by Finley and others. Peter Garnsey and Richard Saller note that groups "distinguished from both the elite orders and the humble masses" were "sizeable" in the Greco-Roman world.[30] Neville Morley speaks of "the existence of a range of [economic] groups" in the ancient world.[31] Greg Woolf speaks of there having been a "huge middle bracket between paupers and nobles" in the ancient world that was filled by an array of people.[32] Willem Jongman notes that "[e]ven many ordinary citizens were moderately prosperous, and there were also many moderately wealthy people in between the masses of modest means and the rich but small political elite."[33]

Consequently, Friesen's proposal of 7% for ES4, which is ultimately attributable to a Finleyan perspective of the ancient economy, is quite vulnerable. Since Finley's day, there have been "considerable changes in our factual knowledge and interpretation of ancient technology and economics."[34] In

29. Patterson, *Landscapes and Cities,* p. 261.

30. Peter D. A. Garnsey and Richard P. Saller, *The Roman Empire: Economy, Society and Culture* (London: Duckworth, 1987), p. 116. Garnsey and Saller do not allow their perception of this "sizeable" group to do much to offset a binary distinction between the *honestiores* and the *humiliores,* even while recognizing that a "rough, binary classification . . . run[s] the risk of oversimplifying and thus distorting the social reality."

31. N. Morley, *Trade in Classical Antiquity* (Cambridge: Cambridge University Press, 2007), p. 44; see further pp. 44-45.

32. G. Woolf, "Food, Poverty and Patronage: The Significance of the Epigraphy of the Roman Alimentary Schemes in Early Imperial Italy," in *PBSR* 58 (1990): 197-228, p. 205.

33. Jongman, "The Early Roman Empire: Consumption," p. 597. See too his Review of *Poverty in the Roman World* by Margaret Atkins and Robin Osborne (eds.), EH.Net Economic History Services, accessed Jul 19 2008; URL: http://eh.net/bookreviews/library/1335 (consulted January 25, 2009), where he speaks of "a significant paradigm shift that is currently unfolding" away from Finley's binary construct.

34. Greene, "Technological Innovation and Economic Progress in the Ancient World," p. 29.

his point-by-point rebuttal to Finley, Greene charges that "a change in emphasis has taken place in the interpretation of the classical economy since Finley placed his stamp upon it."[35] Or as Wilson notes, since Finley's day "thinking on the ancient economy has moved on considerably."[36] Or as Jean Andreau notes, Finley's model has not "triumphed"; instead,

> after years in which his conclusions continued to be advanced . . . , this is no longer the case. The questions are Finleyan, the methods and ways of thinking bear the stamp of his influence, but the answers are moving farther and farther away from his own.[37]

Friesen, however, gives his readers no hint that this "change in emphasis" has taken place, that "thinking . . . has moved on considerably," or that scholarly opinion is "moving farther and farther away" from Finley's own. While Finley's views have merit in relation to some important economic dimensions of the Roman world, they exhibit deficiencies in relation to "economies beyond agrarianism."

The consequence of this pertains especially to attempts to model the middling groups. The increasingly prominent role of trade and technology within the Greco-Roman economy undermines the legitimacy of stark binary schemes. Hanging in the balance is the extent to which middling groups might have been evident within the economic spectrum of the Greco-Roman world. For many historians, there would have been a far greater presence of such groups than the Finley model suggests. But Friesen registers nothing of this sort within his article. By tying itself so closely to

35. Greene, "Technological Innovation and Economic Progress in the Ancient World," p. 52. It is important to note, of course, that Greene recognizes that Finley "was no doubt right to stress . . . that traders and manufacturers were in a minority without social status or political or economic influence" (p. 45), and that "gross disparities in wealth, the importance of political power and social status, and the limitations of financial systems, are not in dispute" (p. 52). What is in dispute is the extent of growth in production in the Roman world. In his 2006 article "Archeological Data and Economic Interpretation" (in Bang, Ikeguchi, and Ziche, eds., *Ancient Economies, Modern Methodologies*, 109-36, p. 132), Greene claimed that in the 20 years since his important book *Archaeology of the Roman Economy* (Berkeley: University of California Press, 1986), "the optimistic views expressed in 1986 have been amplified by the quality and diversity of subsequent archaeological discoveries and publications . . . reinforc[ing] my conclusion that the level of economic activity and complexity of production found in the Roman provinces was not matched again until the postmedieval period."

36. Wilson, "Machines, Power and the Ancient Economy," p. 2.

37. Andreau, "Twenty Years after Moses I. Finley's *The Ancient Economy*," pp. 34-35.

Finley, Friesen's analysis disguises the scope and importance of artisanal and commercial wealth, indicating an apparent gap in his imagining of the ancient economic landscape.

Consequently, we need to give a greater exposure to the middling groups of ES4 than Friesen's 7% allows. This proposed adjustment to Friesen's percentages for ES4 has a significant effect on the model of economic stratification in the Greco-Roman world. We have seen reason to believe that Friesen's model might benefit from adjustments not only in relation to ES4, but also to ES6 and ES7, and in equal measure. It has been noted that Friesen's percentages for ES6 and ES7 are potentially too high, perhaps by as much as 14%.[38] And it has been noted that Friesen's percentage for the middling group of ES4 is probably too low. In light of this, I propose three simple adjustments to Friesen's otherwise helpful model:

1. the percentage for the ES4 middling groups should be registered at 17% (note: this figure represents my 2009 view; the percentage is reduced to 15% in chapter 3 above);[39]
2. the percentages for ES6 and ES7 should be comprised of figures from the lower end of Whittaker's estimates: for ES7, 25% in Whittaker's range of 24% to 28%;[40] and for ES6, 30% in Whittaker's range of 30% to 40%; and
3. the percentage for ES5 should be raised slightly from 22% to 25% (note: this figure represents my 2009 view; the percentage is increased to 27% in chapter 3 above).

38. Although it is neither my intention nor within my expertise to do so, it is of course possible that these categories themselves might be refined further. Peter Oakes ("Constructing Poverty Scales for Graeco-Roman Society: A Response to Steven Friesen's 'Poverty in Pauline Studies,'" *JSNT* 26 [2004]: 367-71, p. 368) has offered suggestions about how we might move towards a more refined model, but his own proposals would seem to outstrip the bounds of the extant data.

39. I note that this percentage is in line with William Herzog's description of those in advanced agrarianism who fall between the elite (on the one hand) and the peasants, degraded and expendables (on the other); the middling groups are comprised of "retainers, 5 to 7 percent; merchants, 5 percent; artisans, 3 to 7 percent" (*Parables as Subversive Speech* [Louisville: Westminster John Knox, 1994], p. 59).

40. It is notable that the proposed 25% for ES7 falls roughly in line with Peter Oakes' estimate that 20% of the Philippian population was living below subsistence level (*Philippians: From People to Letter* [Cambridge: Cambridge University Press, 2001], pp. 47-49).

A1.2: Profiling Some Important Middling Groups

When offering descriptors for ES4, Friesen lists the following as falling within this economic level: "some merchants, some traders, some freedpersons, some artisans (especially those who employ others), and military veterans." Such descriptors are adequate as far as they go, but they also conceal something of the stratum at its middle and upper end. Whereas Friesen places "retainers" only within the 3% elite of ES1 through ES3, the term has at least as much relevance to certain groups within the middling level.

One group that would have fallen towards the middle of ES4, perhaps, is the *apparitores*. These men worked for civic magistrates as scribes, messengers, lectors and heralds. They were usually appointed to their apparitorial positions by patronage but, once appointed, could serve any magistrate. They varied in status, performing tasks from humbler to more responsible functions, with honor being accrued to them by virtue of their role in the proper running of the civic order. They consisted of men originally of relatively humble means who, being deemed able and trustworthy to civic goals, were moved into positions of relative security.

As such, the *apparitores* play two key roles in any attempt to profile the economic stratification of the Roman world. First, they represent a sector of society that was generally upwardly mobile.[41] They may have been relatively exceptional in this regard, but their "upward" potential is not without parallel elsewhere in the ancient record (see also the *Augustales*, below).[42] Second, "they represent a liminal group, occupying a position on the social boundary between the elite and non-elite."[43] In his 1983 study of *apparitores*, Nicholas

---

41. N. Purcell ("The *Apparitores*: A Study in Social Mobility," *PBSR* 51 [1983]: 125-73) makes this point repeatedly: "These posts helped the lowly to aspire to the privileges of the higher echelons of the society" (p. 162); "it is surely time to abandon the old contention that there were no bridges across the gulf between men of servile and of free origin, as well as the view that, with a few exceptions, men of less than equestrian rank could never dream of approaching such a distant and lofty status" (p. 171); the "apparitorial position in the *res publica* allowed it to provide an excellent *entrée* into the world of patronage which characterised Roman public life. It constituted . . . a licensed mechanism for social mobility" (p. 171).

42. See also T. F. Carney, *The Shape of the Past: Models and Antiquity* (Lawrence KA: Coronado Press, 1975), p. 94: "It would be wrong . . . to think that there was no chance of upward social mobility in these societies [of the past]. For in fact there were two major avenues for such ascent: warfare and service under an autocrat."

43. J. Edmondson, "Cities and Urban Life in the Western Provinces of the Roman Empire, 30 BCE–250 CE," in David S. Potter, ed., *A Companion to the Roman Empire* (Oxford: Blackwell Publishing, 2006), 250-80, p. 273.

Purcell describes this group as "numerous, powerful, self-aware and self-esteeming."[44] Purcell advised that their "intermediate status must be taken into account if we are to understand the stratification of Roman society."[45]

Another group of notable civic importance is the *Augustales,* who should be registered toward the top of ES4, sometimes spilling over into ES3.[46] This group consisted predominately of freedmen[47] who, due to their servile past, were generally excluded from securing decurial posts but who, upon gaining their freedom and in view of the viability of their economic resources, were willingly conscripted and appointed by decurial patrons to enhance local civic life.[48] Although they usually did not enjoy the enormous resources of the elite, they were nonetheless "upwardly mobile"[49] and were in a markedly different economic location to those who struggled in relation to subsistence living.[50] Among them were men "whose wealth and influence

44. Purcell, "The *Apparitores:* A Study in Social Mobility," p. 127.

45. Purcell, "The *Apparitores:* A Study in Social Mobility," p. 171.

46. Some have suggested that there were notable differences between the *Augustales,* the *magistri Augustales,* the *seviri Augustales,* and the *seviri,* but most likely these terms were somewhat interchangeable, without significant differences between them, at least for our purposes.

It is important to note that the *Augustales* were primarily a western phenomenon, with a lesser profile east of Macedonia. See especially R. Duthoy, "La fonction sociale de l'augustalité," *Epigraphica* 36 (1974): 134-54, pp. 148-51. But as J. H. Oliver has shown ("Gerusiae and Augustales," *Historia* 7 [1958]: 472-96), the same functions that were performed by the *Augustales* in the west were performed by the *Gerusiae* in the east. The *Augustales,* then, are unlikely to be simply a western phenomenon within the empire; they appear to have been absent at Rome, precisely because other groups perform the same functions (i.e., the *vici magistri*), just as they are lesser in the east due to the presence of the *Gerusiae* there.

47. Duthoy's estimate ("La fonction sociale de l'augustalité," pp. 135-36) that 80-90% were freedmen is commonly accepted.

48. Debate exists over whether they served religious roles in relation to the imperial cult, or simply held civic duties apart from the imperial cult. See, for instance, John H. d'Arms, "Memory, Money, and Status at Misenum: Three New Inscriptions and the Collegium of the Augustales," *JRS* 90 (2000): 126-44, p. 129; and Patterson, *Landscapes and Cities,* p. 243. There is little dispute, however, with regard to the view that the *Augustales* served the double purpose of simultaneously affirming the superiority of wealth to poverty and the inferiority of servile birth to free birth; see Garnsey and Saller, *The Roman Empire,* p. 121; Patterson, *Landscapes and Cities,* p. 251.

49. Edmondson, "Cities and Urban Life in the Western Provinces of the Roman Empire," p. 273.

50. Patterson, *Landscapes and Cities,* p. 245; see also pp. 190-91. The classic study of the *Augustales* as a middling group is that of A. Abramenko, *Die munizipale Mittelschicht im*

were not sufficient to enable them to enter the *ordo,* but nevertheless sought involvement in public affairs," and "sons of freedmen who . . . lacked the [economic] resources to enter the *ordo*" of decurions at ES3.[51] Consequently, on occasions when food and money were distributed within the civic arena (i.e., at formal banquets), the *Augustales* received less than decurions but more than the plebs.[52] Similar testimonies to the public perception of the middling status of *Augustales* come in the form of gifts awarded by leading citizens to sectors within the local populace. Such gifts frequently differentiated between amounts awarded per head for decurions, for the *Augustales,* and for the general populace (i.e., sporting events and caring for children), with decreasing amounts in each case.[53] According to Patterson, the *Augus-*

---

kaiserzeitlichen Italien: Zu einem neuen Verständnis von Sevirat und Augustalität (Frankfurt: Peter Lang, 1993). Scheidel ("Stratification, Deprivation and Quality of Life," p. 42) argues (unconvincingly in my view) that they do not form part of the economic middling group but fall wholly within the economic elite. More nuanced is John H. d'Arms, *Commerce: Social Standing in Ancient Rome* (Cambridge, MA: Harvard University Press, 1981), pp. 121-48. With regard to economic status, I place the *Augustales* generally at the top of the middling group (i.e., the top of ES4), with some overlap (and sometimes significantly) with the elite strata (i.e., ES3).

A confused picture of the *Augustales* appears in J. D. Crossan and J. Reed, *In Search of Paul: How Jesus's Apostle Opposed Rome's Empire with God's Kingdom* (San Francisco: HarperSanFrancisco, 2004). There the *Augustales* are initially described as "a lower-class group" who could only make their influence felt by "banding together" and putting their resources together collectively in order to win them civic visibility (p. 300). On Friesen's scale, the terminology tends to correspond with ES5. But what the Corinthian *Augustales* erected in their city was "a huge blue marble step with an enormous statue of Augustus" — something that a band of ES5 freedmen would be unlikely to have been able to resource. Later in Crossan and Reed, discussion of the *Augustales* is couched in terms that apply most appropriately to ES4, sometimes even ES3 (pp. 323-25). Even accounting for the fact that *Augustales* often ended their lives much wealthier than they had been upon gaining their freedom, the description of the *Augustales* as "a lower-class group" (p. 300) is far too skewed to be generally accurate.

51. Patterson, *Landscapes and Cities,* p. 247.

52. Patterson, *Landscapes and Cities,* pp. 246-49.

53. R. P. Duncan-Jones, "Human Numbers in Towns and Town-Organisations of the Roman Empire: The Evidence of Gifts," *Historia* 13 (1964): 199-208. It may even be possible to estimate the general percentage of the urban population represented by the *Augustales* alone, although noting that local variations would obviously apply. In his analysis of private gifts to cities, Duncan-Jones finds two occasions in which evidence can allow us to reconstruct the size of the decurial population and that of the *Augustales.* In the case of Italian Petelia, Duncan-Jones gives an estimate of 80-100 *Augustales* and 100 decurions (pp. 199-200). Although this suggests a ratio of almost 1:1, Duncan-Jones notes that this ratio is probably unrepresentative, since the evidence of most gifts would suggest a higher proportion of *Augustales.* More representative is the case of a generous gift given to Spanish Barcino, where

tales comprised one of the "three central groups in civic life,"[54] sandwiched between the decurions of ES3 and the members of *collegia* below that economic level.[55] It is best to imagine them as falling predominately within the upper band of the middling economic groups, and as sharing with the elites a commitment to the enhancement of the civic environment that the Roman imperial order cultivated.

With the *apparitores* and the *Augustales* in view, ES4 is shown to be a much-elongated economic category, with markedly wealthy members in its upper half. For this reason, there may be merit either in adding an extra level to the economy scale or, preferably, distinguishing between the upper and lower levels of ES4 through ES4a and ES4b designations, respectively (and wherever necessary or helpful). Moreover, it is notable that the upper band of ES4 plays a critical role in oiling the civic mechanisms of the Greco-Roman world. Most likely it is also in the upper band of ES4 that we should expect to see a notable rise in pro-Roman affinities.

---

the ratio is closer to 2.5 *Augustales* for every 1 decurion (p. 205). If we accept Duncan-Jones's reasoning on this, and if we accept Friesen's estimate that 1.1% of the urban population was comprised of decurions, then we can estimate that, in general, the *Augustales* would have comprised somewhere in the order of 2.5% to 3% of the urban population.

54. Patterson, *Landscapes and Cities,* p. 260.

55. Peter D. A. Garnsey ("Grain for Rome," in P. D. A. Garnsey, K. Hopkins and C. R. Whittaker, eds., *Trade in the Ancient Economy* [London: Chatto & Windus, 1983], 118-30, p. 125) lists the *Augustales* as belonging to the middling group of the Greco-Roman economy.

Non-Pauline Configurations
of Generosity and the Mosaic Law

In §9.2 above we saw that Paul regarded "remembering the poor" as a representative moral component of what it means for the Mosaic law to be fulfilled in the lives of Jesus-followers. It is important to note that Paul was not alone in viewing things along these lines. Similar views were attributed to Jesus-followers/Christians by Tertullian, Lucian of Samosata, the Lukan evangelist, and (the author of the letter attributed to) James. Since all of these authors have already been considered for one reason or another, only brief overviews of the point are necessary here.

As we saw in chapter 7 above, in the late second century CE Tertullian imagined that, in the Jerusalem meeting of Gal 2:1-10, the apostles were deciding which parts of the scriptures of Israel should be apportioned to Christians as determinative of their own practice. Whereas the phrase "remember the poor" has generally been interpreted without reference to the scriptures of Israel (i.e., it was solely about a collection for Jerusalem followers of Jesus), Tertullian has the opposite impression. For him, the apostolic discussion was concerned wholly with the interpretation of scripture within communities of Jesus-followers, and this applies even to the phrase "remember the poor." We recall Tertullian's words in this regard:

> [The apostles' agreement] "to remember the poor" was in complete conformity with the law of the Creator, which cherished the poor and needy. It is thus certain that the question was one which simply regarded the law, while at the same time it is apparent what portion of the law it was convenient to have observed [*Marc.* 5.3].

Tertullian does not use the language that Paul uses in Galatians — i.e., of Jesus-followers fulfilling the whole law (ὁ πᾶς νόμος, 5:14) through generous self-giving to those in need. Instead, for Tertullian, remembering the poor is about fulfilling that part of scripture that pertains to Jesus-followers. But the net effect is much the same, and corresponds well with Paul's case in Galatians. In Tertullian's view, Paul and the Jerusalem leaders agreed (1) that the scriptural requirement of circumcision is not essential to the identity of Jesus-followers, and (2) that the scriptural requirement of caring for the needy is essential to the practice of Jesus-groups. Paul probably would not object to Tertullian's formulation of things, even if it is not quite how he put it in Galatians.[1]

As was shown in chapter 4 above, in the mid-second century CE the non-Christian rhetorician Lucian of Samosata held a view about Christian groups in which generosity was front and center. And if Tertullian imagined Christian generosity to be a matter pertaining to the interpretation of scripture, so too did Lucian. Lucian links Christian generosity to the Mosaic law in this way (*Peregr.* 13):

> The earnestness with which the people of this religion help one another in their need is incredible. They spare themselves nothing to this end. Apparently their first law-maker has put it into their heads that they all somehow ought to be regarded as brethren.

Critical here is Lucian's reference to the "first law-maker" of the Christians. To whom does this refer: Moses, or Jesus? Since the phrase implies the existence of a "second law-maker" for Christians, and since that latter designation would more likely apply to Jesus than to anyone else, the phrase "first law-maker" evidently is a reference to Moses. Whatever else Lucian may

---

1. Even if Paul did not express things in quite the same way that Tertullian later did, it is possible that Tertullian's view corresponds with how the Jerusalem apostles understood what they were doing in the Jerusalem meeting of Gal 2:1-10. This speculation gains some credibility if Gal 2:1-10 recounts the meeting described in Acts 15, and if Richard Bauckham is right in understanding the apostolic decision of Acts 15 as one that decided on the applicability of certain scripture passages over and above other scripture passages. See Richard Bauckham, "James and the Jerusalem Church," in R. Bauckham, ed., *The Book of Acts in Its Palestinian Setting* (vol. 4 of *The Book of Acts in Its First Century Setting*; Grand Rapids: Eerdmans, 1995), pp. 415-80. Although Bauckham's thesis prioritizes passages that have to do with "the alien in your midst" rather than "the poor," it might be that the Lukan author has rightly captured the general issue at stake in the meeting (i.e., discernment in prioritizing some scriptures over others).

know about Christians, he knows them to be generous, and he knows that this is in accord with their "first law-maker" Moses. Like Tertullian, Lucian's brief outline of Christian practice and conviction does not follow the precise contours of Paul's case in Galatians, but Paul may not have been too perturbed at the way in which those practices and convictions regarding care for the needy were later to be interpreted by Lucian.

A further parallel in this conjunction between generosity toward the needy and the scriptures of Israel is evident in one of the elaborations of Jesus' message in the Lukan Gospel. In the parable of the rich man and Lazarus (Luke 16:19-31), the rich man ends up in Hades, evidently for his characteristic neglect of the destitute at his doorstep, embodied by Lazarus. Then the rich man begs that Lazarus be allowed to warn the man's father and brothers — presumably to offer a warning about how one's situation in the afterlife is dependent on how one relates to the needy in this life. The answer that comes to the rich man is stark in its simplicity: "They have Moses and the prophets; they should listen to them. . . . If they do not listen to Moses and the prophets, neither will they be convinced even if someone rises from the dead" (Luke 16:29-31). Even if post-Easter interests have shaped the telling of the story, the Lukan evangelist nonetheless imagined the words to be in line with the spirit of Jesus' own teachings. And here, the Lukan Jesus establishes an interpretative lens through which the scriptures of Israel are to be read, and that lens involves care for the needy.[2] This is not a world away from the view Paul expressed in Galatians, in which self-giving care itself is depicted as embodying what the law was about.

If James is shown to be one of the primary figures behind the stipulation to "remember the poor," in the letter attributed to him in the New Testament he is also shown to be one who links care for the poor with the Mosaic law. On two occasions in James 1:22–2:17, the Jacobite author (whose text was considered already in §5.5 above) characterizes the "perfect law" as being intricately bound up with care for the needy. First in 1:22-27, where care for widows and orphans is equated with "religion that is pure and undefiled before God." People who act to care for the needy are presumed to

---

2. The Lukan and Matthean Gospels give independent indication that the historical Jesus highlighted scriptures in which the poor were prioritized, especially Isaiah 61. That Jesus employed this piece of scripture when interpreting his mission is a relatively secure piece of historical bedrock in Jesus research. As we saw in chapter 5 above, Jesus seems to have placed his own life work within the context of the Isaianic narrative of divine sovereignty against the evils of the world — one of the most pronounced of those evils being the harsh situation of poverty.

be those who look into the perfect law of liberty and will be blessed by Israel's deity.

The second instance is in 2:8-17 where, as in Gal 5:14 (and Rom 13:9), the motif "love your neighbor" from Lev 19:18 is used as the interpretative lens for understanding the essence of the law. The motif of neighborly love is expanded to destabilize preferential treatment for the rich and to endorse care for the needy. Precisely this same expansion is evident in Luke 10:25-37, where Lev 19:18 appears again when attention is given to what was "written in the law." In that Lukan account, the parable of the Samaritan is used to destabilize any notion of "neighbor" that fails to include those in need.[3]

In James 1:22–2:17, the scriptures of Israel are claimed to be the "law of liberty" for one of at least two possible reasons. First, when they are viewed through the lens of the sovereign deity's choosing of the poor of this world, those who look into them are thereby freed from having to observe the cultural codes of status acquisition and honor-capture that engulf this world. Or second, because when viewed aright, they sponsor generous action whereby the poor are "released" from the bondage of their situation (cf. Jesus' repetition of Isa 61:1-2 in Luke 4:18-19). So it is not wholly clear whether the freedom pertains to the one who offers care or the one who receives care, or both. But regardless of this nuancing, it is clear that the author of the Jacobite letter viewed care for the poor and needy as the surest sign that the perfect "law of freedom" was playing its rightful role among followers of Jesus. Where care for the needy is absent, the law is not rightly understood. Even if we imagine there to be a difference in the ways that Paul and the Jacobite author construct their theological discourse, there is nonetheless considerable overlap in the way that the Galatian and Jacobite letters depict the law in relation to care for those in need.[4]

Here, then, are four examples from the second half of the first century

---

3. I have argued that, in its pre-Lukan setting, the parable should be seen to feature not only the Samaritan but also the inn-keeper; see my "The Parable of the Samaritan and the Inn-Keeper (Luke 10:30-35): A Study in Character Rehabilitation," *Bib Int* 17 (2009): 422-47.

4. I think it likely that the Jacobite author was apprehensive about Paul's construal of faith in a passage like Romans 4, or at least about how Paul's construal of faith could be interpreted. That apprehension (which was not wholly unfounded, in light of the problems that Paul's gospel of freedom seems to have contributed to in Corinth) lies behind the argument of James 2. Although the point cannot be elaborated here, most striking is the way the two authors handle Gen 15. On this, see especially James D. G. Dunn, *Unity and Diversity in the New Testament* (London: SCM Press, 1977), p. 251: "James in effect refutes the Pauline exegesis of Gen. 15.6."

to the early third century CE, each of which shows some semblance to Paul's depiction of the law as properly interpreted in relation to caring for the needy. Whatever differences they might have, these four examples resonate with Paul's efforts in Galatians in their close association of the law of Israel and the practice of care for the needy by the followers of Jesus.

Dating the Origin of Paul's Collection

A3.1: Preliminary Observations

A3.2: The Date of Paul's Residency in Corinth

A3.3: The Date for the Composition of 1 Corinthians

A3.4: The Date of Paul's Conceptualization of the Collection

A3.1: Preliminary Observations

Dating the origin of Paul's conceptualization of the collection has not been controversial in Pauline scholarship. The reason for this lack of controversy is no doubt clear to the reader of this book: the overwhelming majority of scholars date its conception one way or another back to the Jerusalem meeting described by Paul in Galatians 2:1-10. That meeting, in which Paul and Barnabas met with James, Peter and John regarding "the truth of the gospel" (Gal 2:5), is commonly thought to have occurred in the late 40s CE. And Paul tells the Galatians that the Jerusalem leaders included in their deliberations the charge to "remember the poor" (2:10). It is virtually ubiquitous in Pauline scholarship to view this as a charge to "remember the *Jerusalem* poor." One way or another, then, the collection that Paul brings to Jerusalem in the year 58 CE or so is organically rooted in the Jerusalem meeting of the late 40s, with its stipulation to assist the Jerusalem communities.

For some, the lines of causality between Gal 2:10 and Paul's collection are fairly direct: the Jerusalem leadership expected a collection to be organized by Paul (and Barnabas), and so Paul organized that collection throughout the

50s CE. For others, the lines of causality are less direct, involving a three-stage process: (1) the Jerusalem leadership expected a collection (or a series of them) to be initiated *by Antiochene Christianity*, of which Paul and Barnabas were representatives; (2) when Paul broke away from Antiochene Jesus-groups (i.e., Gal 2:11-14, retold in Lukan terms in Acts 15:36-40), he was absolved of the stipulation placed on Antiochene Jesus-groups by the Jerusalem leadership; (3) later, despite not being tied to Antiochene Jesus-groups, Paul took personal responsibility for the stipulation once again, in a gesture beyond the call of duty. Although specifics vary in different reconstructions, for the majority of interpreters, the date for the origins of Paul's collection lie ultimately in the late 40s, when the Jerusalem leaders commanded him (and others) to send money to the poor of Jerusalem.

Since I do not share this view of things, the onus is on me to give renewed consideration to the temporal origins of Paul's conceptualization of the collection. If the term "the poor" in Gal 2:10 contains no reference to Jerusalem, the dating of the conception of Paul's collection needs to be given fresh consideration.

With that said, I do not deny that the apostolic stipulation played a role in Paul's thinking about the collection. I have already noted how Paul might have seen that stipulation as a general principle and his own collection as a particular application of that principle. But I have also noted that Paul's own efforts on behalf of the poor were not set in motion merely as a consequence of the Jerusalem meeting described in Gal 2:1-10. As Paul suggests in 2:10b, he had already been committed to inspiring care for the poor among urban Jesus-groups long before that meeting — a claim that we should not doubt, especially in view of the evidence noted in chapter 6 above. Consequently, even if "remember the poor" is a principle affirmed by Paul, it is one that does not originate for him in the meeting with the Jerusalem apostles in the late 40s; instead, it predates that meeting by any number of years, perhaps from the very beginning of his apostolic ministry (in conformity to the practices of the earliest followers of Jesus in Jerusalem).

Recognizing this only serves to put more firmly on the table the question of when Paul first conceptualized his collection for the Jerusalem poor. And in this regard, Paul's relationship with the followers of Jesus in Corinth holds the key to establishing a date that is more reliable than the traditional one. In order to arrive at a date for the origins of Paul's conceptualization of his collection, the dates for other key points need initially to be established, including (1) the date of Paul's residency in Corinth, and (2) the date for the composition of 1 Corinthians.

A3.2: The Date of Paul's Residency in Corinth

Acts 18:11 locates Paul in Corinth for an eighteen-month period. Towards the end of that period, according to Lukan reconstruction, Paul stood trial before the local governor Gallio (Acts 18:12-17). If this is historically reliable, it enables us to establish a fairly secure date for Paul's Corinthian residency, since it is likely that Gallio was appointed to the gubernatorial office on 1 July in the year 51. This would put Paul's trial before Gallio into the second half of 51 CE.

Moreover, Acts 18:18-22 recounts a sea journey taken by Paul to Jerusalem not long after his Corinthian trial. Since this journey needed to take place prior to winter months when the sea was rough and dangerous, it needed to be completed by October 51. Paul's trial before Gallio in Corinth, then, must have taken place sometime between July and September 51.[1] Working backwards by eighteen months from the mid to late summer of 51, Paul's arrival in Corinth should be dated to the early months of 50 CE.

Two other pieces of Lukan reconstruction fit nicely with this dating of Paul's residence with Corinthian Jesus-groups from between early 50 to mid 51 CE. First, Acts 16–17 places Paul in Galatia and Macedonia after the "apostolic council," itself having taken place most likely in 48 CE. So Paul's time in Galatia and Macedonia seems to have been concentrated in the years 48-49, just prior to his arrival in Corinth, recounted in Acts 18:1.

Second, Acts 18:2 recounts that Paul met Aquila and Priscilla in Corinth after they had been included in the numbers of Jews deported from Rome. This deportation is usually dated to the year 49, in which case Aquila and Priscilla seem to have left Rome in 49 and settled (temporarily) in Corinth, where Paul met them when he arrived in the early months of 50.

A3.3: The Date for the Composition of 1 Corinthians

Because Paul's first extant reference to the collection appears in 1 Corinthians 16, the date of that letter needs to be established. Paul indicates in 1 Cor 16:8 that he writes 1 Corinthians from Ephesus. Consequently it is important to fix the dating of his time in Ephesus in order to set temporal limits on the writing of this, and other, Corinthian correspondences.

---

1. Acts 18:18 speaks of Paul staying in Corinth for "many days" after his trial before Gallio, which also needs to be fitted in between the time of Gallio's appointment in July and the sea-voyage to Judea in the autumn.

Paul's departure from Corinth in July/August 51 places the writing of his Corinthians letters after that date. Acts 18:18-22 has Paul sailing from Corinth to Caesarea (and then going to Jerusalem, although this leg of the journey is often disputed) in what was probably the autumn of 51, and then after "some time" going through Galatia and Phrygia (18:23) until he arrives in Ephesus (Acts 19:1). This would have him arriving in Ephesus probably in late summer or early autumn of 52.

Acts lists Paul's "public" ministry in Ephesus first in relation to a three-month initial period (Acts 19:8) and then in relation to a two-year period (Acts 19:10). It is not wholly clear whether the two-year period followed on from the initial three months of 19:8 or included that initial period. In a (Lukan) speech that falls late in his public career, Paul recounts to Ephesian Jesus-followers that he had stayed in Ephesus for "three years" (Acts 20:31); in the ancient world, half years were sometimes rounded up, so the actual time is likely to have been less than three years, but we cannot tell how much less. Nonetheless, even if we date Paul's arrival in Ephesus to late 52, Paul is likely to have been based there until early 55 at least. It is within this period of time (i.e., late 52 to early 55) that Paul must have written 1 Corinthians.

In 1 Cor 16:8 Paul speaks of wanting to be in Ephesus "until Pentecost" in the spring. This reference to Pentecost probably pertains to the years 54 or 55, with scholars divided fairly evenly in their opinions on the date. I tend towards the date of 54 for the composition of 1 Corinthians, with Paul having written this letter prior to the spring of that year. But it is possible that the Pentecost in view is that of 55, putting the date of 1 Corinthians to the early months of 55. For our purposes, it needs simply to be noted that either reconstruction supports the argument presented below (§A3.4) regarding the dating of Paul's interests in the collection (with the main point of that section being strengthened further if 1 Corinthians was composed in 55).

A3.4: The Date of Paul's Conceptualization of the Collection

Before the writing of what we know as 1 Corinthians, Paul wrote an earlier letter to the Corinthians, which he refers to in 1 Cor 5:9 (the "previous letter"). If 1 Corinthians dates to early 54, then this previous letter would have been delivered in 53, perhaps mid to late 53. In it Paul instructed the Corinthian Jesus-followers that they should separate themselves from others within their communities who are engaging in sexually immoral behavior.

After sending this "previous letter" to the Corinthians, Paul received a delegation of "Chloe's people," who informed Paul about a rupture in the social fabric of Corinthian Jesus-groups, brought about by allegiances to different leaders of the Jesus-movement.[2] About the same time,[3] Paul received a letter from some other Corinthian Jesus-followers, carried probably by Stephanas, Fortunatus and Achaicus (1 Cor 16:17). This letter requested advice about at least four matters: (1) sexual conduct,[4] (2) meals, worship and food,[5] (3) heavenly speech,[6] and (4) the collection.[7] On the basis of Paul's advice about the collection in 1 Corinthians 16, we can conclude that the collection had not been a long-standing concern by the time he wrote 1 Corinthians. If the collection had been on Paul's agenda during the 18 months that he spent in Corinth during 50-51 CE, for instance, the rudimentary advice of 1 Cor 16:1-4 might well have been prefaced with "as I instructed you when I was with you." But there is no indication in 1 Cor 16:1-4 that the collection has been a long-standing interest of Paul's. Evidently the Corinthians knew nothing about the collection from Paul's residency in Corinth from 50-51 CE.

It is possible that both 1 Corinthians and (the various parts of) 2 Corinthians (i.e., 2 Cor 10–13 and 2 Cor 1–9) are to be dated to the same year (i.e., 54 CE).[8] In this reconstruction, when he mentions in 2 Cor 8:10 that the Corinthi-

---

2. Paul deals with this in 1 Cor 1–4.

3. Or possibly while writing "1 Corinthians" in response to the information from Chloe's people; for this view, see Martin de Boer, "The Composition of 1 Corinthians," *NTS* 40 (1994): 229-245.

4. Paul deals with this in 1 Cor 7 (περὶ δὲ ὧν ἐγράψατε, 7:1; περὶ δέ, 7:25).

5. Paul deals with this in 1 Cor 8–10 (περὶ δέ, 8:1).

6. Paul deals with this in 1 Cor 12–14 (περὶ δέ, 12:1).

7. Paul deals with this in 1 Cor 16:1-4 (περὶ δέ, 16:1). It is unclear whether the issues dealt with in 1 Cor 5–6 and 15 were brought to Paul by "Chloe's people" or by Stephanas and his associates. Jerome Murphy-O'Connor comes to the same conclusion, but for different reasons. He dates the Jerusalem meeting to 51 CE (after an earlier one from the mid-40s), after Paul's residency in Corinth. So he writes (*Paul: A Critical Life* [Oxford: Oxford University Press, 1996], p. 22): "Paul did not preach the collection in Corinth during his founding visit. The only explanation is that it had not yet been decided at the Jerusalem Conference." The dating of the Jerusalem meeting is more likely to have been 48 CE (possibly even 47) rather than 51 CE, however; Paul's "three years" and "fourteen years" (Gal 1:18; 2:1) after his "conversion" of 32 CE (possibly even 31) are likely to be rounded-up figures (representing 2-plus and 13-plus years), which puts Paul's arrival in Corinth (in 50 CE) after the Jerusalem meeting rather than before it. (Notice that Murphy-O'Connor says of the "three years" of Acts 20:31 that it "is a round figure, and therefore suspect" [p. 29]; the same reasoning should be applied to the years described in Gal 1–2.)

8. Although nothing much rides on the matter for purposes of this book, I tend towards the view that 2 Cor 1–9 and 10–13 are two separate letters, with 10-13 having been writ-

ans began their support of his collection "a year ago" (ἀπὸ πέρυσι), we can locate Corinthian support to the year 53 CE, if we date those letters to 54 CE. This would then coincide with the delivery of Paul's "previous letter" to the Corinthians mentioned in 1 Cor 5:9. Upon delivery of that non-extant letter, either its contents or the letter carrier made reference to Paul's collection efforts.[9] Some Corinthians then sent a query to Paul regarding how he envisioned the money being gathered, with his response being recorded in 1 Cor 16:1-4.[10]

Alternatively, while 1 Corinthians and 2 Corinthians 10–13 should be dated to 54 CE (and written from Ephesus), 2 Corinthians 1–9 might best be dated to 55 CE (and written from Macedonia).[11] In this reconstruction, when

---

ten prior to 2 Cor 1–9 and itself being the "severe" or "painful" letter mentioned in 2 Cor 2:3-4, 9; 7:8, 12. For defenses of this view, see Francis Watson, "2 Cor. x–xiii and Paul's Painful Letter to the Corinthians," *JTS* 35 (1984): 324-46; Charles H. Talbert, *Reading Corinthians* (London: SPCK, 1987), pp. xviii-xxi; David G. Horrell, *The Social Ethos of the Corinthian Correspondence: Interests and Ideology from 1 Corinthians to 1 Clement* (Edinburgh: T&T Clark, 1996), pp. 296-312.

9. The letter that Titus delivered (mentioned in 2 Cor 8:6) is more likely to be this previous letter than the "severe letter" (probably 2 Cor 10–13, which Titus also delivered).

10. John C. Hurd (*The Origins of 1 Corinthians* [London: SPCK, 1965], pp. 73-74) argues that the initial instructions about the collection are evident only in 1 Cor 16. But Paul's comments in 1 Cor 16:1-4 suggest otherwise, implying that the Corinthians have already been enlisted in the collection initiative (or that Paul had intended to enlist them at that point, even if it took the instructions of 1 Cor 16 to get them moving with it) and that they only require some procedural instructions. The rationale for the collection initiative must have already been laid by Paul on an earlier occasion — i.e., the "previous letter" of 1 Cor 5:9.

11. Nicholas H. Taylor's interesting six-letter reconstruction of Paul's correspondence with Corinth during this period ("The Composition and Chronology of Second Corinthians," *JSNT* 44 [1991]: 67-87) places most parts of 2 Cor in the year 54 CE, with a few parts of it dating from 55 CE. I imagine 2 Cor to be comprised of only two separate letters. If they weren't composed in the same calendar year (i.e., 54), then 2 Cor 10–13 (= the "painful letter"?) was most likely written from Ephesus after Paul's painful visit to Corinth in 54, and 2 Cor 1–9 was written from Macedonia in 55, while Paul was waiting to hear news about the Corinthians from Titus (7:5-7). Paul's expressions of high regard for the Macedonians in 2 Cor 8–9 would then arise out of this context, with the Macedonians being on hand to hear them.

Hans Dieter Betz (*2 Corinthians 8 and 9: A Commentary on Two Administrative Letters of the Apostle Paul* [Philadelphia: Fortress Press, 1985], pp. 3-35) offers a constructive history of partition theories. One of the most interesting of recent theories is the five-letter partition theory of Margaret M. Mitchell, "The Corinthian Correspondence and the Birth of Pauline Hermeneutics," in T. J. Burke and J. K. Elliott, eds., *Paul and the Corinthians: Studies on a Community in Conflict* (Leiden: Brill, 2003), pp. 17-53; Mitchell, "Paul's Letters to Corinth: The Interpretive Intertwining of Literary and Historical Reconstruction," in Daniel N. Schowalter and Steven J. Friesen, eds., *Urban Religion in Roman Corinth* (Cambridge, MA: Harvard University Press, 2005), pp. 307-38.

speaking of the Corinthians' support for the collection starting as of "a year ago" (ἀπὸ πέρυσι) in 2 Cor 8:10, we would need to imagine that he is referring to the time when he assumed them to take initiatives in earnest. This might have resulted from his advice of 1 Cor 16:1-4 — itself a rudimentary elaboration of instructions sent to the Corinthians in 53 CE and reinforced in what we call 1 Corinthians in 54 CE; or it might have resulted in the wake of the painful letter (2 Cor 10–13) and Titus's involvement in restoring the Corinthians' loyalty to Paul when delivering that letter.

In any of these scenarios, the earliest we can possibly date the Corinthian involvement in Paul's collection efforts is the year 53 CE, and even then, a full-hearted dedication to Paul's collection might have taken root in Corinth only in the year 54 CE. Since Paul was likely to have tried to get the Corinthians on board at a relatively early stage after devising the collection (in view of his strong and recent links to their communities), it would be hard to imagine Paul's collection efforts pre-dating 53 CE.

Bibliography

Abramenko, A. *Die munizipale Mittelschicht im kaiserzeitlichen Italien: Zu einem neuen Verständnis von Sevirat und Augustalität*. Frankfurt: Peter Lang, 1993.

Alcock, S. E. "The Eastern Mediterranean." In *The Cambridge Economic History of the Graeco-Roman World*, edited by W. Scheidel, I. Morris, and R. Saller, pp. 671-97. Cambridge: Cambridge University Press, 2007.

Alexander, Loveday. "Ancient Book Production and the Circulation of the Gospels." In *The Gospels for All Christians: Rethinking the Gospel Audiences*, edited by Richard Bauckham, pp. 71-111. Grand Rapids: Eerdmans, 1998.

———. *The Preface to Luke's Gospel: Literary Convention and Social Context in Luke 1.1-4*. Cambridge: Cambridge University Press, 1993.

Alföldy, Geza. *Die römische Sozialgeschichte*. 3rd ed. Wiesbaden: Steiner Franz Verlag, 1986.

Andreau, Jean. "Twenty Years after Moses I. Finley's *The Ancient Economy*." In *The Ancient Economy*, edited by Walter Scheidel and Sitta von Reden, pp. 33-49. Edinburgh: Edinburgh University Press, 2002.

Arrow, Kenneth. "Gifts and Exchanges." *Philosophy & Public Affairs* 1 (1972): 343-62.

Arterbury, Andrew. *Entertaining Angels: Early Christian Hospitality in Its Mediterranean Setting*. Sheffield: Sheffield Phoenix Press, 2005.

Ascough, Richard S. *Lydia: Paul's Cosmopolitan Hostess*. Collegeville, MN: Liturgical Press, 2009.

———. "The Thessalonian Christian Community as a Professional Voluntary Association." *JBL* 119 (2000): 311-28.

———. "Voluntary Associations and the Formation of Pauline Christian Communities: Overcoming Objections." In *Vereine, Synagogen und Gemeinden im kaiserzeitlichen Kleinasien*, edited by A. Gutsfeld and D.-A. Koch, pp. 149-83. Tübingen: Mohr Siebeck, 2006.

———. *What Are They Saying about the Formation of Pauline Churches?* Mahwah, NJ: Paulist Press, 1998.

Ausbüttel, F. M. *Untersuchungen zu den Vereinen im Westen des römischen Reiches.* Kallmünz: Lassleben, 1982.

Ayerst, D., and A. S. T. Fischer. *Records of Christianity,* Volume I: *The Church in the Roman Empire.* Oxford: Basil Blackwell, 1971.

Bagnall, R. S. "Landholding in Late Roman Egypt: The Distribution of Wealth." *JRS* 82 (1992): 128-49.

Balch, David L. "Paul, Families and Households." In *Paul in the Greco-Roman World,* edited by J. Paul Sampley, pp. 258-92. Harrisburg: Trinity Press International, 2003.

Barclay, John M. G. "'Do We Undermine the Law?': A Study of Romans 14.1–15.6." In *Paul and the Mosaic Law,* edited by James D. G. Dunn, pp. 287-308. Tübingen: Mohr Siebeck, 1996.

———. "Grace and the Transformation of Agency in Christ." In *Redefining First-Century Jewish and Christian Identities,* edited by Fabian E. Udoh with Susannah Heschel, Mark Chancey and Gregory Tatum, pp. 372-89. Notre Dame: University of Notre Dame Press, 2008.

———. *Jews in the Mediterranean Diaspora from Alexander to Trajan (323 BCE–117 CE).* Edinburgh: T&T Clark, 1996.

———. "Money and Meetings: Group Formation among Diaspora Jews and Early Christians." In *Vereine, Synagogen und Gemeinden im kaiserzeitlichen Kleinasien,* edited by A. Gutsfeld and D.-A. Koch, pp. 113-27. Tübingen: Mohr Siebeck, 2006.

———. "Poverty in Pauline Studies: A Response to Steven Friesen." *JSNT* 26 (2004): 363-66.

———. "Thessalonica and Corinth: Social Contrasts in Pauline Christianity." *JSNT* 47 (1992): 49-74.

Barnett, Paul. *Paul: Missionary of Jesus.* Grand Rapids: Eerdmans, 2008.

Barrett, C. K. *Paul: An Introduction to His Thought.* London: Geoffrey Chapman, 1994.

Bartlet, V. "'Only Let Us Be Mindful of the Poor': Gal. 2.10." *The Expositor* 9 (1899): 218-55.

Barton, Carlin A. *Roman Honor: The Fire in the Bones.* Berkeley: University of California, 2001.

Bauckham, Richard J. "James and the Jerusalem Church." In *The Book of Acts in Its Palestinian Setting,* edited by Richard Bauckham, pp. 415-80. Vol. 4 of *The Book of Acts in Its First Century Setting.* Grand Rapids: Eerdmans, 1995.

———. "The Origin of the Ebionites." In *The Image of the Judaeo-Christians in Ancient Jewish and Christian Literature,* edited by Peter J. Tomson and Doris Lambers-Petry, pp. 162-81. Tübingen: Mohr Siebeck, 2003.

Beale, Greg K. *1-2 Thessalonians.* Downers Grove: InterVarsity Press, 2003.

Beard, Mary. *Pompeii: The Life of a Roman Town.* London: Profile Books, 2008.

Becker, Jurgen. "Paul and His Churches." In *Christian Beginnings,* edited by Jurgen Becker, pp. 132-210. Louisville: Westminster John Knox Press, 1993.

Beker, J. C. *Paul the Apostle: The Triumph of God in Life and Thought.* Philadelphia: Fortress, 1980.

Berger, K. "Almosen für Israel: Zum historischen Kontext der paulinischen Kollekte." *NTS* 23 (1976-77): 180-204.

Bernheim, P.-A. *James, Brother of Jesus.* London: SCM Press, 1997.

Berquist, Jon L. *Judaism in Persia's Shadow: A Social and Historical Approach.* Minneapolis: Fortress Press, 1995.

Best, Ernest. *Ephesians.* Edinburgh: T&T Clark, 1998.

Betz, Hans Dieter. *2 Corinthians 8 and 9: A Commentary on Two Administrative Letters of the Apostle Paul.* Philadelphia: Fortress Press, 1985.

————. *Galatians.* Philadelphia: Fortress, 1979.

Boatwright, Mary T. *Hadrian and the Cities of the Roman Empire.* Princeton: Princeton University Press, 2000.

Boatwright, Mary T., Daniel J. Gargola and Richard J. A. Talbert. *The Romans, From Village to Empire.* Oxford: Oxford University Press, 2004.

Boer, Martin de. "The Composition of 1 Corinthians." *NTS* 40 (1994): 229-45.

Bolchazy, Ladislaus J. *Hospitality in Antiquity: Livy's Concept of Its Humanizing Force.* Chicago: Ares, 1977.

Bolkestein, H. *Wohltätigkeit und Armenpflege im vorchristlichen Altertum.* Utrecht: A. Oosthoek Verlag, 1939.

Borg, Marcus, and John Dominic Crossan. *The First Paul: Reclaiming the Radical Visionary behind the Church's Conservative Icon.* London: SPCK, 2009.

Bovon, F. *Das Evangelium nach Lukas 1.* Zürich: Benziger Verlag, 1989.

Bremen, R. van. "Women and Wealth." In *Images of Women in Antiquity,* edited by A. Cameron and A. Kuhrt, pp. 223-42. Detroit: Wayne State University Press, 1983.

Bremner, Robert H. "Jewish, Christian and Islamic Texts on Giving and Charity." In *Giving: Charity and Philanthropy in History,* edited by Robert H. Bremner, pp. 11-20. London: Transaction Publishers, 1994.

Brown, Peter. *Poverty and Leadership in the Later Roman Empire.* Hanover, NH: University Press of New England, 2002.

Bruce, F. F. *The Epistle to the Galatians: A Commentary on the Greek Text.* Grand Rapids: Eerdmans, 1982.

Brunt, P. A. *Italian Manpower, 225 BC–AD 14.* London: Oxford University Press, 1971.

Buel, Denise Kimber. "When Both Donors and Recipients Are Poor." In *Wealth and Poverty in Early Church and Society,* edited by Susan R. Holman, pp. 37-47. Grand Rapids: Baker Academic Press, 2008.

Burton, Ernest de Witt. *A Critical and Exegetical Commentary on the Epistle to the Galatians.* Edinburgh: T&T Clark, 1921.

Cadbury, Henry. "Erastus of Corinth." *JBL* 50 (1931): 42-58.

Campbell, Douglas A. *The Deliverance of God: An Apocalyptic Rereading of Justification in Paul.* Grand Rapids: Eerdmans, 2009.

Campbell, Joan Cecelia. *Phoebe: Patron and Emissary.* Collegeville: The Liturgical Press, 2009.

Capper, Brian. "Jesus, Virtuoso Religion, and the Community of Goods." In *Engaging Economics: New Testament Scenarios and Early Christian Reception,* edited by Bruce W. Longenecker and Kelly Liebengood, pp. 60-80. Grand Rapids: Eerdmans, 2009.

Carandini, A. "Italian Wine and African Oil: Commerce in a World Empire." In *The Birth of Europe: Archeology and Social Development in the First Millenium AD,* edited by K. Randsborg, pp. 16-24. Rome: L'Erma di Bretschneider, 1989.

Carney, Thomas Francis. *The Shape of the Past: Models and Antiquity.* Lawrence, KA: Coronado Press, 1975.

Carrie, J. "Les distributions alimentaires dans les cités de l'Empire romain tardif." In *Demografia, Sistemi Agrari, Regimi Alimentari nel Mondo Antico,* edited by D. Vera, pp. 273-88. Bari: Edipuglia, 1999.

Carter, Warren. *Matthew and the Margins: A Socio-Political and Religious Reading.* Sheffield: Sheffield Academic Press, 2000.

Casson, L. *Travel in the Ancient World.* London: Allen and Unwin, 1974.

Catchpole, David R. "Paul, James and the Apostolic Decree." *NTS* 23 (1977): 428-44.

Chadwick, H. *The Early Church.* Harmondsworth: Penguin, 1967.

Chilton, Bruce. *Rabbi Paul: An Intellectual Biography.* New York: Doubleday, 2004.

Christ, K. "Grundfragen der römischen Sozialstruktur." In *Studien zur Sozialgeschichte,* edited by W. Eck, H. Galsterer and H. Wolff, pp. 197-228. Cologne: Böhlau, 1980.

Clark, Gillian. *Christianity and Roman Society.* Cambridge: Cambridge University Press, 2004.

Collins, John J. *The Sibylline Oracles of Egyptian Judaism.* Missoula: Scholars Press, 1972/1974.

Collins, Raymond. *1 Corinthians.* Collegeville: Liturgical Press, 1999.

Cramer, John Anthony, ed. *Catenae in Sancti Pauli Epistolas ad Corinthios.* Vol. 5 of *Catenae Graecorum Patrum in Novum Testamentum,* edited by John Anthony Cramer. Oxford: E Typographeo Academico, 1841. Reprint, Hildesheim: Georg Olms, 1967.

Critchlow, Donald T., and Charles H. Parker, eds. *With Us Always: A History of Private Charity and Public Welfare.* Oxford: Rowman & Littlefield Publishers, 1998.

Crossan, John Dominic. *The Birth of Christianity.* Edinburgh: T&T Clark, 1998.

———. *The Historical Jesus: The Life of a Mediterranean Jewish Peasant.* San Francisco: HarperSanFrancisco, 1991.

———. *Jesus: A Revolutionary Biography.* San Francisco: HarperSanFrancisco, 1994.

Crossan, John Dominic, and J. Reed. *In Search of Paul: How Jesus's Apostle Opposed Rome's Empire with God's Kingdom.* San Francisco: HarperSanFrancisco, 2004.

Dahl, Nils. *Studies in Paul.* Minneapolis: Fortress, 1977.

Danker, Frederick. "Paul's Debt to the *De Corona* of Demosthenes: A Study of Rhetorical Techniques in Second Corinthians." In *Persuasive Artistry: Studies in New Testament Rhetoric in Honor of George A. Kennedy,* edited by Duane F. Watson, pp. 262-80. Sheffield: Sheffield Academic Press, 1991.

D'Arms, John H. *Commerce: Social Standing in Ancient Rome.* Cambridge, MA: Harvard University Press, 1981.

———. "Memory, Money, and Status at Misenum: Three New Inscriptions and the Collegium of the Augustales." *JRS* 90 (2000): 126-44.

———. "M. I. Rostovtzeff and M. I. Finley: The Status of Traders in the Roman World." In *Ancient and Modern: Essays in Honor of Gerald F. Else,* edited by John H. D'Arms and J. W. Eadie, pp. 157-79. Ann Arbor: University of Michigan Press, 1977.

Davids, Peter H. "The Test of Wealth." In *The Missions of James, Peter, and Paul: Tensions in Early Christianity,* edited by Bruce Chilton and Craig Evans, pp. 355-84. Leiden: Brill, 2005.

Davis, Ellen F. *Scripture, Culture, and Agriculture: An Agrarian Reading of the Bible.* Cambridge: Cambridge University Press, 2009.

Degenhardt, Hans-Joachim. *Lukas, Evangelist der Armen.* Stuttgart: Verlag Katholisches Bibelwerk, 1983.

Deissmann, G. A. *Light from the Ancient East: The New Testament Illustrated by Recently Discovered Texts of the Graeco-Roman World.* London: Hodder & Stoughton, 1910.

———. *Paul: A Study in Social and Religious History.* 1925. Reprint, New York: Harper & Brothers, 1957.

Descat, R. "*L'économie antique* et la cité grecque." *Annales* 50 (1995): 961-89.

Dickey, S. "Some Economic and Social Conditions of Asia Minor Affecting the Expansion of Christianity." In *Studies in Early Christianity,* edited by S. J. Case, pp. 393-416. New York: Century, 1928.

Dignas, Beate. *Economy of the Sacred in Hellenistic and Roman Asia Minor.* Oxford: Oxford University Press, 2002.

Domeris, William. *Touching the Heart of God.* London: T&T Clark, 2007.

Dover, Kenneth. *Greek Popular Morality in the Time of Plato and Aristotle.* Indianapolis: Hackett Publishing Company, 1994.

Downs, David J. "Is God Paul's Patron? The Economy of Patronage in Pauline Theology." In *Engaging Economics: New Testament Scenarios and Early Christian Reception,* edited by Bruce W. Longenecker and Kelly Liebengood, pp. 129-56. Grand Rapids: Eerdmans, 2009.

———. *The Offering of the Gentiles.* Tübingen: Mohr Siebeck, 2008.

———. "Paul's Collection and the Book of Acts Revisited." *NTS* 52 (2006): 50-70.

Drinkwater, J. F. "The Gallo-Roman Woolen Industry and the Great Debate: The Igel Column Revisited." In *Economies Beyond Agriculture in the Classical World,* edited by D. J. Mattingly and J. Salmon, pp. 279-308. London: Routledge, 2001.

Duncan Jones, R. *The Economy of the Roman Empire: Quantitative Studies.* 2nd ed. Cambridge: Cambridge University Press, 1982.

———. "Human Numbers in Towns and Town-Organisations of the Roman Empire: The Evidence of Gifts." *Historia* 13 (1964): 199-208.

———. "Some Configurations of Landholding in the Roman Empire." In *Studies in Roman Property,* edited by M. I. Finley, pp. 7-33. Cambridge: Cambridge University Press, 1976.

———. *Structure and Scale in the Roman Economy.* Cambridge: Cambridge University Press, 1990.

Dunn, James D. G. *Beginning from Jerusalem: Christianity in the Making.* Vol. 2. Grand Rapids: Eerdmans, 2009.

———. *The Epistles to the Colossians and to Philemon.* Grand Rapids: Eerdmans, 1996.

———. *The Epistle to the Galatians.* London: A&C Black, 1993.

———. *Jesus and the Spirit.* London: SCM Press, 1975.

———. *Jesus Remembered: Christianity in the Making.* Vol. 1. Grand Rapids: Eerdmans, 2003.

———. *Romans.* 2 vols. Dallas: Word Publishers, 1988.

———. *The Theology of Paul the Apostle.* Grand Rapids: Eerdmans, 1998.

———. *Unity and Diversity in the New Testament.* London: SCM Press, 1977.

Dutch, Robert S. *The Educated Elite in 1 Corinthians: Education and Community Conflict in Graeco-Roman Context.* London: T&T Clark, 2005.

Duthoy, R. "La fonction sociale de l'augustalité." *Epigraphica* 36 (1974): 134-54.

Easterly, William. *The White Man's Burden: Why the West's Efforts to Aid the Rest Have Done So Much Ill and So Little Good.* Oxford: Oxford Univeristy Press, 2007.

Edelstein, Emma J., and Ludwig Edelstein. *Asclepius: Collection and Interpretation of the Testimonies.* Baltimore: Johns Hopkins University Press, 1998.

Edmondson, J. "Cities and Urban Life in the Western Provinces of the Roman Empire, 30 BCE–250 CE." In *A Companion to the Roman Empire,* edited by David S. Potter, pp. 250-80. Oxford: Blackwell Publishing, 2006.

Eisenbaum, Pamela. *Paul Was Not a Christian: The Original Message of a Misunderstood Apostle.* New York: HarperOne, 2009.

Elliott, J. K. *The Apocryphal New Testament: A Collection of Apocryphal Christian Literature in an English Translation.* Oxford: Clarendon Press, 1993.

Elliott, Neil. *Liberating Paul: The Justice of God and the Politics of the Apostle.* Maryknoll, NY: Orbis Books, 1994. Reprint, Sheffield: Sheffield Academic Press, 1995.

Elliott, S. *Cutting Too Close for Comfort: Paul's Letter to the Galatians in Its Anatolian Cultic Context.* London: T&T Clark, 2003.

Ellis, E. Earle. *Pauline Theology: Ministry and Society.* Grand Rapids: Eerdmans, 1989.

Elmer, Ian J. *Paul, Jerusalem and the Judaisers: The Galatian Crisis in Its Broadest Historical Context.* Tübingen: Mohr Siebeck, 2009.

Endsjo, Dag Oistein. *Greek Resurrection Beliefs and the Success of Christianity.* New York: Palgrave Macmillan, 2009.

Evans, Craig A. "Context, Family and Formation." In *The Cambridge Companion to Jesus,* edited by Markus Bockmuehl, pp. 11-24. Cambridge: Cambridge University Press, 2001.

Evans, Jane DeRose. *The Coins and the Hellenistic, Roman and Byzantine Economy of Palestine.* Boston: American Schools of Oriental Research, 2006.

Finley, Moses I. *The Ancient Economy.* London: Chatto & Windus, 1975.

———. "Technical Innovation and Economic Progress in the Ancient World." *Economic History Review* 18 (1965): 29-45.

Finn, Richard. *Almsgiving in the Later Roman Empire: Christian Promotion and Practice, 313-450.* Oxford: Oxford University Press, 2006.

Fitzmyer, Joseph A. *The Letter to Philemon.* New York: Doubleday, 2000.

Fowl, S. "Know Your Context: Giving and Receiving Money in Philippians." *Int* 56 (2002): 45-58.

Fox, R. Lane. *Pagans and Christians.* London: Viking, 1986.

Foxhall, L. "The Dependent Tenant: Land Leasing and Labour in Italy and Greece." *JRS* 80 (1990): 97-114.

Frank, Robert H. *Luxury Fever: Money and Happiness in an Era of Excess.* Princeton: Princeton University Press, 1999.

Fredriksen, M. W. "Theory, Evidence and the Ancient Economy." *JRS* 65 (1975): 164-71.

Freedman, Charles. *Egypt, Greece and Rome: Civilizations of the Ancient Mediterranean.* Oxford: Oxford University Press, 2004.

Friesen, Steven J. "Injustice or God's Will: Early Christian Explanations of Poverty." In

Wealth and Poverty in Early Church and Society, edited by Susan R. Holman, pp. 17-36. Grand Rapids: Baker Academic, 2008.

———. "Injustice or God's Will: Explanations of Poverty in Proto-Christian Communities." In *Christian Origins,* edited by Richard A. Horsley, pp. 240-60. Vol. 1 of *A People's History of Christianity.* Minneapolis: Fortress, 2005.

———. "Poverty in Pauline Studies: Beyond the So-called New Consensus." *JSNT* 26 (2004): 323-61.

———. "Prospects for a Demography of the Pauline Mission: Corinth among the Churches." In *Urban Religion in Roman Corinth,* edited by Daniel N. Schowalter and Steven J. Friesen, pp. 351-70. Cambridge, MA: Harvard University Press, 2005.

———. *Twice Neokoros: Ephesus, Asia and the Cult of the Flavian Imperial Family.* Leiden: Brill, 1993.

———. "The Wrong Erastus: Ideology, Archaeology, and Exegesis." In *Corinth in Context: Comparative Studies in Religion and Society,* edited by Steven J. Friesen, Daniel N. Schowalter, and James Walters. Leiden: Brill, forthcoming.

Fung, Ronald Y. K. *The Epistle to the Galatians.* Grand Rapids: Eerdmans, 1988.

Furnish, Victor Paul. *II Corinthians.* Garden City: Doubleday Press, 1984.

———. "The Jesus-Paul Debate: From Baur to Bultmann." In *Paul and Jesus: Collected Essays,* edited by A. J. M. Wedderburn, pp. 17-50. Sheffield: Sheffield Academic Press, 1989.

———. *The Moral Teaching of Paul.* Nashville: Abingdon, 1979.

Gager, J. G. *Kingdom and Community: The Social World of Early Christianity.* Englewood Cliffs: Prentice-Hall, 1975.

———. Review of *Social Aspects of Early Christianity,* by Abraham Malherbe. *Religious Studies Review* 5 (1979): 174-80.

———. "Shall We Marry Our Enemies?" *Int* 36 (1982): 256-65.

Garland, David E. *Reading Matthew: A Literary and Theological Commentary on the First Gospel.* London: SPCK, 1993.

Garnsey, Peter D. A. *Famine and Food Supply in the Graeco-Roman World: Responses to Risk and Crisis.* Cambridge: Cambridge University Press, 1988.

———. "Grain for Rome." In *Trade in the Ancient Economy,* edited by P. D. A. Garnsey, K. Hopkins and C. R. Whittaker, pp. 118-30. London: Chatto & Windus, 1983.

———. "Legal Privilege in the Roman Empire." *Past and Present* 41 (1968): 3-24.

Garnsey, Peter D. A., and Caroline Humfress. *The Evolution of the Late Antique World.* Cambridge: Orchard Academic, 2001.

Garnsey, Peter D. A., and Richard P. Saller. *The Roman Empire: Economy, Society and Culture.* London: Duckworth, 1987.

Garnsey, Peter D. A., and Greg Woolf. "Patronage of the Rural Poor in the Roman World." In *Patronage in Ancient Society,* edited by Andrew Wallace-Hadrill, pp. 153-70. London: Routledge, 1989.

Garrison, Roman. *Redemptive Almsgiving in Early Christianity.* Sheffield: Sheffield Academic Press, 1993.

Gaston, Lloyd. "Paul and Jerusalem." In *From Jesus to Paul,* edited by P. Richardson and J. C. Hurd, pp. 61-72. Waterloo: Wilfrid Laurier University Press, 1984.

Gaventa, B. *Acts.* Nashville: Abingdon Press, 2003.

Gehring, Roger W. *House Church and Mission: The Importance of Household Structures in Early Christianity*. Peabody: Hendrickson, 2004.

Georgi, Dieter. *The City in the Valley: Biblical Interpretation and Urban Theology*. Atlanta: Society of Biblical Literature, 2005.

———. *Remembering the Poor: The History of Paul's Collection for Jerusalem*. Nashville: Abingdon, 1992.

Gill, C. "Altruism or Reciprocity in Greek Ethical Philosophy?" In *Reciprocity in Ancient Greece*, edited by C. Gill, N. Postlethwaite and R. Seaford, pp. 303-28. Oxford: Oxford University Press, 1998.

Gill, David W. J., and Conrad Gempf. "Acts and the Urban Élites." In *The Book of Acts in Its Graeco-Roman Setting*, edited by David W. J. Gill and Conrad Gempf, pp. 105-118. Vol. 2 of *The Book of Acts in Its First Century Setting*. Grand Rapids: Eerdmans, 1994.

Goodchild, Philip. *Theology of Money*. Durham, NC: Duke University Press, 2009.

Gordon, Barry. *Economic Analysis before Adam Smith*. New York: Harper & Row, 1975.

———. *The Economic Problem in Biblical and Patristic Thought*. Leiden: Brill, 1989.

Gordon, R. "The Veil of Power: Emperors, Sacrificers and Benefactors." In *Pagan Priests: Religion and Power in the Ancient World*, edited by M. Beard and J. North, pp. 199-231. Ithaca: Cornell University Press, 1990.

Goulder, Michael. "A Poor Man's Christology." *NTS* 45 (1999): 332-48.

Grabbe, Lester L. *A History of the Jews and Judaism in the Second Temple Period*. New York: T&T Clark, 2004.

Gray, P. *Godly Fear: The Epistle to the Hebrews and Greco-Roman Critiques of Superstition*. Atlanta: Society of Biblical Literature, 2003.

Green, Joel B. "Good News to Whom? Jesus and the 'Poor' in the Gospel of Luke." In *Jesus of Nazareth: Lord and Christ*, edited by Joel B. Green and Max Turner, pp. 59-74. Carlisle: Paternoster Press, 1994.

Greene, Kevin. "Archeological Data and Economic Interpretation." In *Ancient Economies, Modern Methodologies*, edited by P. F. Bang, M. Ikeguchi and H. G. Ziche, pp. 109-36. Bari: Edipuglia, 2006.

———. *The Archeology of the Roman Economy*. London: Batsford; Berkeley: University of California Press, 1986.

———. "Industry and Technology." In *The High Empire, A.D. 70-192*, pp. 741-68. Vol. 11 of *The Cambridge Ancient History*, edited by A. K. Bowman, P. D. A. Garnsey and D. Rathbone. Cambridge: Cambridge University Press, 2000.

———. "Technological Innovation and Economic Progress in the Ancient World." *Economic History Review* 53 (2000): 29-59.

Grey, C. "Salvian and the Poor in Fifth-Century Gaul." In *Poverty in the Roman World*, edited by M. Atkins and R. Osborne, pp. 162-82. Cambridge: Cambridge University Press, 2006.

Grig, L. "Throwing Parties for the Poor: Poverty and Splendour in the Late Antique Church." In *Poverty in the Roman World*, edited by M. Atkins and R. Osborne, pp. 145-61. Cambridge: Cambridge University Press, 2006.

Haenchen, Ernst. *Die Apostelgeschichte*. Göttingen: Vandenhoeck & Ruprecht, 1977.

Hamel, Gildas. *Poverty and Charity in Roman Palestine, First Three Centuries* C.E. Berkeley: University of California Press, 1990.

Hancock, Graham. *Lords of Poverty: The Power, Prestige, and Corruption of the International Aid Business.* New York: Atlantic Monthly Press, 1989.

Hands, Arthur R. *Charities and Social Aid in Greece and Rome.* Ithaca, NY: Cornell University Press, 1968.

Hanson, K. C., and Douglas E. Oakman. *Palestine in the Time of Jesus.* Minneapolis: Fortress, 1998.

Hardin, Justin K. *Galatians and the Imperial Cult: A Critical Analysis of the First-Century Social Context of Paul's Letter.* Tübingen: Mohr Siebeck, 2008.

Harnack, Adolf von. *Marcion: Das Evangelium vom fremden Gott.* Leipzig: J. C. Hinrichs, 1921.

Hasselhoff, Görge K. "James 2:2-7 in Early Christian Thought." In *Wealth and Poverty in Early Church and Society,* edited by Susan R. Holman, pp. 48-55. Grand Rapids: Baker Academic Press, 2008.

Hays, Richard B. *The Moral Vision of the New Testament.* San Francisco: HarperCollins, 1996.

Hellerman, J. H. *Reconstructing Honor in Roman Philippi: Carmen Christi as cursus pudorum.* Cambridge: Cambridge University Press, 2005.

Hemer, Colin. *The Book of Acts in the Setting of Hellenistic History.* Tübingen: Mohr, 1989.

Henderson, Suzanne Watts. "'If Anyone Hungers . . .': An Integrated Reading of 1 Cor 11.17-34." *NTS* 48 (2002): 195-208.

Hengel, Martin. *Acts and the History of Earliest Christianity.* Translated by John Bowden. London: SCM, 1979.

―――. *Crucifixion in the Ancient World and the Folly of the Message of the Cross.* Minneapolis: Fortress, 1977.

―――. *The Pre-Christian Paul.* London: SCM, 1991.

Herman, G. "Reciprocity, Altruism, and the Prisoner's Dilemma: The Special Case of Classical Athens." In *Reciprocity in Ancient Greece,* edited by C. Gill, N. Postlethwaite and R. Seaford, pp. 199-226. Oxford: Oxford University Press, 1998.

Herzog, William R. *Parables as Subversive Speech: Jesus as Pedagogue of the Oppressed.* Louisville: Westminster John Knox Press, 1994.

Hitchner, R. B. "Olive Production and the Roman Economy: The Case for Intensive Growth in the Roman Empire." In *La production du vin et de l'huile en Méditerranée,* edited by M.-C. Amouretti and J.-P. Brun, pp. 499-508. Athens: École française d'Athènes, 1993.

Hock, R. E. *The Social Context of Paul's Ministry: Tentmaking and Apostleship.* Philadelphia: Fortress, 1980.

Holland, Glenn. "Paul's Use of Irony as a Rhetorical Technique." In *The Rhetorical Analysis of Scripture,* edited by Stanley E. Porter and Thomas H. Olbricht, pp. 234-48. Sheffield: Sheffield Academic Press, 1997.

Holmberg, Bengt. "Methods of Historical Reconstruction." In *Christianity at Corinth: The Quest for the Pauline Church,* edited by Edward Adams and David G. Horrell, pp. 255-71. Louisville: Westminster John Knox Press, 2004.

————. *Paul and Power: The Structure of Authority in the Primitive Church as Reflected in the Pauline Epistles.* Philadelphia: Fortress, 1980.

————. *Sociology and the New Testament.* Minneapolis: Fortress, 1990.

Hopkins, Keith. "Economic Growth and Towns in Classical Antiquity." In *Towns in Societies: Essays in Economic History and Historical Sociology,* edited by P. Abrams and E. A. Wrigley, pp. 35-77. Cambridge: Cambridge University Press, 1978.

————. "Elite Mobility in the Roman Empire." *Past and Present* 32 (1965): 12-26.

————. "Introduction." In *Trade in the Ancient Economy,* edited by P. D. A. Garnsey, K. Hopkins and C. R. Whittaker, pp. ix-xxv. London: Chatto & Windus, 1983.

————. "Taxes and Trade in the Roman Empire, 200 BC–AD 400." *JRS* 70 (1980): 101-25.

Hoppe, L. J. *There Shall Be No Poor Among You: Poverty in the Bible.* Nashville: Abingdon, 2004.

Hopwood, K. "Bandits, Elites and Rural Order." In *Patronage in Ancient Society,* edited by Andrew Wallace-Hadrill, pp. 171-88. London: Routledge, 1989.

Horden, P., and N. Purcell. *The Corrupting Sea: A Study of Mediterranean History.* Oxford: Oxford University Press, 2000.

Horrell, David. "Aliens and Strangers? The Socio-Economic Location of the Addressees of 1 Peter." In *Engaging Economics: New Testament Scenarios and Early Christian Reception,* edited by Bruce W. Longenecker and Kelly Liebengood, pp. 176-202. Grand Rapids: Eerdmans, 2009.

————. "Domestic Space and Christian Meetings at Corinth: Imagining New Contexts and the Buildings East of the Theatre." *NTS* 50 (2004): 349-69.

————. *The Social Ethos of the Corinthian Correspondence: Interests and Ideology from 1 Corinthians to 1 Clement.* Edinburgh: T&T Clark, 1996.

Horsley, Richard A. *Covenant Economics: A Biblical Vision of Justice for All.* Louisville: Westminster John Knox Press, 2009.

————, ed. *Hidden Transcripts and the Arts of Resistance: Applying the Work of James C. Scott to Jesus and Paul.* Atlanta: Society of Biblical Literature, 2004.

————. *Jesus and the Spiral of Violence: Popular Jewish Resistance in Roman Palestine.* San Francisco: HarperSanFrancisco, 1987.

————, ed. *Paul and Empire: Religion and Power in Roman Imperial Society.* Harrisburg: Trinity Press International, 1997.

————, ed. *Paul and Politics.* Harrisburg: Trinity Press International, 2000.

————, ed. *Paul and the Roman Imperial Order.* New York: Trinity Press International, 2004.

————. *Scribes, Visionaries, and the Politics of Second Temple Judea.* Louisville: Westminster John Knox Press, 2007.

Houston, Walter J. *Contending for Justice: Ideologies and Theologies of Social Justice in the Old Testament.* Rev. ed. London: T&T Clark, 2008.

Humfress, C. "Poverty and the Roman Law." In *Poverty in the Roman World,* edited by M. Atkins and R. Osborne, pp. 188-203. Cambridge: Cambridge University Press, 2006.

Hurd, John C. *The Origins of 1 Corinthians.* London: SPCK, 1965.

Hurtado, L. W. "The Jerusalem Collection and the Book of Galatians." *JSNT* 5 (1979): 46-62.

Jeremias, J. "Sabbathjahr und neutestamentliche Chronologie." In *Abba: Studien zur neutestamentlichen Chronologie und Zeitgeschichte*, edited by J. Jeremias, pp. 233-38. Göttingen: Vandenhoeck & Ruprecht, 1966.

Jewett, Robert. "Ecumenical Theology for the Sake of Mission: Romans 1:1-17 + 15:14–16:24." In *Pauline Theology*, Volume 3: *Romans*, edited by David M. Hay and E. Elizabeth Johnson, pp. 89-108. Minneapolis: Fortress, 1995.

———. *Romans*. Minneapolis: Fortress, 2007.

———. *The Thessalonian Correspondence*. Philadelphia: Fortress, 1986.

Johnson, Paul. *A History of Christianity*. New York: Touchstone, Simon and Schuster, 1976.

Jongkind, D. "Corinth in the First Century AD: The Search for Another Class." *TynBul* 52 (2001): 139-48.

Jongman, W. M. "Beneficial Symbols: *Alimenta* and the Infantilization of the Roman Citizen." In *After the Past*, edited by W. Jongman and M. Kleijwegt, pp. 47-80. Leiden: Brill, 2002.

———. "The Early Roman Empire: Production." In *The Cambridge Economic History of the Graeco-Roman World*, edited by W. Scheidel, I. Morris, and R. Saller, pp. 592-618. Cambridge: Cambridge University Press, 2007.

———. Review of *Poverty in the Roman World*, edited by Margaret Atkins and Robin Osborne. EH.Net Economic History Services (July 19, 2008), http://eh.net/bookreviews/library/1335 (accessed January 25, 2009).

Jordaan, W., and J. Jordaan. *People in Context*. 3rd ed. Johannesburg: Heinemann, 1998.

Joubert, Stephen. *Paul as Benefactor: Reciprocity, Strategy and Theological Reflection in Paul's Collection*. Tübingen: Mohr Siebeck, 2000.

Judge, Edwin A. "Paul's Boasting in Relation to Contemporary Professional Practice." *ABR* 16 (1968): 37-50.

———. "The Social Identity of the First Christians." *JRH* 11 (1980): 201-217.

———. *The Social Pattern of the Christian Groups in the First Century: Some Prolegomena to the Study of New Testament Ideas of Social Obligation*. London: Tyndale, 1960. Reprinted in D. M. Scholer, ed., *Social Distinctives of the Christians in the First Century: Pivotal Essays by E. A. Judge* (Peabody: Hendrickson, 2008), pp. 1-56.

Kammel, Mariam. "The Economics of Humility: The Rich and the Humble in James." In *Engaging Economics: New Testament Scenarios and Early Christian Reception*, edited by Bruce W. Longenecker and Kelly Liebengood, pp. 157-75. Grand Rapids: Eerdmans, 2009.

Kassoff, David. *The Book of Witnesses*. London: Collins, 1971.

Kearsley, R. A. "The Asiarchs." In *The Book of Acts in Its Graeco-Roman Setting*, edited by David W. J. Gill and Conrad Gempf, pp. 363-76. Vol. 2 of *The Book of Acts in Its First Century Setting*. Grand Rapids: Eerdmans, 1994.

Keck, Leander E. "The Poor among the Saints in Jewish Christianity and Qumran." *ZNW* 57 (1966): 54-78.

———. "The Poor among the Saints in the New Testament." *ZNW* 56 (1965): 100-129.

Kehoe, Dennis P. "The Early Roman Empire: Consumption." In *The Cambridge Economic History of the Graeco-Roman World*, edited by W. Scheidel, I. Morris, and R. Saller, pp. 543-69. Cambridge: Cambridge University Press, 2007.

————. "Landlords and Tenants." In *A Companion to the Roman Empire,* edited by David S. Potter, pp. 298-311. Oxford: Blackwell Publishing, 2006.

Kent, John Harvey. *The Inscriptions, 1926-1950.* Corinth VIII.3. Princeton: ASCSA, 1966.

Kim, B.-M. *Die paulinische Kollekte.* Tübingen: A. Francke Verlag, 2002.

King, Martin Luther, Jr. *Symbol of the Movement.* Vol. 4 of *The Papers of Martin Luther King, Jr.,* edited by C. Carson. Berkeley: University of California Press, 2000.

Klauck, Hans-Joseph. *Magic and Paganism in Early Christianity.* Edinburgh: T&T Clark, 2000.

Kloppenborg, John S. "Agrarian Discourse and the Sayings of Jesus: 'Measure for Measure' in Gospel Traditions and Agricultural Practices." In *Engaging Economics: New Testament Scenarios and Early Christian Reception,* edited by Bruce W. Longenecker and Kelly Liebengood, pp. 104-128. Grand Rapids: Eerdmans, 2009.

————. "Associations in the Ancient World." In *The Historical Jesus in Context,* edited by Amy-Jill Levine, Dale C. Allison Jr., and John Dominic Crossan, pp. 329-30. Princeton: Princeton University Press, 2006.

————. "Collegia and Thiasoi: Issues in Function, Taxonomy and Membership." In *Voluntary Associations in the Graeco-Roman World,* edited by John S. Kloppenborg and S. G. Wilson, pp. 16-30. London: Routledge, 1996.

————. "Egalitarianism in the Myth and Rhetoric of Pauline Churches." In *Reimagining Christian Origins,* edited by E. A. Castelli and T. Taussig, pp. 247-63. Philadelphia: Trinity Press International, 1996.

————. Untitled article that edits a collection of inscriptions from Achaia. In a volume provisionally entitled *Collegia, Cult Groups, and Guilds: Associations in the Ancient World.* Forthcoming.

Kloppenborg, John S., and S. G. Wilson, eds. *Voluntary Associations in the Graeco-Roman World.* London: Routledge, 1996.

Knox, John. *Chapters in a Life of Paul.* Rev. ed. London: SCM Press, 1989.

————. *Philemon among the Letters of Paul.* Nashville: Abingdon Press, 1935.

Koester, Helmut. "The Silence of the Apostle." In *Urban Religion in Roman Corinth,* edited by Daniel N. Schowalter and Steven J. Friesen, pp. 339-49. Cambridge, MA: Harvard University Press, 2005.

Konstan, David. *Pity Transformed.* London: Duckworth, 2001.

Kuecker, Aaron. "The Spirit and the 'Other,' Satan and the 'Self ': Economic Ethics as a Consequence of Identity Transformation in Luke-Acts." In *Engaging Economics: New Testament Scenarios and Early Christian Reception,* edited by Bruce W. Longenecker and Kelly Liebengood, pp. 81-103. Grand Rapids: Eerdmans, 2009.

Lampe, Peter. *Die stadtrömischen Christen in den ersten beiden Jahrhunderten: Untersuchungen zur Sozialgeschichte.* Mohr Siebeck, 1989. Translated by M. Steinhauser as *From Paul to Valentinus: Christians at Rome in the First Two Centuries* (Minneapolis: Fortress, 2003).

Lenski, Gerhard E. *Power and Privilege: A Theory of Social Stratification.* 2nd ed. Chapel Hill: University of North Carolina Press, 1984 [1966].

Lentz, J. C. *Luke's Portrait of Paul.* Cambridge: Cambridge University Press, 1993.

Levene, D. S. "Pity, Fear and the Historical Audience: Tacitus on the Fall of Vitellius." In

The Passions in Roman Thought and Literature, edited by S. Morton Braund and C. Gill, pp. 128-49. Cambridge: Cambridge University Press, 1997.

Levine, Lee I. *The Ancient Synagogue: The First Thousand Years.* New Haven: Yale University Press, 2000.

Levison, John R. "Did the Spirit Inspire Rhetoric? An Evaluation of George Kennedy's Definition of Early Christian Rhetoric." In *Persuasive Artistry: Essays in Honor of George Kennedy,* edited by Duane F. Watson, pp. 25-40. Sheffield: JSOT Press, 1991.

Ligt, L. de. "Restraining the Rich, Protecting the Poor: Symbolic Aspects of Roman Legislation." In *After the Past,* edited by W. Jongman and M. Kleijwegt, pp. 1-46. Leiden: Brill, 2002.

Ling, Timothy J. M. *The Judaean Poor and the Fourth Gospel.* Cambridge: Cambridge University Press, 2006.

Litfin, Duane. *St. Paul's Theology of Proclamation: 1 Corinthians 1–4 and Greco-Roman Rhetoric.* Cambridge: Cambridge University Press, 1994.

Loader, William. "'Good News to the Poor' and Spirituality in the New Testament: A Question of Survival." In *Poverty and Riches,* edited by Geoffrey D. Dunn, David Luckensmeyer and Lawrence Cross, pp. 3-35. Vol. 5 of *Prayer and Spirituality in the Early Church.* Strathfield, NSW: St Paul's Publications, 2009.

————. *The New Testament with Imagination.* Grand Rapids: Eerdmans, 2007.

Longenecker, Bruce W. "Exposing the Economic Middle: A Revised Economy Scale for the Study of Early Urban Christianity." *JSNT* 31 (2009): 243-78.

————. "Good News to the Poor: Jesus, Paul and Jerusalem." In *Jesus and Paul Reconnected: Fresh Pathways to an Old Debate,* edited by Todd Still, pp. 37-65. Grand Rapids: Eerdmans 2007.

————. "Moral Character and Divine Generosity: Acts 13:13-52 and the Narrative Dynamics of Luke-Acts." In *New Testament Greek and Exegesis: A Festschrift for Gerald F. Hawthorne,* edited by A. M. Donaldson and T. B. Sailors, pp. 141-64. Grand Rapids: Eerdmans, 2003.

————. "The Poor of Galatians 2:10: The Interpretative Paradigm of the First Centuries." In *Engaging Economics: New Testament Scenarios and Early Christian Reception,* edited by Bruce W. Longenecker and Kelly Liebengood, pp. 205-21. Grand Rapids: Eerdmans, 2009.

————. *Rhetoric at the Boundaries: The Art and Theology of New Testament Chain-Link Transitions.* Waco: Baylor University Press, 2005.

————. "Socio-Economic Profiling of the First Urban Christians." In *After the First Urban Christians: The Socio-Historical Study of Pauline Christianity Twenty-Five Years Later,* edited by Todd Still and David Horrell, pp. 36-59. London/New York: Continuum, 2009.

————. "The Story of the Samaritan and the Inn-Keeper (Luke 10:30-35): A Study in Character Rehabilitation." *Bib Int* 17 (2009): 422-47.

————. *The Triumph of Abraham's God: The Transformation of Identity in Galatians.* Edinburgh: T&T Clark, 1998.

————. "'Until Christ is formed in you': Suprahuman Forces and Moral Character in Galatians." *CBQ* 61 (1999): 92-108.

Longenecker, Richard N. *Galatians.* Dallas: Word Books, 1990.

Lopez, Davina C. *Apostle to the Conquered: Reimagining Paul's Mission*. Minneapolis: Fortress, 2008.

Louw, Johannes P., and Eugene A. Nida. *Greek-English Lexicon of the New Testament Based on Semantic Domains*. New York: United Bible Societies, 1988/89.

Lutz, C. E. "Musonius Rufus, 'the Roman Socrates.'" *YCS* 10 (1947): 3-147.

MacDonald, Margaret Y. "The Role of Women in the Expansion of Early Christianity." In *Early Christian Families in Context: An Interdisciplinary Dialogue*, edited by David L. Balch and Carolyn Osiek, pp. 157-84. Grand Rapids: Eerdmans, 2003.

MacDonald, William L. *The Architecture of the Roman Empire*, Volume 1: *An Introductory Study*. Rev. ed. New Haven: Yale University Press, 1982.

————. *The Architecture of the Roman Empire*, Volume 2: *An Urban Appraisal*. New Haven: Yale University Press, 1986.

MacMullen, R. *Roman Social Relations: 50 BC to AD 284*. New Haven: Yale University Press, 1974.

Malherbe, Abraham J. *The Letters to the Thessalonians*. New York: Doubleday, 2000.

————. *Paul and the Thessalonians: The Philosophic Tradition of Pastoral Care*. Philadelphia: Fortress, 1987.

————. *Social Aspects of Early Christianity*. Philadelphia: Fortress, 1977/1983.

Malina, Bruce. Review of *First Urban Christians*, by Wayne Meeks. *JBL* 104 (1985): 346-49.

Marshall, John W. "Hybridity and Reading Romans 13." *JSNT* 31 (2008): 157-78.

Marshall, Peter. *Enmity at Corinth*. Tübingen: Mohr Siebeck, 1997.

Martin, Dale. *The Corinthian Body*. New Haven: Yale University Press, 1995.

————. *Inventing Superstition: From the Hippocrats to the Christians*. Cambridge, MA: Harvard University Press, 2004.

————. *Slavery as Salvation: Metaphor of Slavery in Pauline Christianity*. New Haven: Yale University Press, 1990.

Martin, R. P. *James*. Waco: Word Books, 1988.

Martyn, J. Louis. *Galatians*. New York: Doubleday, 1997.

————. *Theological Issues in the Letters of Paul*. Edinburgh: T&T Clark, 1997.

Matthew Henry's Commentary (Condensed). Public Domain Electronic Text, downloaded from the Bible Foundation e-Text Library: http://www.bf.org/bfetexts.htm. Hypertexted and formatted by OakTree Software, Inc., Version 2.5.

Mattingly, David. "The Imperial Economy." In *A Companion to the Roman Empire*, edited by David S. Potter, pp. 283-97. Oxford: Blackwell Publishing, 2006.

Mattingly, D. J., and J. Salmon, eds. *Economies Beyond Agriculture in the Classical World*. London: Routledge, 2001.

————. "The Productive Past: Economies Beyond Agriculture." In *Economies Beyond Agriculture in the Classical World*, edited by D. J. Mattingly and J. Salmon, pp. 3-14. London: Routledge, 2001.

Mauss, M. *The Gift: Forms and Functions of Exchange in Archaic Societies*. Translated by I. Cunnison. London: Routledge & Kegan Paul, 1954 [1925].

McCready, W. O. "*Ekklēsia* and Voluntary Associations." In *Voluntary Associations in the Graeco-Roman World*, edited by John S. Kloppenborg and S. G. Wilson, pp. 59-73. London: Routledge, 1996.

McGuckin, John A. *The Westminster Handbook to Patristic Theology.* Louisville: Westminster John Knox Press, 2004.

McGuire, M. R. P. "Epigraphical Evidence for Social Charity in the Roman West." *AJP* 67 (1946): 129-50.

Meeks, Wayne A. "The Circle of Reference in Pauline Morality." In *Greeks, Romans, and Christians: Essays in Honor of Abraham J. Malherbe*, pp. 305-317. Minneapolis: Fortress, 1990.

————. *First Urban Christians: The Social World of the Apostle Paul.* New Haven: Yale University Press, 1983.

————. *The Moral World of the First Christians.* New Haven: Yale University Press, 1986.

————. *The Origins of Christian Morality: The First Two Centuries.* New Haven: Yale University Press, 1993.

Meggitt, Justin J. *Paul, Poverty and Survival.* Edinburgh: T&T Clark, 1998.

————. "The Social Status of Erastus (Rom. 16:23)." *NovT* 38 (1996): 218-23. Reprinted in Edward Adams and David G. Horrell, eds., *Christianity at Corinth: The Quest for the Pauline Church* (Louisville: Westminster John Knox Press, 2004), pp. 219-26.

————. "Sources: Use, Abuse, Neglect: The Importance of Ancient Popular Culture." In *Christianity at Corinth: The Quest for the Pauline Church*, edited by Edward Adams and David G. Horrell, pp. 241-54. Louisville: Westminster John Knox Press, 2004.

Melmoth, William. *Letters of Pliny the Consul.* Boston: Larkin, 1809.

Milbank, John. *Theology and Social Theory: Beyond Secular Reason.* Oxford: Basil Blackwell, 1990.

Miller, M. P. "Antioch, Paul and Jerusalem: Diaspora Myths of Origins." In *Redescribing Christian Origins*, edited by R. Cameron and M. P. Miller, pp. 177-36. Atlanta: Society of Biblical Literature, 2004.

Millett, Paul. "The Rhetoric of Reciprocity in Classical Athens." In *Reciprocity in Ancient Greece*, edited by C. Gill, N. Postlethwaite and R. Seaford, pp. 227-53. Oxford: Oxford University Press, 1998.

Mitchell, Margaret M. "The Corinthian Correspondence and the Birth of Pauline Hermeneutics." In *Paul and the Corinthians: Studies on a Community in Conflict*, edited by T. J. Burke and J. K. Elliott, pp. 17-53. Leiden: Brill, 2003.

————. "Paul's Letters to Corinth: The Interpretive Intertwining of Literary and Historical Reconstruction." In *Urban Religion in Roman Corinth*, edited by Daniel N. Schowalter and Steven J. Friesen, pp. 307-338. Cambridge, MA: Harvard University Press, 2005.

Moo, Douglas J. *The Epistle to the Romans.* Grand Rapids: Eerdmans, 1996.

Morgan, Teresa. *Popular Morality in the Early Roman Empire.* Cambridge: Cambridge University Press, 2007.

Morley, N. "Narrative Economy." In *Ancient Economies, Modern Methodologies*, edited by P. F. Bang, M. Ikeguchi and H. G. Ziche, pp. 27-47. Bari: Edipuglia, 2006.

————. "The Poor in the City of Rome." In *Poverty in the Roman World*, edited by

M. Atkins and R. Osborne, pp. 21-39. Cambridge: Cambridge University Press, 2006.

―――. *Trade in Classical Antiquity.* Cambridge: Cambridge University Press, 2007.

Mounce, Robert. *The Pastoral Epistles.* Nashville: Thomas Nelson Publishers, 2000.

Moxnes, H. *The Economy of the Kingdom: Social Conflict and Economic Relations in Luke's Gospel.* Philadelphia: Fortress, 1988.

Murphy-O'Connor, Jerome. *Paul: A Critical Life.* Oxford: Oxford University Press, 1996.

―――. *Paul: His Story.* Oxford: Oxford University Press, 2004.

Nguyen, V. H. T. *Christian Identity in Corinth.* Tübingen: Mohr Siebeck, 2008.

Nickle, Keith F. *The Collection: A Study in Paul's Strategy.* Naperville: Alec R. Allenson, 1966.

Nijf, O. M. van. "*Collegia* and Civic Guards: Two Chapters in the History of Sociability." In *After the Past,* edited by W. Jongman and M. Kleijwegt, pp. 305-340. Leiden: Brill, 2002.

Northcott, Michael S. *A Moral Climate: The Ethics of Global Warming.* London: Darton, Longman and Todd, 2007.

Oakes, Peter. "Constructing Poverty Scales for Graeco-Roman Society: A Response to Steven Friesen's 'Poverty in Pauline Studies.'" *JSNT* 26 (2004): 367-71.

―――. "Methodological Issues in Using Economic Evidence in Interpretation of Early Christian Texts." In *Engaging Economics: New Testament Scenarios and Early Christian Reception,* edited by Bruce W. Longenecker and Kelly Liebengood, pp. 9-34. Grand Rapids: Eerdmans, 2009.

―――. *Philippians: From People to Letter.* Cambridge: Cambridge University Press, 2001.

Oakman, Douglas. "Money in the Moral Universe of the New Testament." In *The Social Setting of Jesus and the Gospels,* edited by W. Stegemann, B. J. Malina and G. Theissen, pp. 335-48. Minneapolis: Fortress, 2002.

O'Day, Gail. "Jeremiah 9:22-23 and 1 Corinthians 1:26-31: A Study in Intertextuality." *JBL* 109 (1990): 259-67.

Oliver, J. H. "Gerusiae and Augustales." *Historia* 7 (1958): 472-96.

Osborne, R. "Roman Poverty in Context." In *Poverty in the Roman World,* edited by M. Atkins and R. Osborne, pp. 1-20. Cambridge: Cambridge University Press, 2006.

Osiek, Carolyn, and David L. Balch. *Families in the New Testament World: Households and House Churches.* Louisville: Westminster John Knox Press, 1997.

Osiek, Carolyn, and Margaret Y. MacDonald. *A Woman's Place: House Churches in Earliest Christianity.* Minneapolis: Fortress Press, 2006.

Painter, John. "James as the First Catholic Epistle." In *The Catholic Epistles and Apostolic Tradition,* edited by Karl-Wilhelm Niebuhr and Robert W. Wall, pp. 161-82. Waco: Baylor University Press, 2009.

Parisot, Joannes. *Aphraatis Sapientis Persiae: Demonstrationes.* 2 vols. Patrologia syriaca 1 and 2. Paris: Firmin-Didot, 1894, 1907.

Parkin, Anneliese. "'You do him no service': An Exploration of Pagan Almsgiving." In

Poverty in the Roman World, edited by M. Atkins and R. Osborne, pp. 60-82. Cambridge: Cambridge University Press, 2006.

Parkin, Tim G., and Arthur John Pomeroy. *Roman Social History: A Sourcebook.* London: Routledge, 2007.

Parkins, H. M., ed. *Roman Urbanism: Beyond the Consumer City.* London: Routledge, 1997.

Parsons, Mikeal. *Acts.* Grand Rapids: Baker Academic, 2008.

Paterson, John J. "Production and Consumption." In *The World of Rome: An Introduction to Roman Culture,* edited by P. Jones and K. Sidwell, pp. 181-207. Cambridge: Cambridge University Press, 1997.

Pathrapankal, Joseph. *Foundational Perspectives in the New Testament.* Bangalore: Dharmaram Publications, 2004.

Patitsas, Timothy. "St. Basil's Philanthropic Program and Modern Macrolending Strategies for Economic Self-Actualization." In *Wealth and Poverty in Early Church and Society,* edited by Susan R. Holman, pp. 267-86. Grand Rapids: Baker Academic Press, 2008.

Patterson, John R. "Crisis: What Crisis? Rural Change and Urban Development in Imperial Appennine Italy." *PBSR* 55 (1987): 115-46.

———. *Landscapes and Cities: Rural Settlement and Civic Transformation in Early Imperial Italy.* Oxford: Oxford University Press, 2006.

Patterson, Orlando. *Rituals of Blood: Consequences of Slavery in Two American Centuries.* Washington, DC: Civitas Counterpoint, 1998.

Perrin, Nicholas. "Introduction." In *Questioning Q,* edited by Mark Goodacre and Nicholas Perrin, pp. 1-12. London: SPCK, 2004.

Pitt-Rivers, J. "Postscript: The Place of Grace in Anthropology." In *Honour and Grace in Anthropology,* edited by J. G. Peristiany and J. Pitt-Rivers, pp. 215-46. Cambridge: Cambridge University Press, 1992.

Pleket, H. W. Review of *First Urban Christians,* by Wayne Meeks. *VC* 39 (1985): 192-96.

———. "Wirtschaft." In *Europäische Wirtschafts- und Sozialgeschichte in der römischen Kaiserzeit,* edited by F. Vittinghoff, pp. 25-160. Stuttgart: Ernst Klett Verlag, 1990.

Polanyi, Karl. *The Great Transformation.* Boston: Beacon Press, 1957.

Prell, M. *Sozialökonomische Untersuchungen zur Armut im antiken Rom: Von den Gracchen bis Kaiser Diokletian.* Stuttgart: Steiner Verlag, 1997.

Purcell, N. "The *Apparitores:* A Study in Social Mobility." *PBSR* 51 (1983): 125-73.

Rathbone, D. W. "The Census Qualifications of the *assidui* and the *prima classis.*" In *De Agricultura: In Memoriam Pieter Willem de Neeve (1945-1990),* edited by H. Sancisi-Weerdenburg and H. C. Teitler, pp. 121-52. Amsterdam: J. C. Gieben, 1993.

———. "Poverty and Population in Roman Egypt." In *Poverty in the Roman World,* edited by M. Atkins and R. Osborne, pp. 100-114. Cambridge: Cambridge University Press, 2006.

Ratzinger, Joseph. (Pope Benedict XVI). *Jesus of Nazareth: From the Baptism in the Jordan to the Transfiguration.* Translated by Adrian J. Walker. New York: Doubleday, 2007.

Revell, Louise. *Roman Imperialism and Local Identities.* Cambridge: Cambridge University Press, 2009.

Riesner, Rainer. *Paul's Early Period: Chronology, Mission Strategy, Theology.* Grand Rapids: Eerdmans, 1998.

Ro, Johannes Un-sok. "Socio-Economic Context of Post-Exilic Community and Literacy." ZAW 120 (2008): 597-611.

Rohrbauch, R. L. "Methodological Considerations in the Debate over the Social Class Status of Early Christians." *JAAR* 52 (1984): 519-46.

Rosenfeld, Ben-Zion, and Joseph Menirav. "The Ancient Synagogue as an Economic Center." *JNES* 58 (1999): 259-76.

Rowe, G. A. "Style." In *Handbook of Classical Rhetoric in the Hellenistic Period, 330 BC–AD 400,* edited by Stanley E. Porter, pp. 121-57. Leiden: Brill, 1997.

Russell, R. "The Idle in 2 Thess 3:6-12: An Eschatological or Social Problem?" *NTS* 34 (1988): 105-119.

Rynne, Terrence J. *Gandhi and Jesus: The Saving Power of Nonviolence.* Maryknoll, NY: Orbis Books, 2008.

Saller, R. "Framing the Debate over Growth in the Ancient Economy." In *The Ancient Economy,* edited by Walter Scheidel and Sitta von Reden, pp. 251-69. Edinburgh: Edinburgh University Press, 2002.

Sanders, E. P. *Paul.* Oxford: Oxford University Press, 1991.

Scheidel, Walter. "Stratification, Deprivation and Quality of Life." In *Poverty in the Roman World,* edited by M. Atkins and R. Osborne, pp. 40-59. Cambridge: Cambridge University Press, 2006.

Scheidel, Walter, and Steven J. Friesen. "The Size of the Economy and the Distribution of Income in the Roman Empire." *JRS* 99 (2009): 61-91.

Scheidel, Walter, and S. von Reden, eds. *The Ancient Economy.* Edinburgh: Edinburgh University Press, 2002.

Schleich, T. "Missionsgeschichte und Sozialstruktur des vorkonstantinischen Christentums." *Geschichte in Wissenschaft und Unterricht* 33 (1982): 269-96.

Schmithals, Walter. "Die Kollekten des Paulus für Jerusalem." In *Paulus, Die Evangelien und Das Urchristentum,* edited by C. Breytenbach, pp. 78-106. Leiden: Brill, 2004.

Schnelle, Udo. *Apostle Paul: His Life and Theology.* Grand Rapids: Baker Academic, 2003.

Schwartz, Stephen. "All for the Best." Music Theater International, 1973.

Scroggs, Robin. "The Sociological Interpretation of the New Testament: The Present State of Research." *NTS* 26 (1980): 164-79.

Seccombe, D. "Was There Organised Charity in Jerusalem before the Christians?" *JTS* 29 (1978): 140-43.

Segundo, J. L. "Two Theologies of Liberation." In *Liberation Theology: A Documentary History,* edited by Alfred T. Hennelly, pp. 353-66. Maryknoll, NY: Orbis Books, 1990.

Silver, M. Review of *The Ancient Economy,* edited by Walter Scheidel and Sitta von Reden. EH.Net Economic History Services (January 3, 2003), http://eh.net/bookreviews/library/0570 (accessed March 11, 2008).

Staab, Karl, ed. *Pauluskommentare aus der griechischen Kirche*. 2nd ed. Münster: Aschendorff, 1984.

Stanley, Christopher D. *Arguing with Scripture: The Rhetoric of Quotations in the Letters of Paul*. New York: T&T Clark, 2004.

Stanton, Graham N. *Jesus and Gospel*. Cambridge: Cambridge University Press, 2004.

Stark, Rodney. *The Rise of Christianity*. Princeton: Princeton University Press, 1996.

Ste. Croix, G. E. M. de. *The Class Struggle in the Ancient Greek World: From the Archaic Age to the Arab Conquests*. London: Duckworth, 1981.

Stegemann, E. W., and W. Stegemann. *The Jesus Movement: A Social History of Its First Century*. Minneapolis: Fortress, 1999.

Still, Todd D. "Did Paul Loathe Manual Labor? Revisiting the Work of Ronald F. Hock." *JBL* 125 (2006): 781-95.

Still, Todd, and David Horrell, eds. *After The First Urban Christians: The Socio-Historical Study of Pauline Christianity Twenty-Five Years Later*. London: Continuum, 2009.

Stowers, Stanley K. "Romans 7:7-25 as a Speech-in-Character (προσωποποιία)." In *Paul in His Hellenistic Context*, edited by Troels Engberg-Pederson, pp. 180-202. Minneapolis: Fortress Press, 1995.

Suhl, A. "Der Beginn der selbständigen Mission des Paulus." *NTS* 38 (1992): 430-47.

Talbert, Charles H. *Reading Corinthians*. London: SPCK, 1987.

Tarn, W. W. *Hellenistic Civilization*. New York: Plume, 1974.

Taylor, Nicholas H. "The Composition and Chronology of Second Corinthians." *JSNT* 44 (1991): 67-87.

———. *Paul, Antioch and Jerusalem*. Sheffield: Sheffield Academic Press, 1992.

Tchalenko, G. *Villages antiques de la Syrie du Nord*. Vol. 1. Paris: P. Geuthner, 1953.

Theissen, Gerd. *The Social Setting of Pauline Christianity: Essays on Corinth*. Philadelphia: Fortress, 1982.

———. "The Social Structure of Pauline Communities: Some Critical Comments on J. J. Meggitt, *Paul, Poverty and Survival*." *JSNT* 84 (2001): 65-84.

Thiselton, A. C. *The First Epistle to the Corinthians*. Grand Rapids: Eerdmans, 2000.

Thrall, M. E. *II Corinthians*. Vol. 2. Edinburgh: T&T Clark, 2000.

Toner, J. P. *Rethinking Roman History*. Cambridge, MA: Polity Press, 2002.

Trobisch, David. *Die Entstehung der Paulusbriefsammlung: Studien zu den Anfängen christlicher Publizistik*. Göttingen: Vandenhoeck & Ruprecht, 1989.

———. *Paul's Letter Collection: Tracing the Origins*. Minneapolis: Fortress, 1994.

Turner, E. G. "Oxyrhynchus and Rome." *Harvard Studies in Classical Philology* 79 (1975): 16-23.

Uhlhorn, Gerhard. *Christian Charity in the Ancient Church*. New York: Charles Scribner's Sons, 1883.

Verboven, Koenraad. *The Economy of Friends: Economic Aspects of Amicitia and Patronage in the Late Republic*. Brussels: Latomus, 2002.

Veyne, Paul. *Bread and Circuses: Historical Sociology and Political Pluralism*. London: Penguin, 1990.

Vittinghoff, F. "Soziale Struktur und politisches System in der hohen römischen Kaiserzeit." *Historische Zeitschrift* 230 (1980): 31-55.

vom Brocke, Christoph. *Thessaloniki: Stadt des Kassader und Gemeinde des Paulus.* Tübingen: Mohr Siebeck, 2001.

Vouda, F. *An die Galater.* Tübingen: Mohr Siebeck, 1998.

Wagner, J. R. "The Heralds of Isaiah and the Mission of Paul: An Investigation of Paul's Use of Isaiah 51–55 in Romans." In *Jesus and the Suffering Servant: Isaiah 53 and Christian Origins,* edited by W. H. Bellinger and W. R. Farmer, pp. 193-222. Harrisburg: Trinity Press International, 1998.

Wallace-Hadrill, A. "*Domus* and *insulae* in Rome: Families and Housefuls." In *Early Christian Families in Context: An Interdisciplinary Dialogue,* edited by David L. Balch and Carolyn Osiek, pp. 3-18. Grand Rapids: Eerdmans, 2003.

———. *Houses and Society in Pompeii and Heraculaneum.* Princeton: Princeton University Press, 1994.

Walters, James. "Civic Identity in Roman Corinth and Its Impact on Early Christians." In *Urban Religion in Roman Corinth,* edited by Daniel N. Schowalter and Steven J. Friesen, pp. 397-417. Cambridge, MA: Harvard University Press, 2005.

Watson, Francis. "2 Cor. x–xiii and Paul's Painful Letter to the Corinthians." *JTS* 35 (1984): 324-46.

Wedderburn, A. J. M. "Paul's Collection: Chronology and History." *NTS* 48 (2002): 95-110.

Wees, H. van. "Greed, Generosity and Gift-Exchange in Early Greece and the Western Pacific." In *After the Past,* edited by W. Jongman and M. Kleijwegt, pp. 341-78. Leiden: Brill, 2002.

Weiner, A. B. *Women of Value, Men of Renown: New Perspectives in Trobriand Exchange.* Austin: University of Texas Press, 1976.

Wenham, David. *Paul: Follower of Jesus or Founder of Christianity?* Grand Rapids: Eerdmans, 1995.

Whittaker, C. R. "The Poor in the City of Rome." In *Land, City and Trade in the Roman Empire,* by C. R. Whittaker, Article 7. Aldershot: Variorum Ashgate, 1993.

Williams, Sam K. *Galatians.* Nashville: Abingdon Press, 1997.

Wilson, Andrew. "'The Advantages of Wealth and Luxury': The Case for Economic Growth in the Roman Empire." In *The Ancient Economy: Evidence and Models,* edited by J. Manning and I. Morris, pp. 207-22. Stanford: Stanford University Press, 2005.

———. "Cyrenaica and the Late Antique Economy." *Ancient West and East* 3 (2004): 143-54.

———. "The Economic Impact of Technological Advances in the Roman Construction Industry." In *Innovazione tecnica e progresso economico,* edited by Elio Lo Cascio, pp. 225-36. Bari, Italy: Edipuglia, 2006.

———. "Machines, Power and the Ancient Economy." *JRS* 92 (2002): 1-32.

Wilson, S. G. "Voluntary Associations: An Overview." In *Voluntary Associations in the Graeco-Roman World,* edited by John S. Kloppenborg and S. G. Wilson, pp. 1-15. London: Routledge, 1996.

Winger, M. "Act One: Paul Arrives in Galatia." *NTS* 48 (2002): 548-67.

Winter, Bruce W. *After Paul Left Corinth: The Influence of Secular Ethics and Social Change.* Grand Rapids: Eerdmans, 2001.

————. *Seek the Welfare of the City: Christians as Benefactors and Citizens*. Grand Rapids: Eerdmans, 1994.

Wire, Annette Clark. "Response: Paul and Those Outside Power." In *Paul and Politics*, edited by Richard A. Horsley, pp. 224-26. Harrisburg: Trinity Press International, 2000.

Witherington, Ben. *Grace in Galatia: A Commentary on St Paul's Letter to the Galatians*. Edinburgh: T&T Clark, 1998.

————. *The Letters to Philemon, the Colossians, and the Ephesians: A Socio-Rhetorical Commentary on the Captivity Epistles*. Grand Rapids: Eerdmans, 2007.

————. *The Paul Quest*. Downers Grove: InterVarsity Press, 1998.

Witherup, R. D. "Cornelius Over and Over and Over Again." *JSNT* 49 (1993): 43-66.

Witulski, Thomas. *Die Adressaten des Galaterbriefes: Untersuchungen zur Gemeinde von Antiochia ad Pisidiam*. Göttingen: Vandenhoeck & Ruprecht, 2000.

Wolterstorff, Nicholas. *Justice: Rights and Wrongs*. Princeton: Princeton University Press, 2008.

Woods, T. E. *How the Catholic Church Built Western Civilization*. Washington, DC: Regnery Publishing, 2005.

Woolf, Greg. "Food, Poverty and Patronage: The Significance of the Epigraphy of the Roman Alimentary Schemes in Early Imperial Italy." *PBSR* 58 (1990): 197-228.

————. "Imperialism, Empire and the Integration of the Roman Economy." *World Archeology* 23 (1992): 283-93.

————. "Writing Poverty in Rome." In *Poverty in the Roman World*, edited by M. Atkins and R. Osborne, pp. 83-99. Cambridge: Cambridge University Press, 2006.

Wordelman, Amy L. "Cultural Divides and Dual Realities." In *Contextualizing Acts: Lukan Narrative and Greco-Roman Discourse*, edited by Todd Penner and Caroline Vander Stichele, pp. 205-232. Atlanta: Society of Biblical Literature, 2003.

Wright, N. T. *The New Testament and the People of God*. London: SPCK, 1992.

————. *Paul for Everyone: Galatians and Thessalonians*. London: SPCK, 2002.

Wuellner, W. H. "The Sociological Implications of I Corinthians 1:26-28 Reconsidered." In *Studia Evangelica VI*, edited by Elizabeth A. Livingstone, pp. 666-72. TU 112. Berlin: Akademie Verlag, 1973.

Yoder, John Howard. *The Politics of Jesus*. 2nd ed. Grand Rapids: Eerdmans, 1994 [1972].

Young, Frances. *The Theology of the Pastoral Epistles*. Cambridge: Cambridge University Press, 1994.

Index of Modern Authors

Index of Ancient Sources